MOTHERING BY DEGREES

The American Campus

Harold S. Wechsler, Series Editor

The books in the American Campus series explore recent developments and public policy issues in higher education in the United States. Topics of interest include access to college and college affordability; college retention; tenure and academic freedom; campus labor; the expansion and evolution of administrative posts and salaries; the crisis in the humanities and the arts; the corporate university and for-profit colleges; online education; controversy in sport programs; and gender, ethnic, racial, religious, and class dynamics and diversity. Books feature scholarship from a variety of disciplines in the humanities and social sciences.

Gordon Hutner and Feisal G. Mohamed, eds., *A New Deal for the Humanities: Liberal Arts and the Future of Public Higher Education*

Adrianna Kezar and Daniel Maxey, eds., *Envisioning the Faculty for the Twenty-First Century: Moving to a Mission-Oriented and Learner-Centered Model*

Scott Frickel, Mathieu Albert, and Barbara Prainsack, eds., *Investigating Interdisciplinary Collaboration: Theory and Practice across Disciplines*

Jillian M. Duquaine-Watson, *Mothering by Degrees: Single Mothers and the Pursuit of Postsecondary Education*

MOTHERING BY DEGREES

Single Mothers and the Pursuit of Postsecondary Education

JILLIAN M. DUQUAINE-WATSON

RUTGERS UNIVERSITY PRESS

New Brunswick, Camden, and Newark, New Jersey, and London

Library of Congress Cataloging-in-Publication Data
Names: Duquaine-Watson, Jillian M., author.
Title: Mothering by degrees : single mothers and the pursuit of postsecondary
    education / Jillian M. Duquaine-Watson.
Description: New Brunswick, New Jersey : Rutgers University Press, 2017. | Series:
    The American campus | Includes bibliographical references and index.
Identifiers: LCCN 2016038031| ISBN 9780813588438 (hardback) |
    ISBN 9780813588421 (pbk.) | ISBN 9780813588445 (e-book (epub))
Subjects: LCSH: Single mothers—Education (Higher)—United States. | Poor
    women—Education (Higher)—United States. | Education, Higher—Economic
    aspects—United States. | College student parents—United States. | Mother
    and child—United States. | BISAC: EDUCATION / Higher. | FAMILY &
    RELATIONSHIPS / Parenting / Motherhood. | SOCIAL
    SCIENCE / Women's Studies. | EDUCATION / Students & Student Life. |
    FAMILY & RELATIONSHIPS / Parenting / Single Parent. | SOCIAL
    SCIENCE / Sociology / Marriage & Family.
Classification: LCC LC1757 .D87 2017 | DDC 378.0082—dc23
LC record available at https://lccn.loc.gov/2016038031

A British Cataloging-in-Publication record for this book is available from the British
Library.

∞ The paper used in this publication meets the requirements of the American
National Standard for Information Sciences—Permanence of Paper for Printed
Library Materials, ANSI Z39.48–1992.

www.rutgersuniversitypress.org

Manufactured in the United States of America

To Samara and Annika, my maternal grandmother,
and my Maleku family with love
And to Piper Skye, forever a shooting star

CONTENTS

Prologue: Lessons from My Grandmother   1

1   The Politics of Single Motherhood in the United States   13

2   Trying to Make Ends Meet   43

3   Clocks and Calendars   82

4   Navigating America's Child Care Crisis   110

5   Mothering Alone in a Chilly Climate   141

Conclusion   179

Acknowledgments   195
Appendix: Supporting Single Mothers at
Colleges and Universities   197
Notes   213
Bibliography   241
Index   255

MOTHERING BY DEGREES

PROLOGUE
Lessons from My Grandmother

When my daughters were young, our nightly routine included storytelling. After dinner, they would select several books from their bookcase and bring them to me. We would then climb onto the sofa, snuggle close together, and I would read from the pages of favorites such as *The Rain Babies* or *The Giving Tree* or *If You Give a Mouse a Cookie*. We often indulged in less familiar titles as well, typically books that were borrowed from the children's section at our public library. Story time lasted about half an hour and I would then usher the girls to their rooms, tuck them into bed, and kiss their foreheads before wishing them sweet dreams.

For the most part, our nightly ritual proceeded in this rather straightforward manner. Yet around the time my youngest daughter celebrated her ninth birthday, she no longer wanted me to read to her. Instead, she wanted a different kind of story: she wanted to hear about my childhood. It began with a very simple question: "Can you tell me about when you were little?" She then settled back, smiled her best smile, and waited for me to comply. Initially, I found it difficult to do so. While I enjoyed reading books to her, I was less comfortable with crafting stories on the spur of the moment, even those based on my own experiences. I was worried that I wouldn't do justice to even my fondest memories of growing up in rural Wisconsin and that my daughter would find my childhood tales boring. After all, by age nine she had already traveled extensively in the United States and abroad, was immersed in computers and digital technology, and had experienced all the comforts and privileges of a middle-class childhood. In contrast, I didn't leave my hometown until I reached age eighteen and went to college, I didn't get my first computer until I was twenty-six, and I grew up in a working-class family where poverty always seemed to be lurking just around the corner. But my daughter is persistent and persuasive, and as a result, our nightly routine soon came to include regular installments of my autobiography with particular attention to my formative years.

Initially, I simply recounted some events such as when my kindergarten teacher gave me a soft, small, gray kitten that I hid inside my backpack and took onto the school bus. The kitten meowed all the way home and as I walked toward the front steps of the vehicle to exit, the bus driver gave me a stern look and told me to never bring a kitten on the bus again. My daughter was surprised to hear about the time I got so mad at my parents that I tried to run away but only made it to the end of our driveway because I was too afraid of the fierce animals I was certain were lurking in the shadows on the rural road where we lived. I also told her that when I was growing up, my mom would make me spaghetti every year on my birthday and I would always end up with more sauce on my face than in my stomach. Then, for dessert, she would serve angel food cake with peanut butter frosting. My daughter was delighted to learn about my experience in fifth grade when one of my classmates gave me a hamster from her science fair project. I brought the hamster home in a cardboard box that I held as I rode the school bus. The hamster scratched incessantly at the inside of the box for the entire ride and before he would let me exit the bus, the driver gave me a stern look and very strict instructions to never bring a kitten, a hamster, or any type of animal on the bus again. And then he smiled and told me he once had a pet hamster.

As I shared my memories with my daughter, it didn't take long for my thoughts to turn to my maternal grandmother. I spent significant portions of my childhood with her on the large dairy farm she and my grandfather owned and operated. These experiences were, without a doubt, the happiest times of my youth and I enjoyed sharing these memories with my daughter. I described the long, hot August afternoons spent lounging on a blanket in the shade of the large elm tree in my grandmother's backyard, drinking the lemonade she had made. We would lie on our backs and survey the clouds, hoping to find recognizable shapes among their floating forms. I recounted long, rainy afternoons spent with Grandma up in her attic where we played school with my dolls. Grandma always let me be the teacher and she would pretend to be my helper. When the dolls did well on their tests—and they always did—we would reward them with a tea party that included homemade cookies and peppermint tea with plenty of sugar, all served on the rose-patterned china Grandma had gotten for her wedding and only used for special occasions. I recounted the fun of helping Grandma feed the baby calves on her farm. We prepared a milk replacer in the kitchen and carried it out to the barn in liter-sized livestock baby bottles. The calves would latch onto the bottles with gusto, draining their contents in mere minutes. I also described the rich taste of Grandma's apple pie, the fragrant scent of the lilacs that grew in thick bushes on the north side of her house, and the riot of color on each of the soft, heavy quilts she pieced together by hand and gave to her grandchildren. These were some of my most treasured memories from my childhood and I was rather amused when my daughter, a lifelong resident of the suburbs, drew parallels between my childhood experiences and those she had read about in the *Little House on the Prairie* series.

Yet even as I told my daughter about my childhood and my grandmother, I was aware that I was providing a sanitized version. I focused exclusively on happy times and comforting memories, avoiding any information that might portray my grandmother as anything less than flawless. The reason for this is simple: I adored my grandmother. She loved me generously and unconditionally, gifts for which I continue to be grateful. But if I had been completely honest with my daughter, I would have told her that my grandmother was a complex person, as I believe most people to be. She was capable of unwavering love and incredible generosity, but she was also capable of intense dislike and could be mean-spirited at times. Sometimes, individuals were the target of her dislike. These were typically people who lived in our rural community and who had engaged in some action my grandmother deemed inappropriate. Other times, she focused on groups of people, treating them as a monolithic entity based on either a shared identity (such as race or country of origin) or shared beliefs (such as religion or politics). Over the years, many individuals and groups were the object of her scorn, including single mothers. In fact, it was my grandmother who introduced me to the word bastard. And through her repeated use of that word, she provided my earliest lessons about single mothers and their children.

My first lesson came in the form of an emotional outburst brought on by a traumatic event. It was a crisp fall morning and I was about four years old. I had spent the night at the farm and my grandmother woke me early so I could help her with chores. We put on our boots and coats and then headed outside to feed her chickens and collect their eggs. Although the chickens provided food, with both their eggs and their flesh, my grandmother treated them as pets, especially the half-dozen or so Bantam hens that laid small, perfect eggs no bigger than the end of her thumb. After a quick stop at the grain bin, we walked to the chicken coop and opened the door, expecting to be greeted by the clucking of dozens of hungry hens. Instead, we encountered a room strewn with blood and feathers. The cadavers of the birds were scattered across the floor, surrounded by kitten-sized paw prints. Minks had gotten into the chicken coop, killed the hens, eaten their fill, and fled the scene. My grandmother's response was instant. She dropped the pail of grain, sank to her knees, and let out an agonizing scream: "Bastards! Those bastards killed them all!" She wailed and sobbed until my grandfather, summoned by the sounds of her grief, arrived at the chicken coop, quickly assessed the situation, scooped up my grandmother, and carried her into the house. I followed behind, not really understanding what had happened. Tears streamed down my cheeks. The rest of the day passed in a blur. My grandfather phoned my parents, and once they arrived, they helped my grandfather gather the chickens. They threw away those that had been partially eaten, but they beheaded, gutted, and plucked those that could be frozen until they were needed for a Sunday dinner. My grandmother did not participate in the clearing out of the chicken coop. Instead, she lay in her bed and cried. I sat in the living room, listening to her sobs and feeling sad as the strange word "bastard" rang in my ears. I didn't know what it meant. But the incident in the chicken coop and my grandmother's use of the word had made it clear to me that a bastard was something bad. Whatever a bastard was, it was capable of killing my grandmother's beloved chickens. Therefore, I believed it was something very dangerous.

After this incident, I grew increasingly aware that my grandmother, who was typically a very mild-mannered person, frequently expressed her anger and frustration by using the word bastard. Indeed, it was her favorite curse word. She called the dog a bastard when it bit the milkman and he threatened to sue. The cows were dubbed bastards when they didn't get in the correct milking stalls, an act that slowed the twice-daily milking process considerably and created more work for my grandmother who then had to rearrange the animals. But people could be bastards, too, especially people my grandmother didn't like or people who acted in ways she deemed unacceptable. Lots of politicians were bastards, according to Grandma, especially Democrats, and in particular Jimmy Carter. Men who drank too much were bastards, as were those who hit their wives or girlfriends. She once labeled a close family friend a bastard when she learned he had left our Catholic congregation and converted to Lutheranism. And once, when she was very angry with my grandfather, she told me that she wasn't going to save any dessert for him because he was being a bastard. This was the worst word my grandmother knew and she used it to convey strong, negative emotions while simultaneously denigrating and disparaging those who were the object of her scorn. Thus, when I overheard my grandmother whispering to my aunt about an unmarried neighbor who "gave birth to a poor bastard son" and I recognized her tone of contempt, I quickly reasoned that this woman and her child must be very bad people. I imagined that if I ever met this woman, I would not talk to her. And if I ever met the baby, I would certainly never play with him. It all made perfect sense in my child's mind. Of course I later came to understand that there are several meanings of the word bastard. Yet a quick glance at any dictionary demonstrates that all of these meanings indicate lack or denote a flaw: an *il*legitimate child, a person who is *im*pure or greatly *dis*liked, a thing that is *ir*regular or *un*usual or *in*ferior. A bastard.

Did my grandmother believe children born to single mothers were inferior children? Did my grandmother think single mothers were unworthy or flawed? And did she mean to teach me that single mothers and their children should be avoided? In 2005, weeks after I earned my PhD, my grandmother died at the age of ninety-six. I was able to visit her in her final days, but I never had the opportunity to ask those questions. In the years since her death, I have occasionally found myself imagining her responses. The part of me that creates impromptu stories for my daughter that include only my fondest memories of my grandmother hopes she would have offered responses based on respect and love for all human beings. Yet another part of me is more realistic and remembers not only learning the word bastard from my grandmother but also the venom with which she used it. It is also this latter part of me that remembers my grandmother's reaction when, at twenty-four years old and unmarried, I gave birth to my eldest daughter. My grandmother did not call my daughter a bastard, at least not to my knowledge. In fact, she welcomed my daughter into the family, presenting her with a handmade quilt shortly after her birth, and she was eager to hold the child every time she saw her. Yet my grandmother also made it very clear that she was disappointed in me. She told me not to tell people that I wasn't married, particularly as she worried about damaging our family's reputation in the community. She also worried that my daughter and I were going to be burdens to society, openly lamenting my status as an unmarried mother and presuming, therefore, that I would never be financially self-sufficient. In addition, and despite the fact that she confessed a great dislike for my daughter's father, she encouraged me to marry him so I would have someone to take care of me and my child. Did my grandmother really prefer that I enter into a loveless marriage rather than remain a single mother? Yes, she did. And by articulating this wish for me, she provided me with yet another lesson on single motherhood.

My unanswered questions about my grandmother's opinions on single mothers and their children have been important to me on a personal level, particularly as I have spent a number of years as a single mother. Yet these questions have also been important to me professionally, especially in recent years as I've worked through the various stages of research, writing, editing, and revising that have contributed to this book. What would my grandmother think of the fact that I have spent over a decade doing academic research on single mothers? Would she consider it a waste of time if she knew that a good portion of the books, reports, journal articles, and news stories I've read during my academic career have related to unmarried mothers? Would she disregard my publications on this topic and consider them unimportant? Would she find it silly that several of my university courses include attention to the lives and experiences of single mothers? And what would she have to say about the experiences of the nearly 100 single mothers who participated in this research project and shared their life stories with me?

For example, what would my grandmother think of Alice Brooks? When I met her, Alice was twenty-two years old and the youngest child of a working-class, African American couple from rural Iowa. Although several of Alice's family members had attended college, none had completed their degree. Alice, who had excelled academically in high school and earned a prestigious scholarship to the University of Iowa (UI), nearly followed in their footsteps. She became pregnant during the second semester of her sophomore year at UI, and in the months that followed, she almost dropped out of school. Alice worried that if she tried to raise a child and go to college at the same time, one or the other would suffer. That is, she imagined that if she put most of her energies into parenting, then her grades would slip or that, conversely, if she focused too much on her academic responsibilities, then she might not be a good enough mother.

I spent time with Alice on a number of occasions throughout the spring semester of her senior year at UI. She was a full-time student and had already been accepted into a master's program in business administration. Her daughter, Abigail, at just over a year old, was a stunning child with dark eyes and a calm, inquisitive demeanor. Alice defined herself as a good student *and* a good mother. Her overall GPA of 3.37 demonstrated this, as did the devotion she had for her daughter. Although she admitted that combining the role of student and the role of single mother was difficult, she regarded the arrival of her daughter as a transformative event that helped her mature and become more serious about her academic pursuits:

> My grades were OK before, but they've been better since Abigail. She keeps me out of trouble and on track with my schooling. She keeps me in the house. I don't have time to go and do things like most college students, like going to the bars. I can't just sit at the coffee shop or go out to eat every day or go shopping. I just can't do those things. I don't have the money and I have to use my time a lot more wisely than that. I am pretty efficient. I get my work done on time and I do it well. I don't do what most college students do, like sleep for twelve hours straight and skip class whenever I feel like it or go out and get drunk on a Monday night and then be too hung over to go to classes the next day or sit up all night and watch a marathon of some TV show rather than doing my homework. I have obligations and responsibilities and I meet all of them.

By emphasizing her own high standards, wise use of time, efficiency, and seriousness about higher education, Alice presents herself as more responsible than "most college students," who, interestingly, she depicts in a stereotypical manner. Consequently, and in contrast to the stereotypical college student—an irresponsible partier who doesn't take education seriously—Alice claimed a unique identity, one that asserted her maternal identity as a source of maturity and achievement. It is difficult to dismiss this claim or disregard her achievements. As a single mother attending UI on a scholarship, Alice had established herself as a capable student at the same time that she was raising a happy, healthy, peaceful child. In

May 2005, Alice realized her dream and became the first in her family to earn a college degree, walking across the stage to receive her diploma as little Abigail and the rest of her family cheered her on.

I would also be curious to know what my grandmother would say about the experiences of Neva Rodriguez. I met Neva when she was thirty-four years old. She was divorced and raising two children while also working full time and taking nine credit hours each semester at Texas Woman's University (TWU). While many might be daunted at the prospect of combining full-time motherhood, part-time academics, and full-time employment, Neva didn't think her life was remarkable. Instead, she believed she was simply following the path God had chosen for her. She admitted it had been difficult, particularly during her thirteen-year marriage to an emotionally and physically abusive man. The difficulties continued after she left her husband and when her parents—who she described as "conservative, Catholic, and very traditional Mexican"—disowned her because she was a divorcée. These experiences had shaken Neva and caused her to question the particular course her life had taken. Yet she found comfort in her faith, trusting that God had a plan. And that plan, much to Neva's surprise, included abandoning her roles as "dutiful Hispanic daughter" and "dutiful Hispanic wife" in favor of a role she had not previously imagined for herself: college student.

Neva was initially nervous about going to college. She had been a poor student in high school and she was worried that she wouldn't fit in with the other college students. After all, by the time she enrolled in her first college course, Neva was nearly thirty, a full decade older than the eighteen- to twenty-year-olds she imagined would be her classmates at North Central Texas College (NCTC) in Corinth, Texas. She began with only one class her first semester but quickly gained some confidence in her academic abilities and became increasingly comfortable around the other students who included, much to her surprise, a number of individuals older than herself. For the next three-and-a-half years, she enrolled in two or three courses each semester, ultimately earning an Associate of Arts in Teaching degree in August 2005. Later that month, she began a full-time job as a teacher's aide at an elementary school near her home and began taking classes in the Teacher Education Program at TWU.

During the time I spent with Neva in the early months of 2007, she was working toward her bachelor's degree at TWU, working full time, raising her children, and preparing for a career as an elementary school teacher. She said that time management was her biggest concern. On weekdays, she worked as a teacher's aide from 7:30 A.M. to 4:30 P.M. She also attended classes two nights a week, often remaining on the TWU campus until 9:00 P.M. Neva's children were both active in various sports, academic clubs, and church-related activities. Consequently, on the nights she did not have a class, Neva spent her time chauffeuring them to practices, games, and meetings. Neva maintained a strict adherence to Catholicism, including the Fourth Commandment: keep holy the Sabbath day. This meant that she did not work or study on Sundays but instead devoted these days exclusively to worship. Neva believed that her strong organizational skills made it possible for her to combine the roles of mother, student, and employee. Yet she admitted that it was difficult. There were days when Neva was so busy she didn't have time to eat lunch or dinner. She seldom slept more than six hours a night. She rose long before the sun so she could pack lunches for her children and prepare for her day, and she typically didn't go to bed until around midnight, only after helping her children with homework, studying for her own classes, and tending to household tasks such as laundry. Neva felt that she was never able to spend enough time with her children and believed that her lengthy absences from home—on the days she worked and then went to class and didn't return home until after her children were in bed—had resulted in an emotional distance between herself and her children. Despite these concerns, however, Neva firmly believed this was the path God had meant for her to follow. When things went well, she praised God for his good works and his generosity. When things were difficult and she felt overwhelmed, Neva continued to praise him and reminded herself that "God [will] help me get through it . . . I rely on him every step of the way because I don't have anybody else."

I think my grandmother would also have been interested in hearing about Sarah Beardsley, a full-time student at Kirkwood Community College (KCC) who, at twenty-one years old, admitted that her life was "off track" and that she felt "just kind of lost." As she told me the story of her life, Sarah expressed many regrets and admitted that she "sometimes still wonder[ed] how I went from normal high school student" to a lonely young woman whose life revolved exclusively around caring for her three-year-old son and studying. The path was actually relatively easy to trace. Sarah became sexually active during her sophomore year of high school. Although she knew about and had access to various forms of birth control, her boyfriend, Justin, convinced her that "he would be careful and pull out before he ejaculated." Within months of her first sexual experience, Sarah became pregnant. Her parents, who were disappointed in their daughter, followed the advice of the school principal and enrolled Sarah in the community's alternative school. Many of the other young women who attended the school were also pregnant or already had children. Sarah began classes at the alternative school in the fall of her junior year, just three months before giving birth to her son, Cade. The arrival of her son was a joyful event, and Sarah felt it brought her and Justin closer. In fact, they became engaged shortly after Cade's birth. Their plan was simple. They would graduate from high school, marry the following summer, and then move to Ames, Iowa, where Justin would attend college. Sarah, who had never been interested in attending college, would be a stay-at-home wife and mother.

Sarah initially enjoyed motherhood. She also found the transition to her new school a pleasant one and even formed close friendships with several of the other young mothers who took classes at the alternative school. She also became friends with Marco, a handsome, humorous young man whom Sarah and the other girls at the school flirted with "on a regular basis." Because Justin still attended her old high school, Sarah didn't see him as often as she would have liked. She grew lonely and, in what she described as "a moment of utter stupidity," she skipped school one afternoon and went to Marco's house, where they had unprotected sex. Sarah was thankful that she did not get pregnant. However, the consequences of her indiscretion were devastating. Despite the fact that Justin "would have never found out about it," Sarah was overcome with guilt and decided to tell her fiancé about her encounter with Marco. Justin broke off their engagement and refused to see Sarah anymore. Sarah also had to contend with the response from her parents, who were "very angry and told me I had ruined my life." Although her parents had previously been willing to provide a home and financial support for Sarah and her son, now they were no longer willing to do so. Instead, they informed Sarah they would support her only until she graduated from high school. Lacking any prior work experience and with no high school diploma, Sarah could only find jobs that paid minimum wage. She pleaded with her parents, but they refused to reconsider.

Not knowing what else to do, Sarah made an appointment with a case worker at the Department of Human Services. She intended to apply for whatever state assistance was available to her and Cade, hoping it would sustain them until she could formulate a better plan. Sarah walked out of that meeting with approval for state benefits and a plan to go to college. The plan was simple: Sarah would participate in a workforce development program entitled Promise Jobs (PJ), attend KCC, and work toward her associate's degree. PJ would provide assistance for Sarah and her son that included a monthly cash stipend, Food Stamps, and Medicaid. PJ also paid her tuition, provided a stipend for textbooks, and paid for child care for Cade. Sarah was also able to secure Section 8 housing assistance and moved into a small two-bedroom apartment. In addition, and because she had no earned income, Sarah qualified for a Pell Grant under Federal Student Aid (FSA) guidelines. She also took out $3,000 in student loans each semester to help cover expenses such as groceries, transportation, and her cell phone bill.

Sarah believed that the forms of support she received through PJ and FSA were crucial and that without them, she and Cade would have likely been homeless. Yet she was unhappy. She didn't like her classes and her grades were not good. She stayed in school only so she could continue to receive support through

PJ and FSA. Sarah was also very lonely. She still missed Justin and missed being a "carefree kid whose parents took care of everything." Between attending classes, studying, and taking care of Cade, Sarah had little time to herself. She didn't have any close friends. Sarah also worried because she was only a semester away from completing her associate's degree in social work at KCC; once she finished her degree, the various forms of support she received would end. She worried about job prospects and future finances. Mostly, however, Sarah worried she would never find someone to marry and, thus, that she would remain a single mother forever.

If I could share the stories of Alice, Neva, and Sarah with my grandmother, I would ask her: Do you believe the children of these women are inferior children? Do you think these women are impure or flawed because they are single mothers? Did you mean to teach me that single mothers and their children should be shunned? Of course I will never get my grandmother's answers to these questions. In some respects, those answers matter a great deal. For personal reasons that are likely obvious given my relationship with my grandmother and my own experiences as a single mother, I would like to know how she would have responded. But her answers are also important for another reason, one that is more academic. Part of my own intellectual history includes my grandmother's use of the word bastard, the particular situations in which she used it, and my subsequent association of that word with people that are bad, immoral, harmful, and should be avoided. Whether she intended to or not, my grandmother provided me with lessons that served as the foundation for my thinking about single mothers and their children, a foundation that cannot be disconnected from my intellectual present. This is true regardless of what other lessons I have encountered on this subject and in spite of the fact that my current thinking about single mothers and their children is very different from the ideas and attitudes my grandmother espoused.

Yet in other ways, her answers seem irrelevant. After all, I am no longer a child. I loved her dearly, yet I no longer see her as almost a saint, as I did when I was a child. Despite the fact that I exclusively portray her as a kind and generous woman in the stories I tell my daughter, I am fully aware that my grandmother was judgmental and even hostile at some times and toward certain people. Thus, as an adult, I would not regard her responses to my questions as lessons but instead as mere opinions. Additionally, the childhood lessons my grandmother provided no longer comprise the exclusive or even the most significant lens through which I think about single motherhood. I have firsthand knowledge of what it is like to be an unmarried woman raising children, garnered through the years I spent as a never-married single mother in the 1990s and, more recently, as a divorced mother. Equally important has been my academic training, including my engagement with feminist and critical scholarly analyses of single motherhood in America, specifically its historical, social, economic, and political dimensions. I have also learned about single motherhood by spending a significant amount of time with single mothers, through my research and through professional and personal relationships.

Finally, it is important to recognize that my grandmother's views strongly reflected the type of condescension and blaming that has been and continues to be directed toward single mothers in America. I was born and raised in the United States, in a culture that, in many ways, has regarded single mothers as impure, has treated children born to single mothers as inferior, and has shunned these women and their children. Thus, it seems likely that even if I not learned lessons about single motherhood from my grandmother, I would have gotten them elsewhere, through interactions with various social institutions such as religion, media, education, and politics. During my childhood and adolescence, such institutions reinforced the lessons my grandmother provided. More recently, however, they have become the subject of my own scholarly analysis. My academic interest lies, in part, in the persistent, pervasive, and dominant portrayal of single mothers as bad and in the blaming of single mothers for a variety of social ills, including the supposed decline of the American family. But I am equally interested in the ways that single mothers engage with this dominant portrayal—sometimes resisting and refuting it, at other times internalizing and reinforcing it—particularly in the context of American colleges and universities. This engagement and the experiences of single mothers as they pursue higher education constitute the core of this project.

I want to return to the subject of storytelling. This project is ethnographic, and as such, it is about telling stories. It focuses on the stories that single mothers who are college students tell about their lives, about their paths to single motherhood, about their reasons for pursuing a college education, about their experiences as nontraditional college students, and about other aspects of their lives, including the personal, financial, academic, and social dimensions. I collected their stories through ethnographic research and have replicated those stories through my own unique style of writing. Thus, this book constitutes a retelling of their lives. I have made a conscious effort to ethically and accurately retell the narratives of the women who participated in this project. I have not attempted to sanitize those stories or to purposefully provide positive portrayals of the women, the way I do when I share my childhood memories of my grandmother with my youngest daughter. However, I do not pretend that I engaged in this project as a sort of blank slate or that I wrote this book as a detached, dispassionate observer. Nor I do not present this retelling as a sort of definitive, exhaustive account. Instead, I offer it as an ethnography that is inherently partial and incomplete, an attempt to contribute to the growing body of scholarly work about the experiences of single mothers in America and single mothers who pursue higher education in particular.

Furthermore, given the more than twenty years I have spent in higher education—approximately half as a student and half as an educator—I have a good understanding of how such institutions operate. I believe that educational institutions have a responsibility to support the needs of all of their students, including single mothers. Thus, I raise critical questions throughout the book, urging readers to contemplate the effectiveness of the various strategies single mothers use to address the challenges they face and to imagine other strategies and their potential outcomes. In addition, I offer examples of specific programs and policies that have been designed in an effort to better meet the needs of the single mothers as they pursue higher education. I have made no effort to hide my opinions on these matters, although readers will find that my opinions do not constitute the foundation of this book.

Instead, this project focuses on the experiences of single mothers who are college students and what they had to say about their experiences. It explores both the commonalities and variations among them and illustrates that despite the obstacles they encounter, these women regarded postsecondary education not only as a means of escaping poverty but also as a way to demonstrate to themselves and others that they were good mothers. Even as they struggled to reconcile their competing roles and responsibilities as college students and single mothers, they tended to define pursuit of a college degree as an extension of their mothering work, something they did to help ensure the long-term health and well-being of their children and their family unit. Thus, the project demonstrates how these single mothers challenged traditional definitions of maternal practice and mothering work. Yet even as they did so, they framed their decisions, actions, and goals in the context of the rather narrow rhetoric of middle-class family norms that were promulgated in late twentieth- and early twenty-first-century mainstream popular culture and political debates. Consequently, the women reinforced the ideal of the good mother as all-loving, self-sacrificing, and devoted to her children above all else. They also replicated a definition of good mothering that characterized it as financially expensive and labor intensive. This will be particularly clear to readers in the chapters that focus on the women's financial situations, on the ways they managed their time, on their child care arrangements, and on their encounters with the so-called chilly climate of higher education. But first, for purposes of contextualization, I offer a discussion the political dimensions of motherhood in the United States.

1 · THE POLITICS OF SINGLE MOTHERHOOD IN THE UNITED STATES

A SINGLE MOTHER PURSUES HIGHER EDUCATION, PART I: GINA OCON

As she prepared to graduate from high school, Gina Ocon found herself in an enviable position. She had excelled in both academics and extracurricular activities during high school and had achieved a 3.9 cumulative grade point average (GPA). She had also earned admission to several Ivy League institutions as well as the Air Force Academy. In the fall of 1994, just months after receiving her high school diploma, the eighteen-year-old left her home in Lakewood, California, and traveled nearly 3,000 miles to Cambridge, Massachusetts. There, she began her undergraduate studies at Harvard University with the support of a scholarship valued at approximately $30,000 a year. Ocon's freshman year was a busy one. She devoted considerable time to academics, achieving a nearly 3.5 GPA. She also joined the crew team and the model legislature and worked at the American Repertory Theater. It was, by all measures, a successful year for the ambitious and talented young woman, a year that represented a significant step down the path she had planned for her post–high school life: "an Ivy League degree, law school, a job in international relations, and, one day, an ambassadorship."[1]

After completing final exams for the spring 1995 semester, Ocon returned home for the summer. Shortly after her arrival in the Long Beach area, she crossed paths with Tommaso Maggiore, a young man who had been her high school classmate. Maggiore was also a college student, pursuing academics at Long Beach City College. He also worked in his family's Italian restaurant, Andiamo. Although the Ocon and Maggiore had not dated previously, they soon began what she would later refer to as a "summer fling."[2] They were described as a dashing couple: "she had been a former beauty contestant runner-up, he was a well-dressed, handsome heir to a popular restaurant."[3] By most accounts, Ocon and Maggiore were inseparable that summer, "popping into local dance clubs, lounging at the beach, and cruising on Maggiore's motorcycle."[4] As the fall semester drew near and Ocon prepared to return to Harvard and resume her studies, she and Maggiore decided to continue their relationship long-distance. Several weeks later, not yet midway through her sophomore year at Harvard, Ocon realized she was pregnant. She discussed the situation with Maggiore and the couple decided that Ocon would withdraw from the university, return to California, and move in with Maggiore and his parents.

On June 17, 1996, Gina Ocon gave birth to a daughter, Bailey Marie Theresa Maggiore. Less than two months later, accompanied by her daughter and Maggiore, Ocon returned to the Cambridge area. The couple had worked out what appeared to be a reasonable plan. Maggiore applied at one of Harvard's elite dining clubs and intended to work full time. Ocon intended to, with the support of her scholarship, resume her studies and complete her undergraduate degree. Yet their plans did not come to fruition. By the time they arrived in Cambridge, on-campus housing was no longer available, and as a result, they could not find an affordable place to live. Ocon was forced to delay her education plans for another year, and the couple and their daughter returned to Long Beach, where they continued to live with Maggiore's family. Shortly after their return, however, the couple had a number of arguments and Ocon decided to end the relationship, moving out of the Maggiore home and taking Bailey with her. She applied for welfare benefits, ultimately receiving $453 a month, something she regarded as a temporary, stopgap solution. She still intended to return to Harvard.

Maggiore, however, did not wish to be separated from his daughter. Only days after Ocon ended their relationship, Maggiore filed for custody of Bailey. He also filed a temporary restraining order as a means of preventing Ocon from moving across the country and taking the child with her. Maggiore made it clear that he did not intend to prevent Ocon from resuming her studies. Instead, he claimed that he was looking after the best interests of his daughter, particularly as he believed Bailey would receive better care if she remained with him. However, the case was a complicated one. Maggiore had never paid child support, and he had been arrested on several occasions for alcohol-related incidents. Furthermore, Maggiore admitted that he could not afford to support the child on the approximately $800 a month he earned as a waiter. Yet he still believed he should be granted custody of Bailey, assuring the court that he would continue to live with his parents and they would assume financial responsibility for Bailey. He also indicated that his parents would care for the child while Maggiore worked and attended classes. Maggiore contrasted the multigenerational, stable home environment he intended to provide for Bailey with the less appealing environment he believed Ocon could offer. He did not believe that Ocon could be a full-time student at Harvard and still manage to provide appropriate care for their child, arguing that "the school that she's going to demands that you put 100 percent into school. I don't think she'd be able to handle it as well as if she had family support back over here. I really don't think she would be capable of doing it."[5]

The case was what is commonly referred to as a move-away case, a type of custody dispute that typically involves one parent seeking to move out of state in order to pursue a job opportunity. Such a move results in significantly reduced contact between the noncustodial parent and the child. Although in the Ocon-Maggiore case, the motivation for moving out of state was education rather than employment, the court still had to consider the same rights, responsibilities, and interests that are used in other move-away cases: the rights and responsibilities of Ocon, who sought to relocate in pursuit of educational opportunities, versus the rights and responsibilities of the noncustodial parent, Maggiore, including his right to maintain a meaningful relationship with his daughter. And central to the case were the best interests of the child. On May 6, 1997, Long Beach family court commissioner John Chemelski handed down his decision. Maggiore was ordered to pay child support of $213 a month plus the cost of day care and was granted visitation rights. Ocon, who was still eligible for her full scholarship, was awarded sole custody of Bailey and granted the right to move out of state with her daughter. Soon after, Bailey and her mother were back in Massachusetts. The child attended Bigelow Cooperative Day Care while Ocon attended Harvard.

The case, however, was far from settled. Only months later, Maggiore filed for custody a second time, "alleging that Ocon has failed to take adequate care of their child"[6] because Bailey was attending day care. He argued, once again, that he could provide a better environment for the child because he was still living with his parents and they would help support the child financially and provide care for Bailey so she would not have to be placed in a day care setting. Maggiore's mother, Theresa, believed that day care was detrimental to Bailey because "she's in day care, eight hours a day, five days a week. . . . Every time Bailey has been here, she's been sick. She comes here sick. She goes back healthy. She comes back sick."[7] Ocon managed to retain custody of her daughter. In June 2000, after several years of what she referred to as the "ultimate juggling act"[8] that involved balancing the demands of college coursework with her role as a full-time mother, she graduated from Harvard.

A SINGLE MOTHER PURSUES HIGHER EDUCATION, PART II: JENNIFER IRELAND

Ocon's experiences as a single mother pursuing a college degree in the mid-1990s were not entirely unique. In fact, there are some striking similarities between Ocon's situation and that of Jennifer Ireland, a young woman from the Detroit suburb of Mount Clemens. Ireland was a fifteen-year-old sophomore in high school when she began dating football star Steven Smith, age sixteen. The couple had been together for only a few months before they became sexually active and Ireland became pregnant. When she shared the news with Smith, he encouraged her to have an abortion. Ireland initially agreed, but after driving to the reproductive health clinic to terminate the pregnancy, she changed her mind. Her religious beliefs were particularly important in this decision as Ireland, a Catholic, said she "started thinking that I was going to burn in hell for even considering this. So I left."[9] Ireland decided to continue the pregnancy and on April 22, 1991, she gave birth to her daughter, Maranda Kate Ireland Smith. Although he had not been involved with Ireland during the pregnancy, Smith visited his former girlfriend and the newborn in the hospital. However, he did not indicate a desire to be involved in his daughter's life. Ireland, who was only sixteen at the time of her daughter's birth and was daunted by the prospect of raising a child alone, initially put Maranda in foster care with the intention of allowing the child to be adopted. However, after three weeks, Ireland changed her mind—she decided to raise her daughter. Ireland's mother and thirteen-year-old younger sister offered to help look after Maranda. As a result, Ireland was able to catch up on her studies. She completed her sophomore year on time with an impressive 3.98 GPA.

For reasons that are not entirely clear, Smith refrained from visiting or otherwise interacting with his infant daughter for nearly a year, but then began to show an interest in Maranda around the time of her first birthday. Ireland permitted Smith to see the little girl, but she also filed for child support. Smith was initially ordered to pay $62 a week, but the amount was then reduced to a mere $12. Smith still lived with his parents, and they dedicated one of the bedrooms in their home to Maranda so she had somewhere to stay when she visited her father and her grandparents on weekends. However, Smith and Ireland did not have a harmonious relationship. They often quarreled over visitation and after an altercation on Christmas Eve in 1992, Ireland charged Smith with assault. He denied the charges and responded with a countersuit, demanding full custody of Maranda. As the case wound its way through the court system, there were a number of changes in Ireland's life. She graduated from Cardinal Mooney Catholic High School. Despite the demands of being a teen mom, she had done well in her studies, graduating third in her class and securing both admission and an $11,000-a-year scholarship to the University of Michigan (UM). Ireland moved to Ann Arbor a few months after finishing high school in order to pursue full-time studies at the university. She also enrolled her daughter at a licensed, in-home day care that the university had recommended. While Maranda was in day care, Ireland attended classes, studied, and completed her homework. She and Maranda lived in university-provided family housing on campus. Because Smith failed to pay child support, Ireland was the sole financial provider for Maranda.[10]

Midway through the spring semester of Ireland's first year at UM, the assault case against Smith and the custody case came to court in the same week. The assault case was dismissed. Judge Raymond R. Cashen of Macomb County Circuit Court, an admitted advocate of "family values,"[11] considered the evidence in the custody case. Smith's attorney "attacked Jennifer Ireland's behavior as a mother, accusing her of drug and alcohol abuse and sexual misconduct. Jennifer denied all such allegations."[12] Cashen also considered the expert opinions of two social service agencies he had appointed to independently review the case. Both agencies reported that Maranda's home life with Ireland was a positive one and recommended that Ireland retain custody. In June 1994, the judge issued his decision. Cashen acknowledged that Ireland had provided a stable home for the child and even acknowledged that the little girl "looked to her mother for guidance, discipline, and the necessities of life."[13] Yet he was concerned about the fact that Maranda attended day care: "The mother's academic pursuits, although laudable, are demanding and in order to complete her program it necessitates the leaving of the child for a considerable portion of its life in the care of strangers. There is no way that a single parent, attending an academic program at an institution as prestigious as the University of Michigan, can do justice to their studies and the raising of an infant child. There are not that many hours in the day."[14] In essence, Cashen determined that Ireland could not devote adequate time to being a mother because of the demands associated with being a college student. Consequently, he awarded custody to Smith. The young man was still living with his parents. He worked part-time and, in a rather ironic twist, was also a college student, pursuing an education part-time at Macomb Community College in Warren, Michigan. Because of his work- and school-related demands, Smith's mother, a homemaker, would be Maranda's primary caretaker. In fact, Smith's mother assured the court she "would devote her entire time to raising the child when the father was not available to assume his responsibilities in this area."[15] From Cashen's perspective, awarding custody to Smith was in Maranda's best interests simply because she would be cared for by a blood relative, her grandmother, instead of attending a day care and being cared for by strangers.

Ireland appealed the decision. A temporary stay was issued and Ireland was allowed to retain custody of Maranda during the appeals process. As the case moved forward, a diverse group of more than sixty associations and organizations collaborated to submit amici curiae on the case, including the U.S. Civil

Liberties Union, the National Organization for Women, the United Auto Workers, the Feminist Majority Foundation, the University of Michigan Single Parent Coalition, the Child Welfare League of America, and the National Center on Women and Family Law, to name only a few. After reviewing the case and the evidence presented, the Michigan Court of Appeals issued its ruling in November 1995. The decision affirmed the lower court's assessment of both Ireland and Smith, specifically with regard to the determination that "the parties are equal, or the proofs neutral" as they pertained to emotional attachment to and relationship with Maranda, suitability of home environment, and the "mental and physical health" and "mortal fitness of the parties involved."[16] However, the decision reversed the custody determination Cashen had made on the basis that "it was a clear legal error to consider . . . which party's arrangement was preferable for the child's care while her parent was working or at school."[17] The case was then remanded to the lower court for reconsideration with the stipulation that Cashen be disqualified from any further proceedings on this matter because of concerns that had been raised about his bias. In October 1996, Ireland and Smith agreed to share custody of their daughter. At that time, Ireland also withdrew from UM and moved back to her mother's home in order to honor the shared custody agreement, thereby allowing Maranda to have more frequent contact with her father.[18]

The cases involving Gina Ocon and Jennifer Ireland raised a number of issues concerning parental rights and child custody. As the legal aspects of these cases were debated and decided in the courtrooms of California and Michigan, respectively, corollary debates were happening in the U.S. court of public opinion. Both cases received considerable media coverage. In fact, the coverage was so extensive in the Ireland case that the Michigan Court of Appeals commented that

> in this case, the media frenzy generated by the trial court's decision reached national proportions. Numerous newspaper and magazine articles, as well as radio and television references, appeared throughout Michigan and elsewhere. We are concerned that some of the trial judge's reported comments appear inconsistent with his expressed findings of fact. Because we have found that the record supports those factual findings, we conclude that the nature and scope of the media exposure create an appearance of bias in this case.[19]

While media reports focused on various facets of the case, most of the attention was on Jennifer Ireland herself, specifically her activities and life decisions. A few years later, Gina Ocon also found herself the focus of newspapers, morning news programs, and talk shows across the United States. As they faced their respective custody battles, these two young women made headlines in numerous cities across the country.[20] Some of the media coverage raised issues about "single mother bashing" and gender bias as it pertained to women who put their children in day care.[21] Other articles praised the young women for their ambition.[22] Some focused on concerns about infringement on father's rights while others concentrated on the well-being of the children involved.[23] While the rhetoric of this media coverage is certainly important, of equal importance is what prompted such lively debate in the first place. Why did the U.S. press and, by extension, the U.S. public care so much about the lives of these two young women?

DIVERGENT IDENTITIES AND EXPERIENCES OF MOTHERHOOD

Contemporary debates about motherhood demonstrate the deeply political nature of maternal experience, identity, and practice in the United States. A particular rhetoric of family values continues to be central to constructions of motherhood and is grounded in the imagined norm of the Standard North American Family (SNAF),[24] a norm based on the model of a white, married, middle-class, heterosexual couple that includes a male breadwinner and stay-at-home wife and mother plus their biological offspring. Yet the politicization of motherhood is certainly not a new phenomenon. On the contrary, it is as old as the United States itself, articulated in relation to social constructs of gender, race, socioeconomic status, sexuality, and other identities. Such identities are important individually yet they also intersect with one another within and across existing power hierarchies. Thus, it is at the intersection of such identities that the experience and institution of motherhood is shaped and that cultural ideals of motherhood are politically constituted.[25]

A historical examination demonstrates that motherhood has been promoted, rewarded, and even required for certain women in the United States. Conversely, it has been discouraged, opposed, and denied for others. In colonial America, for example, motherhood was promoted through an emphasis on the white family unit as the foundation of society, a "little commonwealth" or a "little cell of righteousness" intended to reflect and reinforce social norms.[26] Family was the center of society in colonial America, a patriarchal institution that was held responsible for instilling a proper attitude toward work, religion, authority, and society. Thus, the family unit was arguably the most important social institution in the colonies. It helped promote conformity and, by extension, helped maintain social order and stability in the community. As a result, both single adults who lived alone and married couples who lived apart from each other were regarded with suspicion. They faced legal and social penalties:

Town courts fined single persons and couples who lived apart, and taxed bachelors and self-supporting single women for evading their civic responsibility. Unmarried women, in addition, faced social disapproval as dependent girls and incomplete women. Without a husband, a colonial woman was not a "real" woman. Single women with means and widows were respected somewhat more, but newspapers and town gossips often characterized single females as unattractive, disagreeable "old virgins" unable to attract a man.[27]

Unmarried adult white women, including widows, divorced women, those abandoned by their spouses, and those who never married, were often suspected of immorality. They were frequently regarded as both an economic and a social burden to the community, simply because they existed outside a socially sanctioned family unit. Although adult white women who married and bore children garnered social acceptance, they had little power in the family. The husband was head of the household, a status that was regarded as divinely ordained, and he had absolute authority over his wife and children. Indeed, the law of coverture meant that a woman suffered a type of legal death upon marrying, as her entire identity was subsumed under that of her husband. A married woman's primary role was to reproduce in order to expand the population of the colonies. On average, a woman could expect to spend a decade and a half engaged in the reproductive activities of pregnancy, childbirth, and lactation.[28]

Similarly, in the post-Revolution United States, where domestic life, female virtue, childbearing, and child-rearing were linked to notions of morality and civic duty,[29] the maternal role of white women was emphasized, specifically for those with financial privilege. Although such women were encouraged to marry and reproduce, the rationale for doing so was decidedly different than it had been in colonial America. The complex influence of the Enlightenment, the Great Awakening, and the American Revolution—especially the ideas about freedom, citizenship, and the right to representation that formed the core of revolutionary ideology—resulted in an expanded role for women in the new republic. Women were still not regarded as full citizens, but motherhood was no longer simply an activity that took place in the private sphere of the home; instead, it became a role that had decidedly political implications. Women were urged to regard child-rearing as a civic duty, a role through which they would instill in their children the morals and values of the young republic. By doing so, the republican mother would raise her children to be good citizens. Especially important was the raising of sons who, once they reached adulthood and entered the political sphere, would presumably not only defend but also promote American values. Thus, while the role of the republican mother continued to focus on women's role as mothers, the power associated with mothering work was cast in decidedly different terms than it had been in colonial America and was explicitly connected to national politics.

Of course the ideals of motherhood espoused in colonial America and during the immediate post-Revolution era were not ideals that all women were expected or, more accurately, permitted to emulate. While white women with economic means were held to such ideals, women of color and poor women were excluded from them. For women of African ancestry, motherhood was another part of the forced labor they experienced under conditions of slavery. Regarded as property and chattel and likened to livestock by those who bought and sold them, female slaves were valued for the labor they could provide, including both agricultural work and domestic labor in the homes of white families. However, the reproductive labor of female slaves was also noteworthy. Those who were taken from Africa were frequently forced to engage in sexual activities with the crew of slave ships and some were impregnated.[30] In addition, throughout the period of slavery in the United States, female slaves were raped and impregnated by plantation owners and overseers, a practice that was widely accepted due to presumptions concerning Black female sexuality. Such presumptions were reflected in the Jezebel stereotype,[31] a characterization widely endorsed by those who benefited from existing racial and gender hierarchies:

> The Jezebel stereotype was used during slavery as a rationalization for sexual relations between white men and black women, especially sexual unions involving slavers and slaves. The Jezebel was depicted as a black woman with an insatiable appetite for sex. She was not satisfied with black men. The slavery-era Jezebel, it was claimed, desired sexual relations with white men; therefore, white men did not have to rape black women. . . . Slave women were property; therefore, legally they could not be raped.[32]

The children born as a result of the rape of slave women were legally classified as Black and therefore were regarded as part of the "plantation's inventory as though the child were a lamb or a bale of cotton."[33] Within the political-economic-social system of slavery, the reproductive capacity of female slaves became part of their relative value, particularly as their ability to give birth enabled plantation owners to increase their slave population without purchasing additional slaves. Although slave women who gave birth were mothers in the biological sense, their social identity as mothers was not legally recognized. Instead, they were defined as breeders.

Whereas slave women in early America were required to reproduce, poor women were discouraged from doing so. The doctrines of Calvinism stated that social hierarchies were divinely ordained; certain populations were predestined to be wealthy and others to be poor. Consequently, wealthy colonists had an obligation to care for the poor, both because the poor were regarded as "not responsible" for their condition and because caring for the poor provided a means for wealthy individuals, in the words of Puritan leader John Winthrop, "to do more service to the Lord."[34] To this end, the colonists looked to the English Poor Law of 1601, implementing a system that included apprenticeship for poor children and outdoor aid for those with short-term need. Poor adults with longer-term need, including widows and those with disabilities, were frequently placed in the homes of wealthy families and their care was funded through taxes and local dues.[35] Yet as the number of people living in poverty surged, attitudes toward the poor began to shift. They were increasingly regarded as prone to laziness, vice, and moral depravity. With these shifting attitudes came a corresponding shift in support for the poor. By the late 1700s, communities increasingly turned to indoor aid or poorhouses, institutions that served the dual purpose of "offer[ing] respite to those who were desperately in need and stand[ing] as a deterrent to the idle, intemperate poor."[36] In this context, poor women's childbearing became an increasing concern, as their children were deemed a public burden due to their economic situation and the presumed "harmful influences of the poor community" into which they were born.[37]

Similarly, single women were actively discouraged from reproducing, something that comes as no surprise, given the emphasis on the male-headed family unit in early America. A woman who was sexually active outside marriage was regarded as immoral and was ostracized in her community, dubbed a "whore, adulteress, slut, or 'brasen-faced bawd.'"[38] Despite this, it was not uncommon for single women to become pregnant during this period; "it is estimated that during the Revolutionary era, one-third to one-half of all recorded first births were the result of premarital intercourse."[39] Yet given the gendered dynamics of social and economic power, single women's financial resources and their ability to care for their children was quite limited. Furthermore, children born out of wedlock were legally classified as *filius nullius*, "the child and heir of no one," and their identity and lineage was linked to neither their mother nor their father.[40] Such children became wards of the community or parish into which they were born. In an effort to discourage pregnancy among single women and punish those who gave birth outside marriage, so-called bastardy laws were implemented. As part of the proceedings in bastardy cases, courts sought to determine paternity. Although women in labor sometimes "confessed" the name of the father of their child and some fathers identified themselves during court proceedings, paternity could not always be established.[41] Thus, while it was possible for some males to avoid the social and legal consequences associated with out-of-wedlock childbearing, single women could not do so; the birth of a child constituted incontrovertible proof of their illegal sexual activities.

GOOD MOTHERS AND BAD MOTHERS IN TWENTIETH-CENTURY AMERICA

Another fundamental element of the politicization of motherhood in America is the tendency for people to see certain groups of mothers as good and others as bad. In the twentieth century, various psychoanalytic, scientific, and popular discourses drew increasing attention to women's maternal roles and responsibilities and formed the foundation for such categorizations. The emergence of psychoanalytic theory prompted increasing concerns about child-rearing, particularly as the early years of a child's life were thought to impact their long-term mental health. In particular, Freudian theory shifted the goal of child-rearing from socialization to self-realization, and with this shift came the belief that mothers, as primary caretakers, were principally responsible for the psychological development and well-being of children.[42] Attention to child development continued throughout the century as psychologists, pediatricians, and other professionals—including so-called baby gurus such as Benjamin Spock, T. Berry Brazelton, and Penelope Leach[43]—helped popularize ideas about child development and educate mothers about the particulars of healthy child development through books, television programs, and parent education classes.[44] Similarly, medical and scientific discourses emphasized the physical health and well-being of children. Concerns over feeding practices, proper nutrition, personal hygiene, exercise, sanitary conditions of the home and surrounding environment, and even household products such as bathroom tissue were fueled by the opinions of doctors and scientists. Such opinions contributed to the development of "scientific motherhood"[45] and its corresponding "insistence that women require expert scientific and medical advice to raise their children healthfully."[46] Consequently, medical and scientific discourses about child-rearing were incorporated into U.S. political institutions. The Children's Bureau, for example, published the widely distributed booklet, *Infant Care*, and other literature to inform mothers that successful child care required reliance on specially trained physicians.[47] Mothers were told to ignore their instincts, ignore the advice of other mothers, and ignore their cultural and experiential knowledge about child-rearing. Women's magazines, television programs and movies, and other elements popular culture also adopted this attitude.[48]

One consequence of the proliferation of expert scientific and medical discourses was the transformation of cultural ideals, expectations, and definitions of motherhood. Such discourses were central in shaping the ideal of the good mother, an ideal defined by "intensive mothering" and a maternal practice that was "child-centered, expert-guided, emotionally absorbing, labor-intensive, and financially expensive."[49] This ideology became so enmeshed in U.S. culture that as the twentieth century drew to a close, ideals of mothering were defined quite narrowly. The all-loving, self-sacrificing, stay-at-home, middle-class, white, heterosexual, married mother was presented as the model against whom all mothers and against whom all women, including women who are not mothers, were measured: "Imagine a woman who only wants what is best for her children. Whose needs she intuits effortlessly. This mother adores her offspring and finds them fascinating. She is exquisitely attuned to her children and is so resourceful that she is immune to boredom. Nurturing comes as naturally as breathing, and child rearing is a source of pleasure that does not require discipline or self-sacrifice. She is the Good Mother."[50] Despite the increasing likelihood that women would combine motherhood with other roles, U.S. social policies provided little support for mothers. Consequently, mothers were, in many respects, "left alone to juggle the simultaneous demands" they faced, regardless of their marital status.[51] This lack of support, combined with "the new momism," a contemporary idealization of motherhood that insisted that "all mothers become more closely tethered to their kids,"[52] created an ideal of motherhood in the United States that was unattainable yet was the yardstick by which mothers were measured.

Not surprisingly, the twentieth-century image of the good mother was joined by its counterpart, the bad mother, although shifting cultural codes and discourses made this category more fluid and difficult to define. At various moments, for example, women were labeled as bad mothers on the basis of specific actions and practices that included their eating patterns and weight gain during pregnancy, the number of children they bore, the intervals between births of their children, their legal status with regard to child custody, their participation in the labor force, their breastfeeding practices, and their participation in surrogacy programs.[53] Furthermore, just as social identities were significant in shaping the experiences of mothers in early America, these were also key factors in the labeling of certain groups of mothers as bad. Teen mothers, for example, were labeled bad on the basis of their age, African American mothers were targeted on the basis of racial identity, and lesbian mothers were deemed bad on the basis of their sexual identity.[54] Married mothers were regarded as the norm, while those who gave birth outside the institution of marriage or who became single mothers through divorce were deemed deviant. In fact, it is arguable that of the groups of mothers who are targeted as bad, single mothers are among those who have borne this label and its burdens most consistently from the late nineteenth century to present.

REPRODUCTIVE POLITICS: SINGLE MOTHERHOOD IN THE UNITED STATES

In the waning decades of the nineteenth century, social reformers grew increasingly concerned about unwed mothers. Interestingly, such reformers did not blame the women for out-of-wedlock conception and birth; instead, they believed that illegitimate childbearing was a consequence of poverty, specifically the inadequate home life and lack of moral training that were presumed to be synonymous with poverty. Thus, reformers saw unwed mothers as victims of circumstance. They did not label them as bad mothers. Instead, they saw them as deserving of sympathy and assistance from the more fortunate members of society. In this vein, Christian-based benevolent organizations sought to provide direct services and support for the "fallen women and wayward girls"[55] who had "lost the glory of their womanhood."[56] Their chief means of assisting single mothers was the residential maternity home.[57] The goal of such homes was, quite simply, to rescue unwed mothers by providing them with a safe living environment, teaching them "habits of industry and self-help . . . lead[ing] them to Christ for salvation."[58] Perhaps the most well-known maternity homes were those operated by the National Florence Crittenton Mission (NFCM). Founded in New York in 1883 with the opening of the Florence Night Mission, the NFCM was a Christian-based organization that initially sought to provide shelter for prostitutes and help them get off the streets of New York. Yet it soon began to concentrate on unwed expectant mothers. Aided by the endorsement of President William McKinley, who granted a national charter to the organization, the NFCM included more than seventy residential homes in cities across America by 1909.[59] Staffed primarily by volunteers who were "predominantly white middle-class evangelically oriented Protestant women," the early Crittenton homes aimed to provide a safe living environment for unwed pregnant mothers and help them realize their mothering potential through instruction in proper infant and child care.[60]

With the expansion of professional social work in the 1920s and 1930s, however, attitudes toward single mothers began to shift. This is evident in the discourse of deviance that permeated both research on single motherhood during the period and the movement away from supporting and sheltering the single mother and toward rehabilitating her in accordance with middle-class notions of appropriate femininity.[61] Earlier environmental-based explanations for out-of-wedlock pregnancy and childbearing were abandoned as the purported cause of illegitimate childbearing was identified as a problem in the moral code of the single mother. Consequently, maternity homes became "places of treatment"[62] where the woman who became pregnant out of wedlock could undergo a type of moral rehabilitation. This shift was evident in the operation of these facilities and attitudes toward the residents:

No longer was the relationship between worker and unmarried mother to be that of mother and daughter. Seeking to divest this relationship of its moral and familial overtones, social workers recommended that the proper relationship was that of "professional" to "client," with all of the objectivity and distance required by such a relationship. In exchanging the "sisterly" or "maternal" relationship to unmarried mothers for that of the neutral and objective professional, social workers congratulated themselves for jettisoning moralism and condescension. Indeed, underneath proclamations of sisterhood lay moralism and condescension of the highest order. The attitude of evangelicals toward unmarried mothers, implicit in their efforts to redeem and rehabilitate their predominantly working-class charges according to the standards of middle-class domesticity and respectability, occasionally surfaced in day-to-day relationships. One evangelical worker, in a candid moment, spoke to the limits of sisterhood: "It is easy to love the babies . . . but it is not always easy, in ordinary circumstances, to love some of the unlovable mothers."[63]

The daily routine for residents included religious instruction, basic education, and training in child care and domestic arts such as sewing, cooking, cleaning, and personal hygiene. Free time was limited. In addition, each resident was typically expected to stay at the home for a minimum of six months after the birth of her child so social work professionals could continue to monitor her transition to motherhood. The routine of the maternity home and the accompanying guidance of social work professionals were intended to provide the structure and supervision an unwed mother needed to successfully rehabilitate and adopt a morally honorable life.[64]

Numerous social changes in the 1930s and 1940s, however, again altered attitudes toward both unwed mothers and their offspring. The Great Depression brought increased attention to the economic costs associated with maternity homes, and private donations decreased dramatically during this time.[65] In addition, the implementation of New Deal social policies meant that funding for maternity homes began to include more public funds. As a result, the policies and financial aspects of maternity homes drew scrutiny from taxpayers. Cutting costs became an imperative and was facilitated in a variety of ways, including by discouraging and, in some cases, prohibiting lengthy stays at maternity homes.[66] The expansion of adoption laws and the corresponding increase in the number of adoption agencies in this period were also significant factors in changing attitudes toward white single mothers. This combination of economic, political, and social factors helped bring about a new understanding of unwed pregnancy. The white single mother was no longer regarded as lacking morals. Instead, her out-of-wedlock pregnancy was regarded as a symptom of mental illness. This is not to suggest that the discourse of deviance from earlier decades was abandoned. Instead, in the immediate post–World War II decades, social scientists, politicians, psychologists, and maternity home staff constructed the deviance of the white unwed mother as a temporary state that was the result of psychological weakness and maladjustment.

Such maladjustment was most often regarded as a consequence of "gender dysfunction and family dysfunction."[67] Consequently, individual and group counseling sessions were designed to help maternity home residents reflect on their relationships with their parents and how the dynamics of those relationships may have led them down the path to unwed pregnancy.[68] Out-of-wedlock pregnancy was explained as fantasy fulfillment in conjunction with Oedipal and pre-Oedipal concerns, as an impulsive and reckless attempt to solve some problem in the unmarried woman's life. For example, this type of explanation was central to an analysis of Francis Smith, a case study of the supposedly typical, maladjusted single mother that was offered at the 1957 National Conference of Social Work: "Though she had been married two years previously, she was divorced after three months; and in the nature of her problems, and her attempts at solutions, she was not atypical of the unmarried mother. She was a masochistic young woman who suffered from intense feelings of failure, worthlessness, and inadequacy."[69] In an effort to treat what were deemed neurotic tendencies and the maladjustment of women such as Francis, social workers sought to help their clients work through the defensive functions they believed were at the core of the women's psychological problems. By doing so, psychologists reasoned, the unmarried mother could move beyond the pregnancy lest it "become yet another trauma in her neurotic struggles."[70] Relying on psychological theories, the goal of maternity homes shifted from teaching the white single mother how to become a good mother and toward rehabilitation.[71] Such rehabilitation was fairly straightforward: the unwed mother needed to show remorse, give up her child for adoption, and then pursue a "renewed commitment to fulfilling her destiny as a real woman" by adopting the socially accepted pattern of heterosexual dating, then marriage, and then motherhood.[72] It quickly became accepted and even expected that maternity home residents would give up custody of their children. In some cases, they were coerced or tricked into relinquishing their children to adoption agencies.[73]

The discourses of rehabilitation were explicitly racialized. While illegitimacy among white women was cast as a temporary mental problem or weakness that could be cured, among Black women it was regarded as biologically determined, as evidence of the "pathology" of the Black family, an aspect of the "culture of poverty" that was equated with the Black community and of which illegitimate childbearing was considered a by-product.[74] Couching out-of-wedlock pregnancy among Black women simultaneously as evidence of Black women's selfishness, as an economic strategy designed to burden white taxpayers and gain additional support through social service programs, and as a result of the supposed hypersexuality of Black women, politicians advocated for the punishment of Black unwed mothers.[75] Black unmarried mothers were typically required to keep their babies so they would serve as a constant reminder of their supposed inferiority and inability to conform to white social norms. Even if a Black single mother wanted to give her baby up for adoption, she would have had a difficult time doing so. The mid-twentieth-century U.S. adoption market was only interested in securing white, healthy babies and facilitating their legal transfer to heterosexual couples who were white, married, religious, and middle class.[76]

THE PILL, FEMINISM, AND THE RHETORIC OF CHOICE

As the immediate post–World War II decades drew to a close, concerns about unwed mothers were expressed in a somewhat different manner that hinged on changing gender roles and a rhetoric of choice. The combination of two significant events, one scientific and one legal, helped facilitate this shift, particularly as these events altered ideas about women's reproduction in general. After years of experimentation and development by endocrinologist Gregory Pincus, the oral progesterone pill underwent a clinical trial in Puerto Rico in 1954 and was deemed highly successful in preventing pregnancy. In 1957, the Food and Drug Administration approved the pill for treatment of menstrual disorders and in 1960 approved it for contraceptive use in the United States. Although the availability and use of the pill drew heavy criticism from devout Catholics, African American communities, and those who advocated conservative values that included condemnation of premarital sex, use of the pill quickly became commonplace. While forms of contraception had been available in prior decades, the pill was discreet, effective, and user-controlled. By 1965, it was the most common form of birth control used in the United States; over 6.5 million women were taking it daily.[77]

No contraceptive method—except abstinence and sterilization—is 100 percent effective, and even those taking the pill can experience an unintended pregnancy. Options for responding to such a pregnancy changed dramatically for U.S. women in 1973 when the U.S. Supreme Court issued its decision in *Roe v. Wade*. Defining the matter of whether or not to continue a pregnancy a private matter rather than a public one, the ruling declared a Texas law unconstitutional because it prohibited pregnancy termination except in cases where the life of the mother was at stake. The ruling also judged any law prohibiting or restricting access to abortion during the first trimester of pregnancy unconstitutional and declared that access to termination was warranted in both the second and third trimesters if the health of the mother was in jeopardy. Of course, women had terminated their pregnancies in the pre–*Roe v. Wade* era. Those who could afford to do so traveled to other countries while others found sympathetic U.S. doctors who performed the procedure illegally. Some worked with underground groups to secure abortions, while others attempted the procedure on their own, inserting various substances and objects into the vagina and the uterine cavity or

inflicting injury on themselves in an effort to end a pregnancy, often with disastrous results that included infection, sterility, and even death.[78]

The legalization of abortion, however, combined with the increasing availability and social acceptance of contraception, gave women increased control
over their reproductive lives. Such control, in turn, impacted public and political opinions about unwed mothers. Once the pill became widely available and
abortion was ruled legal, single pregnancy came to be regarded as intentional,
something that certain women pursued on purpose. The argument went something like this: if women could prevent unintended pregnancy through the use
of contraception and could end an unwanted pregnancy through legal abortion, then single women who became mothers were doing so by choice. In other
words, they were knowingly violating gender norms and choosing to pursue
pregnancy and motherhood outside marriage. Some applauded such choices,
attributing them to feminism, women's increased independence, and women's
expanded consciousness about their bodies and their lives.[79] A more prominent
discourse, however, condemned single mothers for purportedly contributing
to the disintegration of U.S. values. Such concerns were about more than single
motherhood. They also reflected fears about feminist ideas and the influence of
the second wave of the U.S. women's movement. Those involved in the movement challenged gender bias in U.S. society and advocated for women's economic, social, and legal equality. Not all sectors of society welcomed the growing
equality and independence of women, however, especially those concerned
about the supposed disintegration of the family because of increasing divorce
rates. Although divorce was not unheard of during the first half of the twentieth century, it was still relatively uncommon during that period. Those who
sought legal dissolution of marriage were generally required to produce "proof
of marital fault" such as adultery, impotence, malicious behavior, bigamy, deser-
tion, or lengthy unexplained absences of their spouse.[80] In 1910, the divorce rate
was only 0.9 per 1,000 persons. After World War I, the divorce rate began a slow
but steady increase and by 1941, it had doubled from the 1900 rate. Although
there was an increase in the immediate post–World War II years, the divorce rate
declined during the 1950s and remained stable throughout the 1960s.[81] By 1970,
however, around the same time the women's movement began to grow size and
power, the divorce rate again began to increase, and by 1987 it reached an all-
time high. In 1992, Naomi Miller wrote that "anyone getting married today has
only a 50–50 chance of staying married 'until death do us part'" and the divorce
rate has remained fairly consistent since that time.[82] The increase in divorce rates
was influenced by no-fault divorce laws, which removed notions of blame and
made a divorce easier to obtain.[83] However, conservative politicians were more
apt to "blame it on feminism,"[84] claiming that feminists not only supported no-
fault divorce laws but also encouraged female autonomy. Conservatives believed

this made women too willing to give up when they encountered difficulties in their marriages. According to this perspective, feminists were attacking the family and the traditional male breadwinner: "There are people who want a different political order. . . . Symbolized by the women's liberation movement, they believe that the future for their political power lies in the restructuring of the traditional family, and particularly in the downgrading of the male or father role in the traditional family."[85] Within this political ideology, the divorced mother was portrayed as selfish and arrogant, a woman who wanted nothing more than to emasculate her husband in her quest to increase her own power. Although a woman who became a single mother through divorce escaped the social stigma associated with out-of-wedlock childbearing, she was still regarded as inadequate because she was no longer married.[86] Thus, she faced scrutiny as both an unmarried mother and as a divorced woman.[87] In other words, because she occupied two identities that were "culturally defined as contradictory—single woman *and* primary parent"[88]—the divorced mother was criticized for deviating from gender norms, regardless of whether she wanted the divorce or not. She was a bad mother, regarded as having chosen self-fulfillment and independence over her social obligations as wife and mother.

Such criticisms of never-married mothers and divorced mothers were core features of the rhetoric of the New Right in the second half of the twentieth century. Rooted in the rise of the conservative movement that took hold in the 1960s as a response to progressive social and political movements of the period, the New Right signaled a turning point for the Republican Party. The strengthening of the family was central to the New Right agenda, which launched a full-scale attack on social services and targeted the single mother as the symbol of America's failed welfare state. This attack included an appeal to increasing concerns about "the negro family" and the "culture of poverty" and relied on data from conservative organizations such as the Heritage Foundation and the John Birch Society and from scholars who argued that U.S. social welfare programs were "losing ground."[89] Of course not all single mothers sought support through welfare programs and not all unwed mothers were poor. Conservatives ignored these facts and presented the welfare recipient as the representative of all single mothers, characterizing her as an irresponsible woman whose bad choices had led her to single motherhood and poverty.[90] Claiming that poor populations were only "semisocialized," the New Right deemed poverty both a consequence of and proof of the pathology of single mothers.[91] Consequently, the single mother became a political spectacle, constructed as a fundamental threat to the "fundamental values of work, responsibility, and family," and an "enemy within" the United States.[92]

The power of such rhetoric cannot be overstated. It was a mainstay of political debates and popular media representations in the last quarter of the twentieth century, it was expressed in overtly racist and sexist ways, and it served as a basis for depictions of single mothers as deviants who lacked morality and made bad choices.[93] One of the most notorious incarnations of this rhetoric appeared in a 1976 speech by presidential hopeful Ronald Reagan, who described the activities of a woman from Chicago's South Side who he claimed was committing welfare fraud by receiving benefits under multiple names and social security numbers and by claiming to be the mother of children that did not exist. Reagan claimed that she received so much in welfare benefits that she dressed in furs, owned three new cars, and had nearly $1 million in cash. Although he never named the woman, Reagan's description captured headlines across the United States. Thus, the stereotype of the "welfare queen" was born. This figure "became a convenient villain, a woman everyone could hate. She was a lazy black con artist, unashamed of cadging the money that honest folks worked so hard to earn."[94] The stereotype became a controlling image that was used in political debates and media representations.[95] It reinforced not only conservative political criticisms of the broken welfare system but also the depiction of poor single mothers as bad mothers. Of equal importance, it reinforced the racial and economic hierarchies that were at the core of New Right politics.[96]

The condemnation of single mothers was also evident in comments made by former vice-president Dan Quayle during a 1992 speech. Appearing before the Commonwealth Club of California, Quayle decried the "failure of families," pointing to teen childbearing, absentee fathers, and out-of-wedlock childbearing as part of what he deemed the "war on traditional values" and evidence of the growing "indulgence and self-gratification" among many Americans. He then attacked fictitious single TV mom Murphy Brown, "a character who supposedly epitomizes today's intelligent, highly paid professional woman, mocking the importance of fathers by bearing a child alone and calling it just another 'lifestyle choice.'"[97] A decade later, Quayle launched another attack on a fictitious television character. This time, his target was Rachel Green of NBC's hit show *Friends*, who was "single and pregnant, but the father is apparently planning to be actively involved in the child's life. So we have come halfway."[98] For Quayle, it did not matter that in the context of the fictitious worlds they occupied on the small screen, both Murphy Brown and Rachel Green were financially stable and did not look to social service programs to help them provide for their children. Because they had chosen single motherhood, he regarded these women in the same way Reagan regarded his imagined welfare queen: as ongoing threats to and evidence of the erosion of American values.

SINGLE MOTHERS AS BAD MOTHERS

News and mainstream media representations also helped shape ideas about single mothers in the late twentieth century. Emphasizing themes of welfare,

urban decay, immorality, and broken families, such representations both reinforced and informed political discourse. Inner cities were portrayed as having
been "reduced to hollow shells peopled largely by poor non-whites" and "eddies
of poverty" that ran counter to the values and institutions of mainstream culture,
as places where the American dream had turned into an "American nightmare."[99]
Stories of drug use, rape, murder, and other crimes were standard fare in such
coverage, thereby associating poor single mothers with social ills and criminality, part of a "dangerous society" that continued to weaken American values and
threatened to destroy not only itself but the rest of the country as well.[100]

Morality was a principal concern. News and media sources focused on increasing rates of out-of-wedlock births and changing family structure, claiming that
such changes were the result of a "reduction of the traditional stigma" associated
with single motherhood.[101] Consequently, the act of nonmarital childbearing
became a symbol of immorality, an indicator that America had become a "law-
less social anarchy," a "world gone crazy" that was dominated by a "moral vac-
uum."[102] In the context of such coverage, the single mother became a symbol of
the demoralization of society that included "tolerance for heedless sexual behavior and unwholesome family life and of weakened commitment to competence,
work, and responsible living."[103] The single mother was a bad mother, regarded
as both a consequence and a cause of immorality. Interestingly, both conservative and liberal politicians endorsed the belief that out-of-wedlock childbearing
was immoral, demonstrating yet again that politics makes for strange bedfellows.
In a news conference to announce his candidacy for the 1992 presidential race,
former Ku Klux Klan leader David Duke denounced illegitimacy as immoral and
as a key factor in the "undermining of Christian society."[104] Similarly, when former health and human services secretary Donna Shalala was asked to share her
views on single mothers, she claimed that while she didn't like to put it in "moral
terms," she believed that "having children out of wedlock is just wrong."[105]

Popular news and media sources often provided accounts of supposedly typical single mothers in an effort to demonstrate the assumed immorality of single
mothers in general. One story out of Boston, for example, focused on Clarabel
Ventura, who was described as a "26-year-old drug addict who is pregnant with
her seventh child and reportedly sold food stamps to buy crack cocaine."[106] Ventura was charged with abusing her five-year-old son, Ernesto, whose hands had
been held under scalding water as punishment.[107] Another story, this time from
Queens, told of a single mother addicted to heroin. She was on welfare, had
AIDS, and was accused of killing her four-year-old daughter. According to the
news report, "the woman is 'mother' to four children through a succession of
drug-numbed boyfriends."[108] A story from Chicago detailed the case of Maxine
Melton and her four sisters, all single, all receiving welfare, and all charged with
child abuse and neglect. Taken individually, each of these stories may simply

appear to be a factual account of a newsworthy event. Yet these stories and the hundreds of others like them that appeared in news and media reports during the late twentieth century are significant because of their cumulative effect. Like all news stories, they are constructed accounts. They rely on certain discourses and themes that resonate with cultural narratives, values, and ideologies. Thus, through their repeated focus on drug use, sexual promiscuity (which was alluded to through data on high birth rates, discussion of how many sexual partners a woman had, and a focus on sexually transmitted diseases), and purported criminality, news and media sources reinforced political discourses about the supposed immorality of unmarried mothers.

IRRESPONSIBLE SINGLE MOTHERS AND UPPITY SINGLE MOTHERS

During this period, news and media sources fashioned two dominant caricatures that appeared regularly in their coverage of welfare, welfare reform, and poverty in America. The first caricature was the irresponsible single mother, described as "[a] mother who[se] values have been eroded by the welfare system. This mother is usually African American (and increasingly Latina). She has many children, is not a 'productive' member of the labor force, and does not share the ideals of mainstream Americans. Variations on this theme include unmarried teen pregnancy, drug use, child abuse or neglect, and failure to ensure children's attendance at school or adequate medical care."[109] Irresponsible single mothers were depicted as a rather diverse group in terms of their life experiences. Some were teen mothers while others were in their twenties, thirties, or forties. Many had never been married, some were divorced. Some had an employment history, others had never worked for wages. Some irresponsible single mothers had only one child, others had five or more. Irresponsible single mothers were typically portrayed as women of color and were presumed to have one thing in common: poor judgment. They were thought to have arrived on the dole through a series of unfortunate choices and mistakes.[110] And with a monthly welfare check "supporting them and obscur[ing] the consequences of [their] mistakes," these women continued to make mistakes that frequently endangered themselves and their children and prevented themselves from becoming self-sufficient.[111] In other words, irresponsible single mothers became poor and stayed poor because of their life choices. In some cases, depictions of irresponsible single mothers included a multi-part series in which an investigative reporter sought to provide an in-depth account of one single mother's life, contrasting "the choices she had and the choices she made" to demonstrate that she had repeatedly made bad choices that left her poor, unmarried, lacking basic skills, addicted, and "overwhelmed."[112] Yet given the pervasiveness of the stereotype of the irresponsible single mother, such lengthy accounts were not needed. Instead, media sources could render a single mother irresponsible simply by describing her so-called bad choices. In some cases, this involved discussing a poor teen mother who failed to insist that her partner consistently use a condom.[113] Other times, it was a story about the rebellious nature of a young woman who quit high school, began using drugs and alcohol, became pregnant, and then spent over a decade on welfare.[114] Or it might be a story that focused on two sisters who were both on welfare and were arrested for stealing $172 worth of groceries because they couldn't afford to feed their children.[115]

Whereas irresponsible single mothers were presented as rather pitiful characters, as women who suffered because of their own errors in judgment, the uppity single mother was characterized as defiant, as having actively pursued out-of-wedlock childbearing and child-rearing, and as rejecting conventional family norms in favor of female independence and empowerment. This type of single mother was portrayed as a unique product of the late twentieth century, created through the convergence of several "major cultural shifts" that had taken place in the decades since World War II.[116] Chief among these shifts was the "cataclysmic social change" of increasing numbers of women who had entered the workforce and were no longer financially dependent on a male breadwinner.[117] Changes in women's reproductive patterns and sexual behaviors also received significant attention in depictions of uppity single mothers. Those who criticized uppity mothers bemoaned the fact that reproductive technologies such as artificial insemination and the oral contraceptive pill had helped the "sexual revolution catch fire," had "loosed the ties between marriage and sex," and had "split marriage from childbearing."[118] Reduction in the "traditional social stigma" attached to out-of-wedlock childbearing was another important aspect of patterns of social change, one that some believed had contributed to the "fading nuclear family."[119]

Such changes, however, were seen as consequences rather than causes. It was posited that while women's increasing economic independence, increased reliance on reproductive technologies, and the destigmatization of out-of-wedlock childbearing were associated with the emergence of the uppity single mother, the root cause was not with the mother herself. The real problem was the proliferation of feminist ideology:

The key problem of the welfare culture is not unemployed women with illegitimate children. It is the women's skewed and traumatic relationships with men and boys. In a reversal of the usual pattern in civilized societies, the women have the income and the ties to government authority and support. The men are economically and socially subordinate. Favored by feminists dominant at all levels of government, this balance of power virtually prohibits marriage, which is everywhere based on the provider role of men counterbalancing the sexual and domestic superiority of women.[120]

Although few sources actually used the term feminist to describe single mothers, stereotypes of feminism and feminists were central to depictions of uppity single mothers, who were described as having "truly become single mothers by choice," either by choosing to give birth out of wedlock or by obtaining a divorce.[121] It was common for portrayals of uppity single mothers to promote the idea that such women had rendered men optional.[122] Such women were thought to have traded the financial support of a male breadwinner for the financial support of the state, thereby "usurping the role of the provider" and violating the "most important moral and legal rule of kinship."[123] They were blamed for creating a less "civilized" culture, one that was matrilineal and undermined masculinity and that weakened the family, the "foundation of society."[124] The uppity single mother was, in many ways, an updated depiction of the welfare queen, a woman who was supposedly "living the good life at taxpayer expense."[125]

It was primarily through descriptions of her attitude that news and media sources marked a single mother as uppity, constructing her as a nonconformist who did not know her proper place in the gendered scheme of society. Murphy Brown was a favorite example; some sources criticized the television character as "mocking the new realities of tattered family life."[126] But other fictional single mothers also came under fire, including Mary Jo on TV's *Designing Women*, a show known for its four strong, independent female characters. In an episode that aired in February 1991, the character of Mary Jo, who was divorced, considered having another child and was soundly criticized:

> Mary Jo . . . decided she wants to have another child before her biological clock runs out. Her reasons were expressed purely in terms of personal gratification: the happiest time of her life was when her children were babies, and she now "deserves" a new baby. She doesn't think she needs a husband or that the baby needs a father. . . . It struck me that a show that tends to be heavy on politically correct message-sending was broadcasting a socially devastating message: Babies are to make Mom happy; Dad is disposable.[127]

Mary Jo's desire for another child was also linked to concerns about child poverty, rising divorce rates, and welfare, thus implying that women who become single by choice—even fictional ones—are somehow responsible for various social problems.[128] The proposed solution to the problem of welfare was presented in very simple terms: reward single mothers who get married with a welfare bonus of $80 a month. Although it was acknowledged that marriage might not make a mother happy, that was deemed less important that the institution of marriage.[129]

If popular media helped ground the stereotype of the uppity single mother with characters such as Murphy Brown and Mary Jo, news stories that focused on real single mothers helped refine the image and further illustrate how the attitudes of uppity single mothers toward childbearing, marriage, and gender roles conflicted with mainstream American social norms. The uppity single mother was typically portrayed as lazy, scheming to avoid work, and relying on public assistance programs to support herself and her children, even going so far as to flock to California, New York, Wisconsin, and other welfare magnet states where benefits were higher.[130] She would refuse to identify the father of her child, both as a means of demonstrating her inherently stubborn nature and because she didn't want to risk losing her welfare benefits.[131] Furthermore, she was depicted as not only manipulating the system for her own benefit but also teaching her children to do the same. She was dubbed a "matriarch" and a "welfare cheat," a manipulator who was presumed to have passed on her knowledge of how to commit "fraud" to her offspring in order to "raise a welfare dynasty."[132]

Given the proliferation of political and popular representations of irresponsible single mothers and uppity single mothers, it is not surprising that a carrot-and-stick approach figured prominently in welfare reform policies of the 1990s. The passage and implementation of the Personal Responsibility and Work Opportunities Reconciliation Act of 1996 was a significant turning point in U.S. social welfare policies. It brought dramatic changes to the various programs that constituted the social safety net meant to provide assistance to low-income populations in the United States. The carrots of this policy were intended to modify the behavior of irresponsible single mothers. They were presented as a kind of governmental tough love that encouraged irresponsible single mothers to make better choices, specifically those that more accurately reflected mainstream American values. These programs typically offered financial incentives such as monetary bonuses to welfare recipients who got married. The sticks were measures intended to penalize uppity single mothers for defying American gender roles. Sometimes this meant financial penalties such as reduced benefits. But other measures were implemented as well. These included child exclusion policies, the requirement that teen mothers live with their parents in order to receive benefits, the implementation of strict time limits on benefits, the requirement that recipients of benefits work for wages, and restricted participation in postsecondary education and training programs.

MOTHERING BY DEGREES

This project focuses on the experiences of nearly 100 women who identified as single custodial mothers and who were raising children while pursuing a college degree in the first decade of the twenty-first century. In recent years, scholars have addressed issues single mothers face by focusing on welfare reform policies. There has been much attention to the ways such policies impact the choices and opportunities available to single mothers in the United States, including how they essentially shut low-income single mothers out of institutions of higher education.[133] Others have attempted to combat negative stereotypes of single mothers by representing them as "warriors" and "heroines."[134] Still others have argued that poor, single mothers must continue to have access to postsecondary education, particularly as a means of providing a way out of poverty.[135] While welfare reform policies are part of the sociopolitical framework in which the research for this project was carried out, my work does not center on such policies. It also does not attempt to celebrate single mothers or to portray them in a more positive light. That is, I do not claim to know whether specific single mothers should or should not pursue postsecondary education and I not attempt to evaluate the choices and decisions they make in terms of whether they fit cultural definitions of good or bad mothering.

This project is ethnographic, and like similar research on single mothers, it attends to the specific contexts of single mothers' lives and seeks to frame their experiences in terms that are meaningful to them.[136] It provides a situated, comparative account of the experiences of single mothers who were attending college while also raising children. Drawing from their experiences, this project aims to foster a better understanding of the complex ideologies and social structures that influenced the life choices of these women. It also attends to how these women understood and expressed agency. Consequently, this project provides insight into the highly political nature of single motherhood in early twenty-first-century America.

The following chapters demonstrate that despite the obstacles they encountered, the women who participated in this project placed a high value on a college education, for both practical and symbolic reasons. They were motivated to go to college, in part, by financial concerns. Like many students, the women believed they would have better job opportunities and a more secure financial future once they completed a college degree. Yet they also attached a high value to the process of pursuing a college degree. Quite simply, the women regarded the work they completed for their courses—studying, attending class, exams, research projects—as ways to demonstrate to themselves, to their children, and to others that they were good mothers. The obstacles they encountered were often significant, particularly in regard to financial matters, child care, time constraints, and the chilly climate of higher education. Yet even as they struggled to reconcile their competing roles and responsibilities as college students and single custodial mothers, participants tended to regard the pursuit of a college degree as an extension of their mothering work, something they did to set a positive example for their children and to help promote the long-term well-being of their children. In this way, they challenged both traditional definitions of mothering work and cultural stereotypes of single mothers as bad mothers. Interestingly, however, they also tended to frame many of their decisions, actions, and goals in the context of the rather narrow rhetoric of middle-class family norms. Thus, even as they challenged notions of traditional motherhood and stereotypes of single motherhood, the women also reinforced the ideal of the good mother as all-loving and self-sacrificing, a mother who invested financially in her children's welfare and worked hard at being a good parent.

THE RESEARCH PROCESS: LOCATIONS, PARTICIPANTS, METHODS

The research for this project was carried out over an eight-year period at three postsecondary educational institutions. The first was the University of Iowa (UI), a Carnegie Tier One institution located in Iowa City.[137] The largest educator of undergraduate students in the state of Iowa, at the time of my research UI consisted of eleven colleges and offers undergraduate, graduate, and professional degrees. The second was Kirkwood Community College (KCC), whose main campus is located in Cedar Rapids, Iowa, just fifteen minutes north of UI. Kirkwood also operates several additional campuses and learning centers scattered throughout eastern Iowa, providing high school completion and GED programs, continuing education, and two-year degrees. Texas Woman's University (TWU), in Denton, Texas, the third institution, has the distinction of being the nation's largest university primarily for women. TWU, which operates three physical campuses and a fourth "e-learning" campus, offers undergraduate, graduate, and professional degrees in liberal arts and sciences, business, education, and health sciences. Nearly 40 percent of TWU's total student population identifies as members of racial and ethnic minority groups. Single mothers accounted for an estimated 8 percent of the total TWU student population at the time I was conducting my research.[138] The demography of TWU contrasted markedly with the other institutions included in this study.

A total of eighty-six women participated in this research (see table 1). All were custodial mothers and identified as single mothers. Some had never been married while others were divorced or widowed, had been deserted by their spouse, or were legally separated. All participants were pursuing a degree part-time or full-time. They were a diverse group in terms of age, racial and ethnic identity, marital experiences, and the number and ages of their children. They also varied

TABLE 1. Profile of Participants

	Participants attending the University of Iowa (n = 22)	Participants attending community college (n = 13)	Participants attending Texas Woman's University (n=51)
Racial/ethnic identity	Native American 0 Asian/Pacific Islander 1 Hispanic 1 Black, Non-Hispanic 2 White, Non-Hispanic 17 Multiracial 1	Native American 0 Asian/Pacific Islander 0 Hispanic 1 Black, Non-Hispanic 2 White, Non-Hispanic 9 Multiracial 1	Native American 2 Asian/Pacific Islander 3 Hispanic 5 Black, Non-Hispanic 10 White, Non-Hispanic 29 Multiracial 2
Age	< 20 1 20–30 12 30–40 7 >40 2	< 20 3 20–30 10 30–40 0 >40 0	< 20 5 20–30 19 30–40 20 >40 7
Marital status	Never married 11 Divorced 9 Widowed 0 Separated 1 Deserted 1	Never married 11 Divorced 2 Widowed 0 Separated 0 Deserted 0	Never married 22 Divorced 24 Widowed 2 Separated 2 Deserted 1
Number of children	One 14 Two 5 Three or more 3	One 12 Two 0 Three or more 1	One 29 Two 16 Three or more 6
Ages of children	< 1 year 4 1–5 years 13 6–10 years 7 11–15 years 6 >15 years 3	< 1 year 2 1–5 years 7 6–10 years 6 11–15 years 0 >15 years 0	< 1 year 5 1–5 years 32 6–10 years 23 11–15 years 14 >15 years 5
Student status	Job training prog. n/a Associate's degree n/a Freshman 0 Sophomore 2 Junior 6 Senior 5 Master's student 4 Doctoral/prof. student 5	Job training prog. 2 Associate's degree 11 Freshman n/a Sophomore n/a Junior n/a Senior n/a Master's student n/a Doctoral student n/a	Job training prog. n/a Associate's degree n/a Freshman 4 Sophomore 6 Junior 11 Senior 18 Master's student 7 Doctoral student 5
Enrollment status	Full-time 20 Part-time 2	Full-time 8 Part-time 5	Full-time 12 Part-time 39

in terms of their student status; while the vast majority were undergraduate students, some were enrolled in graduate or professional programs.

I used a variety of methods to collect data, including surveys, interviews, and participant observation. I recruited participants using flyers that I placed in public areas on the three campuses, including in libraries, student housing, residential laundry facilities, cafeterias and food service areas, academic advising offices, and student services offices. I also posted flyers in public locations near each campus, including public libraries, grocery stores, child care centers, pediatric clinics, laundromats, and on public buses. The initial phase of research (2001–2005) focused on the experiences of single mothers attending KCC and UI. For this portion of the research, those who met my criteria and provided consent participated in one-on-one interviews. Interviews were conducted face to face in a location of the participant's choosing and consisted of open-ended questions about the participant's experiences as a college student and as a single mother. Several of the women allowed me to engage in participant observation, and I spent significant periods of time with them in academic, home, and social settings in order to get a better understanding of their lives. The second phase of research (2006–2008) included only participants attending TWU. After providing consent, each TWU participant first completed an anonymous online survey and was then offered the option of participating in one-on-one interviews, either by telephone or face to face.

All interviews were recorded and transcribed for accuracy. Each participant had the option of reviewing the transcripts of her interviews so she could delete information she did not wish to be included or clarify anything she deemed unclear. In all cases, each participant was assigned a pseudonym in order to ensure confidentiality. In addition, and again to ensure confidentiality, names of participants' children were changed and any specific characteristics or activities that might reveal the identity of either participants or their children have been modified. When the experiences of women were quite similar, I created composite characters as an additional way of ensuring confidentiality. Research also involved interviews with faculty and staff at KCC, UI, and TWU in order to get another perspective on the experiences of single mothers attending those institutions. Faculty and staff included individuals who provided support services in offices and programs such as academic advising, student life, financial aid, student affairs, student wellness, and student counseling. When a woman who participated in this project indicated that a particular staff or faculty member had been particularly supportive of her or especially sensitive to her needs as a single mother, I contacted that staff or faculty member and asked to interview him or her. A total of twenty-seven staff and faculty members participated in this project. Interviews with these individuals were especially helpful in terms of gathering additional insight into the specific challenges and needs of single mothers at these institutions. Such interviews also helped clarify information single mothers had provided about institutional policies and practices. Interviews with faculty and staff were recorded and transcribed for accuracy and faculty and staff were assigned pseudonyms in order to provide confidentiality.

LOOKING AHEAD

In the following chapters, I explore the experiences of single mothers attending college by focusing on four key challenges: finances, time constraints, child care, and the chilly climate of higher education. By exploring these challenges and the various strategies the women employed in attempts to overcome such challenges, I seek to promote a more nuanced understanding of the lives and experiences of this unique but understudied group. I have made a concerted effort to avoid simplistic representations of the women and their experiences. I am critical of tendencies to group individuals together on the basis of shared experiences or a shared identity in ways that neglect other aspects of their lives. Such tendencies often ignore traits or experiences that members of a group do not have in common with one another. This is common in U.S. politics, for example where campaign speeches and legislative debates refer to the American middle class as a way of emphasizing the shared income level of this particular group. Such rhetoric minimizes the myriad differences that exist in the middle class in terms of values, goals, and experiences. The American middle class is certainly not a homogeneous group; it includes people of varying races and religions, educational levels and ethnicities, professions and political persuasions. Likewise, the single mothers who participated in this project were not a homogeneous group. They had some things in common, including the fact that they were mothers, were custodial parents, and were enrolled in institutions of higher education. There were also differences among the women, and attending to these differences is part of my effort to avoid the "add women and stir" approach that typified much of early feminist scholarship and was soundly critiqued by women of color.[139]

I have developed chapters 2, 3, 4, and 5 by focusing on the experiences of a few women and discussing their experiences at length. While some may critique this as an overly narrative style of writing, I believe it facilitates a more in-depth understanding of the lives of the women, avoiding a flat representation in which participants are reduced to talking heads. This approach also promotes increased attention to the specific ways participants constructed their narratives, including the specific discourses they used to describe their lives and experiences. Readers will also note that I do not pretend to be completely neutral about this topic. Given my more than twenty years in higher education—half as a student and half as an educator—I have a good under-standing of how such institutions operate and believe that colleges and universities have a responsibility to support the needs of all of their students, including single mothers. Thus, I raise critical questions throughout the volume, and in the appendix I offer examples of specific programs and policies that have been designed in an effort to better meet the needs of the single mothers as they pursue higher education.

2 · TRYING TO MAKE ENDS MEET

As college students, single mothers have some of the same educational concerns as their more traditional peers. They want to be taught by skilled and knowledgeable faculty members, take courses that are interesting and relevant, earn good grades, and complete a college degree in a reasonable amount of time. However, given their dual identities as college students and single mothers, they face a financial situation that is rather unique. They must contend with the costs of both postsecondary education and the expenses they incur as sole custodial parents. Consequently, single mothers are more likely than students who are not parents to identify finances as a primary source of stress in their lives.[1] In addition, while single mothers typically receive income from a variety of sources that may include employment, scholarships, grants, student loans, child support, alimony, or government programs, they are significantly more likely to live in poverty than their peers.[2] They are also less likely to receive financial assistance from their parents, more likely to take out student loans, and less likely to earn income from work.[3]

Even so, evidence suggests that pursuing a college degree is a good economic investment for single mothers. Women of all racial backgrounds increase their likelihood of securing better jobs that pay higher wages and provide health insurance, sick leave, and other benefits if they complete a postsecondary degree.[4] Earning a college degree has been shown to "significantly improve the economic status of single mother-headed families."[5] Education is also more important than prior work experience in helping single mothers achieve long-term financial independence.[6] The potential economic benefits for single mothers who pursue higher education are clear. Yet the economic challenges they encounter often challenge their commitment to postsecondary education, particularly as they struggle to reconcile the promise of long-term economic gains with their short-term concerns related to the economic survival and well-being of their family.[7]

The topic of personal finances was a central theme in my interviews with the women who participated in my study. They were generally quite forthcoming with information about the economic aspects of their lives. They told me about their incomes, detailed their expenses, described their efforts to economize, and explained how they managed through financial crises. They also gave detailed accounts of their day-to-day, month-to-month, and semester-to-semester financial concerns. In a number of instances, they even shared documentation pertaining to checking and savings accounts, alimony and child support payments, Federal Student Aid reports, and credit card account statements. Given my own working-class upbringing and especially my parents' attitude that it was inappropriate to talk about money with anyone except your spouse or a bank loan officer, I was often surprised by how freely the women shared such information. They eagerly provided details that sometimes felt almost too private to share with a researcher, even one who had promised to preserve their anonymity.

Perhaps their openness about such matters was due to the fact that they were seasoned pros about sharing their financial information. Many of them had been called upon to share such information in other contexts, such as when they sought assistance through government agencies, applied for loans through the student financial aid office, or attempted to secure food, clothing, and other necessities from churches and other community organizations. Or perhaps their frankness about financial concerns was an indicator that the women had internalized a dominant American discourse related to poverty and single-mother-headed households. Ronald Reagan's fictional anecdote of the welfare queen who manipulated the system in order to live a Cadillac-driving, luxury lifestyle resonated in profound ways with American taxpayers. It is a stereotype that has contributed to stigma aimed at those receiving public assistance and was a central component of the conservative political rhetoric that drove welfare reform in the 1990s and beyond.[8] Given the pervasiveness of such rhetoric, it seems possible that the women were forthcoming about the details of their financial circumstances because they were attempting to demonstrate to me that they were genuinely, authentically, legitimately struggling to make ends meet. Or maybe they had simply been raised in households that had very different attitudes about discussing personal finances than the household in which I had been raised. Or perhaps it was a combination of these factors. Whatever their reasons, I am thankful that they trusted me enough to share this information about the financial complexities they encountered.

In this chapter, I focus on the economic dimensions of the lives of single mothers who are college students. In addition to identifying the sources and amounts of their income, their efforts to make ends meet, and what they did when expenses exceeded income, my discussion will highlight how they attempted to reconcile their more immediate financial concerns with their long-term goals. I suggest that the women regarded their pursuit of a postsecondary education not only as an economic strategy but also as a type of good mothering, particularly as they tended to believe that completion of a college degree would lead to a job that pays well and enable them to provide a more financially secure life for themselves and their children. Quite simply, the women endorsed the idea that earning a college degree is a central component of accessing the American dream. Their perspective on this is certainly not unique. In its May 2000 report, *Great Expectations: How the Public and Parents—White, African American, and Hispanic—View Higher Education,* the National Center for Public Policy and Higher Education found that

> higher education is perceived as extremely important, and for most people a college education has become the necessary admission ticket to good jobs and a middle-class lifestyle. Parents of high school students place especially high importance on a college education, and African American and Hispanic parents give college an even higher priority than do white parents.... Seventy-seven percent say that getting a college education is more important than it was 10 years ago and a towering 87% agree that a college education has become as important as a high school diploma used to be.[9]

Given these prevailing beliefs, it is not surprising that the single mothers who participated in my study often waxed poetic about this issue, describing a kind of idealized future they imagined they would enjoy once they had completed their education. Indeed, they seemed to regard a college degree as a kind of golden ticket like the one that changes Charlie Bucket's life in Roald Dahl's classic, *Charlie and the Chocolate Factory.* The women believed that the golden ticket of a college degree would bring far greater rewards than a lifetime supply of chocolate; they believed it would bring an escape from the American welfare trap and the ability to create a stable future that put them in the middle class.[10]

Despite the diversity among participants in terms of racial and ethnic identity, life experiences, and routes to single motherhood, concerns about trying to make ends meet surfaced with striking regularity as the women talked about their lives. The vast majority indicated that finances were not only *a* concern but, in fact, was *the* primary concern in their lives. Only a handful of the women—those who were divorced and received sizeable child support and alimony payments—had achieved even a modest degree of financial comfort and were able to meet their financial obligations on time and without hardship. Several had once been members of the middle class but due to divorce or other life circumstances had experienced significant downward mobility. Of the eighty-six women who participated in this study, approximately 60 percent had incomes below the U.S. poverty threshold. This directly impacted their ability to pay for food, shelter, clothing, child care, health care, transportation, tuition, books, and student fees. However, economic woes also impacted other areas of their lives, including their physical and psychological health, their academic performance, and their relationships with friends and family.

Although the women tended to endorse dominant beliefs about higher education as a means to achieving a financially secure future, it seemed unlikely that their monetary woes would completely disappear once they completed their degrees. Most of the women relied heavily on student loans, and many took out the maximum amount available to them every year in order to pay for basic living expenses, child care, and costs related to education such as books, fees, and tuition. Those who were undergraduates generally had student loan debt that ranged from $30,000 to $50,000. Graduate and professional students encountered even greater student loan debt and it was common for their totals to range from $60,000 to $100,000. Three of the women—all of whom were graduate or professional students—had borrowed well over $100,000. These women had not yet completed their degrees and many would incur additional student loan debt as they continued their academic journeys. As I shall discuss at the end of the chapter, reliance on student loans was a short-term economic strategy that was likely to affect the financial stability of the women and their families for decades to come.

$35,000, OR MORE THAN THREE TIMES AS MUCH AS TUITION

Joanna Fitzgerald grew up poor and in what she described as an "emotionally unhealthy household" in southern Nevada. Her mother, Lacy, had gotten pregnant at age sixteen. She then dropped out of school and married her boyfriend, Tim. Seven months later, Lacy gave birth to a son, Derrick, and nineteen months later, baby Joanna joined the family. Tim worked full time as a mechanic and Lacy stayed home and raised the children. With only one income, money was a constant source of stress in the Fitzgerald household and Joanna remembered that her parents fought frequently and that their conflicts were exacerbated by drug and alcohol abuse. In fact, Joanna's earliest memories were of her parents' fights, of them "both being drunk and strung out and getting very violent." When this happened, Derrick would take his little sister by the hand, grab a flashlight and some toys, and lead Joanna into the hallway closet where they "hid, just being as quiet as we could and staying out of their way." Lacy filed for divorce when Joanna was six and was awarded full custody of the children. After the divorce, Tim's involvement in their lives was limited to infrequent child support payments and sporadic phone calls. When I asked her to tell me more about her father, Joanna said there wasn't anything to tell. She couldn't remember the last time she had seen him.

She did, however, have a good deal to say about her mother, most of it conveyed in angry tones. Joanna was convinced that Lacy regretted having kids. She said that after the divorce, Lacy "spent more time caring for her drug addiction than she did caring for her children." She told me that it was common for Lacy to go on what she called "vacations," trips she would take with one of her boyfriends, who were also heavily into drugs and alcohol. When Lacy went on these trips, she would hire a babysitter to stay at the house with Joanna and Derrick. Lacy was sometimes gone for only a few days; other times, she disappeared for weeks at a time, leaving the children in the care of sixteen-year-old Jennifer, a neighbor who went to high school during the day and took care of the kids on the evenings and weekends.

Joanna liked Jennifer, but she admitted that the high school student provided little in the way of supervision. Joanna quickly learned that she could come and go as she pleased. At first, she simply wandered around her neighborhood, went to a friend's house, or went to the park to play. Within a few months, however, Joanna found it much more interesting to hang out with some older kids that she described as "a really bad crowd." Some members of this group were students who were in high school; others were in their early twenties. It didn't take long for Joanna to adopt some of their bad behaviors. By the time she was ten, Joanna was using alcohol regularly. By eleven, she was using marijuana. She quickly moved on to other drugs such as Ecstasy, cocaine, and methamphetamines. She skipped school regularly. Although Joanna's new friends initially gave her the drugs for free, they soon began to demand payment. Too young to get a job, Joanna began trading sexual favors for drugs. That is how she became sexually active when she was only twelve. Around this time she stopped attending school altogether. Although she did not use contraceptives, Joanna didn't get pregnant until she was fifteen.

Becoming pregnant was, according to Joanna, "the best thing that ever happened" to her. The day she found out she was expecting, she went to the emergency room at a local hospital and told them she was pregnant and an addict. She stayed in the emergency room overnight and was admitted to a drug rehabilitation program the following day: "I stopped using drugs the day I found out, and I've been clean ever since. I think having a baby made me be more responsible. I mean, she didn't *make* me grow up exactly, but that was a decision I made when I found out I was pregnant. When you have a child, if you want to be a good mom, you can't just act like a teenager anymore." Joanna gave birth shortly after she turned sixteen. Her daughter, Destiny, was delivered at full term. She weighed just over seven pounds and there wasn't a trace of drugs in her system.

Joanna's decision to quit using drugs and alcohol was a great source of pride for her. Although she admitted that rehab was difficult, she claimed that she was "happy to do it for [Destiny]." Sitting up straight and with her voice calm, confident, and proud, she described her ongoing weekly attendance at AA meetings. At the time of my interviews with her, Joanna had been drug free for over three years. Despite her history of dangerous behavior, Joanna felt justified in claiming she was a good mother because overcoming her addictions was a decision she had made, not something she was forced to do. She believed that in making that decision she had demonstrated appropriate maternal responsibility, prioritizing the well-being of her child (even prior to birth) over her own social relationships and presumably her physical cravings for drugs and alcohol.

It is impossible to miss the implied contrast between Joanna and Lacy in this narrative. As Joanna described her own childhood, her pregnancy, and the early months of Destiny's life, I was struck by the way she spoke about Lacy—in harsh tones and with disapproval that edged toward condemnation. Although Joanna admitted that her father was absent for most of her life, she clearly blamed her difficult childhood and adolescence on her mother. Joanna never referred to Lacy as "mother" or "mom." Instead, she simply called her by her first name and made it clear that she did not believe Lacy should have had children. Joanna's attitude toward Lacy reflected her definition of motherhood. Her refusal to refer to Lacy as "mom" or "mother" suggests that she did not believe that motherhood was simply a biological connection between a woman and her child. Instead, and importantly, she defined motherhood as both biological and social, as becoming pregnant and giving birth (the biological component) and then caring for the child in ways that demonstrate responsibility (the social component). By emphasizing her own decision to give up drugs and alcohol and presenting herself in sharp contrast to Lucy, Joanna created a continuum: Joanna was at one end, the responsible good mother, while Lacy was at the extreme opposite end, the position reserved for the woman who is so irresponsible or bad that she doesn't even deserve to be called a mother. For Joanna, being a good mother was an essential part of her identity and one of her primary motivations for pursuing a college degree.

Initially, Joanna's decision to go to college was prompted by financial worries. She wanted to be financially independent and self-sufficient. After Destiny was born, Joanna tried to earn a living by working the graveyard shift five nights a week at a convenience store. Because she couldn't find or afford day care, the store manager gave Joanna permission to bring Destiny to work with her. Destiny slept in a playpen in the employee break room while Joanna waited on customers, cleaned the store, and stocked shelves. Joanna earned $6.50 an hour and worked forty hours a week. Even so, she admitted, bills often went unpaid, utilities were turned off, and there were times she went without food so she could purchase diapers and formula for her daughter. She frequently relied on the food bank, the free health clinic, and other community services for things she could not afford. Yet even with these forms of support, she couldn't provide what she called a "decent existence" for herself and her daughter. Joanna liked her job and loved being a mother, but she felt like her life had reached a dead end.

Fortunately, Joanna had generous relatives who were sympathetic about her situation. Helen and Bob Fitzgerald, Joanna's great-aunt and great-uncle, were a retired, childless couple who lived just south of Iowa City. Although Joanna hadn't seen her Aunt Helen and Uncle Bob in many years, the couple had maintained contact with Joanna and her brother after Tim and Lacy's divorce, always sending birthday and Christmas cards and small gifts. The couple had learned about Joanna's situation from her grandmother, and motivated by their Christian values, they contacted Joanna and encouraged her to consider moving in with them and going to KCC to earn her GED. Joanna confessed that she was scared about moving to Iowa—after all, she had never been out of Nevada. Yet her relatives had made her an offer she simply couldn't refuse: they were willing to let Joanna and Destiny live with them rent free. Eager to improve her situation and especially eager to "make a better life for Destiny," Joanna gave her notice at work. Two weeks later, she packed up their few belongings, bid farewell to the desert, strapped eight-month-old Destiny in the back seat of her "barely running" Nissan, and drove more than twenty-six hours to their new home in the Midwest.

Joanna took a month to settle in and then began working with the staff at the Learning Center at Kirkwood's Iowa City campus to enroll in the GED completion program and earn her degree. Because she had dropped out of high school during her freshman year, Joanna had no transferrable credits and "basically [had to] start from scratch with classes." However, she moved through the program quickly. She seemed to have a natural aptitude for learning, especially for science. Only twenty months after arriving in Iowa City, Joanna completed her GED. With the support and guidance of her primary academic advisor, Joanna applied to KCC's undergraduate program in nursing. She chose nursing because she believed it would provide her with a stable income and because of her own experiences with drug addiction: she hoped to work with patients in drug rehabilitation facilities. Though she had contemplated attending UI to complete her nursing degree, Joanna decided on KCC for financial reasons:

> It's a lot cheaper than UI. You do the same classes basically and read the same books and do the same requirements. There are a few differences, because at Kirkwood you get the RN and not the BSN degree [like at UI]. . . . So this just made a lot more sense to me in terms of the financial aspects, especially since I have to pay for day care. I couldn't pay for tuition at UI and then also have to pay

for day care. I just couldn't do it, even with student loans. It would eat up all of my money and I would go far into debt.

The difference in tuition between the two postsecondary institutions was considerable. During her studies, undergraduate nursing students who were residents of the state of Iowa paid $2,698 a semester for full-time enrollment at UI, or $5,396 for the academic year.[11] At Kirkwood, Iowa residents paid only $89 for a semester hour.[12] Thus, Joanna's tuition bill for full-time enrollment at KCC was only $1,335 each semester, or $2,670 for the academic year, approximately half of what she would have paid at UI. Student financial aid was one of Joanna's primary sources of income and she admitted that without it, she would not have been able to attend college. She felt fortunate to receive a Pell Grant of $4,050 for the academic year, the maximum amount awarded under federal student financial aid guidelines.[13] The grant enabled Joanna to pay for tuition and books for her classes and left her with a few hundred dollars for gas expenses. If she had enrolled at UI, the Pell Grant would have covered only two-thirds of her annual tuition bill and Joanna would have needed to find some way to pay for the remainder of her tuition plus the cost of books and transportation. Although her Pell Grant was sizeable, Joanna still took out student loans to cover other expenses. In fact, she borrowed approximately $10,000 in student loans each academic year. Most was used for day care expenses:

> I work a few nights a week at a clothing store and sometimes on weekends. And I work because I pay for day care on my own. [The job] is not great money, but at least I don't have to pay for day care when I work because my aunt and uncle watch my daughter. But I do have to pay for day care while I'm in school during the day [because my aunt and uncle work] and that costs me $750 per month. . . . And I was thinking about it, day care costs and all that. By the time I get done with college, with my four-year degree, it will cost me a little over $35,000 just for day care. So what I pay in day care each year is more than three times what it costs for [full-time] tuition at Kirkwood. Even with full time tuition and books, I'm paying over twice as much for day care each semester as what it costs to be a full-time student at Kirkwood.

Joanna looked for other day care providers in the area to try to save some money. However, she only found one other day care that was open late enough to meet her needs. Most child care centers in the area closed at 6:00 P.M. On Tuesdays and Thursdays, she had classes that were scheduled until 5:40 P.M., and nursing classes were offered only at KCC's main campus in Cedar Rapids, approximately half an hour away from Iowa City. By the time Joanna drove back to Iowa City to pick up Destiny, "it [was] about 45 minutes later and I [would] get there just in time before the center closes at 6:30." Although putting Destiny in the less expensive child care center would have saved Joanna $100 a month, she refused to take her daughter there "because the staff people were awful, yelling at the kids, these little toddlers. And when I visited, I could smell that a couple of the kids had dirty diapers and they didn't even change them and I was there for almost two hours." Because she felt that this day care was low quality, because she trusted the staff at the center where Destiny was enrolled, and because Destiny "really loves it where she is," Joanna felt she had no choice but to continue to pay $750 a month for child care. And because Destiny's day care center, like most in the area, required that children remain enrolled throughout the entire year, including the summer months when Joanna did not attend classes, her annual day care bill was $9,000. By the time she completes her degree, Joanna will have incurred student loan debt of approximately $40,000, not including fees and interest. Of that $40,000, 90 percent will have been used to pay for child care.

Despite her mounting student loan debt, Joanna had some economic advantages that many of the other women who participated in this project did not. Aunt Helen and Uncle Bob owned a large house and did not charge Joanna rent. Joanna and her daughter occupied the entire second story of the house, which included a full bathroom, a large bedroom for Joanna, a bedroom for Destiny, and a smaller third bedroom that contained Joanna's computer, books, desk, and a reading chair. Joanna's relatives also paid for all the groceries, the phone bill and utilities, and other "necessities that you usually don't think about but that end up costing quite a bit" such as toiletries, laundry detergent, and cleaning supplies. Some might argue that Joanna had it rather easy: her only expenses were day care, tuition, books, health insurance, gas, clothing, and incidentals. While she recognized that her circumstances meant that she faced less pressing financial concerns than some other single mothers, Joanna's finances were nonetheless strained, a fact that became clear as she discussed her social life:

> I can only do stuff that is free. Like we'll go to one of the local malls when they have "free family night" and we'll ride the carousel or skate in the ice rink. But only when it is free. Otherwise, we'll just walk around the mall and window shop, but not buy anything. And we'll go to the library because that's free. Or to the park, we go to the park a lot. It's time that I get to spend with my daughter, quality time. I don't really have any friends or go out with classmates or date or anything. I have no social life.

Joanna and her daughter had enough to eat and a place to live and Joanna was able to pay her day care bill on time each month. But her financial situation left her socially isolated, unable to foster relationships with classmates or others her own age because she "can only do stuff that is free and most people my age just don't want to hang out at the park with a preschooler."

Joanna's predicament was not uncommon among the women I interviewed. For most of them, the combination of limited income and various expenses related to education and raising children meant that economizing was a way of life. Part of this economizing included limiting unnecessary expenditures such as going to the movies, eating out, attending concerts, going to clubs, and other forms of entertainment and socializing that are common among college students. This is not to suggest that the women never purchased non-essentials. However, they typically saved such purchases for special occasions such as taking the children out for ice cream to celebrate an achievement or purchasing a toy or game for a birthday or holiday. And while the women tended to believe it was acceptable to occasionally purchase such non-essentials for their children, most were less comfortable with the idea of spending even small amounts of money on non-essentials for themselves. For example, Joanna rationalized spending $5.00 to buy Destiny an ice cream cone and have her face painted at a music festival because it was a "special outing." However, she did not believe it was appropriate to buy herself a $5.00 ticket to go see a matinee with a classmate. Because Joanna had no close friends, she faced her parenting and educational challenges without the benefits of camaraderie or companionship.

THE ECONOMIC PRESENT VERSUS THE ECONOMIC FUTURE

When Miranda Brown discovered she was pregnant, the person she most dreaded telling was her maternal grandmother, Emma. Miranda was the only granddaughter on her mother's side of the family and Emma indulged her granddaughter, frequently letting her sleep over and taking her away for weekend shopping trips. When Miranda entered high school and began looking forward to college, Emma persuaded her to pursue a career in science despite the fact that Miranda's parents pushed her to follow a more traditionally feminine discipline such as teaching English. After completing an undergraduate degree in chemistry and graduating summa cum laude, Miranda spent two years working for a small research company before deciding to go back to school for her PhD in chemistry. Emma was delighted. In the fall of 2000, Miranda took the Graduate Record Examination (GRE) and completed applications to several doctoral programs. She admitted, however, that she really had her heart set on UI. She was attracted to it not only because of the school's reputation but also because Emma was a big fan of Hawkeye football.

The following spring, Miranda received a letter notifying her she had been admitted to UI and awarded a substantial scholarship. In addition to providing a full tuition scholarship for Miranda's first year of graduate study, the award included a teaching assistantship that was guaranteed for four years as long as Miranda maintained "sufficient progress" in the program. Miranda called Emma to tell her the news and then phoned her parents. She then contacted Kenneth, a man she had met through friends and had been dating for a few months, and they made plans to go out and celebrate that evening. The festivities lasted until the wee hours of the morning and Miranda was certain this was the night she got pregnant: "We went out to a nice dinner and had lots and lots of wine, and then went dancing and drank some more. I know my cycles and I was ovulating at the time and we had sex—I mean, we were celebrating so *of course* we had sex! And we were both pretty drunk and didn't use a condom. It doesn't take a genius to put two and two together—expose an ovulating woman to semen and forget the condom and you're bound to end up with a pregnancy." Nearly a month later, Miranda began to suspect that she was pregnant. She had missed her period and felt unusually tired. Her breasts were also very sore and rather swollen. Despite her suspicions, Miranda hoped that she just had a touch of the flu and that the symptoms would subside. When they did not, she went to see her gynecologist, who confirmed her suspicions. The pregnancy was unplanned but it was not unwanted. Miranda, who had always known she wanted to be a parent, was thrilled. She wasn't upset at the prospect of becoming a single parent because "[although] it was always a goal in my life to have a child . . . it wasn't necessarily a goal to have a husband." Within days, she shared the news of the pregnancy with her parents and friends. She also told Kenneth. Unlike Miranda, he was not excited about the pregnancy. At twenty-six, he felt he was too young to become a father. Miranda wished him well and they parted ways.

Although telling her parents, friends, and Kenneth had been fairly easy, Miranda agonized over sharing the news with Emma because "she's older and she's really conservative—we're white, middle class, and Catholic and my grandma absolutely believes you must be married before you have a child." Emma was also quite opinionated. Miranda expected that her grandmother would scold her and give her a stern lecture about responsibility. Thus, she waited more than six weeks to tell Emma. However, when she shared the news with her grandmother, Emma did not lecture. Instead, she cried and hugged Miranda repeatedly, telling her that she couldn't wait to be a great-grandmother and listing all the ways she was going to spoil Miranda's baby.

As hard as it had been to work up the courage to tell her grandmother, Miranda said it was even more difficult for her to imagine how she was going to manage the move to Iowa City, begin graduate school, and try to raise a child on a graduate student income. Although the scholarship would cover her tuition, it only did so for her first year of graduate studies. Miranda had nearly $4,000 in savings, but she knew that a sizeable portion of those funds would be used to purchase the layette and prepare the nursery. When she compared her projected monthly income to her projected monthly expenses, she found herself facing a substantial deficit. With her financial future looking bleak, Miranda considered putting off graduate school for a year so she could save more money. She also contemplated forgoing graduate school altogether and staying at her research job where she earned $28,000 a year and had both health insurance and opportunities for advancement.

However, Miranda was determined to get her PhD. Thus, on July 31, approximately twenty weeks into her pregnancy, she made the twelve-hour drive to Iowa City. She moved into her new apartment the following day and began full-time classes and half-time teaching three weeks later. Although it took Miranda several months to adjust to living in a new city, she enjoyed her courses and her teaching responsibilities even more than she had anticipated. She had lingering financial concerns, of course, particularly with the birth approaching. Yet she was confident that her decision to attend graduate school had been the right thing to do and she was optimistic about her ability to financially support her child once she completed her studies. On Christmas Day, less than a week after turning in her own research papers and submitting final grades for her students, Miranda gave birth to her son, Taylor.

Unlike Joanna, Miranda's initial motivation for getting her degree was not economic. In fact, economic considerations weren't all that important to Miranda before she became a mother. Instead, she made her decision to pursue a graduate degree because she enjoyed doing research and wanted a career that would provide her with the opportunity to conduct research at a large university. Initially, then, Miranda regarded the intellectual aspects of a research career as far more important than the pay associated with such work. After Taylor's arrival, however, finances became increasingly salient and Miranda worried about her ability to provide a secure economic future for her child:

> My life is completely different than what is was like before . . . I use to go out with friends every single night when I was working on my [undergraduate] degree and even when I was working full time after that. Seven nights a week, I'd be at bars or parties and whatever. I was careless with my money. I'm sure I would have been the same way in graduate school if I didn't have my child. Now, I just have more motivation [to succeed], more focus on what I'm doing and why. I think a lot of students without kids, at least a lot of the graduate students I know, are aimlessly going through their programs and they think they want a career or whatever, but it's not urgent. I have a definite motivation—I need to have a good career to be able to support my child and give my child a good life. That's my goal; it's what drives me, the need to do well because I don't want my child to have to live

without things. I want my child to have the things that children need to learn and grow and be healthy and happy. I want to have a comfortable lifestyle for us. And once I finish my PhD, I'll be able to [provide those things].

In a way that was typical for many project participants, Miranda organized her life narrative in relationship to her maternal identity, drawing a sharp distinction between her experiences before and after becoming a mother. Miranda said that before Taylor was born, she was careless with money and socializing was a priority in her life. Motherhood altered her motivation for pursuing a PhD and a career; her initial wish for intellectual self-fulfillment gave way to her desire to provide for Taylor, give him a "good life," and make certain he wouldn't have to "live without things." It is arguable that this ideological shift occurred simply out of necessity; Kenneth was not involved in Taylor's life and did not provide financial support for his son and Miranda was solely responsible for the expenses associated with raising Taylor. Yet it is important to note that Miranda's economic goals went beyond basic support and aligned squarely with middle-class patterns of consumption. Although Taylor's health and happiness were certainly important to her, making certain that her son wouldn't "have to live without things" was equally important to Miranda.

Miranda was confident that earning her PhD would lead to a secure economic future. She had investigated this issue thoroughly and said that she expected to earn an annual starting salary of $60,000 or more once she graduated from UI. However, her financial circumstances during graduate school were challenging. Under her contract as a half-time teaching assistant for the 2003–2004 academic year, Miranda earned just over $15,000. She acknowledged that the UI graduate student union, UE-COGS, had been instrumental in raising wages for research assistants and teaching assistants across campus. Despite the union's influence, however, she found graduate student wages insufficient for graduate students with families:

[My paycheck] might be enough for a single person with no dependents to live on, or even a married couple with no dependents. But for someone with a child in day care, it's a joke. I don't make enough money to support the two of us. I make a little more than $15,000 a year—who can afford day care on that? Nobody. I still have to pay rent and utilities and transportation and groceries and phone and for my books. And my tuition was covered my first year, but now I have to pay tuition as well. [My expenses are] more than I make, especially after you take out taxes and health insurance. And so I have to take out student loans. I take out almost as much in student loans as I make in wages each year, and we're still barely scraping by. I constantly feel this nagging concern, all of this debt piling up on my shoulders, and that's a huge source of stress for me.

Miranda did not qualify for federal programs such as Temporary Aid to Needy Families (TANF) or food stamps. As a result, and because the wages she earned through her half-time appointment as a teaching assistant weren't enough to support her and her son, she borrowed approximately $12,000 a year in student loans. She estimated that the amount would increase after she completed her fourth year in the program. She was guaranteed a teaching assistantship for only four years and after that, "I'm sort of on my own . . . and unless I get a grant, I'll have to max out my student loans for a year or two until I can finish my dissertation." Miranda and Taylor certainly weren't destitute, but even with the combination of her salary and student loans, there were things Miranda could not afford. For example, while her family was supportive and they loved Taylor, Miranda couldn't afford to take her son back to Ohio very often because the price of gas was too high. They typically made the trip only twice a year. As a result, Taylor didn't have a close relationship with their extended family. This was particularly troubling to Miranda because Emma was nearing her ninetieth birthday and was in poor health.

Miranda believed that once she completed her PhD, she would be able to repay her student loan debt and travel to Ohio more frequently. However, she also voiced doubts about her ability to finish her course of study. Citing tremendous demands on her time and the "breakneck pace" she maintained as she attempted to balance her responsibilities as a single mother, a full-time graduate student, and a half-time teaching assistant, Miranda admitted that she sometimes thought of dropping out of graduate school and getting a nine-to-five job. She imagined that doing so would significantly reduce her stress levels. She also believed it would enable her to spend more time with her son. Yet Miranda also believed that if she did not complete her PhD, she would be less likely to find a lucrative career and would be less able to provide the middle-class lifestyle she wanted for Taylor. Thus, Miranda continued to work on her degree. Despite the fact that tenure-track faculty positions have become increasingly scarce at U.S. colleges and universities over the past three decades,[14] Miranda remained optimistic that she would secure one of those coveted positions and move into a high-paying job. However, her optimism was somewhat difficult to understand in light of the student loan debt she was accumulating. Miranda estimated that by the time she earned her PhD, she would owe approximately $80,000 in student loans. Thus, even if she managed to secure a well-paying job, student loan payments would likely consume a significant portion of Miranda's budget and hinder her ability to secure a place for herself and Taylor in the ranks of the American middle class.

VOTING, TUITION, AND BUS FARE

Kendra Washington was born in St. Charles, Illinois, to what she describes as "very intellectual Black parents . . . overachievers who believe that each generation is supposed to surpass the achievements of the previous generation." Her parents were professionals who expected all four of their children to not only go to college but also to earn "at least a master's degree if not a PhD or professional degree." In addition, they expected their children to pay for their own education because "they don't believe in handouts." Kendra's three siblings, two brothers and a sister, all fulfilled their parents' wishes—one brother became a doctor, another completed a doctorate in education, and her sister earned an MBA. Kendra had similar intentions and initially hoped to finish her bachelor's degree in four years and then go on to graduate school. After graduating from high school in 1992, she began courses at UI on a full scholarship, but her initial attempt at college "just didn't go well because I was so homesick and depressed I just stopped going to classes" after the first few weeks. During her first semester, Kendra earned all Ds and Fs in her courses and was placed on academic probation. Though she "intended to turn things around" during the next semester, by spring break she "couldn't stand being there anymore" and withdrew from the university, moved back to Chicago, and rented an "extremely small, kind of shabby" apartment with friends. After returning to Chicago, Kendra worked a variety of jobs. Initially, she found "just low-wage stuff here and there," but that changed when a family friend hired her as an assistant in his downtown office. Though Kendra says she "only got the job because this guy and my dad went back a long way, like back to kindergarten," she excelled in her new position and quickly earned raises and promotions. She then took on a sort of "modified supervisory role" when Gloria, the office manager, went on maternity leave. When Gloria decided to be a stay-at-home mom instead of returning to work, Kendra was hired as her permanent replacement. Kendra liked the work but didn't like the pay. She worked overtime nearly every week and split rent on an apartment with three other young women, but after her bills were paid, she didn't have much money left for recreation and "certainly none for savings." These economic circumstances prompted Kendra to reapply to UI to finish her degree and "try to do it right this time." In October 1997, she filled out the necessary paperwork and sent it to the UI Office of Admissions. When she received her acceptance letter a few months later, she shared the news with her parents, who were "absolutely thrilled, of course!"

Around the first of March of 1998, Kendra discovered she was three-and-a-half months pregnant. The father was a man she had met at work and had been dating off and on for some time. He was "very unhappily married" and although she "really loved this guy," she had ended the relationship in mid-January because "I spent the holidays alone while he was home with the wife and kids and I just couldn't do the 'mistress' thing anymore." The pregnancy was initially a shock, particularly as Kendra had "always been really irregular with my cycles" and her gynecologist had told her that since she didn't ovulate on her own because of low hormone levels, she would need to go on fertility drugs if she ever wanted to become pregnant. Though she considered "all the options," including abortion and adoption, she decided to continue the pregnancy and keep the child because "it just seemed like the right thing to do." Because she was due in September, Kendra decided to delay her return to UI; instead of resuming her undergraduate course of study in August, she would start classes at the beginning of the spring semester in January.

Although Kendra was "really pretty excited that I was going to be a mom," her parents were disappointed about the pregnancy. They feared it would prevent their daughter from returning to college: "When I told them the news, that I was expecting a child and had no intention of marrying the father, all they could think about was that it was over for me—you know, 'she's gonna be caring for this kid for the rest of her life, by herself, and she's never gonna get anything accomplished.' And that was their idea about what was going to happen. That was probably most of the family's fear, that because I was going to be a single mother, my life was over." For Kendra, however, becoming pregnant "made me think differently about going back to college . . . mostly because I realized it was time to grow up and be serious about moving on with my life, with or without their support." She gave birth to her daughter, Jaleesa, in September 1998. During the first week of 1999, she and Jaleesa moved into an apartment in Coralville, Iowa, a suburb of Iowa City that is "cheaper than renting in Iowa City." Kendra began classes at UI two weeks later.

At the time of my first interview with Kendra, she was approximately six months away from completing her degree in the liberal arts. When I asked her to describe what it's like to be a single mother student and a college student, she responded by saying that she is "flat broke all the time" and then laughed as she considered her economic circumstances. But her laughter was "only to keep from crying!" Despite the fact that her job in Chicago "didn't pay well at all," she didn't really have an understanding of what it meant to live in poverty until she resumed her studies as a single mother. Prior to moving back to Iowa City, she had "anticipated our expenses" and established a monthly budget that included rent, day care, groceries, transportation, and utilities plus an allowance for tuition and books. She also took out "a little extra in student loans, to cover things but also give us like an extra $200 a month for emergencies and stuff." However, upon arriving in Iowa City, she discovered that there were some major expenses she hadn't considered:

I knew about [the cost of] day care, but I didn't know about the deposit at day care. At my day care, you had to pay for your first and last month of day care up front, kind of like a deposit and so that was more money I had to come up with. And I didn't even think of out-of-state tuition. I was on scholarship last time I was here and because of that, I was considered a resident for tuition. So I guess I still thought I'd still be considered in-state, even though I'm not on scholarship anymore. And so I got here and got my tuition bill and it was more than triple what I expected it to be. I couldn't afford that.

I thought about dropping my registration down to only six semester hours and doing only part-time classes that first semester . . . but then I would have lost most of my financial aid anyway, so I wouldn't have been any better off. My financial aid check came in and most of it went to pay for my tuition. But I still had expenses to meet. I had bare cupboards. I had brought some food with me and my parents sent a few things, but it wasn't much. And I had to figure out how to buy diapers and formula for my child. I ended up going to the [Johnson County] Food Bank because I didn't have enough money to feed myself and my child.

Though Kendra tried to increase her student loans, a financial aid counselor told her "we can't give you any more because financial aid is pretty much assigned in the fall." After some sleepless nights, she mustered up the courage to ask her parents for help, but they refused and told Kendra that "I had made my bed so it was my responsibility to figure all this out." She felt she had no choice but to sell her car and take "less than what it was worth just because I needed the money in a hurry."

Kendra had lived in Iowa City continuously for nearly four years since her return to UI and she had established residency in the state of Iowa. However, she still paid out-of-state tuition. As the UI residency regulations stated:

> In determining resident or nonresident classification, the issue is essentially one of why the person is in the state of Iowa. If the person is in the state primarily for educational purposes, that person will be considered a nonresident. For example, it may be possible that an individual could qualify as a resident of Iowa for such purposes as voting or holding an Iowa driver's license and not meet the residency requirements as established by the Board of Regents for admission, tuition and fee purposes.[15]

Thus, because Kendra was not a resident of Iowa before she began her studies, the university charged her the nonresident rate for tuition and fees. This was true not only for the fall and spring semesters, when she enrolled for twelve semester hours, but also during summers, when she took six credits to "make sure I graduate in four years." The difference between resident and nonresident tuition was significant; nonresident students were charged more than three times as much as their resident peers. This was a source of great frustration to her:

> So back then [when I was on scholarship], when I first came here and the university was paying my tuition, they classified me as a resident even though I moved here to go to school. I guess it was to save themselves some money. But now that I'm not on scholarship and I'm paying tuition myself, they consider me a nonresident.
>
> I pay out-of-state tuition even though I live here year round. The city considers me a citizen and the state considers me a citizen, but the university does not. So I can vote here, I'm registered to vote in the state of Iowa, and I don't have a home somewhere else, and I pay taxes only in the state of Iowa, but the university does not consider me a resident for tuition purposes. It's ridiculous, especially considering that tuition continues to go up every single year. My dad just mailed me an article last week—he and my mother get the *Daily Iowan* [the UI campus newspaper] to keep up with what's going on here—and he sent me this article that says tuition is going up 8.3 percent next year [and there was] a note attached that said "Get out now!"
>
> You know, I picked a really great time to come to Iowa—they've had a tuition hike every year since I've been back. And my dad figured it all out for me. He sent me something that said tuition had gone up something like 43 percent overall since I returned. And that's not including this current year, the 17 percent increase. It's ridiculous. I don't live anywhere else. I live here. If I am considered a resident for voting, I should be considered a resident for tuition.

Kendra's frustration about the cost of tuition was understandable. During her final year at UI, which included the summer of 2003 and the fall and spring semesters of the 2003–2004 academic year, Kendra's tuition bill amounted to $19,131.25. If she had been classified as a resident, that amount would have dropped to only $6,265.25, or roughly one-third of what she was charged.

As part of her attempts to make ends meet, Kendra worked fifteen to eighteen hours a week at a bookstore in Iowa City. Yet her primary source of income was student loans, and she borrowed "the absolute maximum I can each year" in loans. In addition to tuition, books, fees, housing, and living expenses, Kendra's financial aid counselor—at Kendra's request—also included day care expenses as part of her "cost of attendance." This enabled Kendra to take out additional student loans, "without which we'd probably be homeless." Yet even with student loans and her wages, Kendra struggled financially and had to seek assistance through various programs for low-income families. Although she applied for support through the Iowa Department of Human Services, she was unable to receive assistance "because they [wouldn't] approve my liberal arts major.

My caseworker told me to do a degree in business or computers so I could get a job when I was finished. I don't even like business or computers." Unwilling to switch her major and therefore ineligible for government assistance, Kendra turned to university and community programs. She received a child care subsidy of "about $75 per month" through the UI Family Services Office. In addition, she participated in the federal Women, Infants, and Children (WIC) nutritional program. When things were "really tight," Kendra went to the Crisis Center, the Food Bank, or the Salvation Army to get food and other "essentials like shampoo or tampons or diapers when I can't afford them." For Kendra, these types of support weren't simply helpful, they were "crucial, because even though I budget things out, by the end of the semester, I'm pretty much digging through the couch cushions for change for the bus." And on the occasions when the couch yielded no coins, Kendra simply packed Jaleesa into her stroller and walked more than two miles from her apartment to UI family housing to catch the free campus bus. For Kendra, her inability to afford bus fare of seventy-five cents was "the biggest reminder of how poor we are, especially when we're doing that walk in winter."

DAYCARE, BOOKS, AND LEGAL FEES

Brenda Wilson met William Butler at a dance club in St. Louis. Brenda had gone there to visit a friend over winter break during her first year of undergraduate studies at UI and was "absolutely charmed" by William's good looks and dance moves. William seemed similarly enamored, and despite the distance between Iowa City and St. Louis, they soon began dating. Since William didn't have a car, Brenda shouldered the responsibility of driving back and forth nearly every weekend to see her new boyfriend. The relationship quickly became serious and William "even introduced me to his parents," who, despite Brenda's worst fears, didn't mind that she was white and their son was African American. Indeed, they liked Brenda so much they invited her to spend spring break with their family in Florida. After several months of their commuter relationship, William decided to leave St. Louis and move in with Brenda in Iowa City. He intended to get a job and help support her until she finished her degree.

Only days into her second year of college and less than nine months into her relationship with William, Brenda discovered she was pregnant. Not yet nineteen years old, Brenda went through a "few days of denial" and then considered her options. She was leaning toward abortion until William told her how much he really wanted them to have a baby so "we could become the family he always dreamed of." She decided to continue the pregnancy and the couple began discussing marriage. Shortly before Thanksgiving, however, Brenda found out that William had been cheating on her with "some college girl he met at the bars" in

Iowa City. She asked William to move out, effectively ending their romantic relationship. However, Brenda made it clear that she expected William to be a father and be involved in all aspects of their child's life. William responded by telling her that if they weren't going to be together as a couple, he wasn't going to "play daddy." The next day, he got on a bus and moved back to St. Louis. Brenda went through the remainder of the pregnancy by herself, although William came back to Iowa City about two weeks before her due date. He was present at the birth of their son, Brandon, and stayed overnight at the hospital that first night, sleeping in the reclining chair in Brenda's room. He left the following morning and Brenda didn't see him again for over two years until he showed up unexpectedly on Brenda's doorstep with a new girlfriend in tow. He informed Brenda that he was "ready to start being a father" and intended to gain full custody of Brandon. Brenda immediately hired a lawyer.

The "custody war," as Brenda called it, lasted for almost a year and a half and plunged Brenda into a serious financial crisis. Although William's attempt to gain custody was unsuccessful, he did receive visitation privileges that allowed him to spend every other weekend with Brandon. William kept to this visitation schedule for approximately three months before disappearing from Brandon's life once again. He moved out of Iowa City and stopped paying child support. When Brenda contacted the Child Support Recovery Unit of the Iowa Department of Health and Human Services, she learned that "they can't take action unless they know where he is." Although Brenda called "all of his friends and family members," she was unable to locate William. She described the emotional toll of the "custody war" as "tremendous and draining," but the financial toll was also significant. Though she had nothing but praise for her lawyer, he wasn't cheap. By the time the case was finally resolved, Brenda's legal expenses totaled nearly $20,000. She paid for them with what she called the "credit card trap":

> Initially, I accepted every credit card offer I got and I probably had about ten or twelve and used those to pay for my lawyer and everything. But the interest rates were killing me. And I was working twenty hours a week during the school year and full time in the summer, but even with that, I couldn't make even the minimum payment on all of my credit cards and the balances just kept getting higher and higher and higher. And so I just decided that I had to take out more in student loans. Prior to this, I only took out enough to pay for day care and books and we just lived really cheap, in subsidized housing and getting WIC and medical assistance and shopping at Aldi [a wholesale grocery chain]. But after like a year of those legal fees being on my cards, the total was up near $28,000, and so I take out the maximum I can for student loans each year until the cards are paid off. I take out loans for day care, books, and to pay off the debt on my legal fees.

Brenda still owed approximately $8,500 on her credit cards, but she was certain that after "two more semesters of financial aid," they would be paid off.

Though Brenda recognized that she would face "mountains of student loan debt when I graduate," she believed that using student loans to pay off credit cards was a wise decision. The interest rates on her credit cards ranged "between 18 percent and 24 percent." Interest rates on her direct loans from the U.S. Department of Education were much lower, ranging from 2.77 percent to 4.17 percent.[16] Thus, by using student loans to pay off her credit cards, Brenda was reducing not only the interest she incurred but also reducing her long-term debt. Furthermore, many of her student loans were subsidized and would not begin accruing interest until after she graduated from college. Finally, monthly payments on credit card debt posed a significant strain on Brenda's already limited budget. By using student loans to pay off that debt and because repayment of student loans was deferred,[17] Brenda was better able to meet her living expenses.

Despite these advantages, Brenda's debt was not disappearing. Instead, it was being transferred to a different lender and repayment was simply being delayed. Upon graduation, she would again have to contend with these financial obligations. And while Brenda hoped she would be able to "get a job that will make it possible for me to repay [the debt] without having to starve," she also recognized that even with a bachelor's degree, her earning potential "probably won't be all that great." Given the wage gap the persists in American culture, even for those with postsecondary degrees, and given the fact that the cost of raising a child continues to increase, finances would likely continue to be a struggle for her for some time to come.[18]

LIFE AFTER THE STORM

St. Bernard Parish, Louisiana, a community located just outside New Orleans, is the place Angela Beauchamp called her "real home." She was born and raised in the community, loved it, and intended to spend her entire life there. In fact, most of Angela's family—including her parents, grandparents, siblings, aunts, uncles, and cousins—lived within a 100-mile radius of the Big Easy. Her ex-husband, James, also lived nearby. Although she sometimes wished James was farther away so she didn't have to interact with him so often, she believed it was best that her toddler twins, Stephen and Sophia, lived near James and had a close relationship with their father.

Many of the women who participated in this research divided their life story into two parts: life before and after becoming a mother. Angela also divided her life story into two parts, but her division did not correspond with her maternal identity. This is not to suggest that motherhood was an insignificant part of Angela's life story. On the contrary, Angela talked about her children with great affection and pride and wholeheartedly claimed her maternal identity. Yet unlike the other mothers, Angela divided her life in a rather unique way: life before and after the storm. On August 29, 2005, Hurricane Katrina slammed into the Gulf of Mexico, decimating the coastline of Louisiana, Mississippi, and Alabama. It was one of the deadliest hurricanes in U.S. history. Although Katrina had decreased from a Category 5 storm to a Category 3 storm before making landfall, it was nonetheless catastrophic, resulting in nearly 2,000 deaths, thousands of injuries and storm-related illnesses, and over $80 billion dollars in property damage. Angela's hometown of St. Bernard Parish is located just east of downtown New Orleans and was completely flooded as levees failed and storm surge inundated the community.

Before the storm, Angela was a full-time student at a university in the New Orleans area, pursuing her bachelor's degree in social work. She had also worked twenty hours a week at a work-study job on campus. Between her wages, student loans, alimony, and child support, Angela and her children lived a "comfortable but certainly not extravagant" lifestyle. She sometimes struggled with credit card debt and complained that her savings account was poor, but she was always been able to pay the bills on time and kept her family fed and clothed. Angela's grandmother, Betsy, cared for Stephen and Sophia while Angela worked and attended classes. In addition, members of the Beauchamp extended kin network eagerly took the children overnight when Angela had evening classes or on weekends when she had to work. Angela was grateful that her children were surrounded by such a loving, caring family. She was equally thankful that she did not have to pay for child care.

Virtually every aspect of Angela's life changed in the aftermath of Katrina. On Saturday, August 27, 2005, New Orleans mayor Ray Nagin issued a call for voluntary evacuation. Angela, who had been watching the news while doing laundry at her mother's house, decided to wait to see if the storm would worsen. After all, she was not a newcomer to hurricane season and had already lived through Tropical Storm Frances in 1998. The following day, Mayor Nagin declared a state of emergency, calling for mandatory evacuation. Angela thought he was overreacting. Still, at the urging of her mother, Mary, Angela packed enough clothes and personal items to last herself, Stephen, and Sophia for three days and buckled the children into the back seat of her mother's car. After picking up Grandma Betsy, the family began what should have been a three-hour drive north to Natchez, Mississippi, a location where Angela assumed they would be out of danger. The children thought they were going on vacation and couldn't wait to spend a few days swimming in the hotel pool. Angela did not take her textbooks or school materials because she assumed she would return home in plenty of time to put the finishing touches on her short sociology paper that was due four days later.

The drive took longer than expected. Traffic was heavy on Interstate 55 as thousands of cars moved slowly northward out of New Orleans. Mary drove while Angela and Betsy tried to keep the children occupied with songs and car games. When they reached Natchez, the family checked into a budget hotel, reserving a suite for only two nights. After settling the children in, Angela accompanied her mother to a local grocery store. Mary, who Angela described as "very nervous about the storm," purchased several bags of groceries and more gallons of bottled water than Angela felt they would ever need. They returned to the hotel and, with her children, mother, and grandmother all safe, Angela prepared to wait out Katrina. She assumed the storm would be windy and rainy, but otherwise uneventful.

Although Hurricane Katrina was frightening for Angela and her family, they survived unharmed. The hotel lost power, water service, phone service, cable, and a portion of its roof, but the building remained standing and structurally sound. For the next few days, Angela and her family stayed close to the hotel, sweltering in their first-floor suite and waiting for power and water to be restored. They tried phoning friends and family members to get information about the situation in New Orleans but couldn't reach anyone. The city of Natchez had suffered considerable damage—buildings were destroyed, cars were upended, large trees were uprooted, and power lines hung into the street like strings of thick, heavy black yarn. The streets were impassable, cluttered with branches and debris. During the day, the community remained eerily quiet. At night, looters roamed the area. Feeling helpless and completely cut off from the world outside Natchez, Angela and her family remained unaware of the full extent of the damage caused by Katrina and the emergency response fiasco that ensued.

It wasn't until several days after the storm, when a convoy of National Guard trucks rolled past their hotel in Natchez, that Angela began to grasp the severity of the situation. The trucks were headed south, toward New Orleans. It was a sight Angela will never forget. Her thoughts turned to her sister, brothers, and other family members who had stayed behind. Were they hurt? Had they survived? She thought of her rental house in St. Bernard Parish. Was it still standing? Had her car been damaged? She had many questions but no answers. With the roads to New Orleans closed to everyone except law enforcement and relief crews, Angela's family felt they had no choice but to heed the advice of relief workers, and they made their way to the Reliant Center in Houston. Days later, while lying in a cot and surrounded by thousands of other Katrina survivors, Angela realized that she and her children were homeless:

We weren't getting any information from the city. When I watched the news, I only saw the same pictures and the same reports over and over. I knew something was going on but I didn't know [the extent of it]; I didn't believe I could be homeless. And that made me think about people who are really homeless—they know that they're homeless. They stink, they don't take showers. They're dirty.

[My children] thought we were on vacation. They didn't know. They were clueless. But I was, too. I didn't have any clothes. I had on some sandals that I had for like six or seven years that were actually hand-me-downs from my mom. That's all I had for shoes. I had some old jogging pants, just some other stuff that I threw in the bag when we left because I thought we'd be going back home.

Then I was watching the news reports and I guess it just occurred to me that I was homeless. I was homeless. I didn't have a car anymore. I had ridden in a car with my mom and my grandmother but they were homeless, too. We had no clothes, nothing with us. All I had were these kids, my mother, [and] my grandmother. I was at the shelter for days before I realized I was actually homeless.

Angela and her children lost their home and all of their possessions, including clothes, furniture, photographs, appliances, books, toys, and Angela's laptop computer. Even her car had been destroyed.

Unlike many who were affected by Katrina, Angela managed to formulate a plan fairly quickly. She didn't wait for the Federal Emergency Management Agency (FEMA) to come through for her family. Instead, she contacted "friends who knew friends in the Houston area" and arranged for herself, Mary, Betsey, Stephen, and Sophia to stay with them. They were able to get some clothes from the Salvation Army and a Houston-area church. Angela and Mary began looking for work and found jobs almost immediately—Angela as an assistant teacher in a child care center and Mary as a receptionist in a health clinic. By the end of October, they had enough money to move into a small furnished apartment and they began to rebuild their lives.

As part of this rebuilding process, Angela set her sights on returning to college, a decision she described as economically motivated. Angela hadn't taken out rental insurance on the house in St. Bernard Parish and did not receive financial compensation for the belongings she and her children had lost to Katrina. In addition, her ex-husband had lost his house and job and was no longer paying child support or alimony. Angela earned only $6.75 an hour at the day care center where she worked at in Houston, while Mary made just over $10.00 an hour at her job. Even after combining their incomes, splitting expenses, and with the help of food stamps and medical assistance, the two women struggled to support themselves, Betsy, and the children. Angela realized that without a college degree she would be stuck in "dead end" jobs with low pay and no benefits. After reviewing online job advertisements, she was eager to finish her social work degree and secure one of the $30,000-a-year positions in social services she had read about. She believed that her outgoing personality and empathy skills made her a good candidate for this type of work. She explored a variety of universities in the state of Texas but finally chose TWU because of its low tuition rate and because after transferring the sixty-nine credits she had already completed back in New Orleans she would be able to complete her bachelor's degree with only two more years of coursework. In August 2006, approximately one year after Hurricane Katrina had turned her life upside down, Angela said good-bye to her mother and grandmother and moved her children north to Denton, Texas. She began classes at TWU the following week.

Although she managed to do well academically at TWU, Angela's return to college was difficult for her financially. Grandma Betsy was in Houston and Angela had to locate and pay for child care for the first time in her life. It was much more expensive than she had anticipated, despite the fact that she was able to find space for both children at a church-based preschool that was more economical than other centers in the area. However, her weekly child care bill totaled $160 for part-time care for Stephen and Sophia. Angela received a financial aid award of $14,500 for the 2006–2007 academic year that included a Pell Grant and subsidized and unsubsidized loans. However, child care expenses consumed nearly one-third of her total financial aid. Rent was also a considerable expense, costing Angela $655 a month. As a result, she quickly got behind on bills, including rent and utilities. Her phone and Internet were disconnected for nonpayment. She also received a late rent warning from the apartment manager. By the time December arrived, her checking account was overdrawn, and Angela had to rely on a charitable program to provide Christmas gifts for the children. She also made regular trips to the food bank in order to put food in her nearly empty cupboards.

The stress of her financial woes took a significant toll on Angela and challenged her commitment to completing her degree. Over winter break, as she and children "lived on the noodles, powdered milk, beans, rice, tuna, canned peaches, and generic cereal" they received from the food bank, Angela contemplated dropping out of school. In mid-January, however, her financial situation improved when she received her financial aid disbursement for the spring semester and was able to catch up on her rent. She decided to stay in school. She also paid to have her phone turned back on but decided that Internet access was beyond her means. Angela managed her money carefully. However, by the beginning of April and with five weeks remaining in the spring semester, her money had run out. Her financial aid was simply not enough to cover her expenses for the entire semester. Desperate and fearing she would have to withdraw from the university prior to completing her courses, Angela met with

Louise, one of the financial aid counselors at TWU. The meeting was initially quite frustrating for her:

> I said I'm telling you, I am a full-time student, I have zero income. Me and my kids are living off of loans and it's not enough. She asked if I had anything that I could sell, like a car or jewelry . . . I lost it in Katrina. I've got nothing. I do have the car, but it's my mother's *and* I need it to get the kids to day care. It isn't mine to sell. I'm sleeping on an air mattress . . . every day we come home, every night we have another need, something missing that we [need]. . . . She asked if I thought about getting a job. I don't have a job so I can spend time with my kids and study. If I had a job, I'd never see them.
>
> She asked if I had family members who could help me. They lost it all [in Katrina]. I am my own household, me and my kids, and I don't have access to any other money or any more credit cards or things like that. I said that I am poor and it was like she had this picture in her head of what poor looks like. My clothes were clean. I had showered. I didn't fit her expectation of poor. And I tried not to let my emotions take over the situation but I was so upset. I wanted to ask her, "What does poor look like to you? How do you want me to act when I come in here so you will help me? How do you want me to look?" It was like because I wasn't homeless, then I wasn't poor enough for her.

Angela felt that because she didn't "look poor," Louise hadn't taken her situation seriously. However, once Angela provided Louise with a list of her monthly expenses and a copy of her Federal Student Aid Report (SAR), the course of the conversation changed dramatically. Instead of being dismissive, Louise grew concerned. She first verified the information on Angela's SAR. Next, she calculated Angela's total annual child care bill and informed her that she was eligible for an additional $937 each semester in student loans to help cover child care expenses. Finally, she helped Angela secure an emergency loan of $350 through the TWU Office of Student Life to help cover food and other expenses until the end of the semester. Although generally such loans must be repaid in thirty days, Louise worked with her supervisor to arrange for it to be repaid in July after Angela received her summer financial aid disbursement.

After her meeting with Louise, Angela's financial situation improved somewhat. The additional student loans she took out during the fall, spring, and summer terms helped ease her financial strain and provided almost $3,000 in additional funds a year. She no longer fell behind on rent or utilities, although she continued to rely on the food bank from time to time. The family's basic needs were met, but there was no money for extras. They did not have health insurance. During the 2007 holiday season, for the second year in a row, Angela again relied on a community assistance program for Christmas gifts for Stephen and Sophia. In addition, she hadn't changed the oil in her mother's car for almost nine months because she couldn't justify the expense. She also stopped purchasing some of the books for her classes. Although she acknowledged that this had a negative impact on her grades, taking her from As and Bs to "mostly Cs and Ds," she felt she simply could not afford to "waste" money on books when she was barely able to feed and clothe her family and keep a roof over their heads.

STUDENT LOANS ARE KIND OF LIKE GAMBLING

My interviews with Genevieve O'Neil were some of the most memorable of this project. We met three times during the spring of 2004, and each interview lasted an average of two hours. For several years afterward, Genevieve continued to e-mail me from time to time, providing updates about herself and her children, sending links to recent news articles on welfare policies as they have developed nationally and in the state of Iowa, and sharing my name and contact information with other single mother students and encouraging them to get in touch with me. She was what most ethnographers would regard as a key informant, but she also stood out from the other participants because she was one of the few women who had been a welfare recipient both before and after the passage of welfare reform legislation in 1996.[19]

Genevieve was born and raised in "a really small town in Iowa" and had always planned on going to college. When she became pregnant in the fall of 1987, during her senior year of high school, her plans didn't change. Although her family worried that the pregnancy meant "there goes college" and her mother wanted her to get an abortion, Genevieve said she never thought becoming a mother meant she would have to give up her dream of attending UI. She had visited the campus during her junior year and "fell in love with the place . . . I knew it was a good school with strong academic programs." Though she was briefly engaged to the father of her child, she reconsidered when he entered the military and despite "all kinds of promises," offered "no emotional support and the financial support would come and go." Genevieve broke the engagement. She then formulated what she referred to as a "backup plan" with her cousin, Natalie, who had also been accepted at UI. The two young women intended to rent an apartment together, and Natalie offered to help with childcare while Genevieve attended classes. In fact, as her high school graduation and due date neared, Genevieve believed she had "worked everything out and was looking forward to starting school the following semester."

Shortly after earning her high school diploma, however, Genevieve had to reconsider her options. Her daughter, Alexia, who was born six days after Genevieve's high school graduation, was "a difficult baby." Though her physician initially dismissed the infant's frequent bouts of crying and fussiness as simple colic, after several weeks of "this baby just crying almost nonstop," Genevieve finally took her to the emergency room and "demanded that they find out what was wrong with her." Alexia was diagnosed with a minor intestinal malrotation, an abnormal development of the intestines that was causing blockages. At twenty-nine days old, Alexia underwent surgery to repair the condition. Shortly after Alexia's intestinal problem was rectified, Natalie's mother was diagnosed with ovarian cancer. Though the doctors were optimistic, particularly as the disease was confined to her ovaries and hadn't spread to her abdomen, Natalie decided to "take the year off of school to be with her mother through all the treatment." Genevieve tried to figure out how she could still move to Iowa City and begin classes even without Natalie, but soon realized that she "couldn't afford rent on my own and also pay for day care." With a heavy heart, she withdrew from the university only weeks before classes were scheduled to begin.

Though Genevieve had continued to live with her parents after Alexia was born, they made it clear that since she was not going to school, they would no longer support her and she had to find her own apartment. Unemployed and without any source of income, Genevieve applied for Aid to Families with Dependent Children (AFDC), food stamps, and medical assistance through the Iowa Department of Human Services. She also applied for Section 8 housing assistance. Her applications were successful, and with a "recovering and much happier" baby Alexia, she moved into a small two-bedroom apartment on September 1, 1988. In the three months since her high school graduation, she had given birth, let go of her dream of attending UI, and established her own household. As she reflected on that period of her life, Genevieve suggested that if she had been more mature, she could have been rather content taking care of her daughter for a few months and then getting a job and raising Alexia on her own. However, she admitted that she "wasn't at all grown up" at eighteen and felt tremendous pressure from both her parents and her community with regard to her marital status. Although she didn't feel ashamed of being on welfare "because it wasn't as big a deal back then [in the late 1980s]," she felt stigmatized as a single mother. As she explained, "After high school, girls in my town either went to college or got married—they weren't supposed to have babies on their own." After giving birth to Alexia, Genevieve found that most of her friends drifted away and she felt very isolated, a feeling that was no doubt exacerbated by the fact that she spent most days in her apartment with only her infant daughter for company. In addition, she was "very depressed" about her college plans falling through. Consequently, and in what she referred to as "not the smartest move of my life," she married Ben:

> He was still in his senior year of high school when we got married, so he was a year younger than me. A great guy, really. And we had been friends all through

high school and the whole time I was pregnant, he told me the other guy was no good and then when he left to go into the military, Ben told me there was no way my baby was going to not have a father. He was very, very supportive of me throughout the pregnancy and even afterward. But we were so young. My idea of marriage back then was *so* different than it is now. And so it didn't last very long.

By the time the couple celebrated their second anniversary, they had added another daughter, Celeste, to their family. They didn't have extra money, but they were generally able to make ends meet. Eventually, however, their relationship fell apart and Ben moved out of state, filing for divorce after six years of marriage.

In addition to her roles as full-time mother and wife, Genevieve worked part time as a waitress during the marriage and continued to do so after the divorce. In addition to her wages, she also received child support from Ben, who "always, always, always pays it . . . and has never missed a single month." Still, part-time wages and child support for only one of her children were not enough to live on. Genevieve tried to make ends meet by "patch[ing] together" a variety of jobs, including as a school crossing guard and a telemarketer, "the only kind of jobs I could get with [only] a high school diploma." She also completed a training course and began selling insurance "on the side, you know, out of my home." However, the licensing and renewal fees were too expensive and after only a year, Genevieve let her license lapse and went back to waitressing. She liked her co-workers and the customers, but she didn't like the wages and found that wait-ressing left her little time to spend with her children:

I loved being a waitress. If I could have made more money at it and gotten ben-efits and things like that and not totally wear my body out, I would probably still be doing it. . . . I didn't have any choice on what shift I worked. That's just how they did it at the place I worked. So there were a lot of nights that I had to work, which would have been fine except I had school-aged children—how was I sup-posed to spend any time with them if they're in school all day and I have to work evenings?

And then new owners took over and they rearranged shifts and I had to work two shifts on the weekend, every weekend, so either Friday and Saturday or Sat-urday and Sunday, and these were fourteen-hour shifts. And at the time, I was driving almost forty-five minutes to get to work because I lived out in the middle of nowhere. And whatever tips I made would go to pay my babysitter for that weekend. So I was only taking home the $2.10 an hour that I got paid [in wages]. And I asked them to switch me to another shift, but they would not do it. And I didn't mind working on Saturdays and Sundays, but I couldn't do it every week-end and I couldn't work a fourteen-hour shift. I just couldn't do it anymore. And I told my boss, "Look, I'm a single mother and I need to be able to spend time with my kids," but he wouldn't take me off that shift. He said, "Well, I have other single mothers who would be willing to do those shifts," and I just told him, "maybe their priorities are different. My priorities are that I need to have off every other weekend so I can spend time with my kids and that on the weekends I do work, I will not work more than an eight-hour shift at one time." And he wouldn't go for that.

Unwilling to sacrifice her relationship with her children, particularly for a job that didn't pay her a living wage, Genevieve "began looking for other options."

One of the options she considered was pursuing her college degree. It was something she "had been meaning to get back to for a long time but never got around to." Nearly twenty-eight at the time, Genevieve decided that she "had put off college for almost a decade—and that was long enough!" She made some phone calls to the admissions and financial aid offices at UI. But the cost of tuition was beyond her means. Even though she qualified for Pell Grants and other forms of financial aid, including student loans, Genevieve "did the math" and determined she wouldn't be able to afford tuition and books and still pay living expenses. Though Genevieve still believed she would one day go to UI, she decided to begin her studies at Marshalltown Community College (MCC), which was "only a short drive from my house." She intended to complete her general education requirements at MCC and then transfer to UI to complete her bachelor's degree. In addition to saving Genevieve thousands of dollars in tuition, MCC was also an attractive option because of scheduling:

> They had really flexible hours. There were some classes scheduled during the day, but you could also take the same classes at night. There were multiple sections of almost every class and so I could take classes when it worked best with my sched-ule and when it allowed me to spend time with my kids and when I could get a bab-ysitter. And there were Saturday-only classes, and those might last for three hours but they only met once a week so that worked great for me. And even though this was before online classes really became a big thing like they are now, they did have some online classes and those were really nice because I could do my coursework whenever I had time. I could put the kids to bed and then get on the computer and do the online assignments for the classes I was taking. I could do my work and still be there for my kids and not have to pay a babysitter. And I completed a few of my general education courses that way.

Genevieve took twelve credits each semester, enough to meet the requirements for full-time enrollment and, accordingly, to qualify for student financial aid. She also quit her waitressing job and began working part time, "sixteen hours a week, two eight-hour shifts" as a cashier at a grocery store, a job that worked better with her school schedule and her parenting responsibilities. Despite her various sources of income, however, Genevieve was "still flat broke" and looking for a way to reduce her living expenses.

The solution to her financial problems came in the form of Robert, a mechanic who was also a part-time student at MCC and was working toward his business degree. Though 30-year-old Robert "seemed to drink quite a bit," Genevieve believed he was generally "a really nice guy," and he didn't mind that she had two kids. They began to date. When Genevieve ran into financial trouble around the holidays and feared she wouldn't be able to buy Christmas gifts for her children, Robert "said he would help out and then went to the mall and bought them everything on their lists." This convinced Genevieve that Robert was a "good catch." Two days after Christmas he proposed, and on Valentine's Day, at City Hall, he became Genevieve's second husband. The newlyweds and Alexia and Celeste moved into a three-bedroom apartment, and "for the first time in a long time, money wasn't a huge problem . . . I could even afford to go see a movie once in a while if I wanted to."

Their financial situation, however, changed fairly quickly. Genevieve was taking birth control pills but "still managed to get pregnant almost immediately . . . apparently getting pregnant is one of my specialties." Though she would have considered abortion if she had been single, it "just didn't make sense because I was married." She finished the spring semester at MCC and decided that since the baby was due in mid-November, she would take the fall semester off and return to full time classes the following spring. Yet after her third daughter, Robin, was born, Genevieve and Robert found themselves stretched financially. They didn't believe they could afford to pay for full-time infant child care plus Genevieve's full-time tuition and Robert's part-time tuition. To save money, Genevieve reduced her course load to two classes a semester. By the time Genevieve completed her associate's degree, Robin was nearly three.

Genevieve had not given up on her dream of attending UI. After graduating from MCC, she reapplied to UI and was accepted for the following semester. Genevieve and Robert decided they would move their family to Iowa City to enable Genevieve to pursue full-time studies and complete her bachelor's degree in only two years. Robert had "initially been excited about the move and seemed supportive." He had even lined up a job and looked into business classes at KCC. However, as their moving date drew nearer, Robert "became real moody" and started raising concerns about relocating the family. One evening, he stopped at a bar after work and then came home drunk and in a particularly irritable mood. He yelled at Genevieve, telling her that she was "screwing up his life." The yelling quickly escalated and when he began "throwing stuff around the house," Genevieve gathered up her daughters and went to her mother's house "to let him cool off." She tucked the girls in bed and was just about to go to bed herself when Robert showed up. Genevieve went outside, thinking he wanted to talk, but Robert "got violent and began hitting me and just saying 'you've ruined everything, you've ruined everything' over and over and he said he was going to kill me." Genevieve's mother called the police, but by the time they arrived, Robert had "already done quite a bit of damage." Genevieve was taken to the hospital and treated for "a couple of broken ribs, a fractured wrist, a broken nose, and lots of bruises." Within twenty-four hours, a judge issued a restraining order against Robert. Within a week, Genevieve had hired a lawyer and started divorce proceedings. And within a month, she had relocated to Iowa City, where she began classes in August and "tried to start over and make a new life for myself and my kids."

Starting over was more difficult than Genevieve had anticipated, particularly because of the downward economic mobility she experienced after ending her marriage to Robert. During her first semester at UI, even with student loans, a scholarship of $2,000 for each semester, and child support from Ben, she didn't have enough to pay for tuition and books plus rent, groceries, child care for Robin, and other expenses. By the end of October, she was "completely broke." She didn't want to drop out of school, so Genevieve did the only thing she felt she could—she reapplied for assistance through the Iowa Department of Human Services. This was particularly difficult because she never imagined she would have to go back on welfare. As she discussed her decision to reapply, she cited the so-called welfare reform bill, arguing that it discouraged those in need from applying for assistance:

> Now things have changed with welfare . . . it used to be about helping people when they were in a bad situation, but now it's about Big Brother watching you and judging you . . . justifying intrusions into your personal life by saying that it's going to save the taxpayers money. . . . And it has changed how caseworkers treat people. The thing I would recommend to anybody who is working with a social services caseworker—and I'm sure some people would have a major problem with this, just like I did—is when you go see them, be as meek as possible. Just listen to what they say, don't contradict them, and don't act like you know anything otherwise they are real jerks and will try to make things harder for you. You have to act stupid, because that's what they think about you anyway. I have a 4.0 (GPA), but I have to act like I don't know anything because when I didn't, then my caseworker would give me a hard time and do things that slowed down my application. If you seem too smart or don't seem pathetic enough or don't seem thankful enough for their help, you have a much harder time with your caseworker.

Although Genevieve was awarded food stamps and medical assistance for herself and the children, she was denied cash benefits because of changes in welfare policies. Because she had already completed her associate's degree, Genevieve was classified as "employable" and was deemed ineligible for TANF. Furthermore, because she would not quit school and go to work full time, she was put on a Limited Benefit Plan, something she felt was the government's way of saying, "You didn't do what we told you to do so we're not going to give you a cash grant." Although the food stamps and medical assistance were helpful, Genevieve still had a financial shortfall. Faced with the prospect of having to drop out of school, she went to her financial aid counselor and found out she could request additional student loans. This enabled her to "make it through the semester."

Over winter break, Genevieve investigated support programs in the community, something that "was easier to do on break because I had some free time then." She eventually located and applied for Section 8 housing assistance and a fuel assistance program, but she found it very difficult to locate programs in the Iowa City community. And even when she did locate services, she had a difficult time accessing them: "I didn't have a car and I couldn't get a current street map or the bus routes had changed and I couldn't figure out which bus to take to get to which place." Genevieve acknowledged that services in the community had provided her family with essential forms of assistance such as bus passes for her and the children, groceries when their food stamps had run out, and even school supplies for Alexia and Celeste. However, Genevieve believed that things would have been easier for her if programs were centrally located and easier to find, particularly because she didn't learn about most of them "until we had been in town for a while . . . at least five or six months and some even longer than that." Because she was a student and had already applied for financial aid, she had the option of increasing the amount of her student loans, of "maxing them out" to help meet living expenses. However, it was an option with long-term consequences:

So because I have three kids, I can take out the maximum amount of student loans every year and live off of that. Fine. That seems like a good deal. But remember, I have to pay those student loans back. So it's almost like with welfare reform, they're pushing you to max out your loans if you want to get a degree. And the thing is, the government doesn't have to think about how you're going to pay all of those loans back. They don't care about what happens to me or other single mothers once they're kicked off of assistance and living off of student loans. . . . The system is set up to punish women for wanting to better themselves. I'll be paying off these loans forever. The way the system is set up, it just keeps single mothers trapped in a cycle of poverty.

Student loans are kind of like gambling. You take them out because you need [them] to live, to support your kids. And you just hope that once you're done you can get a job and pay those loans back. But it's a gamble. The economy is awful now. And I know a lot of people who have college degrees and they can't get a job so they go back to things like waitressing or being a shift manager at McDonald's because there isn't anything else out there.

For Genevieve, it was a gamble with a mixed payoff. On the one hand, student loans helped her move closer to completing her degree and thus helped increase her lifetime earning potential. On the other hand, as she pointed out, a college degree would not automatically lead to more lucrative employment and she was well aware that she might have to go back to the kind of low-pay, unskilled jobs she had before earning her degree. Furthermore, she was concerned about repaying her student loans. Though repayment would impact Genevieve most directly, she was also concerned about the long-term indirect effects this would have on her children. Alexia was almost fifteen and was looking ahead to her own college career, and Celeste had expressed similar interests. Both girls hoped to attend UI. While Genevieve was adamant that she wanted her daughters go to college and "be able to stand on their own two feet," she also wondered how she would pay for their education, worrying that "they'll have to gamble on student loans and end up in the same situation I'm in."

And though she worried about the future, Genevieve said that "most days, I have all I can do to just worry about right now." Chief among her financial worries were the bills that went unpaid, including her car insurance—she simply could not afford the annual bill of over $800 a year "even with a $500 deductible on a car that is worth only $5,000 at most." Though she rationalized going without auto insurance by claiming "that's money that keeps my kids from starving," the decision left her feeling guilty, particularly when she thought of "what could happen" if she were ever in a car accident, "especially if the kids were with me and they got hurt or I hurt someone else." In addition, while Alexia was old enough to go through the driver's education program at her high school, Genevieve could not afford the $250 program fee. Though she tried to get the fee waived, even going to the school principal to explain her financial situation, she was unsuccessful. While for many teenagers obtaining a driver's license is a rite of passage that symbolizes their move toward adulthood and independence, in Genevieve's household, the significance ascribed to this event was defined primarily in practical terms. If Alexia had her driver's license, she could pick up Robin from day care. This would help ease Genevieve's time constraints, particularly because it would mean that she "wouldn't always have to rush to day care by a certain time to get Robin." This extra time on campus would have allowed Genevieve additional time to work in the campus computer labs. However, because Genevieve could not afford the fee, Celeste did not complete the training program and could not get her license.

Genevieve could not afford other things, including textbooks. Though some professors put copies of books on reserve, Genevieve and other women who participated in this study indicated this was the exception rather than the rule. Though Genevieve tried to locate the required books at the UI library or public libraries, this strategy was quite hit and miss because "a lot of times the libraries won't have them." Several times a professor or another student had loaned her a copy of a required text, but more often she simply did not read the book and had to "try to pick up everything I can in class discussion."

A home computer was also something that Genevieve had to do without. UI had a program that allowed students to take out a loan to purchase a computer, but this program was separate from student financial aid and when Genevieve applied for a computer loan, she was "rejected because my credit history is so bad." As a result, she had to rely exclusively on the campus computer labs, trying to "fit in time to write papers and other things" between classes. At UI, labs were located in academic buildings and dormitories, and some labs were accessible twenty-four hours a day. However, using the labs was difficult for Genevieve because she couldn't "afford to pay for day care except when I have to be in class," so she didn't "have free time on campus without [Robin]." In addition, because of her parental responsibilities, she couldn't "just be on campus at midnight writing a paper." She had taken Robin to the computer labs with her a few times but found this "very difficult" because Robin was bored and other students "give me these deep sighs and dirty looks for bringing my kid into 'their' space." This intersection of financial constraints and time constraints affected Genevieve's academic performance because she couldn't "get time I need to write the kind of papers I could write if I had a computer at home and could write late at night, after the kids are in bed." It also left her feeling rushed and frustrated when she could not fit her computer work into the only "free time" she had on campus—that is, between classes.

Genevieve devised what she called "creative ways" of dealing with her financial constraints. Because she could not afford to buy notebooks for classes, she developed her own recycling program: at the end of each semester, she went through the recycling bins on campus and retrieved used composition notebooks. The Rhetoric and English Departments, she noted, were "particularly good locations to find these sorts of things because I think they require most students to keep a journal of some sort." She would scour the bins and then remove the used pages of each notebook. She stored the notebooks in her garage until she or one of the kids needed them. She acquired her folders and binders in the same way and was pleased to report that she had "even found some really nice three-ring binders, you know, the ones with the UI logo on them." Genevieve also searched through the trash and recycling bins on campus to retrieve aluminum cans and plastic bottles: "In Iowa, we can get refunds for our pop cans and bottles. It's only five cents apiece, but almost everybody on this campus drinks pop and so I just collect them between classes. I bring a couple of grocery bags in my backpack each day I come to campus and then I dig through the trash. It's disgusting! And once a professor saw me doing it and I felt just humiliated. But it helps pay for gas and parking." Genevieve was supposed to let her social service caseworker know about any change in income that was over $5, regardless of the source or reason for the change, so her food stamp allotment could be adjusted accordingly. However, she did not report the "between $25 and $30" she earned each month from collecting cans and bottles because it would have reduced her food stamp allotment and "then I'd have to pay more for food out of my pocket and then how would I pay for parking?" Though refunds on soda cans and bottles provided only a small amount of income, all of which Genevieve "desperately [needed]," she worried about getting caught. She knew that if her caseworker found out, she could have lost her food stamps and been prosecuted for fraud. She worried about this so much that she had developed anxiety that was so severe that "I couldn't concentrate in class and it was keeping me up at night." At the suggestion of a classmate, Genevieve started seeing a mental health professional at UI's Student Counseling Services, something she could do only because such services were provided free of charge to UI students. Though her anxiety has decreased, she still gets "nervous every time someone unexpectedly knocks on the door at home." She wondered if it was the police coming to arrest her for "scrounging for pop cans and cheating on food stamps." Her fears were not unfounded. The penalty for welfare fraud, a violation of both federal and state law, can include jail time and steep fines.[20] More important, at least from Genevieve's point of view, it would "probably mean my kids would get taken away."

CONCLUSION

One of my primary goals in this chapter has been to demonstrate that there is no singular, definitive financial profile of single mothers who are attending college. Any attempt to create such a profile would be an artificial, static portraiture of "the single mother college student" and would deny the important differences that exist among these women. As the narratives in this chapter have demonstrated, the stories of the women's finances were, in some respects, as unique as their respective life stories. Joanna, for example, lived her entire life in poverty and experienced a relative degree of economic stability only after she moved in with relatives and began pursuing higher education. Kendra and Miranda did not encounter significant financial hardship until after they became single mothers and faced the financial obligations related to their dual identities as sole custodial mothers and college students. In Brenda's case, finances weren't a significant concern until she faced the possibility of losing custody of her son and was forced to hire an attorney. For Angela, poverty came quite unexpectedly and as a direct consequence of Hurricane Katrina. Genevieve's life was punctuated by episodes of serious economic woes and times of relative financial comfort including, most obviously, during her marriage to Robert. Clearly, the financial circumstances of these women were far from monolithic.

Even so, some similarities merit attention. The women tended to assign great significance to personal finances. Issues pertaining to money surfaced time and time again as they discussed their experiences. This was true both for the women who had some economic advantages and those who were part of the millions of Americans living in poverty. Financial concerns were a source of stress for the vast majority of the women who shared their stories with me. Their socioeconomic circumstances dictated, to varying degrees, their decisions and actions in nearly all aspects of their lives, including education, child care, transportation, social life, living arrangements, and employment. As the title of this chapter indicates, the theme of trying to make ends meet was a constant in the narratives of most of the women, as was the sense of despair they felt—sometimes subtle, other times more urgent—about their economic circumstances. Even so, they tended to believe that a college degree would help them secure a comfortable, financially stable future. In this respect, they endorsed dominant American notions of class mobility, particularly the belief that anyone, regardless of circumstances, can work hard and pull themselves up by their bootstraps and earn a place in the ranks of the American middle class.

The "bootstraps" ideology is, of course, a highly individualized and simplistic account of class dynamics. A built-in assumption of this belief is that each individual is solely responsible for their economic success (or failure); it denies the ways that economic inequalities are integrated into and perpetuated by various American social institutions and impacted by gender, race, and other systems of inequality. Put another way, if moving into the ranks of the middle class required only hard work, single mothers who are attending college would already be middle class. They work very hard as mothers and as college students and many are also employed either part time or full time. Hard work alone is simply not enough to achieve middle-class status. Yet, paradoxically, the women tended to solidly endorse this aspect of American class mythology. Part of this endorsement seemed to stem from their desire to be regarded as good mothers. Their belief that they could and would achieve middle-class stability may have insulated them somewhat from the stigma associated with single motherhood in the United States. Yet it is also possible that supporting this mythology functioned as a coping mechanism that enabled the women to regard their current financial constraints as temporary and hold on to the hope that their future would be more financially secure.

Another similarity among the women was their intense attention to financial planning and money management. During the debates surrounding the welfare reforms of the 1990s, dominant caricatures of single mothers were quite unflattering and hinged on the supposed financial irresponsibility of such women. In light of these caricatures, and as numerous critics of the Personal Responsibility and Work Opportunities Reconciliation Act have pointed out, proponents of welfare reform crafted legislation that was envisioned, at least in part, as a stick intended to punish poor single mothers.[21] The narratives in this chapter help counter negative stereotypes of single mothers, particularly by demonstrating the great lengths these women went to in order to manage their finances. Despite what were often difficult circumstances and limited resources, they generally managed to provide basic necessities for themselves and their children by strategizing, planning, networking, scrimping, saving, and digging through couch cushions and recycling bins. Their ability to meet basic needs is particularly noteworthy given the decline in public assistance available to poor populations in the wake of welfare reform and the overall economic scarcity that defined the first decade of the twenty-first century in the United States.

On the other hand, their experiences reveal an equally compelling theme of financial despair and what some critics might deem irresponsibility or bad judgment. Some of the single mothers seemed to lack specific knowledge about their expenses, including things such as child care deposits and tuition. Others chose unapproved college majors instead of pursuing a course of study that met their state's TANF guidelines, thereby cutting themselves off from a potential source of financial support. Still others refused to even investigate government and community support programs such as food assistance, rejecting what they saw as handouts in favor of maintaining their own sense of dignity and self-worth. Unlike other low-income populations, however, these women were attending college and thus had the option of taking out loans through the federal student aid program. Most of them exercised this option, but in doing so, they traded short-term access to much-needed funds for long-term debt. While their reasons for taking out student loans were clear, the long-term financial and related psychological consequences associated with student loans are important to consider. Quite simply, student loans must be repaid. According to the SLM Corporation, more commonly known as SallieMae, the nation's leading provider of educational loans, a student who takes out $10,000 in student loans will pay $98 a month for fifteen years in order to repay that debt. For a $20,000 debt, it will take twenty years and $197 a month. Those whose debt totals $45,000 will make payments of $443 a month for twenty-five years, and for a student who borrows $60,000, it will require monthly payments of $590 over the course of thirty years for their debt to be repaid.[22] For a student who takes out more than $60,000 in loans—as did a number of the women who participated in this project, particularly those pursuing graduate or professional degrees or who had several children to care for—monthly repayments will be even higher. The single mothers who can secure employment that pays a living wage will likely find that student loan payments take a significant bite out of their monthly budget, particularly because many were taking out the maximum available to them in loans each year. However, for those unable to get lucrative jobs, monthly loan payments may keep them trapped in poverty and struggling to afford food, shelter, and other basic necessities. If this is the case, higher education will not have provided a rout out of poverty but will instead be a life decision that perpetuated a state of financial distress for these women and their children.

3 · CLOCKS AND CALENDARS

For those who learn and work at institutions of higher education, life is governed to a great extent by two powerful and related forces: the clock and the calendar. These strict keepers of time affect campus life regardless of whether an institution is a community college, a public university, or a private school and regardless of whether one is a student, a member of the faculty, or a staff member. Over the more than twenty years I have spent in higher education, I have come to think of the time allotted to each semester as shaped like a funnel. The beginning of the semester is the top of the funnel, the widest part, a period when time seems abundant. Of course some members of the campus community end up rushing around in these early weeks, such as students who are attempting to add or drop classes or finalize financial aid and the staff members who help them do so. Yet the first few weeks of the semester are relatively relaxed because the focus is more on the newness of classes and the weeks ahead rather than on deadlines, due dates, and the like. As the term progresses, however, and the academic community works its way down through the increasingly narrow funnel, time becomes a greater concern. When the midterm period arrives, the funnel has narrowed considerably and stress levels increase accordingly. From that point onward, the funnel continues to narrow, and by the end of the semester, the campus has moved into the slender stem at the bottom of the funnel, a place where free time seems a distant memory, schedules are hectic, and altered sleep schedules are the norm for many.

Deadlines and due dates are a core feature of the American educational experience. Beginning as early as kindergarten, we learn that due dates are important and that assignments, permission forms, and other documents submitted late are judged inferior. This is a system that intensifies as we move through the education system and, by college, most American students have been schooled in the consequences associated with late work—looks of disapproval, loss of points, reduced grades, or, in many cases, a professor's outright refusal to accept tardy assignments. College students are generally well aware of these penalties and understand the importance of meeting academic deadlines if they wish to maintain acceptable grades and good academic standing.

The deadlines associated with higher education are not arbitrary. Faculty members have their own deadlines to meet and must adhere to the academic calendar that is established by university administration and the board of regents or coordinating board. As they pertain to teaching responsibilities, these deadlines include ordering books and required course materials, finalizing and tendering course syllabi, submitting midterm and final grades, and assessing course learning objectives in accordance with accreditation standards. There are additional time-sensitive requirements for faculty members who conduct research that pertain to research and grant proposals, budget reports, evaluation by institutional review boards, and completion of documents for journals, book publishers, and online venues. For those who have tenure-track positions, there is also the constant ticking of the tenure clock, often a nagging source of pressure because of the inflexible way that tenure decisions seem to be made at many institutions. Like students and faculty, university staff members are not immune to the demands of time; in many respects, they face quite rigid constraints. On a day-to-day basis, staff personnel are generally required to be physically present on campus for lengthier periods than students or faculty members, and they typically work eight hours or more a day in an office or a cubicle, at a counter, or in various behind-the-scenes locations around campus as they serve the diverse needs of faculty, students, and other staff members. They are responsible for a great many things and if they don't meet deadlines, the operations of the university can slow considerably.

This fixation on time is not exclusive to colleges and universities. It is a defining feature of American life: quality time, family time, time off, down time, work time, leisure time, being on time, lack of time. Americans are seemingly obsessed with time, particularly because of their tendency to equate time with money:

> We Americans are very time-conscious and very money-conscious. Many of us get paid by the hour for the work we do. We give the employer time in order to get money.
>
> The idea that *time is money* has gotten into our minds so deeply that it affects our whole lives. Wasting time is as bad as wasting money, so we schedule everything and hurry everywhere. We often signal the end of a phone conversation or a meeting by saying, "Well, I don't want to take up any more of your time." If you really want to annoy an American, sit down and talk as if you have nothing to do for the rest of the day.[1]

During a work-related trip to Costa Rica in 2011, I became acutely aware of American attitudes toward time when I encountered a phenomenon known as

Tico time. Schedules, I discovered, tend to be fairly free flowing in Costa Rica, and appointment or meeting times are regarded as rough estimates rather than strict commitments. One evening on this particular trip, I was scheduled to have dinner with two colleagues from Costa Rica and another who had recently arrived from the Dominican Republic. After one of my hosts gave me a tour of San Jose, we were detained in rush-hour traffic and arrived nearly fifteen minutes late for our 7:30 dinner engagement. As we entered the restaurant, I was fully prepared to apologize to the others, but it was unnecessary. They were nowhere to be found. In fact, they didn't arrive until nearly 8:30, almost an hour late by American standards, and after entering the restaurant, they greeted us, took their seats, and casually began to look over the menu. When I gently commented on the time and my resulting ravenous appetite, my Costa Rican hosts laughed and told me that I would simply have to get use to operating on Tico time. In Costa Rica, arriving after the appointed time is not regarded as rude or insulting but instead reflects the relaxed attitude toward time and schedules that is part of the culture.[2] Despite my own tendency to maintain a fairly well-organized schedule, I must admit that after a few days in Costa Rica, I embraced this aspect of the culture and greatly enjoyed the stress reduction associated with the gradual letting go of my American sense of punctuality. Indeed, as my work now takes me to Costa Rica several times a year, I find myself looking forward to this aspect of Tico life, and when I am there, I am generally so *tranquila* about time that I do not even wear a watch or check the clock.

In this chapter, I attend to the time-related challenges single mothers who are college students face. Like many Americans, these women regard time as fleeting and perpetually in short supply, something that must be maximized through strict management of schedules. Their narratives provide insight into the widespread anxieties about time that are common in contemporary American society. While these women may not be typical American parents or even typical American college students, they face a time crunch that is not that different from other American populations, including college students who must balance full-time academic work with full-time employment or parents who must patch together two or more jobs in order to meet the needs of their families. My aim in this chapter is to shed some light on contemporary American attitudes toward time and time management by examining them through the experiences of single mothers who are college students. I attend to the women's attitudes toward time, their perception of time as a limited resource, and the different ways they attempted to manage time. Effective time management is regarded as a requirement for success in American society. Indeed, mastering this skill is considered to be highly predictive of success in many aspects of life, including work, relationships, parenting, and academics. The women I interviewed endorsed these beliefs about the importance of time management skills even as they chronicled the various challenges they faced in this regard.

In light of these challenges, it may be tempting for some readers to feel sorry for these women, to regard them as lacking power and control in relation to the calendar and the clock. Yet I caution readers to refrain from pitying these women, for doing so casts them as passive and powerless victims. Nothing could be further from the truth. Although time was a central concern for most of the women, they exercised a great deal of agency as they responded to the demands on their time. Within the contexts of their lives, they created effective ways of managing time, striking a balance between parenting responsibilities, student responsibilities, and, for those who worked for wages, employment responsibilities. They did this by dividing their days into parent time and student time. As the following examples demonstrate, the women believed that time management was crucial to both their academic success and their ability to be good mothers.

A TYPICAL DAY

After completing final exams at the end of her sophomore year of high school, Rochelle Jimenez boarded an airplane and flew to Seattle, where she had been hired as a nanny for the summer. Born and raised in a large city in Arizona, Rochelle accepted the job at her parents' insistence. They believed it would keep her away from some of the problems of other teens in their neighborhood; these problems included drugs, crime, and teen pregnancy. Initially, Rochelle didn't like Seattle. She missed home and didn't particularly like the damp climate. Her feelings about the area changed, however, when she met Evan. He owned a small landscaping company and was building a large koi pond in the backyard of Rochelle's employer when the two met. Rochelle thought he was very handsome and didn't mind that he was eight years older than her. What started as a summer romance quickly developed into Rochelle's first love. When the end of the summer arrived, she and Evan decided to continue the relationship and even made plans for Rochelle to visit Seattle over the winter holiday.

Shortly after she returned to Arizona, however, Rochelle was in a panic—she had missed her period. She postponed taking a pregnancy test. She opted, instead, to pray each night, and in a ritual that many religious, sexually active, single heterosexual women have performed, promised God that if he would please let her not be pregnant, she would never have sex again until she was married. After a month of praying, she finally took a pregnancy test, cried when the results were positive, and then called Evan to tell him the news. She hoped he would want to marry her. Instead, he demanded that she get an abortion. When

Rochelle refused, citing her religious beliefs, Evan told her he didn't want anything to do with her or the baby and hung up. He never called back.

Rochelle put off telling her parents, who are conservative, working-class, Catholic Mexican Americans, about the pregnancy for over two months. She was their only child and they expected her to graduate from high school and get married before she started a family. Rochelle knew they wouldn't be happy that she had been having sex while she was in Seattle; they had sent her to Seattle to keep her *out* of trouble. Yet as she neared the end of her first trimester and the swelling in her lower abdomen became visible, Rochelle decided to tell her mother and father. The day she turned seventeen, feeling "more like an adult" because of her age, she sat with her parents and informed them she was going to be a mother. Her father got angry; her mother cried and prayed. Like Evan, they told her to get an abortion. When she refused, her father stopped speaking to her. Within weeks, Rochelle's world was turned upside down. Her parents withdrew her from the public school she had attended since kindergarten and sent her to live with relatives near Fayetteville, Arkansas. When she arrived there, Rochelle learned that she would be attending what locals referred to as the "pregnant school," an alternative school exclusively for pregnant girls:

> It is some subsidiary school of the regular high school, the local high school there, so pregnant girls or girls who already have their babies can still get their high school degree from a regular high school rather than getting a GED. They sent all of the girls there from all of the different school districts in the area, all the pregnant girls. And it was really, really sad, the ages of some of these girls. The youngest one was eleven, and I was the oldest. I was there when I was seventeen. I was only one of two students who were over the age of sixteen. There were 100 girls when I was there, and that was [full] capacity. . . . In that school, they were really just trying to get us out the door, not necessarily focusing on the quality of our education. So just the minimum we needed to be able to pass a test in whatever subject so we could pass all of our classes and get a diploma.

During her months at this school, Rochelle decided she would go to college. Her mother tried to talk her out of it and believed that she should be more realistic, arguing that college would be a waste of her time. She told Rochelle she should move back to Arizona after the baby was born, get a job, and "focus on her relationship with God and making things right with him." Rochelle was not persuaded. She wanted to focus on her future and that of her unborn child. She was determined to make a "good life" for the two of them that included "owning a house with a backyard and in a good neighborhood with good schools." She believed that in order to do this, she would need to earn at least a bachelor's degree and perhaps even a master's degree. As she said, "For women who have bachelor's degrees, their lifetime [income] is like twice as much as it is for women who only have a high school diploma. And there's no way I'd be able to work some low-paying job and have enough money to take care of my child." Like many single mothers, Rochelle's primary motivation for pursuing a college degree was economic. She also wanted to get "as far away as possible" from her parents and the rest of her family. She resented her parents for sending her to Arkansas, resented her relatives for making her attend the alternative school, and longed for a chance to find a community where nobody knew her so she could make a "fresh start." She used the Internet to investigate colleges in the Midwest and finally settled on UI because it had family housing and because she "fell in love" with the Iowa City community during a three-day visit to the campus. By the time I met Rochelle, she was a junior at UI and had declared a major in elementary science education with a minor in Spanish. In addition to pursuing full-time studies, Rochelle was solely responsible for raising her son, Emmanuel. I was struck by how grown-up and mature Rochelle seemed despite the fact that she was only twenty years old. She was an old soul and wise beyond her years. Rochelle and Emmanuel were living in the 630-square-foot, two-bedroom apartment they had occupied since their arrival in Iowa City nearly three years earlier. The apartment was located in Hawkeye Court, the UI family housing complex located approximately three miles from the university's main campus.

Like many single mothers and many college students, a typical day for Rochelle began early and ended late. At 4:30 A.M. on a brisk, Wednesday morning in November, her alarm went off. It was still dark outside, but Rochelle rolled over, shut off the alarm, and began what would end up being a nearly nineteen-hour day. After getting out of bed, she made her way to the kitchen, where she turned on the coffee maker and headed to the bathroom. By the time she had finished taking a shower, her coffee was ready and she poured herself a large mug before making her way to the small desk that was wedged into the corner of her living room. She spent the next two hours there, sipping her way through an entire pot of coffee as she tended to homework, including the semester research paper she was writing for her English class. At 7:00 sharp, Rochelle closed her books and headed to the back of the apartment to the smallest bedroom, where Emmanuel was sleeping. She gently shook him awake and they spent the next few hours together. Rochelle made scrambled eggs and toast and they ate breakfast in front of the television, watching cartoons. Next, she did the dishes and started a load of laundry before getting herself and her son dressed. She then packed herself a lunch, gathered her books and the other materials she would need for her classes, and packed Emmanuel's diaper bag with an extra change of clothes, diapers and wipes, snacks, and a few toys.

By 8:45, they were out the front door and headed to day care. The trip took approximately fifteen minutes. At the day care, she put Emmanuel's coat and bag in his cubby, talked briefly with his teacher, and kissed her son good-bye. She then drove to a private residence where she had rented a parking spot for the academic year. She chose to park there because it was much cheaper than the campus parking lots and because renting a space meant that she was always guaranteed a parking spot. She grabbed her backpack and began the 1.2-mile walk to the English-Philosophy Building for her first class. Rochelle made a quick stop at the restroom before starting her first two classes of the day. They were scheduled back to back; one ran from 9:30 to 10:20 and the second from 10:30 to 11:20. She then had a two-hour break during which she ate lunch in the student lounge and did homework in the campus library. She also made a brief visit to one of the campus computing centers to check her e-mail before walking to her afternoon classes. These two classes were also back to back; one from 1:30 to 2:20 and the other from 2:30 to 3:20. When her last class ended, she went to the language lab to complete a short assignment for her Spanish class. At 4:00, she logged off the computer, left the lab, and began her walk back across campus so she could retrieve her car and make it to the day care center by 4:30.

After picking up Emmanuel, Rochelle stopped at the grocery store for a few things and then drove home. Back in the apartment, Emmanuel played with his toys while Rochelle made chicken soup. While the soup simmered, she retrieved the morning laundry from the dryer and folded and put away the clothes. Dinner followed a short time later, and after they had eaten, Rochelle and her son played together. By 7:30 P.M., Rochelle had read him a story, kissed him goodnight, and tucked the child into bed for the night. She then returned to the kitchen to wash dishes and by 8:00 was back at her desk doing homework, which included studying for a Spanish test that was scheduled for the following morning. Rochelle finally headed to bed after 11:00 P.M. She slept for five and a half hours, rising once again when her alarm rang at 4:30 the next morning.

One of the most interesting aspects of Rochelle's day was her clear division between student time and parenting time. This was a strategy many of the women adopted, primarily because they found it difficult to actively parent while also engaged in the work of being a student, such as studying or completing homework. By dividing their time in this way, they were able to better manage their responsibilities and the various tasks they had to complete each day. As Rochelle's schedule demonstrates, these tasks are numerous. In the course of a 24-hour period, she attended four classes and studied for over five hours. She also engaged in a variety of parenting-related activities that included feeding, dressing, and bathing her son; reading to him and tucking him into bed; and cooking, cleaning, shopping, and doing laundry. Throughout her day, Rochelle regularly shifted between her role as parent and her role as student, almost like a light being switched on and off. Rochelle's schedule was highly regimented and relied on a strict compartmentalization of her roles as parent and as student.

Notably, there was also a conspicuous absence of free time for such things as socializing, relaxation, recreation, or simply catching up on sleep. When I asked her about this, Rochelle explained that her current schedule was a necessity, something she simply had to do.

Rochelle's time management strategy suggests that she regarded her dual roles as mother and student as somewhat incompatible. She explained that she was simply not able to actively be a mother and a student at the same time. She found herself unable to study for an exam while also trying to watch Emmanuel. Likewise, she could not provide her son with the attention she believed he deserved if she was also trying to memorize vocabulary for Spanish. She confessed that she had tried to combine her dual roles on a number of occasions but found it impossible to do so. Such attempts had left her feeling "stressed out," and she believed it diminished both the quality of her academic work and the quality of her time with Emmanuel. Consequently, she carefully divided her time. During certain periods, she was Rochelle the student. Prioritizing her academic responsibilities at these times increased her ability to retain what she had read and to write papers that were more coherent. She also believed this strategy was the main reason why she had an impressive 3.82 cumulative GPA and had earned a place on the dean's list every semester of her college career. At other times, she was Rochelle the mother and caring for Emmanuel was her main concern. Rochelle felt that because she focused exclusively on her parenting duties during these times, she was a better mother, one who devoted appropriate time and attention to her child. This time management strategy required a great deal of discipline to maintain, but Rochelle deemed it essential in order to cope effectively with the demands on her time. Indeed, she accomplished a great deal in the course of a 24-hour day, and from what I observed, she was a devoted mother and a dedicated student.

However, Rochelle did not maintain this schedule every day of the week. Although she was a full-time student and took four courses each semester, Rochelle had managed to arrange her schedule so all of her classes met on Mondays, Wednesdays, and Fridays. This helped her save money because she was able to limit Emmanuel's enrollment in day care to part-time. This scheduling strategy also permitted her to work part-time on Tuesdays and Thursdays; she babysat two neighbor children in her home while their mother and father—both graduate students—attended classes at UI. Financially, the job was important to Rochelle because it reduced the amount she borrowed in student loans each semester. Yet the addition of employment responsibilities also impacted Rochelle's schedule, requiring her to divide her time on Tuesday and Thursdays. The parenting and caregiving work she did in relation to her son and the neighbor children took up the majority of her time on these days, literally from breakfast time until bedtime. As a result, she was able to attend to her academic responsibilities only before breakfast and after Emmanuel had gone to bed. In order to make certain she had some time for studying on Tuesdays and Thursdays, Rochelle maintained her practice of rising at 4:30 A.M. and retiring at 11:00 P.M.

In theory, Saturday and Sunday were her free days. Rochelle did have more flexibility in her weekend schedule. She got extra sleep on the weekends, typically a full eight hours each Friday and Saturday night in order to compensate for the meager amount she got during the week. She also frequently found time to take her son to the park or the library or to socialize with others in the family housing community. Yet she continued to divide her time on the weekends, creating clear distinctions between her parenting responsibilities and her student responsibilities and organizing her time accordingly. And while it was not uncommon for her to complete homework after her son had gone to bed on Friday and Saturday evenings, Rochelle made it clear that parenting was her priority on the weekends. It was the only time during the entire week that she and Emmanuel had sustained, uninterrupted time together.

THE STUDENT WHO (ALMOST) NEVER WENT TO CAMPUS

Isabella Lopez, who described herself as "a devoted Baptist and a woman who tries to live God's word each day," never imagined she would go to college. She had been a poor student throughout elementary school, middle school, and high school, "barely scraping by" in terms of grades. She believed that college would be too difficult for her. After earning her high school diploma in 1987, she continued to live with her parents and split her time between what she regarded as her two jobs: one as a full-time cashier at a grocery store near her home in Parker, Texas, and the other as a volunteer working more than twenty hours a week at one of the megachurches in the area. Isabella planned to lead a very traditional life that centered on marriage, motherhood, and the church.

At first, her plan fell neatly into place. At the age of twenty-one, Isabella met and married Henry, a department store manager and avid golfer she met on a blind date arranged by a family friend. Because Henry was earning a solid income, the couple decided that Isabella no longer needed to work. She became a homemaker and continued to devote much of her time to the church. The couple's first child, Peter, arrived in 1991. Two years later, Isabella gave birth to a daughter, Grace, and in 1998, to another son, Christian. Isabella described this period of her life as filled with happiness, for she was "fulfilling the destiny that God had planned for her" through her roles as wife and mother and church volunteer. Isabella's happiness was shattered when her marriage ended in 2002. She provided few details about this part of her life and made it clear that she and the children had little contact with her ex-husband.

After her divorce, Isabella took a job at the same grocery store where she had been employed after high school, working thirty hours a week. Yet even with her wages and the alimony and child support payments she received each month, she and the children were "living hand to mouth." These economic circumstances were part of her motivation for going to college. However, she also wanted to set a positive example for her children:

> I always thought I was too stupid to go to college and I think that everyone else thought the same thing—my parents, my husband. But to survive as a single mother, I knew I had to further my education for [my kids], to be able to give them a life outside of the crowded apartment we were living in. . . . I'm doing it mostly for my children, so they can see that I can do this, despite all we've been through. They need to know that even when things seem darkest, they can rise to the challenge, to better themselves, to improve themselves. . . . A higher power provided this opportunity for me. He wants me to teach my children the value of taking on something that feels bigger than you and facing that challenge, the value of being independent.

Isabella was initially nervous about attempting college-level courses, particularly given her previous academic performance and the fact that she was "sure I was going to be the oldest person in my classes." However, in 2003, she enrolled part time at Collin College in Plano, Texas, which offers two-year degrees and continuing education courses. She chose Collin College because the main campus was only a ten-minute drive from her home and because tuition was "affordable at only around $25 per credit."[3] Isabella was also attracted to the school because it offered online courses. This allowed her to more easily manage her work and parenting responsibilities as she pursued her associate's degree and completed the Texas Core Curriculum requirements.[4] It took her three years of part-time classes to finish her associate's degree. During her last semester at Collin College, prompted by the fact that she had been awarded three scholarships, Isabella began to think about a bachelor's degree. The combined financial support from these scholarships and a federal Pell Grant would enable her to complete her bachelor's degree without taking out additional student loans.

While Isabella was delighted about the scholarships, she had a nagging concern. The scholarships required her to attend school full time. Initially, she experienced "a sense of total panic" as she tried to imagine how she would handle full-time student responsibilities and parenting and employment. In fact, she initially believed she would have to turn down the scholarships because "I just didn't see how I could fit everything into my schedule—there's only so much time in a day, you know!" Her fears subsided, however, after she met with an academic advisor at Texas Woman's University. The advisor explained that

Isabella could complete her bachelor's degree in general studies by taking all online courses. Although many of the four-year college and universities in the Dallas–Fort Worth metroplex offer such courses, TWU's undergraduate program in general studies is rather distinct because it offers students the option of completing all upper-level courses using Blackboard, a software-based learning platform that enables instructors and students to engage with one another entirely through the Internet.

Isabella had been a full-time student at TWU for just over a year when she contacted me and agreed to participate in this project. She had completed nine courses—four during the fall semester and five in the spring—and had just started two summer session courses. She was very positive about her experiences with online courses:

> I never have to come to campus. I have only been to campus twice, just twice in a whole year—once when I visited the campus and another time when I decided to drive up here to pay my tuition in person [rather than online]. I register for classes online, do everything with my academic advisor online, even buy my books online. I love it! I don't really know where anything is on campus. I was thinking about it and I don't even know where the computer labs are at Texas Woman's. I don't even have a student ID from there because I haven't been on campus enough to take the time to get the picture taken. I have a student number, but no actual ID.

In addition to pursuing full-time studies at TWU, Isabella maintained her job at the grocery store and continued to be the primary caregiver for her children. Juggling these three roles—student, mother, and employee—was sometimes difficult, but she claimed that "most of the time, it works really well and I have time for everything." All three of her children attended school, so Isabella worked at the grocery store during the day Monday through Friday. She most often did her homework in the evenings, after the children had gone to bed, but she also tried to "get in a few hours on Saturdays." On Sundays, Isabella did not do homework or work at the grocery store. She and her children spent most of the day at their church, attending services in the morning and then participating in various groups and activities throughout the afternoon.

There were times when Isabella was not able to get all of her school work done, and her grades had "slipped a bit" since she had started attending TWU, falling from a 3.73 GPA to just above 3.0. She also missed having face-to-face classes like those at Collin College. She didn't know any other TWU students except by their name and the comments they posted on course Blackboard pages. Isabella had never spent time in the physical presence of other TWU students. Furthermore, she hadn't met any of her instructors, which left her feeling rather "disconnected from the campus." Still, she believed this type of isolation from the campus community was worth it. She had achieved a manageable balance between her various responsibilities as mother, employee, and student. Smiling, Isabella boasted about her ability to "have it all" in this regard. Yet she also acknowledged that her schedule left her with little time for socializing or relaxation:

> If I wanted to have a social life, I don't know how I'd do it. Right now, I just have to focus on the things that are important; personal time and time for fun, those are luxuries, things that are just not important to me at this point in my life. Things get stressful because I have all of this stuff to do and I just have to be really organized with my time. Sometimes, at night, I lie in bed and there are all of these thoughts that run through my head about did I do my best on this and did I spend enough time with the kids or on school stuff. So having a social life, well, I don't really care about that because right now my main goal is to complete this journey, finish my education. That was a huge goal for me. And I'm doing well in school, I'm proud of what I've accomplished and my kids are seeing me do well in school, so not having a social life doesn't matter. That's not what is most important at this point in my life.

Isabella regarded free time as a luxury. She accepted the stress associated with the demands on her time and the lack of free time she experienced as a student, mother, and employee.

DAYS, NIGHTS, AND WEEKENDS

Like Rochelle Jimenez, Beth Jacobs became pregnant when she was seventeen. Beth, who described herself as a twenty-year-old white college student with one daughter, remembered an argument she had with her parents as a "defining moment" in her life. Beth was a senior in high school and didn't think she should have a curfew. Her parents said that "as long as I lived in their house I had to be in by midnight." Feeling rebellious, Beth decided that she no longer needed to live in their house and moved in with her boyfriend, Jeff, a military reservist four years her senior. It was a defining moment, Beth said, because she "ended up getting pregnant right away, like three weeks after I moved in." When she told Jeff about the pregnancy, he didn't seem particularly surprised and later "confessed that he hadn't used a condom for the past two weeks we had been sleeping together." Though Jeff began to discuss marriage, Beth knew he wasn't someone she wanted to spend the rest of her life with because "he wants the little wife that stays home and has more and more babies and whatever, and that's just not me." After a confrontation, Beth moved out and decided to raise her child on her own.

Before she became pregnant, Beth had planned to go to a four-year college and earn a bachelor's degree. However, after giving birth to her daughter, Andrea, she believed that community college was a more viable option because "it was cheaper and I could finish in just two years." Beth first visited Hawkeye Community College in Waterloo, Iowa, located only fifteen minutes from the small town where she lived. However, after spending time on the campus and sitting in on a few classes, she decided against it because the institutional climate didn't fit with how she saw herself as a parent or as a student. According to Beth, "It was mostly teen parents or people who don't really know what to do with their lives so they're just kind of taking classes to fill the time. It's more like high school than college." She finally settled on Kirkwood Community College because it was affordable and had a program in paralegal studies that was approved by the American Bar Association. Beth began classes as a part-time student in the fall of 2003. She enrolled in two classes that semester. Both courses met on Tuesdays and Thursdays, one in the morning and the other in the early afternoon. Despite the one-hour drive from her home to the KCC campus, Beth found it "very easy to be a single mother and a student" during this time and felt she had plenty of time to finish her homework and take care of her daughter. Her brother moved in with her temporarily during this time and helped with child care.

In the spring of 2004, however, her brother moved into his own apartment and Beth had to rethink her child care situation. Because she couldn't afford to pay for day care on her own, she decided to participate in a child care assistance program through the Iowa Department of Human Services. The Workforce Investment Act (WIA) of 1998, which took effect in Iowa on July 1, 2000, and replaced the Job Training Partnership Act of 1980, was designed to help adults and dislocated workers achieve self-sufficiency through employment. WIA-funded programs provided services to adults who faced significant barriers to employment.[5] It assisted them with job-search and placement services that included career counseling, pre-employment training, and workshops in specific skills such as résumé writing. Participants who were unable to find jobs through these basic services or those who were deemed unemployable because of a lack of basic skills or work experience and met income guidelines were eligible for occupational skills training and support services that included grants for tuition, books, and child care. Because KCC was a WIA-certified training provider and because Beth met WIA program guidelines, she received a grant that paid for her child care expenses while she attended classes. However, her eligibility was restricted to a maximum of two years and she was required to maintain full-time enrollment at KCC. In order to participate in the program, she had to increase the number of class she was taking. When I met Beth, she was enrolled in six courses for eighteen semester hours.

Much like Rochelle, Beth described her typical day as beginning early and ending late. She also divided her time into distinct periods: some devoted to mothering responsibilities and some to student responsibilities. In the morning, she got up, got herself and Andrea ready for the day, then drove Andrea to the day care center where she is enrolled full time. Dropping Andrea off at day care was the most difficult part of her morning. The task required a good deal of time and energy:

> It's across town, but since we live in a really small town it only takes seven minutes to get to the day care center. And when we get there, I take her inside and she's at this stage where she throws a fit every morning—she won't let me put her down, won't take off her coat, won't take her hat off, doesn't want me to leave. So it usually ends up being like twenty minutes or half an hour that I have to spend there, settling her down. I mean, I'm not one of those mothers that is just going to put her kid down and walk out and leave her screaming. I know some people say that you should do that, but I just can't. I would feel too horrible.

After leaving day care, she drove an hour to campus. She typically arrived around 8:30. If it was a Monday, Wednesday, or Friday, her first class didn't begin until 10:10.[6] She typically went into the classroom and used the extra time to study, work on homework for other classes, or "look over notes and review what we went over in the last class so I feel more like I know what the professor is talking about in class." By the time she left campus at 3:30, Beth had attended four classes, each lasting between fifty-five minutes and two hours, all of them scheduled back to back. On Tuesdays and Thursdays, Beth attended two classes and completed the lab component required for one of her courses. She arrived on campus at approximately 9:00 A.M. on these days and left at 3:00 P.M. After picking Andrea up from day care, Beth drove home and spent the next few hours cooking dinner and playing with her daughter before putting the child to bed around 8:00 P.M. Beth said that she occasionally took "an hour or so to unwind a little, watch some TV like *Law and Order SVU*, or *The Practice*." More often, however, she worked on homework until she went to bed around 10:30 P.M.

Beth's transition from part-time to full-time student had made it more difficult for her to manage her time. This was especially true after her brother moved out and was no longer available to help with child care:

> I don't know. There are some people who just seem to have this time to sit around. Like those three girls sitting right over there, laughing and talking and relaxing.

They're probably in-between classes and they will take some time later and do homework, but right now they're just having down time. Like regular college students. I don't really have any time to do that when I'm on campus, to have down time. I don't have time to relax... there's a huge different between being a college student and being a college student with a kid. Like college is where you're supposed to meet people and socialize and be able to go out and do different things. But I can't do that.... This is my time for being a student, not a mom. Like those girls over there—they're talking about what they did last night, who they went out with, what bar they went to or whatever, or what they're going to do this weekend. And I don't fit in. I can't relate to that. And most of the things that typical girls my age, typical college girls, most of the things that they are doing, well I just don't understand them. I could find so many better things to do with my time than going out drinking every night or trying to snag a different guy every night at the bars.

Beth's comments reveal as much about how she thought about herself as a student as they do about her perception of her student peers. Because of her class schedule and parenting duties, she regarded herself as different from those she referred to as "regular" college students, particularly women around her own age. She believed that as a parent she had to be responsible in a way that "regular" students did not. In order to meet her student responsibilities, she was a "student, not a mom" while she was on campus, spending her time either in classes or studying. In contrast, Beth imagined that "regular" college students, like the three young women seated two tables away from us during our interview, did not have time commitments other than those they had as students. The implication was that without additional demands on their time, "regular" college students could put their student responsibilities aside when they were not in class or studying and enjoy periods of recreation and fraternization. Beth clearly felt out of place among other students her own age. It is also clear that she desired both "down time" and social interaction with her peers. However, rather than admit these feelings, she presented her demanding schedule as beneficial, particularly as her student and parenting responsibilities took up the vast majority of her time and, as her comments suggest, kept her from engaging in excessive alcohol consumption and being sexually promiscuous.

Such challenges were impacted by Beth's financial circumstances. She wasn't able to afford a personal computer and the library in her small town did not have computers available for public use. As a result, Beth often had to drive to the Kirkwood campus on weekends and spend time in the computer lab in order to finish whatever computer-related coursework she could not complete while on campus during the week. She tried taking Andrea to the computer lab but said that she only did that twice: it "never works because she doesn't want to just sit there and watch me write a paper or do research on the Internet or whatever. It doesn't work and I end up getting really frustrated." In order to manage, Beth extended her strategy of compartmentalizing student time and parent time into the weekends. This meant that she often hired a babysitter to care for Andrea so she could use the campus computer labs on Saturday or Sunday. Although the additional expense was one that Beth could "barely afford," it allowed her to complete her assignments on time. But there was a psychological cost to this time management strategy. Beth worried that she was not striking an appropriate balance between her parent and student responsibilities. She said, "Right now I feel like I'm not even raising my daughter, that the people at day care and the babysitter are raising her because they see Andrea more than I do."

Beth's guilt seemed fueled by two competing ideologies. On the one hand, the American ideology of good mothering insists that women place childrearing at the very top of their priority list, staying home and putting their maternal duties above all else lest they be deemed bad or irresponsible mothers.[7] On the other hand, the "intrusive and patriarchal" ideology of mid-1990s welfare reform cast poor unmarried mothers who receive assistance as "an omnipresent icon of motherhood gone wrong."[8] This ideology demanded that in order to redeem themselves, such mothers had to adhere to middle-class ideals of hard work and responsibility by supporting their children economically. Beth seemed caught between and unable to reconcile the two perspectives. By earning a postsecondary degree, she would increase her likelihood of being able to support herself and her daughter without government assistance. However, in order to maintain full-time student status, which she was required to do in order to receive child care assistance, and in order to complete the assignments for the full-time course load she was taking, Beth felt she had no choice but to sacrifice time with her daughter. And this, as her comments make clear, left her feeling like a bad mother.

A LIFE CRISIS

Karen Coffman had married Ken, her high school sweetheart, the summer after she turned eighteen and spent the next several years supporting him while he completed his bachelor's degree and then his master's degree. After that, the couple settled into what Karen describes as a "very traditional marriage." Ken began a lucrative career in business administration while Karen quit working in order to become a full-time homemaker. The couple's first child, Sarah, was born in 1985, and the second, Noah, arrived in 1989. Ken worked "more than full time," supporting Karen and the children financially while she assumed primary responsibility for childrearing and domestic responsibilities. Though Karen stayed home full time while the children were young, she began taking classes part time at a nearby college when her son started preschool. When Noah entered kindergarten, Karen became a full-time student; she finished her bachelor's degree three years later. She then began working part-time in the school system, from 8 A.M. to 12 P.M. Monday through Friday, then returned home in the afternoon to "take care of the house stuff for a few hours" before picking up the kids at 3:30.

The year Sarah started high school, Ken filed for divorce. It wasn't a complete surprise for Karen, who says that she wasn't happy in the marriage and that they "had been growing apart for some time. He was a nice enough guy and all, but he was just so boring and we weren't interested in the same things." What did surprise Karen, however, was the financial situation she encountered after the divorce. Her husband had taken charge of all the finances during their marriage. Before filing for divorce, he liquidated their stocks and "took almost everything out of the savings account so there was nothing left for me and the kids." Knowing she couldn't afford to feed and clothe herself and the children and pay the mortgage, insurance, and other bills on her income plus the alimony and child support she received, Karen decided to go back to school and earn her PhD at UI. The decision was prompted, in large part, by a self-help book for women going through divorce:

> The study found the women who survived best, who were the happiest and had what they needed to live, were the ones that had rebuilt their lives and made positive decisions about what to do instead of being caught up in how they use to live and what they miss about being married. So by acknowledging that they need to make some changes and do some new things with their lives, these women moved on and found a better place.

Working on a PhD was Karen's way of moving on, of trying to be happy and make a new life for herself and her children. When she contacted me to participate in this project, Karen had attained the status of an ABD student (all but dissertation) and was only months away from defending her thesis. She was also teaching half-time as a graduate instructor at UI.

In some ways, Karen's situation was not typical. As an ABD student, she was no longer taking classes. In addition, her children were teenagers and did not require the kind of supervision that is necessary with young children. Therefore, Karen should have had significant periods of unstructured time or at least a much greater degree of flexibility with regard to her schedule than most of the other women. This might have been the case if Karen's daughter, Sarah, hadn't experienced a life crisis. Though Sarah had "been a very happy child and was very creative and so sunny," her demeanor changed after the divorce. She seemed to resent her dad and things gradually disintegrated to the point that they "no longer had a relationship." Sarah began to exhibit signs of depression; her moods had grown "darker and darker and worse and worse" by the middle of her sophomore year of high school. She also began skipping school "almost every day and would just sit in a parking lot somewhere, either sleeping or reading these dark, depressing novels." When Sarah's report card came home, Karen expected "the usual 4.0 because she had always been a straight-A student." Instead, Sarah had earned all Ds and Fs. On the advice of a friend, Karen took Sarah to see a therapist, who diagnosed her with depression and prescribed a combination of antidepressants and weekly therapy sessions.

Things began to improve, and Karen thought her daughter was "getting better" until one day Sarah called Karen on her cell phone and "told me that I really needed to come home because she wasn't feeling well." By the time Karen got to the house, Sarah had swallowed an entire bottle of antidepressants, "somewhere between fifty and sixty pills," and a whole bottle of ibuprofen tablets. In addition, she had made several cuts to one of her wrists, "not very deep, but her arm was bleeding pretty good." Karen rushed her daughter to the emergency room. She was treated and then admitted to the psychiatric ward, where she spent "a considerable amount of time."

Sarah's suicide attempt was followed by "a year of one catastrophe after another." Shortly after being released from the hospital, Sarah caused a serious car accident. Within the next several months, Sarah was arrested for shoplifting and Karen found marijuana in her daughter's purse. Karen said that the hardest part was when Sarah became pregnant and had an abortion. Sarah's doctor assured Karen that these types of behaviors were not uncommon among teens who were dealing with depression. Still, as she described her daughter's "downward spiral of depression," Karen's voice grew low and quiet and tears appeared in her eyes, signs that she was still quite shaken from the experience:

> But the next day, I still had to get up and to go work and teach my classes and then go and try to work on the chapter that was due soon and try to take care of the house and then go up to the hospital to spend time with my daughter. Well there was just no time left for me. I couldn't even stop long enough to think about what was happening to my daughter—I just had to move from one thing to the next to the next to the next and didn't even have a moment to process what was happening, to grieve for this horrible thing that had happened to my child. And a few days after she was admitted, the nurses called and said they wanted me to come in so they could talk to me. And they wanted me to come right away that morning. And I couldn't, I couldn't go in the morning because I had to be at work. There was nobody else who could cover my class that day, so I had to tell the nurses no and go teach my class instead and go to the hospital later in the afternoon. And I felt terrible about that. I couldn't be there after what my child had gone through.
>
> And [Sarah] has a friend who is a few years younger and also has depression and has done even worse things as a result. But her mother doesn't work, her

father is a physician, and the mother went to school every day with her daughter to make sure that she was OK. And the mother met with all of the high school teachers like every other week about how her daughter was doing and what they could do to help her. But I didn't do that because I didn't have time to meet with all the teachers and the therapists and create this whole plan about how to help my daughter. I will always feel bad about that.

Karen's circumstances were difficult, to be sure. They clearly demonstrate how unexpected situations—in this case, Sarah's health crisis—can impact the time-related challenges single mothers who are college students face. Yet her description of this particular situation also revealed a great deal about Karen's perception of herself as a mother. Her reference to Sarah's friend who "also has depression" seemed to be offered as a protective measure, intended to keep me from thinking badly of Sarah. It was Karen's attempt to shield her daughter from the judgment of a researcher. Put another way, by describing the friend as having "done things much worse" than Sarah, Karen presented depression as something unexceptional among teenagers and invited me, as a researcher and a mother—and by extension, those she knew would be reading about her life and experiences in this book—to refrain from blaming Sarah for the things she has done. In this respect, Karen demonstrated one of the core traits associated with good motherhood in U.S. culture: a good mother is protective of her children.

However, Karen also compared herself to the married, middle-class parents of Sarah's friend, claiming that they handled their daughter's depression "so much better." Thus, rather unintentionally, she reinforced the idea that children are better off if they are raised by two parents, particularly if those parents adhere to a traditional gendered division of labor that includes a stay-at-home mother and a breadwinner father. Furthermore, Karen also implicitly compared her life as a married mother to her life as a single mother and doctoral student. She lamented the fact that teaching part time and working on a dissertation left her without the ability to spend time with her children the way she believed a stay-at-home mom would do. As a result, she experienced significant guilt as she attempted to reconcile her maternal responsibilities with her academic ones. This was especially clear when Karen shared her concern that her decision to pursue a PhD had "not only aggravated but perhaps even caused" Sarah's illness.

A LAW STUDENT WHO WAS BUYING TIME

One Tuesday morning in January, Melinda Douglas knocked on my office door nearly thirty minutes before the time we had set for our interview. When she saw that I was grading papers, she apologized for being early, and despite the freezing temperatures and her already pink cheeks, offered to walk a block to the local coffee shop to get beverages for both of us while I finished my task. I was more than happy to put the grading aside, and Melinda and I made the trek together to buy steaming decaf lattes. We spent the next two and a half hours engaged in a leisurely, conversational interview that focused on Melinda's experiences. Melinda was the only single mother student I interviewed for this project who arrived more than five minutes early, didn't check her watch even once during our interview, and didn't have to rush off to a class or office hours or to pick up a child at day care when we were finished. In short, she did not experience the same kind of time constraints as the other women. As shall become clear in a moment, her financial status had a great deal to do with this.

Melinda was in her second year of law school at UI. She was the mother of six-year-old "very energetic" twin sons, David and Daniel, and a three-year-old daughter, Samantha. Melinda had been married for eight years before getting divorced in 2001. She described her marriage as "doomed from the start." She and Jason had dated throughout college, but they weren't in love. Still, after graduating, Jason proposed and Melinda accepted, "mostly I think because so many of my friends were getting married and because I thought that Jason might be my one chance to get married." Initially, they both worked full time and Jason went to night school to complete his master's degree. The couple celebrated their four-year anniversary shortly after Christmas in 1996, and in February 1997, they welcomed their sons, who arrived two months earlier than expected. Melinda became a full-time, stay-at-home mother after the twins were born. Shortly after Samantha's birth, Melinda began to suspect that Jason was having an affair. Her suspicions were confirmed when Jason moved in with "a girl he was dating from the office" around the time Samantha was six months old. After a "brief breakdown when I realized my marriage was ending," Melinda filed for divorce and decided to pursue a law degree, "something I had always been interested in doing."

As Melinda described her typical day, a familiar narrative emerged. She devoted certain periods of the day to student responsibilities such as attending class, doing research in the law library, and reading cases to prepare for upcoming class discussions. Other times, however, were "just for the kids," times when she put aside academics and prioritized her mothering responsibilities, including "cooking breakfast for them, dropping the boys off at school, and taking them to soccer practice and games." For Melinda, managing time in this way was a very important strategy that allowed her to "be a mother when I need to be a mother, and a student when I need to be a student."

Hiring a full-time live-in nanny was another strategy that enabled Melinda to manage the demands on her time. Because she wanted someone available "around the clock" for her children, Melinda hired Heather White to help care for her children. A part-time student at KCC, eighteen-year-old Heather lived with Melinda and her family and was "the primary caretaker in the household." Heather was responsible for doing laundry, doing the grocery shopping, cooking dinner most evenings, picking up Melinda's dry cleaning, and "keep[ing] the house from looking too much like a disaster." Heather also stayed home with Samantha during the day so Melinda was able to attend classes, and she frequently "tuck[ed] the children in at night" when Melinda stayed on campus late. The job requirements for Heather were very clear: be "on duty and available" twenty-four hours a day, Monday through Friday and every other weekend. When the boys become ill at school and needed to be picked up, the school nurse called Heather, not Melinda. Though Melinda described Heather as "one of the family, like an aunt to the kids," in reality, Heather was a hired caregiver. And her time and labor did not come cheap. In addition to a bedroom and private bathroom in Melinda's house, Heather also had use of the family vehicle and earned a salary of $1,200 a month, nearly the full amount Melinda received in child support from her ex-husband. Though she shook her head when she talked about Heather's salary, Melinda felt that this arrangement was the only option for her, concluding "it's the only way I would be able to do law school as a single parent." As a result, and because of her economic situation, Melinda had formulated a unique time management strategy that left her feeling she had fulfilled her obligations as a student and a mother "without having to take care of the kids all by myself." In buying Heather's time and labor, Melinda had found a way to balance her roles as full-time student and single mother to three children.

Despite this, Melinda identified time constraints as one of her primary challenges. Though she believed employing a live-in nanny gave her enough time to study and still have "plenty of quality time" with her children, Melinda had very little leisure time: "Maybe single moms aren't supposed to say this, but I want some time left for me. I want time to be able to go out for a beer with my classmates after class, or to go out on a date with a man I like. I want a little time left over for myself." Though she felt she had been able to successfully balance her identities as graduate student and single mother, Melinda faced a challenge familiar to single mothers without her relative economic privilege: finding time to tend to the parts of herself that were not related to mothering or being a student. As our discussion ended, this point became especially clear. As she put on her coat and prepared to head back out into the cold, Melinda thanked me for allowing her to participate in the project. She then apologized: "I'm sorry I talked so much and took so much of your time, but this is the first fun thing I've done in months. I guess I got a little carried away."

WORKING THE THIRD SHIFT

My interview with Stephanie Sergeant was markedly different than the time I spent with Melinda. Stephanie arrived twenty minutes late for our 9:00 A.M. meeting on the last day of the first week of spring semester. She was clutching what I later learned was her fourth cup of coffee and her hair was still wet from her shower. As she dropped her backpack in the corner and claimed the chair next to my desk, she apologized for running behind schedule. She also informed me that she had very limited amount of time for the interview, "only . . . fifty-five minutes because I have to be out of here by 10:15 at the latest. I have a 10:30 class that I can't miss." I offered to reschedule the interview, but Stephanie preferred to proceed as planned because "I don't know when I'd have time to do this again. It probably won't be until after the semester is over." Initially, I thought Stephanie was exaggerating, making an offhand comment after what may have been a particularly stressful start to her day or even a hectic week of being back in classes after the long winter break. What she described to me during the ensuing fifty-five minutes, however, left me with little doubt that she was being anything but perfectly honest about her schedule. In addition to being a full-time single mom and a full-time undergraduate student at UI, Stephanie was also a full-time employee, working a third shift that often included mandatory overtime. Given these demands, it is not surprising that Stephanie characterized her situation as a "constant trade-off" as she continually navigated the competing time demands she faced as a parent, a student, and an employee.

Despite "practicing safe sex and using a condom every single time," Stephanie became pregnant during January of her junior year of high school and gave birth to her son, Jeffrey, in late September of her senior year. Adults in her life, including her parents and the principal of her school, pressured her to attend the alternative high school in her community. But after visiting the school, Stephanie knew that she "wouldn't fit in" and "didn't have anything in common with the students there." She remained enrolled at the public high school. In addition, she took three extra classes that were offered at night through the community college in a nearby town. By January of her senior year, she had accumulated enough credits to graduate five months ahead of schedule. Around this same time, she and Jeffrey's father, Adam, split up, a decision that they both agreed was in their son's best interest, as "we were just fighting all the time anyway." Stephanie split her time between raising her son and working full time as a hotel desk clerk, saving whatever money she could in the hope that she could someday afford to go to college. Yet after three years of working and saving, she had "very little money in the bank" and wondered if she would ever save enough to pay for tuition, books, living expenses, and day care.

At her mother's insistence, Stephanie scheduled an appointment with Janelle Roberts, a caseworker with the Iowa Workforce Development Program, to discuss the possibility of earning her college degree. Janelle helped Stephanie understand the various types of assistance that were available and plot a course of action:

> If I didn't work and just went to school, I would be able to qualify for some programs like housing and grants for school like the Pell Grant and even for day care assistance. But I'd still have to take out student loans because I couldn't get enough in assistance and aid to cover my expenses, like to pay for tuition and books and groceries and health insurance and all of that. And I don't want to take a handout. I can work, so I'm going to work. And that will mean that I don't have tons of student loans when I graduate.
>
> And I didn't want to go on welfare. I didn't want to be a welfare mom. I knew people who were on welfare, and they never had money . . . and I didn't want to live like that. I'm planning to go to graduate school and get my PhD in nursing science. And I need some experience in the medical field, things that I can put on my application to the program. So I have a full-time job. And it was a hard decision, I had to wrestle with it for a while, but I decided to work full time.

As her explanation suggests, Stephanie focused on various economic, educational, and ideological considerations when making her choice. She was adamant about reducing her need for student loans. In addition, she believed that working would give her some practical experience that would make her a more attractive candidate when she applied to PhD programs. Finally, her attitudes about welfare influenced her decision. Stephanie's statements reinforce the kind of discourses that drove welfare reform in the United States in the mid-1990s, specifically the implication that welfare recipients are taking a "handout" instead of going to work. She drew a clear distinction between herself and "welfare moms." Thus, she decided to forgo public assistance and work full time while pursuing her degree.

As a result, Stephanie combined three full-time jobs: single mother, college student, and employee. This made it quite difficult for her to describe a typical day. Instead, she talked about her "typical week" and explained the very strict schedule she maintained. Her student responsibilities were scheduled between the hours of 9 A.M. and 5 P.M. on weekdays. This was the time she devoted to attending classes, studying, preparing for class discussions, and completing assignments. However, for reasons that will soon become apparent, Stephanie occasionally found it necessary to locate a quiet corner of the library during these times and take a nap. Typically, she left the campus at 5:00 P.M. to pick up her son at day care and they spent the next several hours together. The remaining hours of her week were a little less predictable and her activities during those times depended on her work schedule. In order to get some experience in the health care field, Stephanie had completed a six-week certified nursing assistant course at KCC during the summer before she began classes at UI. After passing her certification exam, she quit her job at the hotel and began working full time at Mercy Hospital in Iowa City, located just blocks from the UI campus. Stephanie worked two overnight shifts at the hospital during the week, from 11 P.M. to 7 A.M., leaving Jeffrey at home with her cousin, Olivia, who is also a full-time undergraduate student at UI. Olivia had moved in with Stephanie and Jeffrey to help with child care and split the rent. When her shift ended at 7:00 A.M., Stephanie rushed home "to get my son up and fed and dressed and to day care on time" so she could make it to campus by 9:00 A.M. She frequently found herself running late. On weeknights when she was not scheduled to work, she went to bed around the same time as Jeffrey, sleeping until 7:00 A.M., when she started her day. Stephanie completed the remaining twenty-four hours of her full-time employment on the weekends, working two twelve-hour shifts, most often from 11 P.M. to 11 A.M. on both Friday and Saturday. In general, weekends gave Stephanie more time with her son as she was "usually home by lunch time so I get some time to spend with him." However, it was not unusual for Stephanie's weekend shifts to include "mandatory overtime," additional or extended shifts that she was expected to cover when a co-worker called in sick or took vacation time. This meant her twelve-hour shifts were extended to sixteen hours. On those days, Stephanie reported to work at 11 P.M. and did not leave until 3 P.M. the following day.

In theory, Stephanie should have had no difficulty fitting her three full-time jobs into the 168 hours of each week. If she devoted 40 hours a week to paid employment, 40 hours to student responsibilities, and 40 hours to parenting, she would have committed only 120 hours of her week, leaving her with a surplus of 48 hours. Analyzing Stephanie's time by creating a mathematical equation might be appropriate if she were a robot who did not require sleep. But Stephanie was not a robot. Research has demonstrated that adult human beings generally require a minimum of eight hours of sleep daily and perhaps even as much as ten hours of sleep during a twenty-four hour period.[9] Those who do not meet these requirements, particularly for a number of days in a row or over an extended period of time, suffer from sleep deprivation and are likely to experience a decline in both physical and mental health that includes increased susceptibility to infection, high blood pressure, heart disease, obesity, and an inability to concentrate.[10] Thus, even if Stephanie had been able to devote her remaining 48 hours a week to sleep, she would have averaged only 6.86 hours a night, more than an hour below the recommended minimum.

It is also important to point out that Stephanie's life did not follow the principles of a simple mathematical equation with regard to available time and how she managed that time. Though she certainly tried to adhere to the strict schedule she described to me, doing so was nearly impossible. Stephanie had arranged her five classes to fit into the nine-to-five, Monday-through-Friday schedule she had set aside for student responsibilities. However, because she was taking fifteen semester hours, she frequently found herself unable to complete all of her homework and studying in the time she was on campus. Her student time often extended beyond its planned parameters and she had to do homework after her son had gone to bed or on the weekend after she returned home from work. Furthermore, because she worked overtime "at least one weekend a month," Stephanie found herself with less time available to spend with Jeffrey:

> It's tough. There are some days when I just don't want to get out of bed. I don't want to do anything but stay in and sleep late and then spend the whole day just playing with him. I don't ever get to do that. There is always an assignment that needs doing or I have to be in class or at work. And I can't afford to call in sick just to stay home because I need the money. And there are times when I can tell that Jeffrey feels like he doesn't get to see me enough. I can tell when he is really craving my attention. And I try to spend as much time with him as I can, but sometimes I'm just so tired that I don't want to go to the park or play a game. I feel bad about that. And sometimes when I'm trying to study, he'll just close my book and say, "Look at me, look at me, look at me." And that's really, well, it's awful. I feel like I don't give him enough time. I know that all he wants is some attention, that he's letting me know that "Hey, I haven't seen you in a while and I need some attention!"

Stephanie believed that working her way through college would permit her to take out less in student loans than if she had participated in social services programs. However, she had borrowed "far more in loans" than she had anticipated, even with a scholarship that provided her with $2,500 each academic year. Even with overtime pay and splitting rent with Olivia, Stephanie found it difficult to pay all her bills on time. Because she was intent on pursuing a PhD and believed that she would have to work full time while in graduate school, Stephanie realized that her schedule would probably not be easier to manage until she had completed her education. Still, she remained hopeful that things would improve and fantasized about a future when she would no longer be a student because "once I'm totally finished, things will be better. I'll get to sleep then. I'll be able to have some down time."

CONCLUSION

In *Values Americans Live By*, written in the mid-1980s, the late L. Robert Kohls, former director of training for the U.S. Information Agency and the Meridian International Center in Washington, DC, explained attitudes toward time that are uniquely American:

Time is, for the average American, of utmost importance. To the foreign visitor, Americans seem to be more concerned with getting things accomplished on time (according to a predetermined schedule) than they are with developing deep interpersonal relations. Schedules, for the American, are meant to be planned and then followed in the smallest detail. . . . Time is so valued in America, because by considering time to be important one can clearly accomplish more than if one "wastes" time and does not keep busy. This philosophy has proven its worth. It has enabled Americans to be extremely productive, and productivity itself is highly valued in the United States. Many American proverbs stress the value in guarding our time, using it wisely, setting and working toward specific goals, and even expending our time and energy today so that the fruits of our labor may be enjoyed at a later time.[11]

The high value Americans place on time has not diminished in the more than thirty years since the publication of Kohls's book. On the contrary, evidence suggests that U.S. society has become even more preoccupied with time and its use, especially as it relates to paid employment. In fact, Americans are presently experiencing what is referred to as a speedup, a situation in which employers have demanded increased work hours and productivity from their employees despite the fact that wages have remained stagnant.[12] These increased work-related time demands result in an increase in work-related stress. They also have a negative impact on employees' ability to balance work with family life; additional time spent at work and completing work-related activities at home translates into less time spent with spouses, children, and other family members. At present, American employees experience a significant lack of time away from work each week and have the dubious distinction of living in one of the few industrialized nations that does not require employers to give workers paid annual leave.[13]

Parenting, like paid employment in the United States, comes with its own set of time-related challenges, and the time management principles that dominate American business have also come to govern American family life. Corporate models of time management have been applied to family life, for "time is the scarcest resource, and unless it is managed, nothing else can be managed."[14] Numerous books, magazine articles, parenting websites, and blogs suggest that Americans have embraced this model. Such sources advise parents on how to better manage all time-related aspects of family life, such as preparing their children to begin a new school year, organizing after-school activities, planning holiday celebrations, family planning and the spacing of children, helping overscheduled children de-stress, and taking control of the family calendar.[15] And while many of these sources are ostensibly aimed at both mothers and fathers, the gendered division of labor that persists in American society has a significant impact on parenting roles. Despite evidence of positive outcomes when parents engage in a more egalitarian allocation of parenting duties, women continue to do the majority of the childrearing tasks in heterosexual marriages, even in households where both husband and wife are employed.[16] Social scientists have documented the "double day," or the "second shift" of unpaid household labor that married heterosexual women in dual-career households complete after they return home from the office, factory, or other place of employment.[17] This labor typically includes tasks traditionally defined as "women's work" in the domestic sphere such as cooking, laundry, childrearing, shopping, and housekeeping. As a result, married heterosexual mothers experience a significant "leisure gap" and work, on average, "an extra month of twenty-four hour days a year" that their husbands do not.[18] Women's additional time investment in parenting is a key component of how they are socialized to demonstrate maternal love, and such love is central to cultural ideals of good motherhood.[19]

In many respects, the time crunch single mothers who are attending college experience is simply a reflection of American values associated with time. Their attitudes reflected the high value Americans tend to place on time, including the notion that time is money. This was especially clear in their descriptions of the time they devoted to higher education as an investment, applying a basic return-on-investment explanation as they measured what they regarded as a temporary time crunch against what they perceived to be the long-term gains associated with a college degree. Thus, even as they lamented the demands on their time, their ability to tolerate such demands was bolstered by the belief that completion of a college degree would lead to a more lucrative post-graduation life for themselves and their children and, correspondingly, more free time.

Examining the typical day or typical week of these women revealed how they allocated their time, including the specific strategies they developed in the contexts of their lives. It was common for them to divide their time into distinct periods throughout the day and week into student time, parenting time, and work time. The regimented way that Rochelle toggled back and forth between student responsibilities and parenting responsibilities is a good example of this. Although this was an effective strategy for many of the women, others struggled with time management. Because the demands on their time often fluctuated in accordance with things such as midterm and final exams, the illness of a child (as in the case of Karen's daughter, Sarah), semester research papers and projects, and employment schedules (as in Stephanie's case when she was required to work overtime), many of the women found that their meticulously planned schedules were simply impossible to maintain. Time-related challenges were somewhat alleviated for those who had family or friends who are willing to help with child care or who, like Melinda, could afford to hire help. Yet most could not afford to do so and found themselves caught in a time bind that contributed to their feelings of social isolation and fatigue. In addition, many of the women articulated feelings of guilt as they worried they did not spend enough time with their children.

Although many of the women imagined that there would be long-term economic gains associated with the time they invested in higher education, a closer examination of their narratives suggests that those who were able to effectively manage their time also experienced more immediate rewards. In their discussions, productivity was a key theme. They spoke in great detail about how they organized their time in response to the challenges they faced, most often by listing the numerous parenting, academic, and employment-related work they completed in a way that emphasized productivity. This emphasis suggests that they took a certain amount of pride in being able to define themselves as productive. Their emphasis on productivity indicates that the women had a positive self-concept and regarded themselves as hard-working and responsible individuals. Though intangible, a positive self-concept and healthy self-esteem have been regarded as predictors of academic success and favorable job performance.[20] And perhaps for these women, a positive self-concept is a key part of what makes it possible for them to take on the various challenges they do every day. Taking inventory of all their responsibilities may help single mothers realize that despite the fact that they are only twenty-four hours in a day, they can do it all and do it well. This realization, in turn, may make it possible for them to get up and do it all again the next day.

4 · NAVIGATING AMERICA'S CHILD CARE CRISIS

A CHILDHOOD FILLED WITH EXTRACURRICULAR ACTIVITIES

Unlike many American parents and unlike many other single mothers attending college, Tilda Knox did not experience a child care crisis. Shortly after her divorce was finalized, Tilda moved from Houston to the Dallas–Fort Worth area with her daughter, Baylee, and her son, Asher. She was intent on completing the undergraduate nursing program at Texas Woman's University as a step toward independence that would help her increase her income. Tilda already received nearly $50,000 a year in child support and alimony from her ex-husband. Yet given the wealth she had enjoyed during her marriage to Wesley Knox III, a highly paid, well-known surgeon in the Houston area, Tilda had a difficult time adapting to what she considered a limited income. She initially looked for housing in communities close to the TWU campus. Eventually, she rented an apartment in a wealthy suburb on the north side of Dallas, fifty minutes from TWU, justifying the expense because it provided her children with access to "very, very good schools" and the cultural amenities of Dallas.

Tilda's children were both in middle school. Baylee was an eighth grader and Asher had just started sixth grade. The children attended classes from 8:00 A.M. to 3:20 P.M. Monday through Friday and Tilda arranged her schedule so all of her classes at TWU took place between 9:00 A.M. and 5:00 P.M. Although her children were no longer in elementary school, Tilda felt that they were too young to be left at home unsupervised for several hours at the end of the school day. When I asked her about child care, Tilda smiled. She didn't need child care. Both children were heavily involved in sports and student clubs. Indeed, as she listed their various activities, it seemed that Baylee and Asher participated in nearly every extracurricular activity their school offered. Both participated in sports—volleyball and soccer for Baylee, football and baseball for Asher. They were also involved in the performing arts, student organizations, and special academic-focused clubs such as a book club, a foreign language club, a geography club, and a history club. When I commented on the social and academic opportunities these activities were providing for her children, Tilda shrugged. While she acknowledged that the children enjoyed and likely gained something from being involved in these activities, for Tilda, the primary attraction of extracurricular activities was the fact that they minimized the amount of time Baylee and Asher were left "hanging out" at home with "nothing productive to do." By the time the children finished their after-school activities and took the bus home, they were only alone for less than an hour before their mother joined them. Tilda acknowledged the financial burden associated with the children's participation in extracurricular activities—she wrote checks for things such as uniforms, shoes, and equipment for sports and costumes, script fees, and props for performing arts and other clubs. But her ex-husband was required to pay half of these expenses, and Tilda estimated that her children's participation in extracurricular activities cost her approximately $500 a year.

Readers may find it odd that I have chosen to begin a chapter entitled "navigating America's child care crisis" with Tilda's narrative. With relatively little effort, she had managed to arrange a supervised care situation for her children that was convenient, accessible, and affordable. She did not identify child care as one of the primary concerns in her life and she spent relatively little time discussing this aspect of her experiences with me. Child care was certainly not a crisis for Tilda. However, her experiences help illustrate a simple reality of the American child care system: increased economic resources provide increased access to convenient care. Although Tilda complained about her economic situation, the alimony and child support she received provided her with a solid middle-class income. Tilda did not have to hire a nanny, pay for a before- and after-school program, or arrange some other formal child care situation for Baylee and Asher. Her financial privilege allowed the family to live in a well-funded school district that offered a wide variety of extracurricular activities that functioned as supervised care for Tilda's children. It is likely that without her middle-class income Tilda would have faced a much different—and much more difficult—child care situation.

THE CURRENT STATE OF CHILD CARE IN AMERICA

American families struggled with child care throughout the twentieth century. Commonly cited problems included the low quality, high cost, unreliability, and even unavailability of child care services.[1] Americans also had to contend with competing perspectives on the inherent risks and benefits associated with child care, particularly as such perspectives were influenced by the field of child development and debates over the role of government in providing and regulating child care for its citizenry.[2] By the twenty-first century, child care in the United States had reached a full-fledged crisis:

> The United States continues to experience what has been referred to as a "silent crisis" in child care.... At its most optimal—when the quality of care is good and children's needs are met—child care is synonymous with early childhood education. Unfortunately, not all child care is of good quality—thus not all child care is necessarily educational. In fact, poor-quality child care can jeopardize children's health and safety and actually compromise children's development, putting them at risk for poor school readiness and educational outcomes. From this perspective, the child care problem is far more than a challenge for adults. It is a serious threat to the well-being of our children. In turn, to the extent that children's school readiness and academic achievement are compromised by poor child care experiences, it is also a problem for society, which ultimately relies on the human capital embodied in our children. It is from this ecological perspective that I describe child care in America as tragic.[3]

The situation in the United States contrasts sharply with that in countries such as Sweden, Finland, Norway, France, and Japan, where, as George Thurman noted, "a commitment of public funds, effective regulation procedures, caregivers' qualifications, and program objectives" have led to high-quality, accessible, and affordable day care. In some of these countries, day care is free.[4]

The United States has not been completely lacking in efforts to improve child care. In 2011 alone, the government allocated $5 billion through the Child Care and Development Fund (CCDF) Block Grant and Section 418 of the Social Security Act. These funds were intended specifically to "assist low-income families in obtaining child care so they can work or attend training/education. The program also improves the quality of child care and promotes coordination among early childhood development and afterschool programs."[5] In addition, the CCDF promoted standards of care with regard to safety, training, and health for all child care providers who receive CCDF funds. It has also maintained a voucher program to subsidize child care for low-income families, provided financial incentives to increase research on child care, and sought to improve the quality of child care in America through training, resource and referral programs, and increased monitoring.[6]

There is great demand for child care in America. Approximately 11 million children under the age of five spend an average of thirty-six hours a week at a child care center.[7] Millions more participate in other child care arrangements such as care from a friend, relative, neighbor, or older sibling.[8] For 8.4 million school-aged children, child care takes the form of before- and after-school programs in their school districts.[9] But high demand is only part of the story. The signs of increasing poverty in the first decade of the twenty-first century were abundant: widespread foreclosures on homes,[10] mounting unemployment,[11] decreasing household incomes,[12] and increasing numbers of Americans applying for welfare benefits.[13] Countless families have needed child care for their children but have been unable to afford such care.[14] In light of America's recent economic woes and the unmet need for child care for many families, the government's funding for the CCDF initiatives described above amounts to little more than a drop in the bucket.

While the economic downturn had many negative impacts, evidence suggests that the impact on children was significant in terms of health, food security, housing stability, and maltreatment.[15] Economic well-being has also been linked to child well-being in another important way—through child care. Children who live in poverty are more likely than their more affluent counterparts to encounter low-quality child care:

> In the absence of a nationally subsidized child care system, child care, for most parents, must be bought on the private market. Costs are prohibitive. . . . There is a growing national crisis of unmet need: inferior quality, unstable, makeshift arrangements, and the worst and the cheapest of care for the poorest of children. Multiple studies point to critical concerns about the quality and provision of care, and national reports on child care have documented unsafe, unsanitary centers, poor quality care, lack of regulation, closed access, and chronic unavailability to low-income families, with particular concerns raised about substandard care for infants and toddlers.[16]

In such circumstances, poor families struggle to find safe, reliable, and affordable child care. Yet even in middle-class, dual-income families, child care costs can consume a significant portion of household income. Child care costs vary considerably throughout the country. However, Child Care Aware of America found that on average, American families in all regions of the United States spend more on child care than they spend on food.[17] In addition, average costs of child care for families with two children in care exceeded average mortgage payments in twenty-three states and the District of Columbia and exceeded average rent costs in all states.[18] The cost of infant care is especially high; in 2013, "the average annual cost for an infant in center-based care was higher than a year's tuition and fees at a four-year public college in 31 states and the District of Columbia."[19]

The cost of child care is only one aspect of the child care crisis in America. The availability and quality of care are equally important. Availability constitutes more than the presence of a child care provider in the area where the family lives or works; it is "the degree to which a family has ready access to needed child care: this might include not only convenient geographical location but also the availability of slots for the right age range and the right time of day" to meet family needs.[20] Child care availability tends to be greater in metropolitan areas than in rural ones, and availability is typically more limited for poor rural families who work nonstandard hours such as evenings and weekends.[21] But availability is also limited in urban areas, particularly in low-income communities.[22]

Despite the fact that much attention has been given to this issue, the quality of child care in the United States remains a widespread problem. Various websites related to parenting and child care provide guidelines intended to help parents successfully choose a high-quality child care provider. For example, "Child Care Aware®," maintained by the National Association of Child Care Resource and Referral Agencies, explains five "key indicators of quality" that include guidelines for adult to child ratio, group size, caregiver qualifications, turnover, and accreditations.[23] Similar guidelines have been endorsed by the American Academy of Pediatrics, the U.S. Department of Health and Human Services, state health and child welfare agencies, and researchers who have linked high-quality child care with positive child development.[24] Despite this and the existence of federal and state regulations that govern child care services, the quality of child care in the United States is troubling. Consider the following examples. In South Lake Tahoe, California, Kindertown Preschool and Infant Center was cited for multiple violations of the California state code, including inadequate supervision that "allowed a 7-year-old with Down Syndrome to run away from the facility and end up on Lake Tahoe Boulevard."[25] In Washington County, Pennsylvania, the state Department of Public Welfare ordered the emergency closure of three child care centers due to inadequate supervision after an investigation that was prompted by a near-drowning of a seven-year-old child.[26] In Jonesboro, Georgia, the owner of a day care center and two employees were charged with child cruelty, involuntary manslaughter, and reckless conduct when two-year-old Jazmin Green died in their care. Following a field trip, Green had been left locked in the center's van for more than two hours on a day when the temperature was over 90 degrees.[27]

Some may dismiss these as tragic yet disconnected examples. It is much more difficult to dismiss systematic assessments of the U.S. child care system. A 1994 nationwide study by the Families and Work Institute found that child care was significantly lacking in quality.[28] In 2004, prompted by the suffocation death of an infant in a New York City day care center, the city's health department launched an examination of the more than 9,400 child care centers in the area. The investigation found widespread health and safety violations, lack of appropriate background checks for staff, lack of adequate first aid and other emergency training, poor communication, and infrequent, superficial assessments of day care facilities by city inspectors.[29] A 2006 study by the National Institute of Child Health and Human Development found that while high-quality child care promoted language and cognitive development, most of the child care centers studied—particularly those that provided infant and toddler care—did not meet standards for quality care as established by the American Academy of Pediatrics and the American Public Health Association, particularly as these standards related to adult-to-child ratio, observed group size, caregiver training, and caregiver education.[30]

It is against this backdrop that I return to Tilda's story. Her experiences demonstrate that child care is not a crisis for all single mothers who attend college. Because of her financial situation, she was able to provide Baylee and Asher a childhood filled with extracurricular activities in lieu of making formal child care arrangements. However, the nation's economic troubles have not been resolved, and the school district where Tilda's children are enrolled, like others in Texas and across the country, may be forced to cut funding for extracurricular activities to compensate for budget shortfalls.[31] If this happens before Tilda feels her children are old enough to remain home alone for extended periods, she will have to make other child care arrangements. Thus, despite her economic advantages, it is possible that Tilda, like many other American families and like many of the women whose narratives appear on the following pages, could find herself navigating America's child care crisis.

TRYING TO MAKE A NEW LIFE

Evelyn Davis was born and raised on the South Side of Chicago, in what has been dubbed "a second America," a predominantly black community characterized by high rates of poverty and unemployment, substandard schools, and public housing that was literally crumbling down around the residents.[32] Despite growing up in these conditions, Evelyn had a "pretty normal childhood." Unlike many of her friends, she "didn't become a teen mom," a fact she was very proud of. She and her boyfriend, Terrence, had been together for more than five years before Evelyn gave birth to their son, DeZhay, at the age of twenty-one. The couple had met in high school, and after graduating, both started working "whenever we could find jobs," although Evelyn admitted that finding steady employment had been difficult, especially "a job that paid enough for you to live on, even if you had a high school diploma." When Evelyn became pregnant, she and Terrence moved into a subsidized apartment and set about planning their future. Although neither she nor Terrence wanted to get married right away, they were determined to provide the best life they could for their child, a life that involved moving out of the "dead end, no options" situation of their neighborhood. During the early months of her pregnancy, Evelyn enrolled in the nursing assistant program at one of the seven City Colleges of Chicago, taking out approximately $2,500 in student loans to cover living expenses, books, and tuition while she completed the eight-week course. Around the time Evelyn began school, Terrence found a full-time job as a manager at a convenience store, working the second shift. After completing the course, Evelyn passed the state competency exam and graduated with a nursing assistant certification from the Illinois Department of Public Health. She gave birth to her son a few months later, and three weeks after DeZhay arrived, she began working full time as a certified nursing assistant (CNA) at one of the large hospitals in Chicago. With their combined income, Evelyn and Terrence were able to move out of subsidized housing by the time DeZhay started walking.

Yet the couple soon found themselves in a financial bind. After paying for rent, utilities, transportation, groceries, and other basic living expenses, they couldn't afford health insurance, even with the employee health insurance program where Evelyn worked. In addition, DeZhay began to have seizures and was diagnosed with epilepsy at the age of fifteen months. Though anti-seizure medication helped limit the frequency and severity of his seizures, the costs of medical care and prescriptions added up quickly. When the convenience store where Terence worked closed and he lost his job, money became a "big source of tension" in the household. The relationship eventually ended and Terrence moved out. Unable to afford rent and other living expenses on her own, Evelyn applied for and was granted Section 8 housing assistance. She continued working at the hospital and tried to support her son. It was difficult, but she managed at first. However, when budget cuts forced the hospital to reduce her work hours from forty to twenty a week, it became more difficult for Evelyn to manage financially. When she was laid off three months later, it became impossible. Evelyn applied for welfare and although she was approved for TANF, food stamps, and Medicaid, she found it difficult to get by, "especially in Chicago where things are more expensive anyway." She was soon running behind on her gas, telephone, and water bills. She also could not maintain her student loan repayment schedule or keep up with medical bills.

Evelyn decided to leave Chicago and "try to make a new life" for herself and her son. Her younger cousin, Keisha, who was a junior at the University of Iowa and "really liked the community," encouraged Evelyn to move to Iowa City, telling her it was a "good place to raise a kid" and that Evelyn's CNA credentials would enable her to "get a job pretty easily" at one of the hospitals or home health agencies in the area. Eager to "start earning an income again," Evelyn decided to move to Iowa City and work part-time. She intended to devote the remainder of her time to caring for her son and taking three courses a semester at Kirkwood Community College until she had completed her registered nurse's degree, something she had always wanted to do. Evelyn had her Section 8 housing voucher transferred, packed up her three-year-old son and their belongings, and moved to Iowa City in March 2002.

When I met Evelyn nine months later, she told me that their time in Iowa City had been very difficult. She had applied to the University of Iowa Hospital & Clinics, Mercy Hospital, and various home health agencies, only to learn that her nursing assistant certification was only valid in the state of Illinois. If she wanted to work as a CNA in Iowa, she would need to complete a state-approved course and then pass the certification exam from the Iowa Department of Public Health. She was not willing to do this because "if I was going to take out more student loans, it wasn't going to be to do a training program that I had already completed somewhere else." Disappointed but still eager to continue her education, Evelyn decided to enroll full time at KCC's Cedar Rapids campus. She believed that this was a good solution because it would allow her to complete her RN degree more quickly and get enough financial aid to meet her needs. Evelyn chose KCC's Cedar Rapids campus for two reasons: it was the only Kirkwood campus that offered the RN program and it had a day care center, a key consideration for Evelyn due to DeZhay's medical condition. Evelyn felt more comfortable putting her son in a day care center close to campus so she could "be there for him when he needed me." In late April, she registered for classes and was excited at the prospect of working toward her degree.

Her excitement didn't last long. After leaving Enrollment Services on KCC's Cedar Rapids campus, Evelyn walked over to Kirkwood Kids, KCC's day care center, to fill out an application for DeZhay. When she handed it to the office staff, she was informed that there was a "long waiting list." It was so long, in fact, that it was unlikely that DeZhay would be admitted to the child care center for the fall semester. Although the center was part of the campus and served many Kirkwood students and employees, it was also open to members of the broader community. In addition, it did not prioritize enrollment for Kirkwood students, faculty, or staff. Thus, although the child care center was licensed for over 100 children, Evelyn, like many of the other single mother students I interviewed at KCC who hoped to enrolled their children at Kirkwood Kids, found that she was unable to access this service. When Evelyn investigated other day care centers in the area, she encountered similarly long waiting lists, including some that were "at least six months long and some that were more than a year." In addition, she found that child care centers in the Iowa City community were "much more expensive" than Kirkwood Kids. After contacting 4Cs, Community Coordinated Child Care, an organization that provides child care resources and referrals in the Iowa City area, Evelyn obtained a list of less expensive in-home providers.[33] She visited several, hoping that one would have an opening for DeZhay in the fall. While several had space for another child, none was equipped to "take on a child with a medical condition."

By early August, Evelyn felt she had exhausted her options and "did the only thing I could." She withdrew her student registration at KCC but left DeZhay on the waiting list at Kirkwood Kids. She planned to begin full-time classes when he was admitted to the child care center. In the meantime, Evelyn needed to earn an income and she still wanted to pursue her nursing degree. After completing refresher courses in CPR and first aid, Evelyn was licensed by the state of Iowa to provide child care in her home, which she did from 7 A.M. to 5:30 P.M. Monday through Friday. She also enrolled in one course at KCC's Iowa City campus. Although it wasn't the full-time enrollment she had hoped for, it was all she could manage with her child care responsibilities and all she could afford without the help of student financial aid.[34] At the time of our interview, DeZhay had been on the Kirkwood Kids waiting list for nearly eight months. As I sat in her living room, Evelyn called the child care center to check on the possibility of DeZhay being admitted for the upcoming spring semester. She was told that "it doesn't look promising." Her situation was a far cry from the "new life" she had hoped to find in Iowa City. She was self-employed and working full time but not earning enough to achieve self-sufficiency. Evelyn was confident she would be able to support herself without government assistance when she earned her degree. But unless DeZhay was admitted to Kirkwood's child care center, Evelyn felt she had no choice but to work toward her degree one course at a time while providing child care for other people's children.

THREE KIDS, THREE CHILD CARE PROVIDERS, TWO AND A HALF HOURS A DAY

On a brisk morning in early December, Patty Flanigan sat down across from me at a local café. She let her heavy backpack fall to the floor with a thud and gave a deep sigh as she sank into a comfy chair. The UI doctoral student was in her early thirties, divorced, and the mother of three children, Nicholas (seven), Victoria (three), and Angela (one). Brushing a long lock of brown hair back from her face, she confided, "I feel like I've been in school forever. Forever. I don't know how much longer I can do this." Patty had been in school almost continuously since the age of five: after she graduated from high school, she immediately went to college, where she worked toward her bachelor's degree. During her junior year of college, she participated in a semester abroad program in Italy, where she met and began dating Antonio. Before her semester in Italy ended, Patty was pregnant. She didn't want to raise a baby on her own, and although she loved Italy, she didn't want to live there permanently. Thus, she married Antonio because she saw it as "the only way that he could come back to the U.S. with me and participate in childrearing." Once back in the United States, Patty finished her BA, completed her master's degree, and then began working on her PhD.

During her marriage, Patty found it easy to meet her child care needs. If Antonio wasn't working, he took responsibility for the children while Patty attended classes or completed duties as a graduate teaching assistant. On the rare occasions when they both had commitments, the couple hired a babysitter to come to the house, a practice that was "very affordable since we had two incomes." After the couple divorced, however, child care became much more difficult. The most significant challenges Patty faced in this regard had to do with availability, cost, and transportation.

Patty told me that child care availability was a "real nightmare" because she was unable to locate a single provider that could meet all her child care needs. Shortly after her divorce, Antonio "moved away and now doesn't even take the kids on weekends. He doesn't ever see them." Originally, she tried to get all three into a day care center that provided comprehensive services: care throughout the day for younger children such as Victoria and Angela and a before- and after-school program for older kids such as Nicholas. However, when she investigated these types of centers, she encountered a familiar refrain: waiting lists. Patty added her name to the waiting lists "all over Iowa City" and then began to explore other child care options. After obtaining a comprehensive list of licensed day care centers in the area from 4Cs, she located some possible child care options for her daughters but found nothing for Nicholas. Though most of the schools in the Iowa City Community School District had before- and after-school programs, Patty found that they had something in common with traditional child care centers:

> I checked into all of them in Iowa City and at some of the elementary schools in town here [in a nearby city, and] there are two to two-and-a-half-year waiting lists to get into these programs. . . . So what am I supposed to do? Register my toddler now so she can get in when she starts kindergarten? They won't let you do that; you can't register for the programs until the child is officially enrolled in the school system. So basically they won't let me register and then when I do, they tell me that there is a two-year waiting list. So what am I supposed to do for those two years? Tell my kid, my first grader, to go hang out at home alone until they have an opening?

Unable to find care for Nicholas, Patty moved to Solon, Iowa, twenty minutes north of Iowa City, because the Solon school district had an opening for Nicholas in their before- and after-school program. She also found an opening for Victoria with an in-home care provider in North Liberty, a community approximately seventeen minutes east of Solon.

The financial aspects of child care were also a significant concern for Patty. When she started her doctoral program, Patty was awarded a half-time teaching assistantship. This required her to devote twenty hours a week to teaching classes, grading, and holding regular office hours. In return, she earned "somewhere between $14,000 and $16,000 per year, depending on what class I was teaching and which department it was in." Patty also earned "a little extra money" doing medical transcription for a local physician. When she was pregnant with Angela, however, Patty's obstetrician put her on strict bed rest. She remained there until giving birth to Angela approximately one month before her due date. Unable to teach during this time, Patty took a medical leave from the university and earned no income. She took out student loans to cover her living expenses and suspended her dissertation research temporarily. After Angela was born, Patty was eager to get back to her dissertation and to teaching. Yet when she applied for a teaching position for the upcoming year, Patty was told she was ineligible:

> They said I hadn't made "sufficient progress" and so they no longer would con-sider me eligible for teaching in the department. They just said that I failed to make progress because I couldn't do my dissertation research while I was on bed rest. Well, duh! Of course I couldn't do research while I was on bed rest. Who could? And I understand that departments have to have some guidelines for determining who gets funding and how much and who gets to teach which classes or be a research assistant for which professor. I completely understand that. But I had no idea I was going to have a risky pregnancy, I had no idea that would happen. How in the world did they expect me to keep doing my research during that time? There is really no way. I was on medical leave.
>
> (JDW: Have you appealed their decision to not consider you for funding?) Yes, I appealed the decision to the department and they denied my appeal and they told me that's the end of the appeal process, that there's nothing else I can do. I'm not kidding . . . I don't know what they expect me to live on in the meantime, while I'm not teaching. Student loans aren't enough. I have no [other] income right now. My child support ended, he doesn't send it at all anymore. . . . I need to go through child support recovery and once I find out where he is, I will hope-fully get things taken care of and hopefully get a nice child support check. But what am I supposed to do until then? Day care is crazy. I went to one place and they wanted $900 for the infant and $700 for the three-year-old, per month. Per month. So $1,600 a month. Even when I was teaching as a graduate instructor, my [monthly] take home pay after taxes wasn't even that much.

To try to ease her financial woes, Patty took out additional student loans. She was also able to secure a half-time teaching position in another department on the

UI campus. Even so, she found it difficult to pay her child care bill each month. In order to keep her child care costs as low as possible, Patty decided to keep Angela out of day care. When Patty taught her classes, she had friends watch the infant, and during her office hours, Patty brought Angela to work with her. It was a solution that worked well "since she was this little tiny baby who didn't cry or fuss or anything, she just slept and ate." Yet after a faculty member learned that Patty was bringing her daughter to work with her, he told her it would have to stop "because it would be a distraction for people who were trying to work." Patty, who had never had any complaints from her colleagues or her students, explained her situation but she was told that if she brought her child to work again, she would be fired. Neither the University of Iowa *Handbook for Teaching Assistants* nor the University of Iowa *Operations Manual* included rules that prohibited graduate teaching assistants from bringing their children to work.[35] When Patty questioned the legality of this action, particularly since "there was nothing ever put out in writing about it," the faculty member did not respond to her directly. Instead, he sent an e-mail to all teaching assistants in the department forbidding them to bring their children to work.

Patty felt that if she wanted to keep her job, she had no choice but to put Angela in day care. Although some of the child care centers affiliated with University of Iowa had a sliding fee scale for students, Patty could not afford them because "they can charge whatever they want because the demand is so high in this city. It's a white-collar town so they charge white-collar prices, even the supposedly 'lower cost' places." In addition, the waiting lists at the day care centers were lengthy; one day care worker told her that "you pretty much have to get your kid on the list before you even get pregnant." After "contacting every child care person I could find," Patty was finally able to locate an in-home provider who had space for Angela and who charged significantly less than the child care centers. Once Angela was in day care, Patty's monthly child care bill increased considerably. She paid $150 a month for Nicholas to attend the before- and after-school program at his school, and "the bill for the girls . . . total[ed] over $1,000."

Despite her limited income, Patty was not eligible for child care assistance through the Iowa Department of Human Services because she had already completed a bachelor's degree.[36] The University of Iowa Family Services Office gave her a child care subsidy, for which she was grateful, yet it was only a small amount and made only a minor difference given her total child care expenses:

If the kid is under age two, then [the subsidy] is $100 a month. If they're over two but not yet in school, then it's only $75 [per month]. And then once they get in school, start kindergarten, then there's really nothing to help with before- and after-school care. And the subsidy is only for ten months, but most day care centers, including in-home ones that are licensed, require that you keep your child enrolled through the summer, even if classes aren't in session. So the check you get, it's about $750 and if you have a second child that you have to put in day care, then you only get an additional $30 per month for that child. So even though you have more in child care expenses with two, you don't get more assistance through this program. So the total amount I get as a subsidy for the entire ten months for both of my kids that qualify, the two youngest, it doesn't even cover one month of my child care.

The director of that program is wonderful and she's really trying and it would be worse if she wasn't doing anything. But they need to give her more funding. . . . And I've heard that they fund whoever applies, regardless of what their income is. And so what about people who are living in poverty and have more than one kid and really need it more based on their economic circumstances? It just makes absolutely no sense to me. It's like people are being penalized for being poor. But that's not just at the university. That's something that is really a reflection of how we feel about child care in America.

Even with the subsidy, Patty paid over $1,000 a month out of pocket for child care. And while she tried to "ration out" her student loan money, she often found herself unable to afford her child care bill. This was true "especially at the end of the semester when loan money has run out." In those situations, Patty was "at the mercy" of her child care providers and begged them to "be patient . . . until a tax return came in or until the next semester began and a financial aid check was deposited into my checking account." Though her child care providers were accommodating, her situation was far from ideal. In addition to causing "a great deal of stress," her strategy of postponing child care payments was akin to spending money she did not yet have. When she received the next installment of student loans or a tax refund, she had to use that money to "catch up" and pay off her child care bills from previous months. Like many families living in poverty, Patty practiced a type of "windfall child rearing."[37] Because she paid for past child care expenses at the beginning of each semester, she was inevitably left without enough to meet current living expenses, and as each semester drew to a close, she found herself running behind on child care payments until her next financial windfall arrived.

While locating child care and paying for it were difficult, Patty also found that getting her children to and from their respective care providers each day took a toll. After leaving the house in the morning, Patty would first drive Nicholas to the before- and after-school program at his school, usually arriving "right when it opens at 7:30 A.M." After signing him in and kissing him good-bye, Patty would then head east to North Liberty, where she would drop Victoria at the day care where she was enrolled full-time. She would then "fight traffic again" as she headed to the in-home day care Angela attended. Finally, around 8:45 A.M., after more than an hour of driving from one child care site to the next, Patty would be on her way to campus and to her study carrel in the UI main library to work on her dissertation. At 3:30, she would leave the library and reverse her morning route, first retrieving Angela and breastfeeding her in the car, then picking up Victoria, and finally getting Nicholas before going home for the day. Thus, in order to be "child free" from 8:45 to 3:30 P.M. so she could have time to work on her dissertation, Patty would spend approximately two and a half hours driving her children to and from day care each day. Over the course of a week, this added up to twelve and a half hours, and over the course of a month, approximately fifty hours. Because she couldn't find or afford one child care center for all three of her children, Patty spent more than 600 hours a year driving them to and from three different child care sites, the equivalent of fifteen 40-hour work weeks.

HEAD START IS AMAZING

Samantha Mayer had "dreamed of being a Hawkeye" since she was a youngster. Her brother, Nathan, fourteen years her senior, had attended the University of Iowa and had sent Samantha sweatshirts, T-shirts, banners, and other university memorabilia that she wore or hung on her walls. Samantha's parents visited Nathan at least twice each year at UI, driving four hours from their hometown to Iowa City every year for homecoming and at least once in the spring. Samantha had always accompanied her parents on these excursions and "got the idea that Iowa was a good school, a really great school, and so I wanted to get a degree from Iowa." By the time she was "around seven or eight," she began to refer to her college savings account as the "Black and Gold fund," a name that reflected the UI school colors. Her parents added to this account every month. Samantha was so determined to attend UI that when she met with her high school guidance counselor during the summer before her freshman year to register for classes, she announced that she was going to UI after high school and wanted to know what the admission requirements were because she "would only take classes that would help me get in there." For the next several years, she did exactly that, making the honor roll every semester and refusing to consider any other colleges.

During her last year of high school, however, Samantha's life changed dramatically. In the fall, she met and "fell madly in love" with Maximus, an exchange student whose host family lived just down the block from Samantha's parents. She would often "sneak out" after her parents had gone to bed to spend time with him. When Samantha learned she was pregnant, she shared the news with Maximus, who was "very excited." She was afraid to tell her parents or anyone else, however, and kept the pregnancy hidden for over two months. On New Year's Day, after making a resolution to "stop lying to everyone," she finally told her parents; she described this as "the scariest thing I've ever had to do." They were furious and especially worried about how Samantha's pregnancy might reflect on her father, a member of the city council who endorsed a conservative Republican agenda and who planned to run for office in the Iowa State Legislature one day. Exactly one week after she told them, Samantha's parents woke her up "before it was even light" and informed her that they were taking her to a clinic that provided abortion services:

> It was something like an hour away, just over the state line. An abortion was the only option as far as they were concerned. And I actually went to the abortion clinic. They drove me there and dropped me off in front of the building while they went shopping and then they were just going to come pick me up after it was over. And I went in, but I didn't really know what I thought about abortion at the time. I didn't know if I agreed with it or not. But my parents were really quick to sign off on the consent forms because I was only seventeen and they had to do that. And I handed the woman those consent forms and then she sat me down for a counseling session and after talking to me for a while she told me that she couldn't let me go through with it because I didn't know if it was the right decision for me. I was totally crying. I didn't really want to have an abortion. I knew it was going to be hard to have this baby, but I was already emotionally attached to the idea of a baby. You know what I mean? And the counselor told me, "You can leave here as a seventeen-year-old, or you can leave here as an adult." I decided to leave as an adult.
>
> And so I left and went home and my parents were mad but they kept saying, "That's OK, you can still go back, you have a few more weeks to go back" and they just kept pushing and pushing me to get an abortion. And they would say all kinds of things like, "You still want to have a life, don't you? You still want to be able to go to college, don't you?" . . . And part of it was their status in the community. They didn't want everyone else to know. They didn't want to be ashamed.

Samantha's situation became more stressful as her pregnancy progressed. Her parents, angered by her decision not to have an abortion, "basically ignored me whenever I was home." They also demanded that she keep the pregnancy "hidden until they figured out how to tell everyone." After Samantha accepted Maximus's Valentine's Day marriage proposal, they became "slightly less angry . . . but still wanted to keep it hidden for as long as we could."

Hiding her pregnancy became increasingly difficult because Samantha was plagued by morning sickness so severe that her obstetrician prescribed an antinausea medication. When that failed to work, Samantha was hospitalized three times for severe dehydration before she was even halfway through the pregnancy. By late March, Samantha had missed so much school that her parents were called in for a meeting with the principal and the superintendent. When her parents explained the situation, the school officials were "somewhat understanding." However, they made it clear that if Samantha missed any more school she wouldn't be able to graduate on time. During a bout with the flu in May, Samantha was absent for an entire week of school and received incompletes in three of her classes. However, the superintendent, who had graduated from high school with Samantha's father, said that she would "still be able to walk through the graduation ceremony but just not get a signed diploma so nobody would know" that she hadn't graduated. Samantha felt that this was "typical of schools in small towns where they try to cover up when you do something they think is bad." The following summer was a busy one for Samantha. She gave birth to a daughter, who Maximus insisted they name Athena after his mother. She also married Maximus in a small courthouse ceremony, and they moved into a small apartment. Finally, after completing three courses at Iowa Western Community College (IWCC) in Council Bluffs, Samantha earned her high school diploma.

She spent most of the next year as a stay-at-home mom, taking care of Athena while Maximus pieced together various cash jobs, working over forty hours a week to support the family. However, it soon became apparent to both Samantha and Maximus that the marriage was not what they had hoped it would be. Shortly after Athena's first birthday, Maximus flew back to his country for a family wedding and made it clear that he did not intend to return to the United States. Unemployed and unable to pay rent, Samantha moved back in with her parents. She filed for divorce, and around what would have been their two-year wedding anniversary, the divorce was finalized. For the next two years, Samantha pursued full-time studies at IWCC, completing general education courses. Her goal was to complete her associate's degree and then fulfill her dream of transferring to UI to complete her bachelor's degree. In many ways, Samantha's parents were supportive. They allowed their daughter and granddaughter to live with them rent free. They also paid for Athena to attend a "really nice, expensive" day care center while Samantha attended classes. They watched Athena on the evenings and weekends if Samantha had a night class or needed time to study. They even paid for Samantha's books and tuition with her Black and Gold Fund. However, they did not support Samantha's specific educational goals. They wanted their daughter to complete the 86-semester-hour associate's degree in nursing at IWCC, despite that fact that she was "completely not at all interested in being a nurse." Her parents were so adamant that she pursue a nursing degree that they threatened to stop paying her educational expenses if she failed to comply. After explaining her situation to Marianne, her academic advisor at IWCC and a former single mother, Samantha declared a nursing major so that all of her "official forms and things would say 'nursing' on them." However, she did not take nursing courses. Instead, she enrolled in courses that fulfilled general education requirements and would facilitate her transfer to UI.

In January 2003, at the beginning of her final semester at IWCC, and with Marianne's help, Samantha applied to UI and was accepted. Samantha planned to live with her parents through the summer and then move with her daughter to Iowa City shortly before the fall term began. She knew the move would mean some significant changes for herself and her daughter, specifically in relation to her child care situation. Samantha would have less flexibility in her schedule, wouldn't be able to take any classes at night, and would have to "arrange my study time around her day care schedule." However, she also knew that there was "a lot of money, something like $31,000 left" in her college savings account, enough to cover tuition, books, and full-time day care for the two years it would take her to finish her degree. She planned to take out a small amount in student loans to cover her other living expenses.

On the day of her last final exam at IWCC, Samantha went home and told her parents about her plans. She had hoped they would be pleased that she had earned her two-year degree and was "still planning on going to a real college, to UI like I had always planned on doing." Instead, they spent the next several weeks trying to "talk me out of going, telling me that I should just be a mother or just go to school, but that I couldn't do both by myself." Samantha believed their response was prompted as much by their belief that she shouldn't be going to college "unless it was to do a nursing degree" as it was by her parents' desire for their granddaughter to remain living with them. When Samantha made it clear that she was going to UI and that she was taking Athena with her, things "got so bad that we moved in with my cousin and stayed with her for the rest of the summer." When she and Athena finally moved to Iowa City at the end of July, her parents "wouldn't help us pack and didn't drive here to help us move in or anything." Two days after she arrived, they called to let her know that they had "cut me off financially, thinking that if they [didn't] help me financially then I [wouldn't] be able to make it and [we would] be forced to come home."

Because Samantha's Black and Gold Fund was in her parents' names, she could not access her college savings account. Samantha knew that she could take out additional student loans, but she doubted that they would be enough to cover all of her living expenses plus the $575 she paid each month to the day care where she had enrolled her daughter. Near panic and "seriously thinking about just quitting school and moving back home," Samantha called Michael Knight, the UI academic advisor she had met a few weeks earlier when she had attended orientation. Michael had helped Samantha register for classes and he was "the only person I knew in Iowa City." Michael put her in touch with the UI Family Services Office, which put her in touch with one of the four Head Start child care centers in the Iowa City area. At the beginning of August, Samantha filled out an application for Head Start. She was put on the waiting list and informed that it could be anywhere from "two weeks to four or five months" before her daughter would be admitted to the program.[38] Samantha's classes at UI were scheduled to begin on August 25, less than three weeks away:

> I had no choice but to wait and see if something opened. . . . I was calling the Head Start program every day to check. And they kept saying no, but I kept calling anyway. But then someone cancelled at the last minute and they had a spot for my daughter but she couldn't start until September 1st, a week after classes started. And so it was good that she got in, but it was pretty stressful with the waiting and then having to try to find someone to watch her until the 1st.

Becca, a part-time KCC student who lived across the hall from Samantha in her apartment building, was also a single mother. Samantha had "gotten to know her a little bit when we were moving in." While Becca's class schedule "meant that she couldn't watch Athena all the time . . . [she] did help out a few times during the first week," babysitting Athena for an hour here and there while Samantha went to class and came home right afterward. However, Samantha simply had to skip some classes that first week because she did not have child care. She called or e-mailed her instructors and told them she was ill. While Samantha felt bad about missing classes and admitted that "it was hard and stressful," she justified her absences by claiming that "you don't really do much doing the first week anyway."

Samantha believed that she had "lucked out" in regard to the Head Start program, but in all likelihood, luck had very little to do with Athena's admission into the program. Head Start programs in the state of Iowa, as they do elsewhere across the country, prioritize enrollment for families that are categorized as low income because they fall below the federal poverty line or because they qualify for some form of public assistance such as TANF, food stamps, or Medicaid.[39] Because she was unemployed and had no income, Samantha lived far below the federal poverty guidelines. Thus, Athena was prioritized for participation in the program.[40] In addition, while it is not unusual for Head Start programs to have waiting lists even for those who do meet income eligibility guidelines for priority admission, applications are weighted in relation to various standards of need. Families that meet one or more of these criteria—including if the child was born to a teen parent, if the family is headed by a single parent, if English is a second language for the family, if there is documented or perceived threat of endangerment for the child and or the parent(s), or other child needs or family needs are deemed to be a factor in the household—are moved up on the waiting list.[41] Because Samantha's income was below federal poverty guidelines, because she was only eighteen when she gave birth to Athena, and because she was a single mother, her application was given higher priority than applications by families who did not meet these criteria. It wasn't luck that helped Samantha get Athena into Head Start; it was the specific circumstances of Samantha and Athena's lives and the ways those circumstances resonated with the philosophy of Head Start, particularly because the program seeks to "address a variety of concerns about children living in 'pockets of poverty.'"[42] In addition, it is important to note that a "last minute" cancellation by another family resulted in an available spot in the program for Athena. Had that cancellation not occurred, it seems likely that Athena would have remained on the waiting list, possibly for weeks or even months. Samantha admitted that this would have been "disastrous" and would have likely resulted in her withdrawal from the University of Iowa.

Athena's experience at Head Start was positive and Samantha was enthusiastic about the program:

> I just want to say that Head Start is amazing. Head Start is amazing! They do all kinds of stuff with the kids. They have them brush their teeth after meals and snacks. My daughter never did that at her old day care. They wash their hands all the time. They have [the kids] help set the table and clear their dishes and help clean up. And they do Spanish as part of their curriculum and that's just awesome! It's awesome for her to be exposed to that at such a young age . . . There are clear guidelines and a curriculum and things are well established. And she gets exposed to so many different backgrounds and cultures there, I think it's really good for her. It's incredible, really, to have friends from all over the world.

The significance Samantha attributed to the Head Start program was threefold. First, she was pleased with Head Start because of the positive things she felt Athena gained by attending the program. These included self-care habits such as brushing her teeth and washing her hands, increased independence through things such as helping set and clear the table, increased knowledge through the curriculum, and an appreciation of different cultures through the Spanish classes and through interacting with the other children who participated in the program. Second, Head Start helped Samantha remain in school despite her parents' lack of support. Finally, it provided a service that Samantha was not otherwise able to afford. Although Samantha was several semesters away from completing her bachelor's degree, Head Start had helped her fulfill her dream of "being a Hawkeye."

THE BATTLE OVER BEDTIME

Amber Brown was an easygoing, talkative young woman. She was quite charming, yet I found myself quite irritated during my initial interview with her. Throughout our time together, Amber's cell phone sat on the table between us.

This device revealed a great deal about her life as a single mother, particularly one who still lived with her parents and who relied on them for child care. During the eighty-four minutes I spent with Amber, her cell phone vibrated not once, not twice, not three times, but fifteen times. The first few times, I offered to stop recording our interview so she could answer her phone, but she simply looked at the caller identification display, rolled her eyes, and let the call go to voice mail. As calls continued to come in throughout the interview, Amber told me that "it's my mom, calling to check up on me, to see where I am. She does that all the time, I'm talking like twenty to thirty times a day." I initially thought she was exaggerating, as people sometimes do when they are frustrated. But then she showed me the long list of "incoming calls" for the day—it listed "home" over and over and over from the top of the display to the bottom. Aggravated and annoyed by the situation, Amber described feeling "totally stuck" because of her child care arrangement.

Like Samantha, Amber had become a mother when she was still in high school. Her son, Aydan, was born midway through her junior year. She took two weeks off after the birth to "sort of recover, if you can ever recover from giving birth," and then resumed her full-time course schedule. However, unlike Samantha, she did not marry the father of her child. Instead, she focused on her education. When her son was fifteen months old, and wearing the cords that represented the high honors she had earned due to her 3.94 overall GPA, Amber walked across the stage to accept her high school diploma. The following week, she began working thirty hours a week at a telemarketing company in order to save money for college. Three months later, Amber was back in school, taking nine credit hours of course work at the Iowa City campus of Kirkwood Community College. She intended to complete her associate of arts degree and then transfer to UI to complete a bachelor's degree.

When Amber found out she was pregnant, she "wasn't completely surprised" because she and her boyfriend had never been very consistent about using birth control. She was, however, worried about telling her parents. Her father, an insurance agent, and her mother, a stay-at-home wife and mother who had entered a convent and intended to become a nun before meeting and marrying Amber's father, were "very religious people" and "very traditional." They believed that sex should take place only within marriage and only for procreative purposes. Still, Amber had "always had a close relationship with them," and she felt that she needed to tell them as soon as possible "because I couldn't go through this all by myself." One evening, as she sat across the dinner table from her parents, Amber let them know that she was expecting a baby. They were "very disappointed. Very, very disappointed." Her father began to cry and walked out of the room. Her mother "grabbed her rosary and prayed for like a week straight."

However, Amber's parents were also "very pro-life" and once they got over their initial shock, "they were definitely supportive" of her decision to continue the pregnancy and keep the baby. They also promised to support her in whatever ways they could.

During Amber's pregnancy, they supported her in a variety of ways. They helped her find an OB-GYN who specialized in adolescent pregnancy and took turns accompanying her to prenatal appointments. Both of her parents were in the room with Amber when she had an ultrasound at sixteen weeks. They also helped her locate resources in the Iowa City community, identifying organizations and groups that they believed would support the emotional, social, financial, and spiritual needs of teen mothers and single mothers. First, they contacted Concern for Women, a Catholic-based nonprofit organization they had learned about from their priest. Affiliated with the Iowa Right to Life Committee, Concern for Women "aids women in crisis pregnancy." In addition to offering free pregnancy tests, the organization provided "abortion alternatives . . . referrals to other agencies, clothing, counseling, furniture, hospital calls, labor and delivery coaches."[43] Through a conversation with "a close friend at work," Amber's dad learned about United Action for Youth. While this organization was perhaps best known in the community for its programming and outreach activities such as art workshops, recreational activities, services for runaways, and hotlines such as Teenline/Telefriend and Buddy Line,[44] the United Way–funded organization also operated the Teen Parent Transitional Program through its Family Services Center. The program provided respite child care and prenatal and well-baby checks with a pediatric nurse practitioner and offered weekly support groups to give young parents "a break to take care of their own needs."[45] Through that program, Amber learned about other resources in the community. These included the WIC food program;[46] Birthright of Iowa City, a local chapter of Birthright International, a pro-life organization that "offers positive alternatives to the pregnant woman";[47] and The Nest, an incentive-based educational program that promoted "early and consistent prenatal care and health education in order to increase healthy births and families in Johnson County."[48] In fact, Amber participated in so many groups and group-related activities that she felt overwhelmed:

> I was only eight or nine weeks when I found out I was pregnant, so I participated in those programs really early on in my pregnancy and still do participate in some of them. . . . As soon as I found out I was pregnant, I was calling places and figuring out what I needed and all of that. And I got so busy when I was pregnant, participating in all of the programs and everything. It was like I had something going on every night of the week for a while. Seriously! Every night! And I finally just had to drop a few things because I couldn't do it all and keep up with my

homework. Like appointments here and there and classes and visits with the doctor and then group sessions and then meetings with my social worker at UAY [United Action for Youth] once a week and with somebody else once a week. It just got to be overwhelming. I got exhausted from constantly having to be at one thing or another, so I dropped a few things . . . and that was a little better.

After Aydan was born, Amber's parents continued to be "a very strong support system." In addition to "really loving Aydan and spending lots and lots of time with him," they allowed Amber and Aydan to continue living with them rent free. In addition, Amber's mother, who did not work outside the home, "went from being stay-at-home mom to stay-at-home grandma." She provided child care for Aydan free of charge from the time he was born as Amber completed her high school education, began her job, and then began her studies at KCC. In fact, because of Amber's hectic schedule, her mother spent "more time with [Aydan] than I do most weeks."

Amber recognized that her child care situation provided her with "some unique options that other [single mothers] probably don't have." For example, because she did not have to drive her son to day care, her mornings were relatively stress free and she didn't feel rushed. In addition, because she didn't have to worry about getting to a day care center before it closed, she was able to stay on campus after her classes were finished for the day to study in the library or work in the computer lab to finish assignments before she went home. This was important, she said, both because she couldn't "do homework with a kid hanging off of me" and because it allowed her to "really focus" on her son when they were together in the evenings. Finally, because she did not have to pay for child care, Amber was able "make ends meet" on her rather limited income. Her only regular bills were her cell phone, health insurance for herself and Aydan, and her transportation expenses, which included car payments, gas, and automobile insurance. This left her with "enough money to buy food and clothes for me and Aydan and diapers and toys and other things for him" and pay for her tuition and books each semester. However, after paying for all of these things, she was left with little discretionary income. In fact, her finances were so tight that if she wanted to "do something fun, it has to be pretty cheap, like all-you-can-eat wings on Tuesday nights and even that doesn't happen very often."

Though her child care arrangements provided her with some distinct advantages, Amber identified child care as a major source of stress in her life. She and her parents had different ideas about how her son should be raised and what sorts of things he should and should not be allowed to do. When Amber was at school or work, her mother would "let Aydan do all kinds of things that I don't want him doing, so [we] definitely have disagreements about child rearing." One of the major disagreements concerned Aydan's bedtime:

We have this argument in my household between me and my parents. During the week, I have to get up at 4:45 A.M. in order to get to work by 6:00. And then I work until 2:00 P.M. and then go to classes in the afternoon. And 4:45 A.M. is pretty early to get up. And my parents think that my son should stay up until 10:00 P.M. and then sleep as late as he wants in the morning. If he stays up that late, then he usually doesn't get up until like 8:00 A.M. or even 9:00 A.M. sometimes if he's really tired. He sleeps a long time. And it would be fine if I could do the same, but I have to get up at 4:45 A.M. and so I think he should go to bed earlier, like around 8:00 P.M. or 8:30 P.M. so I can get a full night of sleep. In the evening, he is my responsibility. My mom watches him all day, so at night, I take care of my son. And I think he should go to bed earlier, but my mom doesn't think that's right and neither does my dad.

I don't see what difference it makes. My mom always says that if he goes to bed too early then he's going to get up early in the morning, too, like around 6:30 A.M. or something like that. I don't see what difference it makes. She gets up at 5:00 A.M. to make my dad breakfast and pack his lunch and help him get ready for work anyway. So she's already awake. And it's always this big battle, and they end up winning every time because they say that it's my mom who has to watch him in the morning and so she gets to say how late he should be sleeping in the morning. And I always say that I'm his mom and so I should get to say when he goes to bed at night. And then they always come back and say that it's their house and I have to do what they say as long as I live there, and that pretty much ends the conversation right there. What can I say to that?

Amber was grateful for the support her parents had provided during her pregnancy and since Aydan was born. However, in accepting their support, she also found herself in a difficult situation. She worked almost full time but didn't have enough money for pay for child care. Although her job paid only $7.00 an hour, her income was too high to meet eligibility requirements for Head Start.[49] Because her parents still claimed her as a dependent for tax purposes, she was required to include their income on her Free Application for Federal Student Aid (FAFSA). Amber was not considered to have "unmet financial need" according to the FAFSA standards and did not qualify for a Pell Grant, a Federal Supplemental Educational Opportunity Grant (FSEOG), or other grants that might have enabled her to pursue other child care arrangements. Amber did qualify for student loans and could have used them to pay for child care, but she was "trying to stay away from them at all costs" because she couldn't imagine how she would repay student loans and raise a child on her own, even with a college degree.

Amber felt stuck. She didn't have enough income to pay for child care, but she felt that her parents didn't treat her like an adult and certainly didn't give her the kind of autonomy she believed she was entitled to as a parent. And this, she feared, would have a long-term, negative effect on her relationship with her son. As our interview neared its end, Amber's phone vibrated for the fourteenth time and she finally answered it. It was her mother, calling to find out where she was. Amber reminded her that she was "doing an interview for that research project on single moms" and said that we were just finishing up and she would be home soon. After hanging up, Amber offered a final thought on why she believed improving access to day care was the most important thing postsecondary institutions could do to help single mother students:

> Kirkwood is building this new building on the Iowa City campus, this big building, and there isn't even a day care in it. None at all. Just more classrooms and offices and stuff. Why wouldn't they put a day care in there? They could have added another floor, make it three stories instead of two, and put the day care on the first floor and made some of the space around the building into a playground instead of more parking . . . just having day care and making it more affordable for single mothers who are students, and for all low-income parents.

I asked Amber to explain what access to that type of day care would mean to her. But before she could answer, her cell phone vibrated for the fifteenth time. She picked up the phone and showed me the display: "home." Shaking her head, Amber answered my question: "It would give me some independence. I could be treated like an adult." She tucked her cell phone into her pocket, grabbed her keys off the table, and drove home to her son. And her parents.

FROM ONE STEP BEHIND TO UNEXCUSED ABSENCES

Twenty-five-year-old Jessica Donnelly described herself as a "former bad kid, a really bad kid" who dropped out of school when she was in ninth grade. She spent the next seven years "sort of aimlessly drifting around" with a group of friends who "weren't very good." At twenty-one, she became pregnant. Though it was unplanned, the pregnancy became Jessica's motivation for "turning my life around," and she studied for and passed her GED examination before giving birth. After her daughter, Molly, was born, Jessica enrolled at KCC in Cedar Rapids. She completed her general education requirements and then transferred to UI to pursue her bachelor's degree. When I first interviewed her in March 2004, Jessica was a senior and was nearing the end of her third semester at UI. She was a full-time student, a full-time single mother, and she worked twenty hours a week. Her college graduation was only a little over a year away, and she had already started exploring graduate programs because "I *am* going to get my doctorate. End of story."

Jessica was eager to talk about her child care experiences and told me that they were somewhat different when she was a student at KCC than they had been since she began taking classes at UI. However, child care had been a struggle at both institutions. Jessica had started the process of arranging child care when she was still pregnant. She put her name on the waiting list at Kirkwood Kids when she was only four months pregnant, around the same time she began studying for her GED. This was Jessica's strategy to help ensure that her child would be admitted to Kirkwood Kids—she would stay on the waiting list while she was pregnant and by the time she completed her GED and was ready to start at KCC, a spot would be available. At least that was what she hoped would happen. Of course Jessica knew there were other child care options in the area, but she liked the convenience of having the child care center "right on campus." A strong advocate of breastfeeding, Jessica intended to breastfeed her daughter during breaks between classes. Sadly, Jessica's strategy for getting Molly into Kirkwood Kids did not pay off. In fact, Molly was never admitted to the center during the entire year and a half that Jessica was a student at KCC:

> It's so hard to get into that day care. And they don't seem to like to take younger children, which most places don't. They have a very limited number of spaces for little kids, you know, kids through like six months. . . . And when I finally do get a call, it's that she has been admitted into the infant room for kids who are six months and under and she was already eight months old. So we had to turn it down, of course. And then the next time we got a call that she had been admitted was when she was fifteen months old, almost sixteen months, and it was for the room that is only for kids aged six to twelve months, so we couldn't take that spot either. It was like they were always one step behind. And I know they have a lot of kids enrolled, but there is a high demand for it and they don't have enough space to meet the demand of all the students who need somewhere to take their kids while they're attending classes.

Jessica ultimately paid a friend to watch Molly. While this "worked out fine because she was married and stayed home with her three kids anyway and earned a little money babysitting," it wasn't nearly as convenient as the child care center on campus would have been. In addition to "having to drive twenty minutes completely out of my way" both morning and night to go to and from the babysitter, Jessica couldn't breastfeed Molly between classes. She carried a breast pump with her and expressed breast milk in the only places she could find—her car or, if the weather was too cold, the bathroom stalls on the KCC campus.[50]

As Jessica neared completion of her associate's degree at KCC and was preparing to transfer to UI, she hoped to find a much different child care situation. In particular, she imagined she would "have a better chance" of getting into one of the seven campus-affiliated child care centers she found on the UI Family Services website. She was impressed by the number of lactation rooms that were available across the UI campus.[51] However, things did not work out as Jessica had hoped. The waiting lists at the child care centers were very long. In fact, when I interviewed Jessica, Molly's name had been on those waiting lists for nearly two years and she had still not been admitted. Jessica had managed to make other child care arrangements with an in-home provider she had found through 4Cs. However, she would have preferred to have Molly at one of the campus-affiliated centers, both because of the convenience and "because at a babysitter, you don't have a curriculum. She's three-and-a-half now and it's time for her to start doing preschool stuff, and she's not getting that at her babysitter." In addition, because Molly's babysitter isn't licensed by the state of Iowa, Jessica does not qualify for a child care subsidy through the federally funded CCAMPIS: Child Care Access Means Parents in School program, a child care subsidy that is administered through the University of Iowa Family Services Office.[52] Thus, Jessica must pay for all of Molly's child care expenses on her own.

Child care at UI posed other challenges for Jessica. Molly was a relatively healthy child and did not suffer from any chronic diseases, but she had had the usual childhood encounters with colds, flu, and viruses. If Molly was only mildly ill, her babysitter would still watch her. However, if she had a fever or was vomiting, Molly could not go to the babysitter's house. When she was a student at KCC and these situations cropped up, Jessica would simply stay home with her daughter. The Kirkwood instructors did not seem to think it was a problem "if you needed to miss class because your child was sick" and would consider it an excused absence. There was even one instance when Jessica had a midterm exam and eight-month-old Molly "was only a little sick, with this itty-bitty fever . . . but you can't take kids to day care if their temperature is over 100 degrees." Jessica called her instructor and explained the situation. The instructor gave her the option of rescheduling the exam or bringing Molly with her to campus so she could take the midterm as scheduled. Jessica chose the latter, sitting in the front row of the classroom to take her exam while Molly slept in the stroller next to her.

Jessica encountered a distinctly different attitude about bringing children to class among the faculty at UI. She claimed that they "don't even begin to comprehend child care issues or problems at all." On several occasions, UI faculty members refused to excuse Jessica's absences when she had to miss a class because Molly was ill. Most of her instructors considered Jessica's absences unexcused when Molly had to be hospitalized:

The simple truth is that they dismiss the fact that I have a child and they don't think a sick child is a reason for missing class. And frankly, a sick child should be an excused absence; it is a legitimate reason for missing class. And I'm sure they'd just freak out if I just showed up with a kid in class here. That wouldn't be OK here, it wouldn't be accepted here.

And I had to actually drop out during my first semester here because she got really sick. And my professors didn't care. She spent four days in the hospital with pneumonia and then couldn't go anywhere for a few days afterward, not even to the babysitter, and it was during midterm week, and only one out of my five instructors was willing to consider it an excused absence. The rest didn't care and wouldn't let me make up any work. I was mad. Very mad. But there was nothing I could do.

Having missed midterm exams in all of her courses and with only one instructor willing to excuse the absence and allow her to make up the exam, Jessica withdrew from classes. She felt it was the "only option if I didn't want my final semester grades to be completely awful." Withdrawing, of course, meant Jessica had to retake those same courses the following semester. And this meant taking out additional student loans in order to pay for the courses a second time.

Child care was also an issue for Jessica when she had to participate in out-of-class activities for her courses such as group projects and attendance at guest lectures. Jessica could only afford to pay for child care during the time she was in class or at work. Thus, the group projects she had been assigned for several of her classes at UI had been "so difficult for me to do . . . because I can't afford extra child care." On several occasions, Jessica invited others involved in these group projects to meet at her house so she wouldn't have to hire a babysitter but could still fully participate in the project. However, other group members did not want to meet there; they preferred to "meet at the Java House [a coffee shop] or over drinks late at night which basically means I can't go because I don't have child care." In one course, students were required to attend a guest lecture and write a response to if they wanted to earn higher than a C in the course. Jessica explained her situation, hoping the professor, "a mother of two children . . . would understand that I don't have money to hire a babysitter on weeknights." The professor told Jessica that if she didn't attend the lecture, the best she could hope to earn in the course was a C. Though she would have liked to have taken some sort of action, perhaps by raising a complaint with the university, Jessica didn't feel this was a realistic option:

I feel completely powerless here. I don't have enough time to even think about what to feed my daughter for breakfast much less get together with other single mothers and try to organize around child care issues and make change on this campus. I don't have time for that. It's important, but I don't have time for it. My schedule is packed already. If I added one more thing to my schedule, I wouldn't be able to sleep.

Not wanting her 3.88 GPA to drop because of "the only grade lower than an A I would have ever gotten in college," Jessica dropped the course.

CONCLUSION

Clearly, child care was a vital consideration for many women. Yet the child care issues they faced were not exactly the same. Some women did not have difficulty locating child care or paying for it, particularly women who lived with parents or other family members who assumed responsibility for the children while the mothers attended classes or went to work. For others, child care was not a pressing issue at all, particularly for Tilda, whose children had access to supervised extracurricular activities that occupied their time. However, for the majority of the women, arranging child care was an ever-present concern. Those who were unable to find and or afford child care, including for times when their children were ill, often found themselves unable to meet academic responsibilities such as attending class. For some, this jeopardized their ability to complete academic work and jeopardized their grades. This was certainly the case for Jessica. For others, like Evelyn, the child care challenges they faced resulted in limited access to higher education. Access to child care also had a significant impact on the women's ability to work and earn much-needed income. This was true for Amber, whose mother cared for her son while Amber attended classes and worked. In contrast, Patty's lack of access to child care presented a barrier to employment.

The availability of child care varied from one academic institution to another. Texas Woman's University did not have a traditional child care center on campus or off-campus child care centers. However, it did have an after-school program and a summer program for elementary-aged children.[53] Although both the University of Iowa and Kirkwood Community College had campus-affiliated child care centers,[54] these centers were open to the public. In fact, only one child care center at either institution, the University of Iowa Hospitals and Clinics (UIHC) Child Care Center, also known as Bright Horizons, required institutional affiliation; it enrolled only children whose parents were full-time permanent employees of UIHC or full-time permanent faculty members at UI. And while some other affiliated centers, such as the Mary Jo Small Child Care Center at Brookland Woods on the UI campus, required that a certain percentage of the families they enrolled had to be UI student families, demand far outweighed availability at these centers. In addition, fees were typically high at campus-affiliated centers and often were not feasible given the women's economic realities. Finally, long waiting lists at campus-affiliated centers were generally the norm. According to the single mothers and the support staff I interviewed, the wait depended on the age of the child. Those with infants encountered waits that typically ranged from one to two years. Clearly, university-affiliated centers did not solve the women's child care dilemmas.

Lest readers think this is an exaggeration, I want to share my own experiences with child care on the UI campus. In November 2002, not yet halfway through my second pregnancy, I visited several of the UI-affiliated child care centers and put my name on the waiting lists for their infant rooms, hoping that by the fall 2003 semester there would be either a part-time or full-time opening. In May 2005, as I completed my doctoral studies and graduated from the university, my daughter—who had just celebrated her second birthday—had still not made it to the top of the waiting list for infant care at any of the UI child care centers. Although I was able to make other child care arrangements during her first two years—hiring a part-time nanny and coordinating schedules with my husband so that one of us taught classes or conducted research while the other was responsible for child care—such arrangements were possible only because of the privileges we enjoyed as members of a two-parent, two-income household.

As I discussed at the beginning of this chapter, child care issues in America are tied to the financial circumstances of each family. Some of the women I interviewed were able to ease their child care burdens, at least in part, by applying for child care subsidies through the postsecondary institutions they attended or through grants from social service agencies. Although such assistance was welcome, it was usually a nominal amount that covered only a fraction of total child care expenses. In contrast, free child care programs such as Head Start were immensely helpful for those whose income was below the poverty line, such as Samantha. Yet it was often the case that those who were part of the working poor found themselves in a catch-22 situation. On the one hand, employment provided much-needed income to help meet educational and living expenses. On the other hand, if their earnings exceeded federally established guidelines, they were deemed ineligible for social service programs. In this case, they had to pay for child care expenses out of their wages, make child care arrangements with family or friends, or pay for child care with student loans.

Many of the women took out student loans to pay for child care. However, only about half of the women who participated in this project knew this was an option for them as college students. All of the women who were receiving financial aid were required to fill out a FAFSA and include a federal tax return as part of their application. Tax returns include information about dependents and any child care expenses paid in the previous year. Crucially, however, child care expenses are not automatically calculated as part of the cost of attendance for college students who are parents. Those who wished to take out student loans to pay for child care had to take the extra step of requesting additional loans on the FAFSA verification form under the section marked "exceptional circumstances." For those who knew about this option, additional loans made it somewhat easier to afford child care. However, taking out additional loans was not an ideal solution: although loans helped the women pay for child care, they had the long-term consequences of increasing the amount and the duration of student loan repayments.

It is difficult to know how to best go about addressing the child care situation single mothers who are college students face. There is an increasing need for child care services among postsecondary students overall and there have been strong arguments about how such services function as a crucial means of support for college students who are pursuing degrees while also raising children.[55] At present, student parents constitute a sizeable portion of the overall U.S. college student population: "Nearly a quarter of the postsecondary students in the United States, or 3.9 million students, are parents. . . . Of these 3.9 million student parents, 2.2 million (57%) are low-income; one third of low-income students are also parents. Half of student parents are married, and half are unmarried. . . . Twelve percent of undergraduate students, or 1.9 million students, are single parents, of whom 1.5 million (78%) are low-income."[56]

Given the obvious need for child care among student parents, it seems there is an equally obvious solution to this situation: create on-campus or campus-affiliated child care facilities. Doing so could help alleviate the child care challenges student parents face. Yet simply providing on-campus child care will not sufficiently address the problem. The women who were enrolled at campuses with on-site child care or affiliated off-campus centers still faced a variety of issues such as waiting lists and high costs. Any so-called solution to the current child care crisis on college campuses must address these factors. This might be done in a number of ways, including prioritizing enrollment for children of students and implementing sliding fee scales in order to make child care more affordable, particularly for low-income students. However, doing so may result in unanticipated financial outcomes for the child care centers and jeopardize their existence. If the children of students are prioritized for enrollment, it is possible that campus child care centers will not have full enrollment over the summer months when many college students do not take classes, resulting in a loss of revenue. Furthermore, child care centers that implement a sliding fee scale could find themselves in a financial bind if the tuition they collect each month is not enough to meet expenses. Prioritizing enrollment for children of students and implementing sliding fee scales at campus-based child care centers could jeopardize the financial sustainability of such centers.

It is also far too simple to suggest that campuses that do not currently have child care centers should just build them. Constructing new buildings or remodeling existing structures typically requires a significant capital investment. There are numerous other expenses, such as supplies, salaries and training for staff, licensing for both staff and the facility itself, educational materials, furnishings, and similar considerations. With campuses across the country tightening their belts to curb expenses, it will be a challenge to convince educational institutions to invest their resources in child care. Yet unless the increasing demand for child care among college students is addressed, it seems likely that single mothers and other students with children, like many American families, will remain mired in the current child care crisis.

5 · MOTHERING ALONE IN A CHILLY CLIMATE

On January 14, 2005, Harvard president Lawrence H. Summers delivered a lecture at the conference "Diversifying the Science & Engineering Workforce: Women, Underrepresented Minorities, and their S & E Careers." Summers acknowledged the underrepresentation of women in tenured positions in science and engineering fields at major research universities and expressed a desire to promote equality. Yet it was another portion of his address, in which Summers evaluated various explanations for continuing gender inequalities, that received the most attention. Minimizing the role of gender socialization in perpetuating gender inequalities, Summers suggested it was the innate biological differences between males and females and the resulting natural preferences that in large part explained why women were hired and promoted less often than males in science and engineering fields:

> There may also be elements, by the way, of differing, there is some, particularly in some attributes, that bear on engineering, there is reasonably strong evidence of taste differences between little girls and little boys that are not easy to attribute to socialization. . . . While I would prefer to believe otherwise, I guess my experience with my two-and-a-half-year-old twin daughters who were not given dolls and who were given trucks, and found themselves saying to each other, "Look, daddy truck is carrying the baby truck," tells me something. And I think it's just something that you probably have to recognize. There are two other hypotheses that are all over. One is socialization. Somehow little girls are all socialized toward nursing and little boys are socialized toward building bridges. No doubt there is some truth in that. I would be hesitant about assigning too much weight to that hypothesis.[1]

Summers's remarks incited immediate responses from both individual scholars and professional academic organizations. Some offered evidence from their own campuses that refuted Summers's claims about "taste differences" and pointed to the "growing numbers of women who have demonstrated not only extraordinary innate ability, but the kinds of creativity, determination, perceptiveness, and hard work that are prerequisites for success in science and engineering."[2] Others critiqued Summers's ignorance of current research that "measures . . . gender differences in such areas as verbal, mathematical, and spatial abilities . . . [and is] showing virtually no difference at the present time."[3] Still others called for Summers's resignation, deeming his remarks a reflection of ongoing sexism in higher education.[4] Summers quickly issued an apology, and in what seems to have been an obvious attempt to minimize negative publicity, Harvard University formed two task forces to "develop concrete ways to better recruit women and support the careers of female scholars at Harvard, especially in science and engineering [and] announced plans to create a senior position in the central administration to focus on the recruitment and advancement of women on the faculty."[5] Yet these actions did little to quell the controversy or to dispel the ensuing debates about the pervasiveness of sexism in science and engineering fields overall and about sexism at Harvard.

Several years later, another Ivy League institution, Yale University, found itself embroiled in its own sexism controversy. In October 2010, members of Delta Kappa Epsilon (DKE) fraternity marched across the Yale campus while chanting obscenities that many regarded as promoting rape. The university administration immediately received reports about the event, including video recordings of the fraternity members chanting, "No means yes! Yes means anal!" The administration was initially slow to take action. The situation escalated, however, when various members of the Yale community came forward with evidence and claims of a culture of sexism at the university. Their evidence included a photo of members of the Zeta Psi fraternity posing outside the Yale Women's Center with a sign that read "We Love Yale Sluts" and copies of a widely circulated e-mail with the subject line "The Preseason Scouting Report" that rated incoming freshman girls on the basis of perceived attractiveness and sexual desirability. In early 2011, in response to these and similar complaints, including the administration's alleged failure to respond adequately to reports of sexual harassment, rape, and sexual assault, the U.S. Department of Education's Office for Civil Rights launched an investigation that functioned as a "climate check" to determine if the institutional climate at Yale was unwelcoming or hostile to women.[6] As a result of the investigation, Yale voluntarily implemented changes to policies and procedures in order to make the institution more compliant with Title IX.[7]

The chilly climate of sexism is certainly not new in higher education. In the early 1980s, prompted by increases in female enrollment in institutions of higher education and by post–Title IX concerns about sexual equality and public education, researchers examined women's experiences at colleges and universities across the United States. In their groundbreaking study, Bernice Sandler and Roberta Hall found that although most colleges and universities had adapted their formal policies and practices to reflect Title IX's prohibition of discrimination on the basis of sex, institutional climate remained a significant concern. They found that faculty behavior toward students both in and out of the classroom continued to disadvantage female students:

> Most faculty want to treat all students fairly and as individuals with particular talents and abilities. However, some faculty may *overtly*—or, more often, *inadvertently*—treat men and women students differently in the classroom and in related learning situations. Subtle biases in the way teachers behave toward students may seem so "normal" that the particular behaviors which express them often go unnoticed. Nevertheless, these patterns, by which women students are either singled out or ignored because of their sex, may leave women students feeling less confident than their male classmates about their abilities and their place in the college community.[8]

Their results detailed how seemingly small behaviors—such as grouping students according to sex, interrupting female students, making comments that deem women intellectually inferior to men, and using sexist humor in the classroom—created a detrimental climate for female students. Furthermore, they found that particular groups of women may be especially affected, including racial and ethnic minorities, older students, graduate students, and those in traditionally male-dominated fields such as science and mathematics. Subsequent research has documented additional dimensions of the academic climate for women, including how everyday behaviors of faculty, students, staff, and administrators contribute to an atmosphere that often reinforces gender stereotypes and positions women as "outsiders or marginals."[9] This positioning or marginality has been linked to negative intellectual outcomes for female undergraduate students and to the reinforcement of professional barriers that "limit women's productivity and advancement," including their likelihood of being granted tenure.[10]

One of the key aspects of studies of the campus climate has been their attention to previously unexamined facets of women's experience in postsecondary institutions, such as how those experiences are shaped by the intersection of women's reproductive and intellectual lives. Such investigations have helped illuminate some of the struggles female faculty members who are mothers face and have illustrated how the "simultaneous demands of family and career weigh heavily on women who continually balance the two obligations and discard, modify, or question traditional (gender) expectations."[11] In recent years, discussions of the "family track" in academia have moved beyond simply identifying the problem and have stressed the importance of creating and instituting policies to make college campuses a more "family-friendly" environment for scholars.[12] While most analyses continue to focus on the experiences of married women, the particular challenges of faculty members who are also single mothers have received increasing attention.[13]

As important as these examinations are, they have provided only a limited understanding of the experiences of women on college and university campuses, particularly because the experiences of students who are also mothers have been largely ignored. I do not mean to suggest that there have been no studies of this demographic. In the early 1980s, researchers investigated the experiences of female graduate students and concluded that they were evaluated according to a particular set of assumptions that hinged on women's reproductive and maternal roles:

> If women students are already married, faculty may assume they will have children and then drop out of school or leave their profession. If they have young children, faculty may feel that women students should be at home caring for them, and may advise them that a woman cannot properly combine school and a demanding professional career with a family. Indeed, prospective female graduate students may be asked how they plan to combine their career with family—a question rarely asked of male applicants.[14]

Subsequent explorations have indicated that the campus climate poses specific challenges for students who are mothers. However, attention to this issue is infrequent, and it tends to privilege the experiences of married female graduate students.[15] In assessments of the chilly climate, there is a conspicuous absence of attention to the treatment of single mothers who are students on college and university campuses, including both graduate and undergraduate students.

This oversight is particularly important to address in light of the family values rhetoric in American political discourse. This rhetoric dominated the welfare reform debates of the late twentieth century and was the foundation for the sweeping welfare reform of the 1990s that abandoned AFDC and replaced it with TANF. It also put strict time limits on receipt of aid and empowered individual states to experiment with and implement additional welfare reform measures, including marriage promotion policies[16] and child exclusion policies.[17] As numerous scholars have argued, the legislative debates that drove welfare reform relied heavily on stereotypes that characterized single mothers as social deviants who deserved to be punished, particularly if their social and economic circumstances led them to seek public assistance.[18] In other words, poor single mothers were stigmatized. The social uses and consequences of stigmatization are significant:

> Society establishes the means of categorizing persons and the complement of attributes felt to be ordinary and natural for the members of each of these catego- ries. Social settings establish the categories of persons likely to be encountered there. . . . While a stranger is present before us, evidence can arise of his possess- ing an attribute that makes him different from others in the category of person available for him to be, and of a less desirable kind—in the extreme, a person who is quite thoroughly bad, or dangerous, or weak. He is thus reduced in our minds from a whole and usual person to a tainted, discounted one. Such an attribute is a stigma. . . . Note, too, that not all undesirable attributes are at issue, but only those which are incongruous with our stereotype of what a given type of indi- vidual should be.[19]

In the late twentieth-century U.S. political climate that gave rise to welfare reform, a climate that privileged heteronormativity and the nuclear family and was bolstered by nostalgic notions of the "traditional family" and by Christian beliefs, single mothers were deemed different, un-American, and a problem that needed to be addressed.[20] Stigmatization of single mothers was a pervasive component of U.S. society during this period, and it impacted single mothers' personal relationships and their self-concept and identity.[21] It also permeated various social institutions, including human service agencies, where it deterred some needy families from applying for assistance.[22]

In this chapter, I examine the chilly climate of higher education in order to demonstrate how broader contemporary American attitudes toward single motherhood are manifested in the context of higher education. The narratives I have included illustrate the multiple ways that social actors, practices, poli- cies, and expectations aggregate and help shape the academic experiences of sin- gle mothers. I argue that these women faced a challenge unique to the context of postsecondary education institutions: a chilly climate that stigmatized them spe- cifically because of an identity created on the basis of their marital status and their status as parents.[23] I do not mean to suggest that single mothers who are not col- lege students escape stigma or that single mothers attending college are somehow more or less stigmatized than single mothers who are not college students. Rather, my aim is to detail the unique dimensions of the stigmatization single mothers face within the very particular context of the American postsecondary institu- tion. As I shall demonstrate, such stigmatization is evident in both obvious and subtle ways, including in the actions and attitudes of faculty, staff, and students and in formal and informal institutional policies. This stigmatization impacts single mothers across the educational spectrum, including both undergraduate and graduate students and those completing certificate, job-training, and professional programs. However, college campuses are not monolithic when it comes to the treatment of single mothers. As the narratives in this chapter illustrate, some of the campuses had a more welcoming and supportive climate than others. I also do not wish to imply that all of the women had the same experience regarding institutional climate, even when they attended the same institution. It is also important to remember that those who encountered a chilly climate did not bear this stigmatization or its effects passively. On the contrary, they used a variety of strategies to manage their identity that included passing, using techniques of information control, and covering.[24] They also actively challenged the stereotypes of single mothers they encountered in classrooms and across campus. In doing so, they helped shape knowledge and counter stigma and took important steps to help adjust the thermostat and make institutions of higher education a bit less chilly for themselves and other single mothers.

SINGLE MOTHERHOOD AS UNACCEPTABLE

Serena Chen arrived at UI with lofty academic and career goals. The twenty-three-year-old Chinese American woman moved to Iowa City in August 1999, eager to begin graduate studies in the humanities. Her boyfriend, Collin, accompanied her and planned to find a job and help support her while she completed her studies. Serena had just completed her bachelor's degree at a prestigious East Coast university. She had received a substantial scholarship to UI and had her future "completely planned out." She intended to earn her master's degree and then her PhD. Afterward, she planned to move directly into a tenure-track position at a university where she would combine research and teaching. Although Serena knew she eventually wanted to have a child, she didn't plan to pursue motherhood until "long, long after I was tenured somewhere."

Things were going according to plan until the spring of 2001, when Serena, who was writing her master's thesis, became pregnant. She was "initially shocked . . . because I hadn't planned it and had been using birth control and this didn't fit into my plans at all." Yet she soon found herself feeling excited about the idea of having a baby, particularly as she and Collin were planning on getting married before the end of the year, and "that seemed to make it OK, that we were going to be married." Collin, however, was less enthusiastic about the pregnancy. Initially, he didn't believe that Serena was pregnant; when Serena began to experience morning sickness, he told her "you're probably just getting the flu or something." After Serena confirmed the pregnancy with her doctor, however, Collin told her to have an abortion. Serena refused, explaining that she had "really started to like the idea of this baby growing inside of me." Collin responded by "ma[king] it clear that he wasn't ready to have a child yet."

He packed up his belongings and moved back to the small town in Pennsylvania where he grew up. Since his departure, Serena had not had any contact with Collin.

Despite the fact that Serena had what she characterized as a "close relationship" with her parents before the pregnancy, their response to the news that they were going to be grandparents was not what Serena had expected or hoped for. Her mother "screamed . . . and told me I was a disgrace to the family, that we weren't the kind of people who had children without being married." Though her father's reaction was "less dramatic because he's not really an emotional person," he made it clear that he didn't approve and "just got real quiet and wouldn't talk to me." In fact, Serena's father didn't talk to her throughout the entire pregnancy. He and Serena's mother "gradually came around some" after the birth of their first grandchild, a lovely, dark-haired little girl named Ella, but Serena's relationship with her parents was irreparably damaged. As she explained, things have "never been the same because they said some pretty awful things to me that I can never forgive them for."

Serena had hoped the response to her pregnancy would be somewhat more positive from her "academic family," the term she used to describe the graduate students and faculty members she had become close to at UI. She had hoped that their "more progressive attitudes in general" and particularly the "sort of feminist sentiment among a lot of them" would mean that they were less judgmental about single motherhood and "not be hung up on the idea that you have to have a husband in order to have a child." When she announced her pregnancy, the graduate students were a "divided camp." Those who had children, including some who were married and one who was divorced and had a teenager, were "supportive and wonderful and it was beautiful the way they responded and offered to help in whatever ways they could." Those who did not have children, however, "drifted away pretty quickly." Serena felt that this was because "they figured now that I was going to be a mom, I couldn't go out to the bars anymore or go see bands that came through town or those sorts of things."

Responses among faculty members were also mixed. Serena waited until after she had successfully defended her master's thesis and been awarded her master's degree to tell the chair of her department, Dr. John Williams. She decided to approach him first because of her perception that he was a "family-friendly kind of man"—he had two children of his own and had recently become a grandfather for the first time—and because she wanted to discuss her teaching appointment for the following year and assure him that the pregnancy wouldn't affect her teaching responsibilities. Dr. Williams expressed some concern about Serena's pregnancy, particularly with regard to how she would manage a half-time teaching assistantship, a full-time course load, and the final months of the pregnancy in the fall. He was also concerned about the following spring semester, wondering how Serena would juggle her classes and teaching responsibilities with the care of a newborn. However, Serena indicated that Dr. Williams was "very supportive." He assured Serena that her teaching appointment was secure and "he even showed me the UE-COGS [graduate student union] contract, the part about medical leave for the birth of a child." Dr. Williams also suggested that Serena "slow down a bit." He recommended that she take only two classes in the fall and then put together a couple of independent study courses for spring so she could "have a more flexible class schedule" as she adjusted to parenthood. He even offered to supervise the spring independent study courses if she couldn't find other faculty members who were willing to work with her.

As fall semester began, Serena was enrolled for six credits and "figured things were going to be fine." Yet she quickly began to notice some changes, including the fact that "other faculty members [in the department] were treating me differently." Though Dr. Williams was the only faculty member she had told about her pregnancy, Serena "sensed that other people in the department knew." During a lunch meeting with Dr. Rebecca Smith, the faculty member who had initially attracted Serena to UI and had become her advisor and mentor, Serena learned that Dr. Williams had announced the pregnancy during a faculty meeting. From what Dr. Smith told her, Dr. Williams had "seemed to be trying to set the tone for other faculty members, you know, that they should be supportive." Dr. Smith, however, was not enthusiastic about her advisee's situation:

> She flat out told me that I should have gotten an abortion and that this was going to ruin my life, ruin my chances for an academic career. She's married, but she made the decision not to [have kids] because she wanted to focus on her career. And she just looked at me and told me I should have gotten an abortion, just like that. I didn't even ask her [for her opinion]. She said it was "unacceptable" to be having a child by myself while I was in graduate school and she emphasized the "by myself" part. For her, it had to do with the fact that I was single. She was chairing the committee of another graduate student who was married and had recently had a baby and it was no problem. And it was just different, how she treated me because I wasn't married. And I started to feel that, well, like she was just waiting for me to fail in some way, to make a mistake or write a paper that wasn't the best paper I've ever done or not get something finished on time just so she could say "I told you so."

Serena continued to work with Dr. Smith throughout the fall term, but by the end of the semester, she "just couldn't take it anymore." While Dr. Smith had been interested in Serena's research before the pregnancy, she began to "be real critical of my work, wouldn't respond to my e-mails, just didn't seem to care anymore." Over winter break, Serena sent Dr. Smith a message informing her that "I couldn't work with her anymore" and began looking for a new mentor.

Though some faculty members in her home department were "supportive in their own way, certainly not jumping for joy but a few asked how I was doing," Serena felt that most faculty simply ignored her pregnancy. Those who did acknowledge it were "fixated" on her marital status:

> They would come right out and ask me if I was married. And when I said no they would ask if I had a boyfriend. What does that matter? Why is that any of their business? I consider that completely inappropriate—to have a professor ask about my personal life and situation. I mean, you could never ask someone that during a job interview or anything so why is it OK to pry into my personal life just because I'm single and pregnant and because I'm a graduate student?

Serena considered their questions so "intrusive and unprofessional" that she considered filing a formal complaint and even talked to "someone in the graduate college" about doing so. However, she was told it would be difficult to take any action unless she could document the comments made by faculty members. Because "people seemed to only say stuff when nobody was around and never wrote anything in an e-mail or anything," Serena soon abandoned this course of action.

Serena gave birth to Ella in early January 2002 and returned to classes and teaching only fifteen days later. She had taken Dr. Williams's suggestion and registered for two independent study courses for the semester, thus reducing the amount of time she had to be on campus and the amount of time she had to leave Ella with a babysitter. Still, Serena says she began to recognize things about campus that she hadn't noticed before she was a mother:

> I had read about sexism before, about who gets hired and who gets which graduate assistantships and who gets tenure and who doesn't, and all of that. But now it's a reality. This is going to sound strange, but I think the university campus is designed with this mind/body dualism.... It's a philosophical position that translates into the physical aspects of the university. I didn't realize this until I became a mom. . . . I'm a breastfeeding mom, and there are so few lactation rooms on this campus. I'm glad the lactation rooms are here, but they are only a real recent addition and there are only a few of them. There should be one in every single building. They don't include lactation rooms when they're designing a new building on this campus because they think of students and faculty only as brains and not as having physical needs. I have a physical need—I'm a breastfeeding mother and I need to express breast milk or nurse my child every three to four hours. And in order to do that, I have to leave my office [which she shares with three other

graduate students] and walk a few blocks to the nearest lactation room. . . . And there are buildings on this campus that aren't accessible, that I can't get into with a stroller. . . . And the only changing station I've found near my office is in the History Department. There should be one of those in every building. But they just don't think that the people on this campus, the students or the faculty, have kids so those things aren't seen as important. Not having those things, it just says that if you have a kid, you don't belong here.

After the birth of her child, sexism was no longer just a theory to Serena. Instead, it became a productive lens through which she began to make sense of the physical structures of the university. The issue of space was an important one for Serena, particularly as it impacted where she could express breast milk or breastfeed her daughter, where she could change Ella's diaper, and which buildings were accessible when she was pushing Ella in her stroller. These activities were important on a day-to-day basis as Serena navigated the space of the university. Yet, as Serena's comments indicate, space-related issues became important to her in a larger sense, particularly as they reflected a "philosophical position" about the place of parents and their children on a university campus, indicating that they "don't belong here."

Because of her experiences, Serena adamantly believed that single mothers who pursue a college degree are stigmatized in ways that "reflect attitudes about single mothers in this country." As she detailed the ways faculty members had responded to her new status as a single mother, particularly female faculty, who have been "so much worse than males," she also pointed to the "scrutiny that women who are faculty members face in general." She believed that the sexist nature of higher education forced many women to choose between motherhood and career. As a result, Serena felt that many female faculty members who had no children were "kind of bitter and don't want to see anyone else doing both, being a mom *and* on their way to having a successful career." After ending her working relationship with Dr. Smith, Serena had hoped to foster relationships with faculty members who were also mothers. Her reasons were twofold. On the one hand, she wanted to see how they balanced academic and family responsibilities, to "see women who were doing it and good at both." She also hoped they would be more supportive of her or "at least more understanding" of the challenges she faced as a mother. However, developing these kinds of relationships proved more challenging than Serena had anticipated. She found it difficult to determine which faculty members had children because "they never seemed to talk about them or bring their children to campus." Faculty who had children often seemed to be "hiding" them, particularly those who "didn't have tenure yet." Serena understood why a junior faculty member might do this—"after all, it's very political . . . there is still the idea that if a woman has kids then her personal life would be competing with her professional duties . . . and this might affect her job." Yet she was also angry, believing that women who did this were reinforcing the status quo instead of taking steps to "redraw boundaries . . . and do some trailblazing."

By the end of November, less than a year after giving birth to Ella, Serena had had enough of what she perceived as an unwelcoming environment for single mothers in her graduate program. She was tempted to "just pack it in and leave over Thanksgiving break," but she finished out the semester, submitting final grades for her students and turning in "the last paper I'd ever write at Iowa" during finals week. She then officially withdrew from the university, resigned from her teaching position, and moved back East to live with her sister and brother-in-law and their two children "just in time to celebrate Ella's first birthday." She sent me an e-mail three months later that explained her decision to leave the university:

> By the end, I didn't want to go to class anymore because I felt I was on display, like faculty thought of me only as a single mother all the time. That's who I was to them and nothing more. And so I felt like I had to be this radical mom, like I had to be the one always bringing things up like "will there be child care when this speaker comes and everyone in the department is expected to be there?" And it was hard for me to always be the one to bring those things up. I just wanted to be a parent and not have that be considered unusual.

In the months since she had left the university, Serena had managed to secure what she deemed a "fairly good job" and she and Ella had moved into her own apartment. Serena enjoyed "living near my sister again and Ella having her cousins to play with." Yet she regretted the fact that she had not completed her PhD. She hoped to go back to graduate school to finish her doctorate, although she made it clear that she intended to be "very selective" about the program she would choose. She hoped to find a department "with lots of parents and lots of kids and where everyone brings their kids to the office and get-togethers and everywhere." However, her excitement about the prospect of returning to graduate school was tempered by skepticism. Her experiences at UI had left her "doubt[ing] that such a place even exists."

A VERY CHILLY SNOW DAY AND THE CUTE FACTOR

Kasey Stevens was an Iowa City native who had lived in the community her entire life, except for a brief period during her marriage. She attended elementary, junior high, and high school in the Iowa City Community School District, and as her high school graduation approached, she enrolled at UI. Her plan was to complete a double major in chemistry and pre-med and then attend UI's Carver College of Medicine to pursue a career as a medical researcher. Kasey was very aware of the university's strong reputation, having read the "America's Best Colleges" and "America's Best Hospitals" articles in *U.S. News & World Report*. However, she enrolled at UI "mostly because I love Iowa City and I wanted to stay here my whole life."

During her first year of undergraduate studies, at a Halloween party thrown by one of her friends, Kasey met Warren Hampton, a 26-year-old UI law student. Kasey initially wasn't interested in him, "mostly because I thought he was too old for me." Warren, however, asked for Kasey's phone number "so we could go out some time." Kasey refused, lying and telling him she had a boyfriend. She left the party thinking she would never hear from him again. The next day, however, Warren called her dorm. It seemed he had gotten Kasey's phone number from one of her friends. He told her that he knew she didn't have a boyfriend and asked her to dinner that night. Kasey told him she had plans. He called and extended the same offer the next day. And the next. And the next. In fact, he called Kasey every day for almost a month until she finally agreed to go out with him. Kasey "tried not to like him too much, because I was only nineteen and he was seven years older," but she soon found herself attracted to him. She thought he was "so smart and sophisticated in ways that boys my age just aren't." The relationship progressed rather quickly, and by the end of Kasey's second semester at UI, Warren had begun to talk about marriage. While she was flattered, Kasey told him that she wouldn't consider it until after she had completed medical school. Warren was "frustrated" by her response, but he "seemed to understand that school was important" to Kasey and agreed to wait.

During the following semester, however, and despite the fact that she was disciplined about taking her birth control pills at the same time every day, Kasey became pregnant. It prompted her to reconsider marriage, "mostly because my family started pressuring me, telling me 'You *need* a husband!' and I didn't want to be a single mother." Though she declared herself a pro-choice advocate, she said she was "really in love and having a baby seemed like, well, like it would be a really wonderful thing." She and Warren were married over winter break and both returned to classes in January. It was Warren's last semester of law school, but the couple intended to stay in Iowa City until Kasey could finish her BA. Their plans changed, however, when Warren got "a job offer that he couldn't refuse" in Colorado. Kasey withdrew from UI after completing the spring semester. In June, the newlyweds and their newborn daughter, Malika, moved to Denver.

Kasey described her five-year marriage as "not happy at all." As a full-time stay-at-home mom, she cared for the couple's home and Malika. Warren worked long hours, usually "70-hour weeks," and that, coupled with the fact that she didn't know many people in the Denver area, left Kasey feeling "isolated and lonely." She and Warren quickly grew apart. Kasey believed she was partly to blame for the breakup of her marriage because she was "so young and probably didn't know what marriage was supposed to be about." But she also blamed Warren for "being gone *all* the time . . . it was almost like being a single parent anyway . . . except, of course, we had a huge house and were living on a lawyer's salary." During her final year in Denver, Kasey enrolled part-time at a community college near her home, partly because she wanted the social interaction but primarily because she was eager to complete her undergraduate degree and then go to medical school. Warren was not supportive; he told her that "education is overrated . . . and to just get a job at the mall if I wanted something to do." Kasey persisted, however. Initially, she took only two courses per semester, "far less" than what her course load had been at UI, but she was glad to be back in school. In fact, she became more dedicated than ever to completing her studies. In early spring, Kasey filed for divorce. She then moved back to Iowa City and applied for readmission to UI. She was accepted, and she resumed her studies in August.

The transition back to UI and full-time coursework as a single mother was more challenging than Kasey expected. Time constraints were a significant challenge at first, particularly because it was difficult for Kasey to coordinate her class schedule with her daughter's school schedule. For Malika, who began first grade in Iowa City at the same school where Kasey had attended elementary school, the school day didn't begin until 8:30 A.M. and was finished by 3:00 P.M. On Thursdays, however, Malika's school had early release and students were dismissed at 2:00 P.M. Although Kasey was able to schedule her classes during her first semester back at UI to accommodate Malika's school schedule, she knew she would not able to do so every semester and that she would inevitably have to "take classes that ran later in the day or have a lab in the late afternoon." Fortunately, during Kasey's second semester back at UI, Malika was admitted to the before- and after-school program at her school. For $145 a month, Kasey could drop her daughter off as early as 8:00 A.M. and leave her there until 5:45 P.M. This gave Kasey some flexibility with her academic schedule and "really, really helped make it easier for me to get the classes I need."

Finances were also a source of stress when Kasey returned to UI, particularly because "money was really tight that first year." Aside from the $557 per month she received in child support from Warren—an amount that "almost covers our $600 rent"—her only other sources of income were student loans and a Pell Grant. The grant covered most of her tuition, and although she "took out what I thought was a lot in loans," Kasey couldn't afford all of her books and simply went through the semester without access to some of the required readings for her courses. As the semester drew to a close, she had spent all of her loan and grant money. She couldn't afford to pay her phone or electric bills, didn't have enough money to pay for Malika's child care tuition, and "had nothing to eat." Kasey was fortunate that her parents gave her $500 to help her "catch up" and buy groceries. Still, the experience of "having basically no money and having to beg my parents" was stressful and prompted Kasey to alter her approach to financial aid. She began taking out the maximum amount available to her in student loans, and in subsequent semesters, she found that she was better able to make ends meet.

Although Kasey found ways to manage her time constraints and economic challenges, she found it more difficult to manage the climate at the university. She felt that as a single mother, she was "treated differently" by her instructors, her student peers, and "by the university in general." According to Kasey, "most faculty don't really care one way or the other" if she is a single mother "as long as I get [assignments] turned in on time." However, she had several instructors who treated her "negatively and with a bad attitude." During her first two semesters back at UI, Kasey made a point of meeting with her instructors at the beginning of the term to inform them that she was a single mother. She did this "not because I expect special treatment or anything like that" but because she wanted to let her instructors know about her circumstances "early in the semester in case something came up and I had to miss class because Malika got sick or something." Kasey felt she was "being responsible" with these meetings, which she believed could accomplish two things. First, she could let the instructor know that she had "other responsibilities besides just school" and that on occasion, because of things she could not control—like her daughter becoming ill—she might be absent. Second, Kasey felt that meeting with her instructors allowed her to convey that she was a responsible student who was "serious about getting things in on time, even if my daughter is sick or whatever . . . and find out the best way to do that if I have to miss class."

In these meetings, Kasey got "all kinds of reactions." A few faculty members and graduate instructors simply told Kasey that if she was going to miss a class, she needed to contact them in advance whenever possible, especially if an assignment was due. One even told her she could "turn in assignments over e-mail so they wouldn't be late." She felt that no faculty members or graduate instructors had "gone out of their way to be supportive or done me any favors" but mostly, they seemed to "not care at all" about her circumstances. Typically, instructors responded by informing Kasey she had the "same number of excused absences as everyone else in the class before it would start bringing down my grade," regardless of the reason. She believed that this policy posed a disadvantage to single parents, particularly because they have responsibilities that traditional college students do not and they "don't have another person in the house to watch the child" like married parents do. However, Kasey also believed that this policy was fair because it treated all students the same and she was adamant that she did not want special treatment because she was a single mother.

Some instructors, unfortunately, seemed to make a particular effort to "treat me like I'm less of a person." One faculty member, Dr. Herbert Westing, seemed particularly unsupportive; Kasey described him as "hostile." It started the first week of classes, when Kasey stopped by during his office hours. When she told him she was a single mother, he "looked at me real weird and asked, 'Then why aren't you home with your kid?'" He also asked her why she wasn't married and when she told him she was divorced, Dr. Westing told her she "should have stayed married." His attitude, which made Kasey uncomfortable, translated into practice. When the public schools were cancelled one day because of a snowstorm, Kasey e-mailed Dr. Westing to let him know that she wouldn't be in class because her daughter's school had closed and she wasn't able to find a babysitter on such short notice. He didn't respond. When she went to the next class meeting, Dr. Westing addressed Kasey's absence in front of the entire class:

> He made a big deal out of the fact that I wasn't in class and that I didn't come because I had to stay home with my child. I could have never brought her to his class, he never would have gone for that, so what choice did I have? And he just embarrassed me in front of the whole class, making this big announcement that I thought I should be excused so I could "stay home and play mommy." And he has his own kids, two of them, and they are both in the [public] schools here and so I know they didn't have school that day either. But he told me I couldn't come back to class until I brought "proof" that the schools were closed. That just seemed ridiculous to me, that I needed proof when he already knew! And I didn't know how to give him that proof. So I had to go to the principal of my daughter's school and have her write a letter saying that school was cancelled. And then when I brought it to class, he made a big deal out of it in front of everyone. It was humiliating.

When I asked Kasey if she had considered complaining about Dr. Westing's behavior, perhaps by going to the chair of the department, she laughed. Dr. Westing was the chair, and Kasey wasn't aware of any other locations on campus where she could lodge a complaint. When the semester ended and final grades were posted, Kasey was surprised when she received a lower grade than the B+ she believed she had earned in Dr. Westing's course. When she e-mailed him to find out why she had received a C+, he sent her a two-word reply: "Unexcused absences." The snow day was the only class session she missed with Dr. Westing during the entire semester.

Kasey admitted that her experience with Dr. Westing was the worst she had encountered at UI, but it did make her much more cautious about revealing her status as a single mother to other faculty members. Instead of automatically going to office hours and telling faculty about her circumstances, Kasey "will

[now] only tell them if I absolutely have to." Thus, if Malika got ill or her school was cancelled and Kasey had to miss only one session of a particular course, she would "just tell the instructor that I had the flu or something . . . like any other student." In other words, Kasey's experience with Dr. Westing prompted her to engage in a type of stigma management referred to as passing, withholding information about her identity in order to "pass as normal during various forms of social interaction."[25] By telling her instructors that she herself was ill in these instances and not mentioning her daughter, Kasey was able present herself as no different from her nonparent student peers and to interact with her instructors "like any other student." This form of passing worked well most of the time, and in some courses, Kasey was able to "get through the entire semester without ever having to tell [the instructor]" she was a single mother.

When Kasey had to miss multiple sessions of a course in order to care for her daughter, however, passing became more difficult. During the spring 2004 semester, Malika contracted whooping cough. The school district's policy was that Malika was not allowed to return to school until she had been on antibiotics for five full days and was no longer considered contagious. Kasey's parents, who also lived in Iowa City, were both employed full time but each took one day of vacation to help care for Malika. Even with this help, however, Kasey had to miss three days of classes. Though she considered telling her instructors that she herself "had a bad flu or something," she decided against it, mostly because she had missed an exam in one class and needed to produce a doctor's note in order for her absence to be excused and to be permitted to take a makeup exam. Although Kasey had been able to "get by as a normal student"—that is, a student without children—until that point in the semester, she found it difficult to continue to do so under the circumstances. In the end, she told her instructors about Malika and her illness. Because Kasey provided a doctor's note, she was allowed to make up the work she had missed so her grades did not suffer. In addition, she did not experience any hostility from those instructors when she told them she was a single mother. However, in those courses and in all her future interactions with those particular instructors, hiding her identity was no longer an option for Kasey. Her ability to successfully pass at UI had been somewhat compromised because more members of the university community knew she was a single mother.

Kasey also used passing in an effort to manage her relationships with her student peers. She described her efforts to conceal her identity as a single mother as a way of "blend[ing] in with other students," of making herself seem just like any other student on campus. Though Kasey was twenty-five, several years older than most of her undergraduate peers, she admitted that she "looks very young . . . most people think I'm still in high school." When she initially returned to the university, Kasey sometimes mentioned that she was a single mother during class discussions or it came up when she was talking informally with other students while they were waiting for class to begin. Some students reacted negatively. Kasey cited "eye rolling, deep sighs . . . [and] turning up their noses like they just smelled something real nasty" as some of the behaviors that indicated disapproval from her peers. Others would voice their feelings, sometimes by whispering to others sitting near them and "then just laughing to each other." A few students made their feelings known to the entire class; they would make disparaging comments about single mothers in general "and then say that I probably wasn't 'one of those single moms,' like that was supposed to make what they said OK."

Not all of her peers responded in an overtly negative manner. In fact, some students that Kasey described as "well-meaning," primarily young women, were very interested in the fact that she has a child. However, these students seemed to have very little interest in the reality of Kasey's experiences or what it was like for her to raise a child on her own while working toward her college degree:

> [They] get stuck on the "cute" factor . . . like, "Oh, how *cute* that you have a little girl!" And they just get stuck there, going on and on about how sweet and cute it all must be. And they didn't ever seem to think, "Wow, how do you get all the reading done for this class?" or "That must be hard to take care of a kid all by yourself and be in school, too." And they would never ask "What is it like to be a single mom?" They would just say things like, "Oh, that's *so cute!* How old is she?" Or "Why don't you bring her to class?"—like I was going to bring her for show and tell or something! It was good that they were being positive, I guess, or trying to be positive and not just saying, "You don't belong here." But I don't think they have any idea at all what it really means, what it's like to be a single mother and a student, and none of them ever asked what it is like.

Although these types of comments did not contribute to a climate that was explicitly unwelcoming, they contributed to the chilly climate in subtle ways because they indicated only a superficial interest in the experiences of single mothers and demonstrated an inability to recognize that Kasey had any other interests other than being a mother. In other words, students who "get stuck on the 'cute' factor" saw Kasey solely in terms of her status as a single mother. As a result, they defined Kasey "in terms of [her] stigma"; they saw "single mother" as her "master status" or "master trait," the primary identity that "well-meaning" students focused on and emphasized when interacting with her.[26]

Such responses factored heavily into Kasey's decision to conceal her identity as a single mother from other students. In order to keep other students from "judging or stereotyping" her or from "treating me like I'm *only* a single mother," she would "usually stay pretty quiet . . . and wouldn't share any personal stuff" in her classes. This strategy was one way Kasey attempted to exercise power within the context of the chilly climate at the university. She reported a relatively high degree of success in hiding her identity from her peers. Kasey believed that by "staying quiet," she was able to avoid being stigmatized as a single mother in her day-to-day interactions with other students. However, when Kasey or other single mothers attending college conceal their identities, they are likely to suffer from negative psychological outcomes associated with passing such as internalized oppression, marginalization and social isolation, the stress of concealing their identity, and fear that their identity will be discovered. In addition, passing has an impact on the university. When the experiences of a stigmatized group are excluded, their perspectives, experiences, and unique knowledge are both devalued and cannot inform the theoretical and practical aspects of university matters as they relate to academics and student services. While passing enabled Kasey to manage the stigma she encountered on an individual level, it may have helped perpetuate a chilly climate for single mothers and increased the likelihood that the university will remain a place where she and other single mothers are treated differently, encountering both obvious and subtle forms of negativity, simply because of their identity.

A SHAMEFUL LITTLE SECRET ON CAMPUS

While Clarissa Bennett never experienced any of what she referred to as "obvious stereotyping" with regard to single mothers at UI, she was furious about university policies and practices regarding family housing and support services for student families. She felt that the policies contributed to the "shame and humiliation" she felt as a single mother. Clarissa described herself as "a white, divorced woman in her late thirties, with two teenagers, who finally decided to go to college and earn my degree." Born in 1965 in a small community in northern Iowa to a "traditional family with deep farming roots," Clarissa never planned to attend college. In fact, her post–high school aspirations focused exclusively on marriage and motherhood. During her sophomore year of high school, she began dating her classmate Harry, a "quiet, but smart boy" whose family owned a nearby farm. Clarissa had known him "as long as I could remember." She and Harry graduated in June 1983, and it was a surprise to no one when Harry proposed to Clarissa at her graduation party. Clarissa accepted and they were married a little over a year later. Afterward, Harry worked in the mill at the local farmer's cooperative while Clarissa threw herself into her new role as stay-at-home wife. Both Harry and Clarissa worked part time on Harry's parents' farm, helping out "with chores, milking and baling hay and things like that" to earn additional income. The couple saved whatever money they could and planned to purchase the farm from Harry's parents when they retired. Clarissa became pregnant around the time the couple celebrated their second anniversary, and in 1987, she gave birth to their first child, Julia. Sixteen months later, a second daughter, Olivia, was born.

Things were going smoothly for the couple until the summer of 1993. As persistent, heavy rains fell on the Midwest, rivers and streams in the Upper Mississippi River Basin exceeded flood levels. Hundreds of levees along the Mississippi and Missouri rivers failed. The result was "certainly the largest and most significant flood event to ever occur in the United States."[27] The incident affected nine states, including North Dakota, South Dakota, Nebraska, Kansas, Minnesota, Iowa, Missouri, Wisconsin, and Illinois. Fifty people died, hundreds of homes were destroyed, thousands of people were evacuated, and approximately 15 million acres of farmland were flooded.[28] Although the farms of Clarissa's parents and her in-laws suffered relatively little damage compared to others that were closer to the rivers, they experienced considerable losses, both financially and in terms of usable farmland. The flood made Clarissa "rethink the future." Deciding that farming was "too risky," she told Harry that she no longer wanted to buy the family farm. She stopped working on the farm and got a full-time job as a receptionist in a large medical building in a nearby city. This became a "turning point" in her marriage. Harry refused to give up his dream of purchasing his parents' farm. Clarissa believed that farming was not a viable future for their family. Unable to reach a compromise, the couple separated in the spring of 1994. After a decade of marriage, Harry moved back in with his parents and filed for divorce.

Clarissa spent the next six years "working and raising my kids." Although she received child support from Harry, she found it difficult to support herself and her children on her receptionist's salary. Although she liked her job and received praise for her performance at work, she was never able to get promotions because she did not have a college degree:

> When other jobs would open up, jobs that were higher up the chain of command than a receptionist, things like office manager or assistant to somebody, I would apply but it would never work out. I got employee evaluations that were stellar with the exception of the portion that focused on my credentials—it would always say things like, "she really needs to get a degree." . . . And I also wanted to be able to provide for my children, to set an example for my daughters—that if you want to get somewhere in life, you have to work hard for it. And for me, getting somewhere meant I had to get an education. And once I did that, I would be able to get a better job, to have a choice about different kinds of jobs than I had without a college degree. There is a certain amount of freedom that comes with education. If there's a word to describe what I'm talking about, it's independence.

Clarissa began taking classes at a community college near her home. She enrolled full time, working an eight-hour day at her job and then going to classes at night. Clarissa dedicated her weekends to spending time with her daughters and studying for her classes. As she moved through her general education courses, she "learned that I'm really, really good at psychology" and took as many psychology courses as her academic plan would allow. As she neared completion of her associate's degree, she applied to four-year colleges with the intention of completing her bachelor's degree in psychology. Though she was accepted into several institutions throughout the state, she decided on UI "because it had a good [psychology] program and I liked the city." At the time of my initial interview with Clarissa, she was preparing for final exams during what was her third semester at the university. In addition to raising two teenage daughters, ages sixteen and fourteen, she was enrolled in fifteen semester hours and worked an average of twelve hours per week in a work-study position that "mostly involves doing filing and secretarial kind of stuff." She was also an honor student, "on the honor roll every semester so far," and had begun to investigate MA and PhD programs in psychology.

Clarissa believed that because she was older than traditional undergraduate students, her experiences were different from those of most single mothers on the UI campus. Because her children were older and "a little more self-sufficient," she didn't have the kind of child care worries that many single mother students faced. In addition, because her children "have their own activities and friends and all that," time constraints were a "less pressing" issue for her. Although she admitted that raising teenagers "can be challenging . . . because they're still in that 'bumping their heads' stage and still need a lot of guidance," Clarissa found it easier to get uninterrupted study time because Julia and Olivia were older and "can understand the connection between time with the books and good grades." Since her daughters were in high school and had "plenty of homework themselves," it was not unusual for the three of them to spend the evening sitting around the kitchen table or on the living room floor after dinner, huddled over their respective books or notes and sharing a pot of tea late into the night.

Clarissa believed that her age gave her another advantage over other single mothers. She felt it had a positive impact on her relationships with faculty, other students, and staff members, particularly because "being older" enabled her to "escape the single mother stigma" that she felt younger single mother students had to deal with, "especially those who had their kids real young." On the few occasions Clarissa had to miss class because one of her daughters was ill or had a doctor's or orthodontist appointment, her instructors "have been fine with it because I think they expect me to have kids because I'm older." She characterized her relationships with her classmates and academic advisor as positive:

Having my own kids has helped me connect with other students a little more than I would have otherwise. And some of my classmates see me as this mom figure, because I have kids around their age and I'm older than them, so they'll look to me for mom-like advice, like dealing with roommate situations or things like that. It's kind of sweet. I'd say that other students seem to think it's cool that I'm older and I'm in school. They think it's pretty cool. And you have to remember, I'm as old as their parents and as old as the professor in some classes, so a lot of it is my age, they respect my age. . . . And my academic advisor, she's also a single mother and she's around my age, so I probably have a different relationship with her than most students do. She recognizes some of the challenges I face as a single mother—money, scheduling, being the only parent and having to deal with the kids *all* the time. Sure, she helps me with my course schedule, but I don't feel like she sees me [only] as a student. She also understands that I have this other life outside the university, that I have other responsibilities.

Though having kids set Clarissa apart from most other undergraduate students, she felt that it had not done so in a negative way. Instead, it allowed Clarissa to relate to her younger peers through what she described as a rapport that was like that between parents and children. In addition, and primarily because single motherhood was an experience and identity that she and her academic advisor had in common, Clarissa's relationship with her academic advisor was one that that involved both "recognition" and "understanding," attitudes that seemed to suggest respect.

While Clarissa had never experienced any "outright negative attitudes or hostility myself" at UI, she believed that the university did not support single mother students or consider their needs important. She felt that the lack of support services for student families demonstrated a dismissive attitude toward this student population:

I've been waiting for somebody to do a study on single mothers on this campus. I think that this is one of the voices that is ignored on this campus—single mothers who are students. . . . It's really frustrating for me to look around and see all of these wonderfully supportive things that exist on this campus—like for first-generation students, and there are so many types of support services for student athletes, and some services for international students. And some are academic, but others are social. And I don't mean to minimize these forms of support because they should be there. It's the university's job to help support the student body.

But what about single mothers? It's like it's this shameful little secret on campus, the fact that there are single mothers who go to school here. The fact is, they are here and it isn't easy for them, and yet nobody seems to be doing anything to try to support them. And they need support, but they are completely ignored. . . . There are all kinds of things that could be done and they wouldn't have to cost a lot . . . [like] some activities for students with children so we feel more like we're part of this campus. I think they've arranged one family movie for next semester and that's fine, but it needs to be more than just a movie once a year. Those kinds of opportunities to get together with other students, other single mothers and other married student parents would be wonderful . . . for networking, for just feeling like I'm not the only one here. But does anybody in administration or student life even talk to single mother students to find out what they need? What kinds of activities they would be interested in? Nobody has ever asked me.

Clarissa believed that compared to the support services the university provided for various student populations, the support it provided for student families was minimal. To be fair, some forms of support were available. These included child care subsidies through the Family Services Office, a program that provided free child care during finals week, several on-campus child care centers, and, as Clarissa mentioned, an occasional "UI Student Families Movie Break" event.[29] However, child care subsidies through the university were nominal and the need for child care at UI far outweighed availability. While the child care program during finals week was helpful, it was available only for two weeks of a sixteen-week semester. Compared to the resources the university had invested in supporting other student populations on the UI campus, Clarissa's claim that the voices, needs, and interests of single mother students were "ignored" seemed to have merit.

Student family housing was another hot topic for Clarissa. She believed the location and general condition of these dwellings was symbolic of the university's attitude toward student families in general and especially toward single mothers who were "more likely to be poor and needing inexpensive housing." When Clarissa attended UI, the Family Housing/University Apartments complex consisted of two clusters of apartment buildings located approximately three miles west of the UI campus. The apartments were available to any student of the university who was in good standing, but students with children were given priority so long as their housing application was received before the deadlines for each enrollment period. The complex consisted of 694 units that included both one- and two-bedroom apartments. Units were modest in size, from 521 to 630 square feet each, and rental fees were moderate, ranging from $435 to $600 per month with no security deposit required. The apartments were a regular stop on the free campus bus route and were close to public schools. In addition, residents had access to on-site coin-operated washers and dryers and outdoor clotheslines and there were a number of common areas that included grills, picnic tables, and playground equipment.

Before moving to Iowa City, Clarissa had looked at housing in the Iowa City community but found that she couldn't afford the "high rent at most places." Feeling that she "had no other choice," she rented an apartment from the university. It was an act that made her feel "ashamed," particularly the first time she brought her children to what became their new home:

> When I opened the door the first time my children saw where we were going to be living, I apologized. I said, "I'm so sorry that I can't do any better than this, that you have to live here." It was a dump and I know my kids thought it was a dump. . . . And a lot of people choose not to live out there because of the way they look and smell. But the university figures that they'll just stick the low-income people who have kids out there, put all the single mothers out there, and kind of hide them, not let them live by everyone else. And now that we live out there, we've met some neighbors and I really like the people because it's a diverse community with diverse race, ethnicities, families, and religious beliefs. But nobody chooses to live out there. If they could afford something better, they would move out.

The poor condition of the apartments, which were built in the 1960s from what the university has acknowledged were "poor materials," was well documented.[30] Concrete staircases are crumbling, the apartments are infested with roaches, the units are poorly insulated and ventilated, doors and windows let in drafts, and high humidity seems to invite mold and mildew growth on the cinder-block walls. The overall environment of the housing complex prompted some residents to refer to it as a "second campus . . . practically invisible" to university administrators, who were publicly accused of "gross neglect" of the units and residents.[31]

My own experiences with the apartments confirm these ongoing concerns. After being accepted to a master's program at UI in spring of 1997, I traveled from my home in Green Bay, Wisconsin, to Iowa City and spent five days in the community. I spent some of my time attending to academic matters such as getting my student ID, meeting the chair of my graduate program, and registering for classes. The rest of my visit was devoted to personal matters such as finding child care for my three-year-old daughter and finding a place for us to live. When I asked for tips on apartment hunting, a UI staff member told me about UI family housing and indicated that it was more affordable than other apartments in the Iowa City area. After locating it on the campus map, I drove to the complex, eager to find an apartment that would be kind to my budget and would allow my daughter and me to live in a community with other UI families. My enthusiasm deflated when I toured the apartments. They were in poor condition. Dirt and cobwebs covered the floors and walls and countertops. The smell of mold and mildew—visible in the bathroom and the bedrooms of the two units I toured—was heavy, making the air thick and difficult to breathe. I immediately made the decision to not live there because of the general condition of the apartments.

As I was conducting research for my doctoral dissertation, I again visited the apartments to follow up on the information that Clarissa and other project participants had provided about the housing complex. It was the fall of 2004, nearly eight years after my initial visit to the facility, and it was obvious that the university had made some small improvements. The walls of the two units I toured had been freshly painted. They were free of mold and mildew and the scent of cleaning products still lingered in the air. The floors and other surfaces were clean, including the bathtubs, which appeared to have been recently installed. The apartments certainly looked and smelled cleaner than on my previous visit. However, things like paint and new bathtubs are only cosmetic improvements. No amount of paint or cleaning products can revive what Clarissa referred to as "dying buildings."

Reviving the apartments was not on the university's agenda. In 2004, the UI Department of Resident Services Facilities and Operations announced a feasibility study to "determine the financial viability of replacing University Apartments."[32] At the time, many residents considered the plan to replace the apartments a "mixed blessing."[33] While new construction would likely have meant better living conditions in terms of the physical state of the buildings, the number of available campus apartments for students with children would have been significantly reduced. Clarissa believed that the proposed plan was a clear indicator of the university's attitude toward her and other single mother students:

> They're building all the time on this campus. New buildings for classrooms even though so many just sit empty each day. And a new [learning] center for student athletes—I guess they don't get enough already! And so I can't help but think that this plan for the apartments, that it's just an attempt to get rid of low-income students who need to live out there and who don't have any other choice. . . . For me, it just lets me know how much the university cares about me as a low-income single mother who is trying to get an education: not at all! They don't care about us at all!

Interestingly, for several years, the university made no decision about replacing the buildings that form the Family Housing Complex. However, in light of the findings of an external team that was commissioned in 2010 to review housing and dining operations at UI, the university was not able to remain indecisive. The review listed the poor condition of the university apartments as one of the most significant housing concerns for the university: "University Apartments (Hawkeye Court and Hawkeye Drive) are over 40 years old and are past the end of their useful lifecycle. Within five years, the department will need to spend a significant amount of money on the exterior building walkways or abandon the apartments. The initial pro forma show that we are unable to build new apartments at below market rates."[34] If the university simply abandoned the apartments, there would be no designated housing at UI for student families. If administrators decided to demolish and then rebuild a smaller complex, they would likely create a housing shortage on campus. The UI administration chose another route: it created the Aspire at West Campus community, described as "the only on-campus, pet-friendly housing community catered to graduate students and University faculty" and their immediate families.[35] The first phase of the complex, which included 270 apartments, opened in time for the fall 2014 semester. The second phase, which opened in August 2016, added another 252 apartments. On the surface, the creation of this housing complex seems to address the concerns that Clarissa voiced about on-campus family housing, but the Aspire at West Campus community carries a hefty price tag: rent for one-bedroom apartments in the complex starts at $959 and rent for two-bedroom apartments starts at $1,039,[36] nearly double the rates that Clarissa and others paid to rent apartments in Hawkeye Drive and Hawkeye Court. After the Aspire at West Campus complex opened, university administrators admitted they knew that rental rates would be prohibitive and that most of those living in the older family housing apartments would not be able to transfer to the new complex.[37] Thus, the university has failed to make on-campus family housing more accessible. Given the limited economic resources of single mothers and the limited availability of low-income housing in the Iowa City community,[38] it seems likely that some single mothers attending UI will experience this ongoing lack of accessible family housing as a crisis. Within an institutional climate that already stigmatizes single mothers, it isn't difficult to imagine that a lack of affordable family-friendly campus housing might discourage single mothers from attending UI and perhaps to choose a more family-friendly institution. It may discourage them from pursuing a postsecondary degree at all.

COUNTERING STIGMA ON THE COLLEGE CAMPUS

While many of the women described the various ways they attempted to cover or hide their identity, Sally Atkins, a second-year student at KCC, adamantly stated that she would "never do that." In fact, Sally believed it was part of her responsibility as a student to draw on her experiences as a single mother during class discussions. Although she felt that some of her instructors and students in her courses might not agree with her decision to have a child without being married, she believed it was important to actively engage other members of the learning community in discussions about single motherhood.[39] Sally thus positioned herself as a student-teacher: by actively confronting stereotypes about single mothers and raising critical questions "about how single mothers are treated as a social problem in this society," Sally felt that she actively encouraged other members of the university community to examine their attitudes about single mothers.⁴⁰

Sally did not begin college as a single mother. In fact, when she began attending KCC in the fall of 1996, she had just graduated from high school and "was a pretty typical eighteen-year-old." She shared an apartment with three other young women who were also KCC students, worked a part-time job, was a full-time student, and "spent a lot of time partying." Though she was excited to be at college, she didn't study much, and at the end of her first semester, she had earned a GPA that she describes as "embarrassing, it was so, so low, almost as low as you can get." She resolved to bring her grades up, but only a few weeks into the following semester, Sally became pregnant. She had been "only casually dating" another student, Theo, for four months and "knew it wasn't really going anywhere." When she told Theo about the pregnancy, he told her to get an abortion. She briefly considered taking Theo's advice, but she ultimately decided against it. She had "always wanted to be a mother . . . and figured 'how hard can this be?'" When she told her parents, they yelled and said she was "stupid and crazy for even thinking about doing this." Feeling that she probably couldn't afford to raise a child on her own and attend college, especially since her parents "didn't seem like they were going to be there for me at all," Sally made some changes in her life. First, she got a full-time job working on an assembly line in a factory in Cedar Rapids, Iowa, "so I could make decent money and support us." Next, she moved into her own apartment. And finally, she withdrew from KCC.

After giving birth to her son, Elliot, in August 1997, Sally spent her days caring for her child. Then she would go to work from 11 P.M. to 7 A.M., which was possible "only because my sister came to live with me and would stay with my son while I went to work." As for sleep, Sally "got it when I could," napping with Elliot in the afternoon and sleeping for a few hours after he went to bed at night and before she had to leave for work. Although she was able to earn enough to support herself and her son, it was difficult for her to maintain the schedule, and it "left me tired all the time." She thought about returning to college to earn a degree and "then get a better job with decent hours," but didn't think she could afford tuition on top of her living expenses. Furthermore, if she attended classes all day, she would have to find daycare for Elliot. Even if she could "somehow scrape up enough for classes . . . I couldn't pay for someone to watch him." Feeling that she needed a college degree in order to get a "better job" but unable to afford college, Sally resigned herself to the likelihood that she would work in the factory forever.

Sally's forever lasted only five and a half years, until she was laid off in January 2002 when the factory unexpectedly cut out the third shift. A few of Sally's co-workers were able to move to the second shift, but Sally didn't have enough seniority to join them. The break from work was "nice at first," particularly because it allowed her to "sleep normal hours" and she was able to collect unemployment. However, she soon discovered that it was difficult to pay her bills and began looking for another job. After filling out "what must have been about fifty job applications" over a four-month period, Sally was still unemployed. She believed that this "was a sign that I was supposed to do something else with my life." Instead of continuing her job search, Sally made an appointment with an academic advisor at KCC and learned that it was "real easy" for her to return to the school. Elliot was already in kindergarten, so daycare was not a consideration from 8:30 A.M. until 3:30 P.M. This was a crucial factor in Sally's ability to return to school because her sister had moved out earlier in the year and could no longer help with child care. Sally decided she would take classes only during the time when Elliot was in school. She filed the necessary paperwork, including forms for student financial aid, and registered for classes. In late August, Sally resumed part-time studies, hoping to complete her associate's degree in nursing in four years. In the months after her return to KCC, Sally had "no complaints" about managing her dual roles as single mother and college student. Her life was not stress free, however. She worried about money, contended with a number of scheduling conflicts, and often found it difficult to get all of her reading done for classes and still get enough sleep. Even so, Sally enjoyed being a student again and found her studies "a lot more interesting" than her factory job. And when challenges arose, she didn't complain but tried "to do something about them."

Sally adopted a similar approach to dealing with staff members, instructors, and other students at KCC, particularly when they would "disregard or disrespect" her because of her status as a single mother, which she said was a regular occurrence. She believed that frequently their attitudes and actions were unintentional. For example, she described a meeting with Ruth, her academic advisor:

> This person was trying to help me plan out my classes and I told her that I can't schedule classes that run later than 3:20 because my son gets out of school at 3:30 and I have to pick him up. And even after I told her that, she kept suggesting classes that met until like 5:00. So I had to keep reminding her over and over that I have a child, not just from one semester to the next, but from one meeting to the next within the same semester. It was like she didn't or couldn't remember that one thing. And maybe it was a small thing to her, and I know she meets with lots of students. But this is a pretty important thing to me and it's pretty important to my schedule and what I'm able to do as a student—I can only be on campus during certain times of the day because I can't afford to pay for before- and after-school care for him. And so I don't think it's too much to expect a staff member who is supposed to *help* students to keep that in mind as they're advising me. I don't think she was trying to be mean, but it's not OK for her to ignore that either.

Sally considered several options for dealing with this situation. She could have switched advisors or she could have continued to work with Ruth and "keep reminding her over and over" at each meeting. Sally rejected both of these in favor of a third option, one she believed would also help other single mothers attending Kirkwood. She waited until winter break when there were few students on campus and staff members seemed to have less work to do. Then she scheduled an hour-long meeting with Ruth, not to complain but to remedy the situation. Sally used the entire hour to talk to Ruth about how forgetting that she had a child and related time constraints made it seem like she "didn't care about what it might be like to be trying to [go to school] and raise a child alone. And I told her I was going to help her figure out how to do something about it." Ruth apologized and was receptive to Sally's suggestion that she make notations in each student's file, "you know, when I tell her that I can't take classes before 8:30 A.M. or after 3:30 P.M. because I have a kid, she can write that in my file, just to remind herself." During Sally's next advising appointment with Ruth, things went quite smoothly. She didn't "need to remind [Ruth] even once" about her scheduling needs. Of course there was no way for Sally to know if the change in Ruth's treatment of her was due to their meeting and the resulting notation Ruth made in Sally's file or for some other reason. Yet Ruth's behavior toward Sally had changed. And, as Sally pointed out, "maybe now she'll treat other [single mothers] differently, too."

Sally described most of her interactions with KCC faculty members as "really good" in terms of feeling supported as a single mother. Whenever Elliot was ill and Sally had to miss class, she would simply call her instructors and leave a message explaining her situation. She always made certain to provide her phone number in case they needed to call her back "in case they have any questions." When she returned to class, Sally always provided a note from Elliot's doctor and her instructors had always considered these to be excused absences. Even though Sally characterized most of her experiences with faculty members in a positive way, she admitted that some of them seemed to harbor stereotypes about single mothers and make assumptions about her because she was a single mother. She described an incident in one of her classes when the instructor, Dr. Mary Evans, unexpectedly asked Sally to stay after class:

> We were going to be starting to talk about welfare laws and programs the following week and she wanted to know if I would be comfortable sharing my experiences with the rest of the class. I never even got welfare. . . . I guess I should be glad that she was thinking that what I had to add to the discussion is valuable, but I think that sometimes it's just, I don't know, kind of like looking at the single mother as this kind of, well, like an oddity or something, like it's a thing that makes me unusual. She never asked me to share my experiences before, but now

all of a sudden because we were going to talk about welfare, then she comes to me. . . . And I know there aren't a lot of single moms in my classes or whatever, but [a teacher] would never ask a black person to speak on behalf of all black people, or to give "the black perspective," so I don't think it's really appropriate for a teacher to ask me to speak like that, like on behalf of all single mothers, to give "the single mother perspective." We don't all have the same experiences. . . . She wanted me to say what it was like to be a single mother on welfare. I hadn't ever been on welfare.

In some ways, Sally's experience was very similar to what Kasey experienced with her student peers. In both cases, the women were reduced to a single aspect of their identity: single mother. By drawing a comparison between single mothers and "black people," Sally was able to illustrate just how reductive it was for Dr. Evans to ask a single mother student to "speak on behalf of all single mothers," particularly as they "would never ask a black person to speak on behalf of all black people." However, instead of sharing her thoughts with Dr. Evans—partly because she worried that doing so might affect her grade in the course—Sally politely declined her instructor's request.

Sally also discussed her interactions with other KCC students. In most of her classes, she "usually will say something" to identify herself as a single mother. The responses of some of her peers left her "really disappointed and frustrated." In a course titled Social Problems, for example, during a group project that focused on marriage promotion policies, other students described single mothers by relying on some well-worn cultural stereotypes:

We had to present this in front of the class and debate these policies. And during our presentation, everyone else in my group was just talking about how good they are and how they would solve all kinds of problems. They were saying that if you get pregnant, then you should have to get married. And their logic was that two parents are better than one. . . . They didn't know I had a kid and they were saying some pretty awful things about single mothers. How they're all lazy. Calling them sluts. Saying they all just keep having babies to get more money.

And I listened to all of them and then when they were finished I had my turn. I told them that I'm a single mom. I told them that before I came back to school, I worked a full-time job at a factory until I got laid off. I told them that I only have one child. I told them that I have only had sex with three different people in my whole life. And I said that sometimes I think that there are parts of my life that might be easier if I had another adult in the house, a spouse or whatever. I would have someone to help pay bills and someone to help take care of my son so I didn't have to do it all the time. But I also told them that if I had been forced to marry my child's father, I know we would have been divorced pretty quickly. And

I wasn't mean about it. I even had the whole class laughing. But it was really interesting to hear what they thought about single mothers and the idea that marriage is the solution to everything.

There were a range of responses. Some of the students told Sally she was "one of the 'good' ones" because she was in college and "doing something" with her life. One young woman waited for Sally outside the classroom and told her that she was a single mother too, "but then asked me not to tell the rest of the class." Mostly, however, students "just smiled and laughed nervously . . . or looked down at their books."

It is difficult to know whether or not Sally's comments had an effect on the attitudes her peers have toward single mothers. However, in sharing her experiences, Sally was able to present an alternative perspective on marriage promotion policies and counter the perception that all single mothers are lazy "sluts" who "just keep having babies to get more money." The fact that some of her peers regarded her as "an exception" and "one of the good ones" indicates that they still harbored negative stereotypes about single mothers. It is possible that others simply dismissed her comments. Still, in articulating her position, Sally exercised a certain degree of power in the classroom, taking on the role of student-teacher as a way of combatting the stereotypes that had dominated the discussion. In doing so, she not only contributed to the learning that happened in that particular classroom but also worked to combat the chilly climate for single mothers at KCC.

CREATING A SENSE OF COMMUNITY

By the time she settled in Denton, Texas, and began her undergraduate studies at Texas Women's University, twenty-nine-year-old Farrah Williams had lived all over the state of Texas, had attended four other postsecondary institutions, and had been married and divorced. She was raising one child, a seven-year-old son named Luther, on her own. Born into a working-class family near Houston, Farrah credited her deep religious roots and her strong relationship with God for getting her through the hardships in her life and especially for getting her "back on track" with her education. She did not wish to discuss her past educational struggles or her failed marriage except to say that they made up what had been a "difficult" part of her life. Instead, Farrah focused on the present and the future. She was eager to talk about her experiences as a single mother and as an undergraduate student pursuing a degree in management. Farrah was also enthusiastic about the active role she had taken in a student organization for single parents at TWU. As a newly elected officer in the organization, she hoped to help address some ongoing struggles and increase the membership of the organization as a way of promoting the interests of single parents attending TWU and "creating a sense of community" among them.

Farrah became a TWU student due in large part to a chance encounter. In April 2005, she traveled from her home near Houston to take a tour of the University of North Texas (UNT) campus in Denton, a large public research institution that is the flagship institution of the UNT system.[41] She had completed her associate's degree at a community college near her hometown and was eager to finish her bachelor's degree so she could get a better-paying job. UNT had already admitted Farrah for the following semester, but she wanted to check out the campus before accepting. After touring UNT, Farrah and her sister, Latrice, who had accompanied her, went to dinner at a popular restaurant near the UNT campus. They were discussing the lack of family housing on the UNT campus when their waitress, who happened to be a single mother, suggested they visit the TWU campus located just ten minutes east of UNT:

> Originally when I came to Denton, I came to look at UNT. It just happened to be that night when me and my sister went to dinner our waitress said, "Oh well you should go check out Texas Woman's University. You know, it's right there [close by] and since you're here." It was a total fluke. You know, we went . . . and we asked, "Do you provide housing and what do you have for campus housing?" And they had just built the apartments. I was going to be able to move into them the year they opened up and that just sealed the deal right there. We went back to UNT and I said, "Well, do ya'll offer family housing?" And they said no, they just told me about some apartment complexes in the [Denton] area. . . . And I asked, "Do ya'll offer child care?" Well, no they didn't [at UNT]. And then I was done. After that, I was done. And I came back to TWU. [Family housing] was the deal maker for me. I mean, having it is just so convenient for me. Having it right here on campus.

While TWU had several traditional college dormitories on its main campus, it had completed a new family-friendly housing complex just before Farrah's visit. This housing complex, known as the Lowry Woods Community, included seven buildings and 168 apartments. Each building had its own laundry room; each apartment was wired for Internet, cable, and telephone services; and a there was a community center for group activities and social events. Although the Lowry Woods apartments were open to any student attending TWU, the majority of the residents were students with families.

While the availability of on-campus family housing was a key factor in Farrah's decision to attend TWU, the on-campus child care program was equally important to her. This program, called The Clubhouse, operated out of the Lowry Woods community center and was available to children ages five through twelve whose parents are TWU students, faculty, or staff. In 2011, approximately 20 percent of those enrolled in The Clubhouse were children of students who lived on campus, 40 percent were children of students who lived off campus, and 40 percent were children of TWU faculty and staff.[42] The Clubhouse, which is licensed by the Texas Department of Family and Protective Services, offered programs that included summer care and an after-school component during the regular academic year. Children whose parents were TWU students and living on campus received priority enrollment. Those who participated in the academic year program were picked up from their respective schools by The Clubhouse van and transported to the Lowry Woods community center, where they had a snack and then engaged in various age-appropriate activities that included "games, movies, cooking, sports, arts/crafts, fitness activities, music, motor skills, storytelling, reading, skating, bowling, swimming, field trips, and other fun activities."[43] The program operated from 3:00 P.M. to 6:00 P.M. Monday through Friday and charged reasonable tuition rates that ranged from $515 to $625 per semester. The program also offered Clubhouse Extended Days that ran from 1:00 P.M. to 6:00 P.M. on early release days when the public schools dismissed students at 12:50 P.M. These days did not require additional payment; they were included in the per-semester rates. In fact, the only additional fees associated with The Clubhouse were a $25 application fee and a Special Days fee of $25 per day per child for days when the public schools were closed for teacher training. On Special Days, the program operated from 7:30 A.M. to 5:30 P.M. Children who attended on those days brought a lunch from home and the program provided a snack in the morning and again in the afternoon. The Clubhouse Summer Program operated for two four-week sessions and was open from 7:30 A.M. until 5:30 P.M. Monday through Friday. Children attending the Summer Program brought their lunch from home and were given two snacks each day.

Like many of the TWU single mothers whose children attended The Clubhouse, Farrah had positive things to say about the program. She believed it provided high-quality care for her son and she went on and on about how much Luther enjoyed the activities the program offered. Although Farrah considered the rates at The Clubhouse to be reasonable for after-school child care, her income was insufficient to pay the regular program fees. Fortunately, she was approved for a child care subsidy through the Workforce Solutions Office of the Texas Workforce Commission. The subsidy, which is available to low-income families that include adults who are pursuing education or job training activities, covered the majority of Farrah's child care expenses. Because her work-study job provided her with only about $500 per month in take-home income, Farrah was required to contribute only $21 per month—or $84 per semester—to Luther's tuition and the child care subsidy covered the remainder. Farrah also appreciated the convenient location of The Clubhouse in the Lowry Woods apartment complex. Since she had to walk right past the Lowry Woods community center to get to her apartment, she could easily retrieve Luther once her classes were finished for the day. In addition, the transportation the program provided helped alleviate Farrah's stress about scheduling issues. Although her classes were typically finished for the day by mid-afternoon, she went directly to her work-study position after classes and remained there until 5 o'clock every weekday. If transportation had not been provided during the academic year, Farrah would have had to walk to her apartment to retrieve her car, then drive to Luther's school to pick him up, drive back to their apartment, drop Luther off at The Clubhouse, then walk back to the main part of campus to go to her work-study job. Farrah estimated that in addition to complicating her schedule, providing this transportation would have meant a loss of approximately one hour of work time each day, reducing her twenty-hour-per-week work-study position to only fifteen hours per week. The resulting loss of wages would have further strained her already limited budget or required that she take out additional student loans in order to meet her expenses.

Overall, Farrah found TWU to be a fairly supportive environment for single mothers. She had not encountered any situations when TWU faculty or staff members had mistreated or disrespected her because she was a single mother. Yet she did identify some aspects of the university that she felt might make some single mothers feel unwelcome. For example, while Farrah was thankful for the presence of a child care center at TWU, she also recognized that this program had some limitations. The Clubhouse was available exclusively for elementary-school-aged children; therefore, single mothers who had infants or toddlers were likely to find child care a challenge. In fact, several of the mothers who attended TWU identified lack of on-campus child care for their young children as a significant aspect of what they considered to be an unwelcoming climate at the university. In addition, while Farrah described her experience at TWU as positive overall, she also described some encounters that were very similar to those of Kasey Stevens. Some of Farrah's student peers seemed to have a very limited understanding of what it was like to be a single parent and a college student:

They think he's so cute. You know, I find it funny to watch the younger students and how they, I just don't think they understand yet how easy they have it. And I say easy but to them it's hard. Because they don't know. I mean, they just think he's so cute . . . I just don't think they get it. . . . They just haven't had their eyes opened to a situation like this. And they haven't had to deal with anything like this. I mean, in a sense, they are still kids themselves. Their parents are probably supporting them, probably still helping them [financially]. You know? And it's two completely different worlds. Everything changes after you have a kid. They just don't get it.

Yet unlike Kasey, Farrah was not upset by this treatment and it did not make her feel unwelcome. She simply regarded it as a sign of the immaturity of her peers, a symptom of their lack of life experience and lack of understanding about "how easy they have it."

Farrah pointed to other ways the university supported student parents. For example, she thought that the Angel Tree program was "awesome!" This program, facilitated by the TWU Office of Commuter and Non-Traditional Student Services, enabled low-income parents enrolled at TWU to obtain holiday gifts for their children through an anonymous donation program. The parents provided information about the age, sex, and clothing sizes of their children and listed any toys their children wanted that were age appropriate. Information about each family was then put on the back of a paper ornament and hung on the Angel Tree, which was located on the main floor of the TWU Student Union. Supporters chose an ornament, purchased gifts for the children listed on the back on that ornament, and returned the wrapped gifts to the Office of Commuter and Non-Traditional Student Services. The gifts were distributed in mid-December. The Angel Tree was a popular program at TWU, and it was common for academic departments, sororities, and staff groups to adopt a family by choosing an ornament and collectively purchasing gifts for that family. Farrah, like many of the single mothers at TWU, regarded the Angel Tree program as a notable form of support, particularly because their financial circumstances limited their ability to purchase non-essentials such as gifts. It wasn't that the gifts were extravagant—typically, each child received a few toys and some clothing items. The value Farrah attributed to the program was primarily emotional, particularly because she "wouldn't have been able to get him anything" and the program ensured that Luther had gifts to open on Christmas morning.

Farrah also had positive things to say about a unique form of support at TWU: the Single Parents Student Organization (SPSO). Although it is unclear exactly when the organization was founded, it was relatively new when Farrah arrived at the university in the fall of 2005. All of the members were single mothers. She learned about the organization from the TWU Family Resources Manual, an eight-page booklet that is provided to all residents of Lowry Woods that lists family-related services at the university and in the broader Denton community. Farrah attended her first SPSO meetings only weeks after beginning her studies at the university and found that the organization made a good effort to foster community among TWU students who were parenting alone. It also provided ongoing information about various resources and opportunities that might be of interest to members, such as a free Halloween party for children at an area religious center. The SPSO also organized a variety of events. They scheduled an outing to the Frank Buck Zoo, a popular, family-friendly, low-cost attraction located in Gainesville, just thirty minutes north of the TWU campus. On several occasions, they had counselors talk to the group about topics such as "dating issues for single parents and effective discipline for single parents." Other times, the group rented bounce houses for the children or organized a potluck or a family movie night in the Lowry Woods community center.

Farrah appreciated the fact that the SPSO existed at TWU, particularly because she believed that few universities had this type of organization. Yet she also had several criticisms of it, including the fact that planned events often did not materialize and that "it just seems that it is disorganized, like it's not clear who is supposed to be doing what." She also identified poor communication as a problem within the organization, citing several instances when an event was planned but not appropriately publicized to SPSO members. As a result, the events were often poorly attended. Roughly two months before my interviews with Farrah, she had been elected as an officer of the SPSO. Through her new position, she hoped to address some of these issues and help create a more supportive environment for single parents attending TWU. Yet even in the short amount of time she had held her leadership position, she had come to realize that improving and expanding the SPSO was going to be difficult. Only two women showed up to a "meet the officers" potluck the SPSO organized that was "well-publicized—we had flyers all over campus and sent emails to everyone." Farrah attributed this to the time constraints SPSO members faced:

> These women, some just don't have the time to give up, to get together for the support. . . . And it's just so hard to coordinate time, you know, because I leave every other weekend to go drop my son off with his dad. . . . And everybody else has their own schedules and just coordinating things where we can all get together at once is just impossible. And so it's hard to set things up and do things together, to get a big group of people to come to the meetings. This semester I think the only people that have come to the meetings are the officers plus one or two people. And it's just hard. I just think it's hard all around. Because we are so busy with school and work and kids.

Although she hoped to help increase the SPSO membership and attendance at events, Farrah worried about the future of the organization. Her fears were not unfounded; shortly after my interviews with Farrah, the SPSO organization stopped meeting. However, a new organization, Student Parents Also Raising Kids (SPARK), took its place only a few months later. SPARK had a broader membership base than SPSO because it recruited both single and married TWU student parents. And while it is possible that the needs and voices of single parents may be less prominent in SPARK activities and discussions, the organization's greater size may help ensure its sustainability and, in turn, help promote the sense of community Farrah had hoped to accomplish.

CONCLUSION

In previous chapters, I have examined three significant challenges single mothers who are college students face: time constraints, child care, and finances. It is important to point out that these three challenges are not uncommon among single mothers in general, whether they are college students or not.[44] Yet whatever similarities exist between single mothers who are and those who are not attending college, it is important to remember that single mothers are not a monolithic group. Their experiences, opportunities, and challenges are, in both profound and subtle ways, bound up with the particular contexts of their lived experiences, including relevant social institutions. This chapter has focused on the chilly climate for single mothers who are attending postsecondary institutions. I do not mean to suggest that the climate is the same at all institutions or that all single mothers experience it to the same degree or in the same ways. However, in both their survey responses and in interviews, the majority of the women indicated that they encountered a chilly climate and felt marginalized, were treated like outsiders, and even experienced outright contempt and hostility because they were single mothers. This stigmatization affected the women in various ways. For some, like Kasey and Clarissa, it contributed to feelings that they didn't fit in or that their specific needs were ignored or were not taken seriously by faculty, staff, and administration. Others attempted to minimize and avoid stigmatization and its consequences, particularly by hiding the fact they were single mothers and trying to appear like "normal" students who were not parents. For women such as Serena, the climate was so unwelcoming that they were humiliated and shunned to the point of leaving the university altogether.

The presence and pervasiveness of the chilly climate for single mothers did not go entirely unnoticed by others who learn and work at institutions of higher education. Faculty and staff members were very much aware of the often demeaning treatment of single mothers at their institutions. They cited the lack of institutional services and support for single mothers and the specific behavior of faculty, staff, and students as evidence that single mothers, as one academic advisor put it, "haven't really been fully incorporated into the university yet, into the life of the campus. We still tend to forget that they are here, despite the fact that they *are* here and have been here for years." The university professionals I spoke with were quite aware of the presence of single mothers on their campuses. They acknowledged that single women who attend college while raising children have needs beyond those of traditional students and said that they were very familiar with the "chilly" climate facing these women.

It was common for faculty and staff I spoke with to empathize with the single mothers on their campuses. This was true of Andrew Merrick, a psychologist at the UI Student Counseling Center, who had been employed at the university for over a decade and worked with students "from all walks of life." In some respects, Andrew regarded the issues facing single mothers at UI as similar to those facing other students: "academics, relationship issues, money problems, depression and anxiety, and they have too much to do and not enough time." But he also believed that students who were raising children faced challenges that went beyond those of traditional college students, particularly because being a parent "just exponentially magnifies all of those [student] issues." Perhaps the most significant challenge, Andrew said, was the climate of the university and faculty attitudes toward these students:

> Faculty, some faculty, don't think that students who have kids belong here on campus because they can't devote their time exclusively to their student responsibilities. And this seems to be particularly true for graduate students and those who are in medical school or dental school, professional students. It's the idea that you can't be a good dental student or graduate student and be a parent at the same time. And the faculty don't come right out and say that, but I've talked to enough students and to enough faculty on this campus to pick up the subtle ways that attitude operates. But sometimes it's more obvious.
>
> I know that we've made some strides, but it's a struggle even making this university hospitable for faculty and staff who have families. There are still all kinds of issues there as well, and it's not easy to be a faculty member with kids. But I do think it is harder for students, a lot harder. There's little of the tolerance and acceptance that one would hope for with students that may have competing priorities. And children are definitely thought of by most of the faculty I've talked to as competing priorities.

Others expressed similar sentiments and connected the chilly climate to broader cultural attitudes toward single motherhood. For example, Rihanna Rivera, a student life staff member at TWU, indicated that faculty and staff members at her institution sometimes made comments that reinforced the U.S. cultural stereotype of single mothers as lazy. She described a "dismissive and disrespectful" attitude toward single mothers on the part of several of her colleagues. Although this bothered her a great deal, Rihanna did not know how to address the issue. In this respect, Rihanna was like many faculty and staff members I interviewed—they recognized that the institutional climate was an issue, but few had concrete suggestions for making their college or university more welcoming to and supportive of single mothers. The suggestions they did offer related primarily to offering child care on campus and creating scholarships specifically for single mothers. However, their enthusiasm for such ideas typically wavered when I asked them how such programs might be funded.

So what can be done to effectively combat the chilly climate single mothers encounter in postsecondary institutions? The climate of an institution is not fixed. It is dynamic and organic, in a constant state of growing and becoming. It is possible to change an institutional climate. But it is essential to remember that effective, lasting change is likely only when such change is approached in a conscientious, systematic manner and is directed by several guiding questions. These questions include: What type of change is needed? What steps can be taken? What models of support and services for single mothers currently exist at colleges and universities? How might these models be modified and implemented at other institutions of higher learning? How can such programs be initiated and sustained given that economic scarcity is an ongoing concern at many institutions? Who might be involved in formulating plans for and implementing these types of programs in order to effectively address institutional climate issues for single mothers? These are issues I address in the appendix.

CONCLUSION

In many ways, single mothers are similar to other postsecondary students. They have many of the same concerns, such as class schedules, degree requirements, and academic performance. Some to go college because they place a high value on education or want to get a degree in order to pursue their chosen career. Others regard higher education as a natural step in the course of their lives. Some others regard the completion of a college degree as a long-term strategy to increase the odds of obtaining the financial security associated with a stable career. However, as this project has shown, single mothers also pursue postsecondary education for rather unique reasons. These women tend to regard their academic pursuits as a way to set a positive example for their children and teach them about values such as hard work, responsibility, sacrifice, discipline, and goal setting. Single mothers also pursue college degrees because they want to prove to themselves and others that they are good mothers. America's colleges and universities, however, have not been designed with the specific needs of single mothers in mind. As a result, members of this student population face challenges that are distinct from those their more traditional peers face. These challenges impact both their academic experiences and their personal lives and can even jeopardize their ability to complete their education.

For most of the women who participated in this research, financial concerns were a significant source of stress. Like many college students, the women often worried about the costs associated with education such as rising tuition rates, student fees, and the purchase or rental of textbooks. They also contended with the costs associated with raising their children as single custodial mothers. They adopted a variety of strategies as they attempted to economize and manage within the confines of their limited economic resources. It was common for the women to adopt strict household budgets; doing so generally enabled them to better manage their academic, child care, and living expenses. However, their budgets typically did not include any disposable income, and things such as social activities were often beyond their means. The women typically were not able to set aside money for emergencies. Unforeseen legal expenses, car repair costs, or charges associated with illness or hospitalization for themselves or their children meant a financial crisis and a different financial strategy than they had planned. Some took out additional student loans if they were available. Others maxed out their credit cards. Both strategies enabled them to access much-needed funds in the short term, yet they had the long-term implication of mounting debt that would require years or even decades to repay.

The single mothers who had good support networks often had less financial stress, particularly when family or friends provided free housing or babysitting. Those who received child support or alimony or whose parents provided occasional financial assistance typically expressed less concern about their financial circumstances. However, most of the women did not benefit from these types of support, and despite their best efforts to manage their finances, found their income inadequate to meet their expenses. When student loans and credit cards were maxed out, the women often went without essential academic materials such as textbooks and computers. In other cases, they sold personal belongings to bring in additional income, went without food or other essentials, or even dug through trash in order to retrieve bottles and cans to cash in on the deposit money. Although the women were certainly not passive about their economic situations, most lived in poverty as they endeavored to complete their postsecondary education.

The women also faced significant time constraints. The dual demands of coursework and their parenting responsibilities meant that they typically struggled to meet academic deadlines, devote adequate time to parenting and household responsibilities, and still have enough time to care for themselves. Those who worked part time or full time faced even greater challenges in this regard. However, the women were quite active about managing their time, formulating various methods to help them balance their parenting, academic, and employment responsibilities. Many compartmentalized their days into student time and parenting time. Although organizing their schedules in this way was typically quite effective, this strict organization of time left the women with little free time. In addition, sleep deprivation was a common complaint; many of the women studied late into the night after their children were in bed. Although most of the women attended traditional face-to-face classes, some found online courses preferable, particularly because such courses offered flexible scheduling, which helped them better manage their time.

Those with some degree of economic privilege, such as the women who received child support or alimony, faced less pressure with regard to time constraints. They could afford to place their children in child care for more hours per week or, in some cases, hire a nanny to help with child care and household responsibilities. However, this privilege was the exception rather than the rule. Time constraints contributed to a sense of guilt and shame among the women. More specifically, they worried that their demanding schedules did not enable them to devote sufficient time to their children and that they were not good enough mothers because they dedicated part of their time exclusively to academic work.

Child care was another source of stress for the women. They struggled with its high cost. They also encountered problems locating child care that was high-quality, convenient, and met their needs with regard to class schedules or employment schedules. Child care was an essential resource for the women; placing their children in the care of others allowed them to attend classes and tend to other academic responsibilities. For those who worked, child care enabled them to earn much-needed income. The women with children enrolled in elementary school often had an easier time accessing child care because they could place them in before- and after-school programs. Such programs were generally convenient and relatively affordable.

Some of the women had family members or friends who helped care for their children. Others were able to participate in government child care programs such as Head Start. However, many did not benefit from these forms of support and were well acquainted with America's child care crisis. Even on campuses where child care was available, high demand often meant lengthy waiting lists. Women who had more than one preschool-aged child or who had children with special needs faced additional barriers to child care. And while most of those with young children had arranged for child care in a way that permitted them to devote parts of their day exclusively to academic responsibilities, their access to that care could be jeopardized by such things as inclement weather or the mild illness of their child. In such cases, and if other child care arrangements were not available, the women typically had to set aside their academic responsibilities in order to take care of their children. They did not complain about doing so; on the contrary, they took pride in the fact that they prioritized their mothering work. They presented it as a natural response to situations when child care was not available. However, they worried about the consequences of such actions, particularly as missing class and forgoing study time could negatively impact their grades.

Concerns about financial scarcity, time constraints, and child care are certainly not unique to single mothers who are pursuing postsecondary education; many American mothers must contend with these issues. However, single mothers who are college students face a challenge that is unique: the chilly climate of higher education. The women often felt marginalized, stigmatized, and unwelcome at the institutions they attended. The chilly climate they encountered was sometimes overt and took the form of disparaging comments from faculty, staff, and other students. Some faculty took punitive actions against them. But more often, the women experienced subtler forms of marginalization and exclusion, such as institutional policies and practices that did not take their particular needs as single mothers into consideration. A good example is the rigid excused absence policy of some professors.

The women certainly did not bear the chilly climate passively. They used a variety of strategies to negotiate and even challenge it. Chief among these was managing their identities as single mothers within the context of the postsecondary institutions they attended. Sometimes they chose to pass and other times they attempted to control how much people knew about their personal lives or hid the fact that they were single mothers. On occasion, they also actively challenged stereotypes they encountered in classrooms and across campus, particularly those that defined single mothers as bad mothers. In doing so, the women opposed the stigmatization of single mothers and actively sought to impact the ideological landscape of the postsecondary institutions they attended. However, even as they attempted to do so, the women frequently relied on discourses of good motherhood to describe themselves and their reasons for pursuing postsecondary education, embracing the themes of self-sufficiency, sacrifice, and maternal love that permeate those discourses. Thus, as part of their ongoing efforts to navigate institutions of higher education, the women also had to navigate their own complex relationships with cultural ideals of motherhood in the United States. Sometimes they rejected these ideals, particularly those that promote disparaging attitudes toward single mothers. At other times, they reinforced those ideals, laying claim to the status of good mothers by defining themselves in accordance with ideals of intensive mothering and demonstrating their self-sacrificing nature and seemingly limitless love for their children.

In some ways, scrutiny of single mothers seems less intense that it was at the end of the twentieth century, when welfare reform rhetoric still occupied a prominent place in the U.S. political psyche. However, households headed by single mothers continue to be defined as a social problem, and concerns about the supposed social, economic, and criminal consequences of such households continue to receive much attention in conservative political discourse. In pursuit of their party's nomination for the 2016 presidential race, for example, Republican candidates relied on single-mother-headed households as a sort of moral touchstone, a means of drawing attention to the supposed continuing decline of the American family. In June 2015, as he reflected on comments he had made in 1995 when he advocated public shaming of unmarried women who give birth, Jeb Bush reaffirmed his position against nonmarital childbearing: "We have a 40 percent-plus out-of-wedlock birthrate and if you think about this from the perspective of children, it puts a huge—it's a huge challenge for single moms to raise children in the world that we're in today, and it hurts the prospects, it limits the possibilities of young people being able to live lives of purpose and meaning. . . . To assume you can have a fatherless society and not have bad outcomes is the wrong approach."[1] Similarly, Bobby Jindal detailed what he believed to be the harms associated with out-of-wedlock births by discussing crime. Jindal delivered his comments on his campaign blog, where he blamed the October 1, 2015, tragedy at Umpqua Community College in Roseburg, Oregon, in part on "the young men who have either no father figure in their lives, or a broken relationship with their father."[2] And Ben Carson, a staunch advocate of so-called traditional values, religious morals, and the nuclear family, raised concerns about the supposed economic and criminal consequences of childbearing outside marriage: "We need to face the fact that when young girls have babies out of wedlock, most of the time their education ends with that first baby. . . . And those babies are four times as likely to grow up in poverty, end up in the penal system or the welfare system. You know, I'm not making this stuff up. That's well-documented. That's a problem."[3]

Interestingly, all three candidates offered their remarks shortly after the National Center for Health Statistics (NCHS) issued a report that documented a reduction in nonmarital childbearing in the United States during the first decade of the twenty-first century. According to the report, out-of-wedlock births declined by approximately 7 percent overall, with the sharpest decreases noted among Black and Hispanic women. Additionally, although both Bush and Jindal equated out-of-wedlock with "absent fathers," the NCHS found a significant increase in the percentage of nonmarital births that occurred between cohabiting couples: while only 41 percent of babies born to unmarried parents lived in such households in 2002, that number had increased to 58 percent by 2010.[4]

With criticism of single mothers still circulating within the American political sphere, I have not been surprised when I've encountered similar attitudes when I present my research findings on single mothers who are college students. I have shared my findings at formal presentations at academic conferences, at invited talks and guest lectures to college students and community groups, and in the form of book chapters and journal articles. I have also shared my research with my university students in courses I have taught that focused on gender, American culture and society, or social inequalities and when I have been a guest lecturer in such courses. Sometimes I spoke with others about my work in informal conversations in a coffee shop or library when I was writing and revising chapters and a stranger asked what I was working on. Like many academics, I have been quite eager to share my work with others. However, I have encountered a variety of responses that suggest that the stigmatization and marginalization of single mothers is not limited to statements made by conservative political candidates trying to garner support for their campaigns. I have found that such attitudes continue to permeate our postsecondary institutions and our communities. In the following discussion, I address some of the dominant themes in the reactions I have received in response to my research.

Such reflection is useful as a way of moving toward the practical dimensions of this project, specifically toward a discussion of ideas about how colleges and universities can provide better support for single mothers on their campuses. Some have cautioned me against practical applications. A former colleagues advised me, "Don't get political about this. You should just stick to the scholarly dimensions of the project." Such cautions have typically been offered by peers, prospective editors, and well-meaning friends as "in my best interest," frequently with the warning that if I address the practical dimensions of my research, some readers may reject the entire project as "lacking objectivity" and as "too critical of colleges and universities." Others have suggested that such an approach would be "a waste of [my] time" and would distract me from "more important duties" such as continued research, publishing, and teaching. I appreciate it when others try to look out for my best interest, but I wonder if I would have received similar warnings if I had conducted research on a population that is less stigmatized than single mothers. For example, would similar warnings have been issued if I had studied the role of older caregivers to individuals who were HIV-positive as a means of better understanding the dimensions of daily life for those caregivers so steps could be taken to support them in ways that make their care-giving work less burdensome and thus reduce the social and economic impacts of HIV?[5] Would I have been warned about the possibility of coming across as critical of postsecondary institutions if I had studied the effectiveness of university massive open online courses (MOOCs) and discussed practical applications of that research in order to improve student learning outcomes?[6] And would I have been warned about not being objective enough if I was part of a team of ethnographers who examined the design, marketing, and distribution of various products in order to increase productivity and promote industry success?[7] Applied ethnography has a lengthy history.[8] It is widely accepted in the social sciences and more broadly in academia. Contemporary scholars continue to advocate for applied research as a way of fostering social change, particularly in an effort to combat social inequalities.[9] The cautions I have received about the application of my research are not grounded in the merits of applied research. I regard them as a reflection of the ongoing marginalization and stigmatization of single mothers.

DISBELIEF

One of the most common responses I have received to my research findings is perhaps best described as disbelief. This response is typified by questions and remarks such as, "Do single mothers even go to college? I thought most were lucky to finish high school," and "I don't think we have any of them [at our university]." Individuals who make these comments cannot seem to grasp the reality that single mothers are part of the U.S. postsecondary student population. And it seems even more difficult for them to accept the fact that single mothers likely exist as part of the student body on their own campus. It is as though these audience members make their remarks in a moment of genuine cognitive dissonance and cannot seem to reconcile the fact that "single mother" and "college student" are not mutually exclusive identities. In reality, single mothers are not a rarity among the U.S. postsecondary student population. A November 2014 report demonstrated that approximately 4.8 million U.S. college students—26 percent of all registered postsecondary students—were raising children; nearly half of them (2,049,242) were single mothers.[10] To put that number in perspective, the total number of single mothers who attend college in the United States is greater than the total college enrollment in forty-nine of the fifty U.S. states. There are more single mothers attending college in the United States than the entire postsecondary student population in any single state except California.[11] To consider it from another perspective, there are currently 460,000 student-athletes who participate in NCAA programs.[12] Thus, for every NCAA student athlete, there are approximately 4.45 single mothers attending college. Clearly, single mothers are part of the U.S. college student population and their numbers are far from insignificant.

It is tempting to dismiss expressions of disbelief regarding the presence of single mothers among the U.S. postsecondary student population as inconsequential or as simply reflecting a lack of awareness. While this may be true to some extent, those who are unaware of the existence of this student population are not able to take the steps necessary to provide services and support to the single mothers on their campuses. Thus, disbelief and the corresponding lack of awareness are not entirely benign, particularly as they can contribute to a chilly climate. It is also important to consider the reasons for this lack of awareness. The Civil Rights Act of 1964, Title IX of the Education Amendments of 1972, and similar antidiscrimination measures mandated that U.S. postsecondary institutions put diversity, equity, and inclusiveness initiatives in place. Such initiatives were intended to promote diversity in higher education and were grounded in the belief that diversity, equity, and inclusiveness fundamentally enhance the postsecondary educational experience. Research has demonstrated the benefits of such initiatives, such as helping students develop critical thinking skills, exposing students to new perspectives and ideas, confronting stereotypes, fostering critical self-examination, and promoting leadership.[13]

Contemporary understandings of diversity and equity within higher education are still somewhat limited; they focus primarily on the triad of race, class, and gender and seek to level the playing field through programs for racial or ethnic minorities, initiatives for students from impoverished backgrounds, and measures to promote gender equity. Such efforts are important and I do not mean to minimize their impact. However, it is also important to recognize that they represent a limited understanding of contemporary postsecondary students in the United States, in terms of both their identities and their experiences; such efforts do not adequately address the reality of diversity and inequality as they exist on American college and university campuses. Some student populations—such as single mothers—are simply overlooked. We must continue to expand our understanding of diversity, equity, and inclusiveness in ways that help promote a more accurate understanding of the broad range of identities and experiences among our student populations. Doing so can bring increased attention to the myriad ways that exclusion, marginalization, and discrimination are manifest in U.S. culture and on our campuses. However, such attention is only the first step toward the creation of inclusive campuses that reflect an awareness of diverse student populations—including single mothers—and that successfully support all student populations in ways that promote success and achievement.

PITY

Some audience members have responded with pity that is typically expressed through remarks such as "those poor women," or "I really can't imagine how they do it," or "What kind of toll does that take on them and on their children?" Given the various challenges single mothers who are college students face, such responses are not entirely surprising. The audience members who have expressed pity for single mothers seem to genuinely empathize with the women and the challenges they encounter as they pursue postsecondary degrees. However, pity is a rather superficial way of responding to and attempting to make sense of the lives and experiences of these women. Pity is predicated on the notion that single mothers attending college are rendered powerless by their circumstances. The challenges the women who participated in this research identified were significant, to be sure. Most of them struggled financially and many were living below the federal poverty line. They faced numerous obstacles with regard to child care, particularly those who had young children or who had more than one child. Many found it difficult to manage demanding schedules that included parenting responsibilities, attending class and studying, and, in some cases, employment. And, of course, there were the challenges associated with navigating the "chilly" climate of higher education. It is important to acknowledge and understand the dimensions of such challenges, including their causes and their consequences.

Pitying single mothers who are college students runs the risk of denying their subjectivity and of diminishing or perhaps erasing the multiple ways they can and do express agency. For the women who participated in this research, agency sometimes took the form of meticulously organizing their schedules in accordance with parent time and student time. At other times, they expressed agency by confronting peers, university staff, and faculty members who made disparaging remarks about single mothers. They also expressed agency in the decisions they made about how to parent their children and how to manage their limited finances. And it is important to remember that the women tended to regard pursuit of a college degree as an expression of agency—it was a path most of them embarked upon intentionally and as a means of moving toward a better future, one they envisioned as providing the financial security and lifestyle of the American middle class. I certainly do not mean to discount the challenges facing single mothers who are college students. However, to pity these women is to take a one-dimensional view that fails to recognize and honor the ways they recognize, claim, and assert their power in their personal lives and in the context of the academic institutions they attend.

SINGLE MOTHERS AS HEROINES

Perhaps the response that has been most surprising to me has been the exaltation of single mothers who attend college by offering them up as role models for "hard work and determination." This perspective depicts single mothers as modern-day heroines. As a former student remarked, "These women are probably the strongest women on the planet, the kind of women that can do anything they set their mind to. The rest of us [students] just need to sit back and let them teach us how to manage our lives." These comments seem to have been offered in a generous spirit and were likely meant as compliments. However, they represent a limited understanding of the lives of single mothers attending college. Just as responses based on pity ignore the ways that single mothers access and exercise power within the context of their lives, the "single mothers as heroines" response ignores the very real hardships these women endure. To be fair, I often found myself in awe of the women who participated in this project. They typically worked very hard, many maintained grades that earned them a regular place on the academic honor roll, and they tended to have close and affectionate relationships with their children. However, they also struggled as women, as mothers, and as students. When single mothers are characterized as heroines, it becomes quite easy to dismiss the challenges they face or to imagine that they have the skills and resources needed to respond to such challenges on their own and to take care of themselves and their children without support or assistance. This may be true for some single mothers. As examples throughout this book demonstrate, however, most of the women struggled with finances, with managing their time and various responsibilities, with child care issues, and with feeling accepted and welcome within the context of the postsecondary institutions they attended. Therefore, just as it is important not to pity the women and characterize them as powerless, it is equally important to avoid revering them in ways that deny the challenges they face or that somehow cast the women as all-powerful. Neither characterization is an accurate representation of their lives and experiences.

DISMISSAL

Some audience members have listened politely as I have discussed my research but then have quickly dismissed the experiences of single mothers attending college as unimportant and as disconnected from their own lives and experiences. These individuals have made comments such as, "Try being a transgender student and then you'll understand how it feels to be an outsider on this campus," or "I struggle to go to college, to pay my tuition, and nobody is studying me." They have also asked questions such as, "Are we supposed to fund 'special programs' for *all* the different student groups on our campus?" I understand the frustration that gives rise to such comments. Transgender students face ongoing marginalization on campuses across the United States that includes lack of support and documented evidence of the various forms of violence and hate crimes they encounter.[14] Many students struggle with the ever-increasing costs of tuition, student fees, and textbooks. Institutions certainly do not have unlimited budgets, and administrators must make difficult decisions about how to allocate limited funds in a way that best serves their student population. But I still cannot help but be disappointed by such comments, particularly because they reflect and reinforce the notion that the marginalization of particular groups is to be expected within the context of higher education, that such marginalization is simply part of the postsecondary status quo, and that there is nothing to be done about it. Such comments also reflect a kind of social disconnect, as though the marginalization of single mothers is not a problem for the entire university community but is only a problem for single mothers. This tendency to divorce oneself from the plight of others is very much a reflection of the competitive, individualist mentality that remains prominent in U.S. culture. As long as marginalized groups continue to see one another as competitors and are detached and disconnected from one another, they seem doomed to remain in a situation wherein each group is left to face its own challenges. I am not suggesting that transgender students, low-income students, and single mothers who are college students face the same issues. However, all three groups have something in common: they continue to be marginalized within the context of postsecondary institutions. It is from this point of commonality that these groups might work together and create strategic alliances. The importance and effectiveness of such alliances as a component of social change efforts are well documented. While collective numbers are important, equally important is the sharing of ideas and resources, particularly as a way of working more efficiently and effectively to challenge the status quo and combat marginalization, exclusion, and oppression in whatever forms they exist.[15] Thus, instead of remaining divided and struggling separately, marginalized groups can work together to support one another and collectively promote more inclusive campuses for all student populations, including transgender students, low-income students, and single mothers.

BLAMING

One of the most frequent responses I have encountered blames single mothers for the challenges they face in the context of higher education. This response has surfaced most often during the discussion or question-and-answer portion of presentations, particularly when I have asked audience members to imagine how colleges and universities might better meet the needs of these students. This is often met with a good degree of irritation and vitriol and with comments such as, "What did they expect when they enrolled here?" and "They should have known what they were getting themselves into." Some audience members have even suggested that if single mothers can't handle the various challenges they face, they should simply "work harder." One particularly angry faculty member shouted at me, "If they can't handle the demands of my classroom, they should drop out!" I find such responses quite frustrating, yet they do not surprise me. Such responses are quite familiar and reflect the mother-blaming that continues to dominate U.S. discourses of motherhood. They are also grounded in the notion of rugged individualism and the notion that everyone should pull themselves up by their bootstraps.[16] Both of these notions permeate U.S. attitudes toward marginalized and oppressed populations. The central tenet of rugged individualism is really quite simple: if an individual wants to accomplish something and desires to improve her lot in life, that individual simply needs to set goals and then work hard in order to achieve success. According to this mindset, is imperative that the individual engage in this type of goal-seeking journey on her own, without the assistance or support of others. If this individual achieves her goals, she is deemed as having realized all that America has to offer, to be a shining example of someone who has realized the American dream. If the individual doesn't realize her goals, the blame is placed squarely on her own shoulders. This philosophy denies the very real and pervasive structural inequalities that persist in U.S. society that provide certain groups with unearned privilege while marginalizing and oppressing other groups on the basis of identities such as gender, race, socioeconomic status, religion, marital status, and sexual identity. And while privilege and oppression exist in relation to single social group identities, they are exacerbated at the intersection of multiple identities.

In the context of higher education, many of these structural inequalities stem from the fact that despite the diverse identities and experiences that exist among the contemporary American postsecondary student population, there is limited support for nontraditional students. Postsecondary institutions have, to some degree, moved away from the idea that most of their students will fit the traditional college student profile: eighteen to twenty-two years old, unmarried, starting university immediately after high school, and still receiving financial and emotional support from their parents. Indeed, there has been increasing discussion of so-called nontraditional students and, as part of this discussion, various definitions have been offered:

> The concept of non-traditional students does not have a standard definition and at least three definitions can be found in the international literature. The first approach uses age as a differentiation criterion and includes older students (usually defined as 23 or 25 years old at the time of enrollment). The second approach includes those who are different from the majority of students in terms of background, including ethnicity, lower socio-economic status, first-generation, and employment status. The third approach places emphasis on the risk factors for dropping out: for example, the U.S. Department of Education has identified non-traditional students that have at least one of the following characteristics: delayed enrollment (does not enter postsecondary education in the same calendar year that the student finished high school); attends part time; works full time; is financially independent; has dependents other than a spouse; is a single parent; does not have a high school diploma.[17]

These definitions suggest that contemporary notions of nontraditional students reflect a good degree of awareness of diversity in terms of identities and background and life experiences.

However, this awareness does not automatically translate into support for diverse student populations. For example, support programs for first-generation students have become part of the mainstay of university academic support programs. Many institutions also offer what is commonly referred to as a bridge program to help first-generation students acclimate to college-level academics and to familiarize themselves with the campus and the social and financial dimensions of college life before they begin their freshman year.[18] These programs are important and continue to have a significant impact on the satisfaction rates and academic success rates of first-generation students.[19] However, while the definition of nontraditional students in the quote above includes specific attention to students who are single parents, support programs for such students remain rare. Single mothers are often left to contend with the challenges they face on their own, typically without the assistance of university personnel with specialized knowledge about their specific needs and without the support of programs designed to help them navigate the particular dimensions of their academic and personal lives.

Limited attention to single mothers as part of the U.S. postsecondary student population also means that existing policies typically do not take the needs of these students into account. Single mothers who pursue a college degree encounter numerous structural inequalities, including at the federal and institutional levels. For example, the FAFSA does not include child care as a school-related expense. Many institutions do not have child care facilities on their campuses. Furthermore, while attendance policies at postsecondary institutions typically excuse absences for such things as work-related travel, student illness or injury, observation of religious holy days, and participation in university-sanctioned activities such as sports or academic teams, such policies seldom include specific language that excuses a student who must take care of a dependent child who is sick or injured. Structural inequalities can also be identified in the context of specific courses. A course that requires meetings outside class for a group project, for example, or a course in which attendance at performing arts events is mandatory can pose a significant hardship to single mothers who might not have access to child care during evenings or on weekends or simply might not be able to afford the expense of additional child care.

Those who blame single mothers for the challenges they encounter as they pursue a college degree perpetuate the notion that these women are outsiders and do not belong in postsecondary institutions. Furthermore, such blaming is based on the idea that any challenges single mothers face within the context of higher education are somehow natural and inevitable rather than socially constructed via institutional policies and practices. Blaming single mothers for the challenges they encounter becomes an effective strategy for avoiding critical reflection about institutional structures and policies, including how they privilege certain student populations and marginalize, punish, and exclude single mothers.

CONFUSION

The response I have found most frustrating is best characterized as confusion. This response is typically expressed by individuals who understand the challenges facing these women and who express concern and empathy for single mothers who are college students. Yet for whatever reason, they are confused about how they might promote a more inclusive environment for single mothers on their campuses. These individuals will throw up their hands and ask, "What can we do to help them? Where does one even start?" or will say such things as "I don't how to locate resources that might be useful for single moms." My frustration about such responses stems from the fact that there are already models for programs designed to meet the needs of specific student populations and for providing such populations with the services and support that have been deemed essential to their success. These programs are grounded in discourses of student retention and achievement and are based on the understanding that many students have needs that extend far beyond the realm of basic academics. For example, programs designed for first-generation college students, students with disabilities, student athletes, international students, low-income students, and students with special academic interests are common on campuses throughout the country.[20] Thus, it is very frustrating to hear faculty, staff, and members of student government say they don't know how to create programs to meet the specific needs of single mothers on their campuses.

Those of us who wish to provide support to single mothers who are pursing postsecondary education need not reinvent the wheel. Instead, we simply need to honor the spirit and scope of our equity and diversity initiatives and to take our cue from existing programs and policies that are designed to promote inclusive environments. Before such change can occur and before colleges and universities can implement measures to better meet the specific needs of single mothers, it is imperative to take what is the most important step in providing any type of support to a marginalized group: talk to the members of that group and ask them what they want and what they need. Single mothers are the experts regarding their own lives. Those who wish to provide better support to single mothers attending their institution must begin by asking questions and then listening to what these women have to say about their experiences, their goals, their challenges, and their needs. Faculty, deans, administrative staff, representatives from student government, and staff in student support services should talk to these women. This means truly listening to what the women have to say. This may not be easy, particularly as single mothers are likely to offer criticisms of existing programs and policies or criticisms about the lack of such programs and policies. However, for genuinely meaningful change to occur, the voices and perspectives of those who are marginalized must be at the very center of the discussion. As this volume has demonstrated, single mothers already know what challenges they face. They already know what they need. If we truly seek to make our campuses more inclusive and if we endeavor to provide better support for single mothers as they pursue postsecondary education, it is imperative that these women be empowered to define their needs rather than allowing others, however well-intentioned they may be, to make assumptions and define the needs of single mothers from their own limited perspective as cultural outsiders.

There is no one-size-fits-all approach. No single program or proposed solution will address the various needs of all single mothers who are college students on all college campuses. What works in an urban setting might not be possible at a rural institution. A program that is successful at a four-year institution may prove difficult to implement at a community college. A program that is successful in meeting the needs of undergraduate students may fall short of providing adequate support for single mothers pursuing graduate or professional degrees. Institutions are not monolithic, and neither are single mothers who are college students. While four specific challenges emerged from my research, not all participants faced all four of those challenges and not all participants faced them in the same way. Thus, it is important to begin by asking questions, listening to the answers, and then using those answers as a foundation for crafting and implementing programs, practices, and policies to help support single mothers within a specific institutional context.

ACKNOWLEDGMENTS

The process of creating this volume has been filled with both moments of absolute joy and numerous trials. At times, the trials took over and seemed unsurmountable, and I would put the project aside for weeks or months at a time. At one point, I even decided to discontinue the project altogether, tucking the completed chapters, observation notes, interview transcripts, and research files into the bottom of my filing cabinet and locking the drawer. I didn't open that drawer again for nearly two years. I was able to return to and complete this project only because of the support, encouragement, and bliss provided by individuals who have enriched my life in numerous ways and demonstrated unwavering belief in my ability to successfully complete it. They have continually reminded me that each one of us has the capacity to create positive energy and to affect social change in ways that make a real difference in the lives of individuals and our communities.

My gratitude goes out to various colleagues who have supported me through this process. These include the two anonymous reviewers whose careful reading and constructive feedback helped me fine-tune the manuscript. My editor at Rutgers University Press, Kimberly Guinta, was equally enthusiastic and patient, and I appreciate her positive attitude and calm demeanor. At the University of Texas at Dallas, Dr. George Fair has provided me with new opportunities for growth and professional development. I am grateful for his guidance, patience, and encouragement. Dr. Erin Smith deserves special recognition for her role as my primary source of wise counsel and healthy doses of on-campus humor—thank you for helping me become more solution-oriented and for always making me laugh. And I will be forever indebted to the administrative staff in the UTD School of Interdisciplinary Studies, especially Monica Krause, Becky Wiser, and Molly Dickinson—you are incredible colleagues and simply wonderful human beings. Thank you for all that you do.

I am also grateful to the dynamic group of feminist scholars, including Florence Babb, Mary Trachsel, Susan Birrell, and Jennifer Glass, who provided feedback on this project while it was still in its infancy and who continue to be shining examples of engaged feminist scholarship. The same is true of Ellen Lewin, who has continued to be my chief mentor and tormentor (but in ways that were desperately needed and very much appreciated) and who has always believed in me, especially at those times when I lacked the courage to believe in myself. I continue to be thankful for your guidance, your unwavering support, and your friendship. And I will be forever indebted to the women who participated in this research and who continue to inspire me. It was such a privilege to get to know and learn from each of you and I appreciate your willingness to share your lives and experiences with me.

But it is those who have shared my personal life who are most deserving of my appreciation. Romeo, Amira, Princess Twinkletoes, and Lily were ready with generous snuggles, happy tails, and warm hearts. Patrick Morgan, despite our vastly divergent perspectives on most topics and the fact that our exchanges are often sprinkled with healthy doses of disagreement, continues to provide much-needed perspective and to remind me of my purpose in this life.

My Tico friends have provided regular doses of amusement, exploration, and relaxation and have taught me that although I was born in the United States, I have the heart, spirit, and appetite of a Tica. My dear friend Medardo Mosco Vidal introduced me to biodigesters, sustainability, and permaculture, and I cherish every opportunity to work with him to improve the health of our planet and strengthen communities. The members of the Maleku Indigenous Tribe of Costa Rica have enriched my life in ways I never anticipated, cannot fully articulate, and can certainly never fully reciprocate. They welcomed me into their homes and their hearts and continue to teach me about the importance of community, educate me about living in harmony with nature, and allow me to witness their unwavering commitment to social justice and a sustainable future. To my Maleku family, and especially to Alcides Elizondo Castro, I offer my most sincere appreciation: *afepaquian narracarreyeca marama*.

My maternal grandmother continues to be a source of inspiration, even years after her passing. I will always be thankful for her unconditional love. And to Piper Skye, a shooting star whose spirit was far too pure to remain on this earth for long: know that you were loved, little one. Finally, I could have never completed this project without the love and support of my daughters, Samara and Annika. My darling girls, your potent combination of joy, chaos, and passion fills my heart to near-bursting on a regular basis. Being your mother has been the greatest privilege of my life and I look forward to more of our epic estrogen-fest adventures in the years and decades to come.

APPENDIX: SUPPORTING SINGLE MOTHERS AT COLLEGES AND UNIVERSITIES

Some postsecondary institutions have implemented measures to provide better support for single mothers. Some measures focus on a single challenge facing single mothers such as child care or financial needs. Others provide a broader range of services and supports. Some have been designed specifically for single mothers, while others have been designed with other student populations in mind—such as low-income students or student parents more generally—but could be adapted to meet the needs of single mothers. The examples I provide are not comprehensive. I offer them as working models that can be adjusted and expanded in ways that are feasible in the context of a particular institution.

PART ONE: FINANCIAL CHALLENGES

Perhaps one of the most obvious ways to help single mothers meet the financial challenges they face is to provide them with scholarship opportunities. Some scholarships are available to women in specific academic fields such as those sponsored by the Society of Women Engineers and the Educational Foundation for Women in Accounting, but they are not specific to single mothers. Other scholarships, such as those offered by the Jeanette Rankin Foundation, the Talbott Scholarship Foundation, and the Philanthropic Educational Organization, are available to women or to mothers in general but are not exclusively intended for single mothers. Some scholarships are available only to individuals who register and become members of an organization, such as the Single Parent Alliance of America, a for-profit entity. Scholarships for women in traditionally male-dominated fields and scholarships for mothers are certainly important as a means of supporting women's educational pursuits. Yet to imagine that women as a group or mothers in general have the same financial needs and face the same financial burdens as single mothers denies the unique aspects of single mothers' experiences. Thus, it is important to expand the number of scholarship opportunities for single mothers and to make information about such scholarships easily accessible to potential applicants.

Models for scholarships include those offered by private organizations, foundations, or groups and scholarships that are specific to a postsecondary institution, district, or system. The Patsy Takemoto Mink Education Support Award, for example, is available to low-income single mothers age seventeen and older who are pursuing a postsecondary degree.[1] In 2015, five scholarships of $5,000 each were awarded. The Rosenfeld Injury Lawyers' Annual Single Mother Scholarship seeks to promote empowerment and long-term job opportunities for single mothers. It provides two awards of $1,000 each year; recipients must maintain a GPA of 3.0 or higher.[2] The James E. "Pete" Peterson Memorial Scholarship, which is available only to nontraditional female students who are attending Westminster College in Salt Lake City, Utah, gives preference to single mothers. Applicants must be enrolled at least half-time, and three scholarships of $5,250 are awarded annually.[3] Single mothers pursuing their associate's degree at any institution in the Kentucky Community and Technical College System may apply for the Kentucky Colonels Better Life Scholarship. Recipients must maintain full-time academic enrollment, have at least one child under the age of twelve, demonstrate academic potential, and have unmet financial needs. Two awards of $2,500 are given annually and the scholarship may be renewed for a second year.[4]

The University of Wisconsin–Eau Claire offers twelve scholarships that are specifically designated for single mothers, single parents, or nontraditional female students; the institution gives special consideration to single mothers. This type of clustering of scholarships reduces the work involved in locating and applying for scholarships. Of equal importance, it both reflects and perpetuates an institutional climate in which single mothers are welcome, valued, and supported as members of the student population. These scholarships include the Patricia A. Henderson Memorial PEO Scholarship, the Susan J. Bruce Single Parent Scholarship, the Richard and Marlene Cable Single Parent Scholarship, the Cheryl DeMaio Blugold Promise Scholarship, the Charles and Deborah Graupner Blugold Promise Scholarship, the Heroes Fund for Single Parents Scholarship, the Lopas and Cicenas Family Scholarships, the M. Terry and Gina McEnany Single Parent Scholarship, the Mother's Day Scholarship, the Single Parent Scholarship Program, the Ken and Mary Smith Single Parent Scholarship, and the Cathy Sultan Single Parent Endowment.[5]

Some colleges and universities offer emergency funds for single parents. The William Randolph Hearst Endowment for Students/Parents, which began in the early 1990s and was expanded in 2002, provides emergency financial assistance to students with dependents who are attending Texas Woman's University and gives special consideration to single parents.[6] The award must be used to cover emergency costs relating to child care, health care, living expenses, or educational costs. The amount of the award varies.[7] Similarly, Helen's Special Fund, facilitated by the University Women's Association at the University of Wisconsin–Eau Claire, provides emergency financial assistance to help offset unforeseen expenses related to the health, education, or welfare of dependent children. The recipient must be a single parent. The maximum total amount available annually is $1,700.[8]

Some colleges and universities make child care more affordable for single mothers by providing child care subsidies. One example is the Child Care Subsidy Program for Student Families at the University of Iowa. The program helps offset child care costs through a reimbursement program. Eligible costs include those associated with both regular, ongoing child care arrangements and with child care so the parent "can study, write a paper, do research, or participate in a study group on evenings/weekends."[9] The program is open to undergraduate and graduate students, regardless of marital status. Participants must submit receipts for child care costs to the UI Family Services Office for reimbursement.[10] Similarly, the Child Care Subsidy Program at Brown University in Providence, Rhode Island, helps offset child care expenses for graduate students and medical students. Priority assistance is given to students enrolled at least half-time who are either unmarried or are legally considered disabled. The subsidy covers expenses for children up to six years old, is based on annual income, and ranges from $1,000 to $4,000 a year.[11] Portland State University aims to help offset child care expenses for undergraduate and graduate students through the Jim Sells Childcare Subsidy. While priority is given to families whose household income is below the federal poverty guideline, families with incomes up to 249 percent of the federal poverty guideline are eligible. The subsidy is part of the students' financial aid award.[12] Another example is the Student Parent Child Care Subsidy Program at the Pennsylvania State University. The subsidy is available to students who have dependent children and whose annual household income is at or below 200 percent of the federal poverty guideline. Priority is given to Pell Grant recipients (including single mothers), veterans, and first-generation college students.[13]

Some campuses have implemented is a sliding fee scale at campus-based child care centers. This model can help make child care more affordable for single mothers and can provide access to high-quality, developmentally appropriate care. The Campus Children's Center at Evergreen State College in Olympia, Washington, provides care for children from infancy through age six and is state licensed.[14] Enrollment is prioritized for children of Evergreen State College students and the center uses a sliding fee scale to help offset monthly child care costs and offers a discount for a second child.[15] The Child Care Program at the Ohio State University offers full-day, half-day, partial week, and evening care programs for children aged six weeks to five years. The program includes two child care facilities and can serve up to 435 children. Facilities are accredited and offer USDA-approved meals. Subsidized child care is provided for graduate students who are employed on campus and meet income guidelines.[16] Iowa State University also uses a sliding fee scale for tuition at its three on-campus child care centers, which provide care for children from six weeks through twelve years old. Priority enrollment is given to children of students and the centers aim for a ratio of 60 percent student usage.[17]

In the past, some institutions have implemented programs to help single mothers gain access to computers. While most colleges and universities have campus computing centers, multiple factors limit women's access to and ability to use such centers.[18] Through the program called CAPRA: Computer Access Promoting Retention and Achievement, the University of Iowa provided computers on "loan" to single mothers. After completing an application, verifying student status, and making a $25 deposit, CAPRA participants were able to check out a computer for the entire semester and take it home. The CAPRA program, which began in 2004, was facilitated by the Women's Resource and Action Center, the campus women's center. CAPRA was discontinued in 2009. A similar program, the Single Parent Resource Information Networking Technology (SPRINT) Scholarship, was implemented at Texas Woman's University in 2009. In addition to providing single mothers attending the institution with $1,250 each semester toward child care expenses and offering personal, academic, and professional guidance, the SPRINT scholarship provided recipients with a free laptop computer. The program ended in 2012 when its three-year grant expired.[19]

The costs associated with textbooks and required course materials are also a concern. In 2004, college students paid an average of $800–$900 in each academic year for books and supplies.[20] By 2014, that figure had risen to $1,200–$1,300.[21] Overall, the cost of college textbooks has risen by over 1,000 percent since 1977.[22] While there is variation in the price of required textbooks by discipline and course, the cost of a single textbook can be as high as $400.[23] While many institutions now offer students the option to rent textbooks instead of purchasing them outright, rental fees can be quite high. There is growing concern about the ways these rising costs can pose hardships for low-income students, particularly because such students may forgo the purchase of textbooks in order to meet other expenses.[24] Given their limited financial resources, many single mothers struggle to afford required textbooks for their courses.

One option for supporting single mothers in this regard is to offer a textbook scholarship, such as the Cap and Gown Scholarship at Antioch University New England in Keene, New Hampshire. This scholarship provides $400 a year to help each recipient, who must be a single parent with unmet financial need, purchase textbooks. The scholarship was established in 2003 by a group of graduating seniors, and in subsequent years, each graduating class has contributed to the Cap and Gown scholarship fund.[25]

Individual faculty members, department chairs, and deans can take an active role in reducing textbook expenses in their courses. Faculty can reduce the number of required books. At Harvard, for example, one professor reduced the number of required textbooks from four to one, using "publicly available, free texts to replace or supplement required readings," while another put required course readings online in order to make them free and accessible to students.[26] Other strategies include putting copies of required course textbooks on reserve in the university library.[27] Administrators can also promote a reduction in textbook costs, specifically by suggesting that faculty follow a "maximum limit" guideline on textbook costs for each course, by encouraging faculty to make materials available online and through library reserves, and by facilitating on-campus discussions about how to make textbooks more affordable and more accessible to all students. They might consider, for example, textbook exchange programs such as the one organized by the Student Government Association at Northeastern University in Boston, Massachusetts, which "allows buyers to compare prices, list books for sale at competitive rates and meet up with other students at NU to buy and sell textbooks."[28] Faculty members and departments can also help make textbooks more affordable by posting required textbook lists as early as possible and by sharing information about low-cost textbook options, including local vendors and online book websites such as textbookrecycling.com and bookscouter.com.

PART TWO: TIME CONSTRAINTS

One way colleges and universities can assist single mothers is through flexible course scheduling options. Many institutions offer multiple sections of larger high-demand, high-enrollment courses, making different sections available at different times of the day. This can help single mothers accommodate the various scheduling constraints they face. However, it is not realistic for institutions to offer multiple sections of all courses, particularly when enrollments do not warrant doing so. Thus, it is important to consider other options to promote flexible scheduling. Courses offered online or in a hybrid format can be helpful in this regard, particularly as "strategies that use the internet to allow more flexible access to education can help student parents fit postsecondary education into their busy lives."[29] Student parents take online and hybrid courses at twice the rate of their peers who are not parents.[30] Other advantages associated with online learning that may be particularly relevant to single mothers include a reduced need for transportation and child care, the ability of each student to work at her own pace, the ability of the student to schedule academic responsibilities around employment responsibilities, and the fact that digital sources are less expensive than many traditional textbooks.[31] Of course online classes are not suitable for everyone; some students prefer face-to-face courses.[32] In addition, there can be significant barriers to online learning and the "digital divide" can include such factors as lack of or limited access to computing technologies and gaps in knowledge of how to use those technologies.[33] However, online education may prove beneficial for some single mothers by providing flexible scheduling options that help ease the time challenges they experience.

The University without Walls at Amherst University, which was designed to help working adult students, has been offering online degree programs since 1971. The program enables students to design their own course of study. Participants may complete their degree 100 percent online or combine online courses with hybrid and on-campus courses. Students may transfer previous coursework or get credit for work or life experiences. The University without Walls offers traditional semester-length courses, six-week accelerated courses, and four-week "uber accelerated" courses.[34] RioLearn at Rio Salado College in Tempe, Arizona, offers another model for online learning. It offers approximately 100 degree and certificate programs, nearly all of which can be completed either partially or completely online.[35] Courses do not necessarily follow a traditional academic calendar; there are over forty start dates throughout the calendar year. Students may control the timing and pace of each course by choosing eight-week, twelve-week, and sixteen-week options. Tutoring, advising, library assistance, and technical support are provided twenty-four hours a day and may be accessed with telephone, e-mail, and chat options. A third model for online learning is the Worldwide eLearning program at Texas Tech University in Lubbock. It provides instruction to students in the United States and internationally through both online and hybrid degree programs. In addition to undergraduate programs, it also offers fully online programs for eighteen master's degrees and four doctoral degrees. The content and requirements for each online program are the same as those offered on campus.[36] The Worldwide eLearning program is one of the few postsecondary institutions to offer completely online degrees at the graduate level.[37]

On-campus facilities can also provide much-needed support to single mothers. Research demonstrates that students who live on campus experience social as well as academic benefits. They are more likely to become integrated into campus life through participation in student activities and organizations and through interaction with peers and with faculty members than students who live off campus.[38] In addition, those who live on campus are more likely to encounter and to be supportive of diverse ideas, experiences, and identities in their social group than students who live off campus.[39] Finally, on-campus housing has long been shown to positively impact academic performance and is associated with higher GPA achievement, higher retention rates, and higher rates of degree completion.[40]

Colleges and universities can help ease the time burdens related to commuting and the stress associated with it by incorporating family-friendly housing and child care facilities on their campuses. With the incorporation of such facilities, the postsecondary campus would become more than a destination where single mothers go each day to attend classes and study. Instead, the college campus would serve as an all-inclusive location where single mothers could learn, live, and care for their children.

PART THREE: CHILD CARE

Postsecondary institutions can help make high-quality child care more afford-able and more accessible to single mothers in a variety of ways. Access to child care is so essential to students who are parents that it is a factor in whether or not they choose to enroll in college. It is "a critical support in helping them succeed once they are there. . . . Difficulties in obtaining child care can be a serious bar-rier to success in and completion of postsecondary programs."[41] In 2011, only 16.8 percent of all postsecondary institutions provided this service and the num-ber of campus child care centers has declined in the period 2012–2015.[42] The number of available spaces for children of students in campus-based child care programs is limited, particularly because enrollment policies may prioritize chil-dren of faculty or staff or the cost of such care may be out of reach of low-income students.[43]

Perhaps the most obvious way to make child care more accessible to single mothers is to provide on-campus child care facilities. A variety of benefits for students, faculty, and the academic institution itself are associated with on-campus child care:

> Once a child care center is established and recognized on a campus, it can be ben-eficial both to parents and the institution. A campus child care center can offer parents a conveniently located, good quality educational surrounding for their children. In turn, the center can contribute to an institution's success in recruiting and retaining faculty and students with child care responsibilities. The center's location on campus can minimize for parents the multiple adverse factors associ-ated with off-campus child care, such as inaccessibility, inconvenience, commut-ing time, inflexibility and regulations imposed by an external child care facility.[44]

For single mothers attending college, the convenience of such centers is a signifi-cant factor in reducing commute time and helping them balance their academic and parenting responsibilities. On-campus child care centers enable single mothers to attend classes but remain in close proximity to their children; this is especially convenient for mothers who are breastfeeding. Such proximity makes it easier for single mothers to spend time with their children during the day, for example by having lunch with their children or by participating in activities at the child care center as their schedules permit. It is also important to note that access to on-campus child care has a positive impact on the retention rates, graduation rates, and GPA of student parents.[45] Conversely, "lack of affordable, high-quality child care emerges as a major barrier to success," particularly for mothers who are pursuing postsecondary education.[46]

Those who wish to establish or expand child care on their campuses can look to the following examples from universities that have made a commitment to providing such care and even to increasing it. From 2005 to 2011, the Children's Centers at the University of Michigan increased their enrollment capacity by 32 percent, including a 150 percent increase for infants, a 53 percent increase for toddlers at one facility, and a 10 percent increase for toddlers at another.[47] The construction and opening of the Towsley Children's House, a 22,000-square-foot facility that provides care for children from three months through five years old, has been the cornerstone of expanding child care on the campus. Several existing child care centers were renovated and expanded, including the North Campus Children's Center and the Health Systems Children's Center. Similarly, in 2013, the Massachusetts Institute of Technology opened the David H. Koch Childcare Center, a 14,000-square-foot facility that serves 126 children from infancy through preschool and has effectively doubled the availability of child care on campus.[48] The center includes eleven classrooms and outdoor play space and is accredited by the National Association for the Education of Young Children. It also has outdoor play space and age-appropriate playground equipment. Another example is the Westwood Child Care Center at UCLA.[49] In response to the growing demand for child care among members of the campus community, UCLA leased commercial, renovated space located near the UCLA Center for Health Sciences. It turned the operation of the child care facility over to Bright Horizons Family Solutions, an international corporation that operates more than 700 child care facilities. The Westwood Child Care Center was opened in 2010, adding to the three existing campus-affiliated child care centers. With a capacity of 221 children, it increased child care availability to members of the UCLA community by 40 percent.[50]

Not all campuses have the space or the resources needed to implement on-campus child care centers. In such cases, colleges and universities can promote access to reliable, affordable, quality child care by affiliating with child care providers and babysitters. For example, in Atlanta, Georgia, Emory University has created the Emory Child Care Network, which includes more than 175 providers and aims to help increase access to child care as part of a broader effort to address work-family balance.[51] Students, faculty, and staff at the university benefit from priority enrollment and, in some cases, reduced fees for use of child care centers that are included in the Emory Child Care Network. At the University of Iowa, the Child Care Partners program, which is facilitated by the Family Services Office, partners with twelve child care centers, all located within

one-and-a-half miles of the university's main campus; some are even on campus.[52]
The list of partners is organized according to ages of children who can receive
care at each center—which range from six weeks through school-aged—and the
university provides a brief description and an e-mail address and other contact
information for each center. The University of Montana offers another option for
campus-affiliated centers through its Caregivers Network.[53] Through the website
www.care.com, the university maintains an extensive listing of alumni who provide child care services, including babysitters, licensed in-home care providers,
and nannies.

The increasing demand for child care in the United States means that it is
not simply enough to have on-campus child care centers and campus-affiliated
child care centers. In many cases, such centers are open not only to the campus
community but also to the broader community. This increases the demand for
available spaces and can make it more difficult for single mothers to secure care
for their children, particularly in light of their financial circumstances, scheduling needs, and access to transportation. Prioritizing enrollment for children of
students can help address this disparity. Northern Illinois University's Campus
Child Care[54] center offers one model for doing so. This facility provides care for
children from three months through five years old. Enrollment is prioritized as
follows: children with siblings already enrolled at the center, children of NIU
students, children of NIU faculty and staff, and children of community members
(individuals with no university affiliation). However, children of community
members are permitted to participate in only the preschool program (ages three
to five). This policy effectively limits enrollment in the infant and toddler classrooms to members of the campus community.

The TCC Child Development Center at Tidewater Community College in
Norfolk, Virginia, offers another model. Through a partnership with the YWCA
South Hampton Roads, the college provides development-focused child care
for children aged two-and-a-half to six years at its Chesapeake, Norfolk, Ports-
mouth, and Virginia Beach campuses.[55] The enrollment policy for all four child
care centers is as follows: "TCC students receive priority registration for their
children. Employees, contracted vendors, and the community may register children for child care based on a limited, space available basis."[56] Child care fees
are reduced for students and are determined based on a sliding fee scale. A third
model is The Clubhouse at Texas Woman's University. It provides care for children five through twelve years old and enrollment gives priority to children
of TWU students. During the fall and spring semesters, the program operates
from 3:00 to 6:00 P.M. Clubhouse vans and drivers pick up children enrolled
in the program from their respective elementary schools and transport them
to The Clubhouse facility, which is located near Lowry Woods, the on-campus,
apartment-style housing complex. On days when the public schools have early

release for teacher training or parent-teacher conferences, the program is available from 1 to 6 P.M. During the summer, The Clubhouse provides care from 7:30 A.M. to 5:30 P.M.[57]

Although child care centers often have hours that accommodate schedules of working parents, these hours may not meet the need of parents who are college students, particularly because parents are "more likely to take night or weekend classes than non-parents."[58] Thus, it is important to consider various strategies for meeting the child care needs of single mothers during these extended hours. The Evening Child Care program at the University of Texas at Dallas, a year-round program, provides evening care for children ages four through eleven from 3:30 to 10 P.M. Mondays through Thursdays while their parents are attending classes. The program is operated through a partnership between the university and the Dallas International School, a private K–12 institution located across the street from the university campus.[59] Children are cared for by licensed providers and are grouped by age. Food is not provided but parents can send a snack for their child. The fee is $6 per evening per child. Child care is provided in the Student Union, a central location on campus.

At La Guardia Community College in Long Island, New York, the Early Childhood Learning Center Programs, Inc., offers another model for extended-hours child care.[60] This nationally accredited, state-licensed child care program and nursery school provides comprehensive care and early childhood education for children ages one to twelve. In addition to daytime hours for all ages, the center provides care until 11 P.M. on Mondays through Thursdays and until 9 P.M. on Fridays. The center also offers a Saturday Program that provides child care from 9 A.M. to 3 P.M. and a summer camp for children so their parents may take classes during the summer term.

Even when they have access to regular child care, single mothers may find that such arrangements do not always meet their needs. A babysitter may become ill or have a family emergency. If a child becomes ill, they may not be able to attend regular child care. School-age children may need occasional child care on days when school is not in session. Some institutions provide child care for such occasions. The University of Iowa's Well Back-Up Child Care and Mildly Ill Back-Up Child Care program provides access to well-child back-up care and care for children who are mildly ill.[61] Participants, who must pre-enroll, have access to care when the student-parent has work or academic responsibilities. Care is provided in the home of the child and is available twenty-four hours a day for children ages six weeks to twelve years. The University of Wisconsin also provides back-up care and care for mildly ill children through its Kids-Kare program.[62] Started in 2002, this program provides child care on an as-needed basis for university-affiliated families. Student fees help support the program and a sliding fee scale is used. Student parents who are enrolled in the Child Care Tuition Assistance

Program are provided with up to twenty hours of free back-up care each semester. All UW-Madison faculty, staff, and students are provided with up to twelve hours of mildly ill care each semester at no cost. At the University of California, Berkeley, the Back Up Child Care program is subsidized.[63] This program can be used when regular child care arrangements are not available or when a child is mildly ill and cannot attend regular child care. Back-up care for healthy children is provided during regular hours of operation at Bright Horizons Child Care Center. Children who are mildly ill receive care in their homes, a service that is available twenty-four hours a day, seven days a week. Students are charged only a co-pay for each service. Subsidized care is available for up to sixty hours in a fiscal year for each student parent.[64]

PART FOUR: COMBATING THE CHILLY CLIMATE

Colleges and universities must address the chilly climate single mothers face in higher education. In some respects, this is a rather challenging prospect. It involves addressing the pervasive public and political discourses in the United States that continue to marginalize, blame, and even demonize single mothers and help perpetuate such a climate.[65] However, the history of increasing inclusiveness and diversity at American colleges and universities indicates that such change is possible, and some institutions have already taken steps to make their campuses and classrooms more welcoming for single mothers.[66]

The addition of on-campus facilities such as child care and family housing are significant forms of support for single mothers. These facilities make the campus more family friendly. In addition, allocating physical space on the campus signifies an institution's recognition of and support for students who are parents. The creation of lactation rooms on campuses can provide support to single mothers and all breastfeeding women on campus. Many institutions still have not addressed this need.[67] With input from lactation consultants, the Family Resources Office of the University of Arizona created fourteen lactation spaces distributed across campus, earning it recognition as a "best practice model for lactation support."[68] The rooms must adhere to standards related to privacy, availability, and cleanliness. The individual departments that oversee or serve as "hosts" to the lactation spaces are responsible for maintaining these standards.

The University of Michigan has also created a network of lactation rooms that includes space in thirty-five buildings across its Ann Arbor campus. An additional fourteen lactation rooms are located on the university's Health Sciences Campus. The university has established a lactation room setup guide that includes lists of minimum requirements and optional features.[69] Through the UM Breastfeeding Clinic, the university also provides free phone consultations and support. Similarly, the University of Iowa provides thirty-three lactation rooms distributed throughout thirty-one buildings across campus. Each room has a sign-up for those who wish to use the room on their lunch breaks or during breaks between classes; women can also use the rooms on a drop-in basis. Facilities and equipment vary from room to room.[70]

Colleges and universities can also provide better support for single mothers by revising their excused absence policies. At present, such policies currently excuse students when they are absent from class for religious observance, serious illness, military service responsibilities, death of a family member, or participation in university-sanctioned athletic or academic activities. These students are permitted to make up any missed assignments. The same is not true for unexcused absences. Such policies could easily be revised to make it clear that if a student must miss class to care for their sick child, that absence would be excused. Individual instructors can include "caring for a sick child" as part of the attendance policies for their individual courses.[71] However, unless there is a formal, campus-wide attendance policy, single mothers and other students who must miss class to care for their sick child are at the mercy of individual instructors with regard to whether or not that absence will be excused.

Some institutions have included caring for a sick child as part of their attendance and excused absence policies, a significant step in making institutions less chilly for single mothers. Single mothers attending Texas A&M University benefit from a comprehensive excused absence policy that includes "illness of a dependent family member."[72] Students are required to provide documentation for the absence to be considered excused.[73] The absence policy at the University of Minnesota makes it clear that missing a class because of the "illness of a student or his or her dependent" is considered an excused absence.[74] In such cases, students are permitted to make up any missed work. The attendance policy at the University of Maryland defines caring for a dependent child who is ill as an excused absence. Students who miss classes for this reason may not be penalized for attendance or with regard to examinations or other forms of assessment.[75]

One way to combat the marginalization of single mothers on the college campus is by creating opportunities for these women to connect with one another. Peer groups provide an opportunity for single mothers to share experiences and strategies and to support one another in academic and personal matters. Such groups can also combat the chilly climate of higher education by providing an opportunity for single mothers to claim space and articulate their own subjectivity in an institutional context that marginalizes them.[76] Such groups can also help women connect with community resources and mentors and can provide workshops and seminars relevant to the women and the challenges they face.

At Lakeland Community College in Kirtland, Ohio, Single Mothers Achieving Real Triumph (SMART) offers various forms of support to single mothers. Participants must be enrolled at least half time and have unmet financial need. Participants receive financial assistance in the form of a scholarship and are required to take two SMART-specific courses (six credit hours) and meet weekly for seminars and workshops designed to promote academic success.[77] The Women's Center at the University of Utah offers a peer group for single women going through divorce.[78] The group connects participants with free legal advice. At Texas Woman's University, students who are raising children may participate in SPARK: Student Parents Also Raising Kids.[79] This is a student organization, which is offered through the university's Non-Traditional Student Organization, and provides information about educational, financial, and social opportunities for participants. The group meets monthly and organizes a variety of social opportunities such as potlucks, movie nights, and holiday celebrations. Another model for peer groups is SPiN: Single Parents Network at Western Nebraska Community College in Sidney, Nebraska. Created for single parents and displaced homemakers, SPiN meets monthly and is designed to help participants "deal with personal, academic, and career concerns." Meetings provide an opportunity for networking and socialization and may include workshops and guest speakers. Participants may also receive a scholarship and free access to educational materials.[80]

PART FIVE: RESIDENTIAL PROGRAMS

It is important to consider the ways the challenges single mothers face are interconnected. For example, simply making child care more accessible does not necessarily mean it is more affordable for single mothers, and improving access to child care does not necessarily address the other challenges single mothers encounter in postsecondary institutions, including the chilly climate and time-related challenges. The models discussed above offer good starting points for those who wish to improve support for single mothers attending their institutions. But other models provide comprehensive support through residential programs for single mothers and their children. Such models are important because they may help improve academic achievement, retention, and degree completion rates for single mothers.

Keys to Degrees: Educating Two Generations Together
Endicott College, Beverly, Massachusetts
Established in 1992, this program starts with the view that single parents are an important part of the student population, they have the potential to succeed, and they have unique needs.[81] The program is based on a two-generation approach that is designed to benefit adult participants and their children. It accepts ten participants each year and is open to single custodial parents with young children.[82] Participants, who live in five shared apartments on campus, are provided

with financial aid, access to child care, workshops related to parenting and finances, three mandatory academic internships, and "wrap-around support services including: academic support, career counseling, pastoral and personal counseling."[83] A 2010 self-study found that 68 percent of program participants graduated in four years. In addition, 100 percent of graduates of the program were employed full time and none of the alumni were receiving support from public assistance programs.[84] The program has been replicated at several other postsecondary institutions, including Eastern Michigan University (Ypsilanti), Ferris State University (Big Rapids, Michigan), and Dillard University (New Orleans, Louisiana).[85]

Mothers Living & Learning Program
College of Saint Mary, Omaha, Nebraska
This program for single mothers, which began in 2000, provides housing on campus in Madonna Hall, a $10 million facility completed in 2012 that can accommodate up to forty-eight mothers with two children each.[86] The residence hall consists of suites shared by two program participants and their children. The facility also provides wireless access, shared kitchens, dining areas, lounges with TVs and play equipment, free laundry facilities on every floor, conference rooms, meeting rooms, and a reflection room for spiritual practice and prayer.[87] The children of program participants eat free on their parent's college meal plan.[88] A full-time director oversees the program and provides support for participants. Participants are required to take a course, "The Successful Single Mother," that "covers the institutional oppression of single mothers and the feminization of poverty to bust stereotypes and enhance self-esteem."[89] The college is also home to "Many Opportunities for Mothering Solo (M.O.M.S.)," a student organization that seeks to build community among single mothers. It offers a variety of social events for participants and sponsors fund-raising activities to support programs for single mothers on campus. The Spellman Child Development Center, located on campus, provides convenient access to quality child care.[90]

Single Parents Reaching Out for Unlimited Tomorrows (SPROUT)
Baldwin Wallace University, Berea, Ohio
The program is available exclusively to unmarried women who have one child and are residents of the state of Ohio.[91] It enrolls a maximum of twelve participants each year and aims to "provide a strong community of support [so] a parent has the best possible environment for personal and academic success" while simultaneously emphasizing personal responsibility.[92] Housing is provided year-round in one-bedroom apartments. The program director helps participants navigate both academic and personal aspects of their lives and assists which such things as locating child care, securing financial aid, selecting a major and

appropriate courses, and securing work-study assignments. The director also organizes mandatory self-development and educational sessions as well as guest speakers, counseling, internships, and mentoring opportunities. The SPROUT program celebrated its twenty-year anniversary in 2010.[93]

The Ruth Matthews Bourger Women with Children Program
Misericordia University, Dallas, Pennsylvania

Designed for low-income single mothers with up to two children, this program emphasizes empowerment, achievement, and growth.[94] It regards single mothers as an underserved student population and recognizes the multiple barriers they encounter as they pursue postsecondary education. Participation is limited to full-time undergraduate students, and maximum capacity for the program is ten single mothers and their children. The program provides up to four years of year-round, free housing in two homes on the university campus. There is also a playground near the homes, and the homes and the playground are secured with a perimeter fence and card-only entry. The program director, coordinator, and support staff help participants locate child care and provide support in the form of parenting classes, financial aid counseling, career workshops, academic support, tutoring, and counseling. They also sponsor social and recreational events. Participants receive priority placement for on-campus work-study positions and receive help with internship placement.[95]

Single Parent Scholar Program
Wilson College, Chambersburg, Pennsylvania

Emphasizing the college's mission to provide collaborative, student-centered, individualized education, this program aims to help participants complete a bachelor's degree as a means of moving toward "a more fulfilling, economically self-sufficient life."[96] It is open to full-time single custodial parents with up to two children. The program can accommodate up to twenty-six participants and their children. Year-round, on-campus housing is provided in two residence halls that are shared by program participants. Housing consists of private suites with two bedrooms and a private bathroom. Participants share the common play space for their children, a common kitchen, a computer room, and laundry facilities. Purchase of a campus dining plan is required, but children of participants eat free in the campus dining hall. Child care is available on campus in walking distance of the residence halls and is subsidized for participants.[97]

Single Parents Program
Champlain College, Burlington, Vermont

Through a variety of workshops and services, this program supports single parents as they pursue their academic and career goals.[98] Started in 1987, the program is available only to undergraduate students who are residents of Vermont and are unmarried custodial parents. The program provides full tuition through the Single Parents Scholarship. It is overseen by a director and two service coordinators who provide academic support, help participants locate community resources, and administer various aspects of the program such as job referrals, free tutoring, free counseling, and free career advising components. The Save the Day fund is available to participants to help with "unexpected emergencies."[99] Ongoing social events and an annual holiday party promote mutual support among participants and their children. Financial support for the Single Parents Program comes from donors and an annual fund-raiser.[100]

NOTES

CHAPTER 1   THE POLITICS OF SINGLE MOTHERHOOD IN THE UNITED STATES

1. Jeff Leeds, "Judge Must Weigh Father's Rights, Mother's Ambition," *Los Angeles Times*, April 27, 1997, accessed January 9, 2014, http://articles.latimes.com /1997-04-27/news/mn-53088_1_fathers-rights.

2. Ibid.

3. David Abel, "Struggling Ivy League Mother Revisits Custody Battle," *Contra Costa Times*, January 16, 2000, A21.

4. Leeds, "Judge Must Weigh Father's Rights, Mother's Ambition."

5. Quoted in ibid.

6. Georgia N. Alexakis, "Junior Will Face 2nd Custody Battle," *Harvard Crimson*, October 5, 1998, accessed January 13, 2014. http://www.thecrimson.com/article/1998/10/5/junior-will -face-2nd-custody-battle/.

7. Ibid.

8. "Gina M. Ocon," *Harvard Crimson*, June 8, 2000, accessed January 11, 2014. http://www .thecrimson.com/article/2000/6/8/gina-m-ocon-pgina-m-ocon/#.

9. Bernard Ryan Jr., "Baby Maranda Case: 1994," *law.jrank.org*, accessed January 11, 2014, http://law.jrank.org/pages/3612/Baby-Maranda-Case-1994.html.

10. Susan Beth Jacobs, "The Hidden Gender Bias Behind 'The Best Interest of the Child' Standard in Custody Decisions," *Georgia State University Law Review* 13, no. 3 (1996): 2.

11. Ryan, "Baby Maranda Case: 1994."

12. Ibid.

13. Ibid.

14. *Ireland v. Smith*, no. 93–385 DS, Macomb Circuit Court, Michigan, 1994.

15. Quoted in Timothy W. Bratcher, "Ireland v. Smith: Who Better Serves a Child's Best Interests, Day Care Providers or Blood Relatives?" *University of Louisville Journal of Family Law* 34 (Winter 1995/1996): 159.

16. *Ireland v. Smith*, 214 Mich. App. 235, November 7, 1995.

17. Ibid.

18. "Mom Who Put Girl in Day Care Now Will Share Custody," *Chicago Tribune*, October 18, 1996, accessed January 16, 2014, http://articles.chicagotribune.com/1996-10-18/ news/9610180300_1_custody-of-maranda-ireland-smith-splitting-weekends-jennifer-ireland.

19. *Ireland v. Smith*, 1995.

20. Examples include Rick Haglund and Judy Putnam, "Child Care Ruling May Be a Blow to Working Moms: Michigan Judge, in Custody Case, Decided Best Place for Daughter Is with Father's Mother," *San Francisco Examiner*, 10 August 1994; Jennifer Loven, "Mother in College Wins Back Custody: Appeals Court Rules Out Day Care as Issue," *Buffalo News*, November 9, 1995; Gene Schabath, "ACLU, Others Join Legal Fight of Michigan Mom Awarding Custody to Father Based on Day-Care Issue: 'Frightening Social Policy,'" *Seattle Times*, August 9, 1994; "Court Reverses Custody Ruling Tied to Day Care: Lower Court Must Decide Again Which

Parent Will Get Daughter," *St. Louis Post-Dispatch*, November 9, 1994; "Day Care Custody Case," *Pittsburgh Post-Gazette*, July 29, 1994.

21. Diana Griego Erwin, "Single-Mother Bashing," *Baltimore Sun*, August 5, 1994; Susan Chira, "Custody Case Stirs Debate on Bias against Working Women," *New York Times*, July 31, 1994; accessed January 13, 2014, http://www.nytimes.com/1994/07/31/us/custody-case-stirs -debate-on-bias-against-working-women.html?pagewanted=all&src=pm. See also "When Justice Is Blind," *Long Beach Press-Telegram*, July 28, 1994; and "Personal Business: Working Woman Double Standards Still Exist in Parental Care of Children," *Atlanta Journal and Constitution*, March 27, 1995.

22. "Harvard Woman Returns with Baby," 1996; "Taking Scholarship, Support for Large Ambition." *Baltimore Sun*, September 23, 1997; "Taking Jennifer Ireland's Daughter." *New York Times*, August 1, 1994.

23. For perspectives that focus on fathers' rights, see "Taking Jennifer Ireland's Daughter," *New York Times*, August 1, 1994; Stephanie Wilson, "Irrelevant Dads," *Chicago Tribune*, September 26, 1997; and Patricia Haley, "Explaining Custody Issue," *Long Beach Press-Telegram*, May 27, 1997. For articles that focus on the interests of the children involved, see Jennifer Cundiff, "Bailey's Rights," *Long Beach Press-Telegram*, May 16, 1997; and "For Once, Court Puts the Child First," *Atlanta Journal and Constitution*, November 14, 1995.

24. Dorothy E. Smith, "The Standard North American Family: SNAF as an Ideological Code," *Journal of Family Issues 14, no. 1* (1993): 50–65.

25. Kimberlé Crenshaw, "Demarginalizing the Intersection of Race and Sex: A Black Feminist Critique of Antidiscrimination Doctrine, Feminist Theory, and Antiracist Politics," *University of Chicago Legal Forum* (1989): 139–167; Adrienne Rich, *Of Woman Born: Motherhood as Experience and Institution* (New York: Bantam, 1976). For more on the matrix of domination, see Patricia Hill Collins, *Black Feminist Thought: Knowledge, Consciousness, and the Politics of Empowerment* (New York: HarperCollins, 1990).

26. "Little commonwealth": William Trattner, *From Poor Law to Welfare State: A History of Social Welfare in America* (New York: Free Press, 1998), 1; "little cell of righteousness": Mimi Abramovitz, *Regulating the Lives of Women: Social Welfare Policy from Colonial Times to Present* (Cambridge, MA: South End Press, 1988), 52.

27. Abramovitz, *Regulating the Lives of Women*, 52–53.

28. Judith Walzer Leavitt, *Brought to Bed: Childbearing in America, 1750–1950* (New York: Oxford University Press, 1986), 20.

29. Linda K. Kerber, "The Republican Mother: Women and the Enlightenment-An American Perspective," *American Quarterly 28, no. 2* (1976): 187–205.

30. Abramovitz, *Regulating the Lives of Women*, 49; Jennifer Lyle Morgan, "Women in Slavery and the Transatlantic Slave Trade," in *Transatlantic Slavery: Against Human Dignity*, edited by Anthony Tibbles (Liverpool: Liverpool University Press, 2005), 62.

31. For further explanation of the Jezebel stereotype and other dominant stereotypes of Black women, see Patricia Hills Collins's discussion in *Black Feminist Thought*, 69–96.

32. David Pilgrim, "Jezebel Stereotype," accessed February 17, 2014. http://fir.ferris.edu: 8080/xmlui/bitstream/handle/2323/4778/Jezebel%20Stereotype.pdf?sequence=1.

33. Christine B. Hickman, "The Devil and the One Drop Rule: Racial Categories, African Americans, and the U.S. Census," *Michigan Law Review 95, no. 5* (1997): 1161–1265.

34. Quoted in Trattner, *From Poor Law to Welfare State*, 17.

35. Catherine Reef, *Poverty in America* (New York: Infobase Publishing, 2007), 25.

36. Ibid.

37. Ibid., 28.

38. John D'Emilio and Estelle B. Freedman, *Intimate Matters: A History of Sexuality in America*, 2nd ed. (Chicago: University of Chicago Press, 1998), 17.

39. Ibid., 32.

40. Trattner, *From Poor Law to Welfare State*, 32.

41. Laurel Thatcher Ulrich, *A Midwife's Tale: The Life of Martha Ballard, Based on Her Diary, 1785–1812* (New York: Vintage Books, 1990), 149.

42. Elaine Heffner, *Mothering: The Emotional Experience of Motherhood after Freud and Feminism* (New York: Doubleday, 1978).

43. Diane Eyer, *Motherguilt: How Our Culture Blames Mothers for What's Wrong with Children* (New York: Random House, 1996).

44. Julia Grant, *Raising Baby by the Book: The Education of American Mothers* (New Haven, CT: Yale University Press, 1998); Sharon Hays, *The Cultural Contradictions of Motherhood* (New Haven, CT: Yale University Press, 1998).

45. Rima D. Apple, "Constructing Mothers: Scientific Motherhood in the Nineteenth and Twentieth Centuries," *Social History of Medicine* 8, no. 2 (1995): 161–178; Lynne Curry. "Modernizing the Rural Mother: Gender, Class, and Health Reform in Illinois, 1910–1930," in *Mothers and Motherhood: Readings in American History*, edited by Rima D. Apple and Janet Golden (Columbus: Ohio State University Press, 1997), 495–516; Molly Ladd-Taylor, *Raising a Baby the Government Way: Mothers' Letters to the Children's Bureau, 1915–1932* (New Brunswick, NJ: Rutgers University Press, 1986); Jacquelyn S. Litt, *Medicalized Motherhood: Perspectives from the Lives of African-American and Jewish Women* (New Brunswick, NJ: Rutgers University Press, 2000); Lynne Y. Weiner, "Reconstructing Motherhood: The La Leche League in Postwar America," *Journal of American History* 80, no. 4 (1994): 1357–1381.

46. Apple, "Constructing Mothers," 161.

47. Ibid.

48. Donna Bassin, Margaret Honey, and Meryle Mahrer Kaplan, eds., *Representations of Motherhood* (New Haven, CT: Yale University Press, 1994).

49. Hays, *The Cultural Contradictions of Motherhood*, 8.

50. Jane Swigart, *The Myth of the Bad Mother: The Emotional Realities of Mothering* (New York: Bantam, 1991), 6. For the application of these attitudes to women who are not mothers, see Elaine Tyler May, *Barren in the Promised Land: Childless Americans and the Pursuit of Happiness* (New York: Basic Books, 1995).

51. Daphne Spain and Suzanne M. Bianchi, *Balancing Act: Motherhood, Marriage, and Employment among American Women* (New York: Russell Sage Foundation, 1996).

52. Susan Douglas and Meredith Michaels, *The Mommy Myth: The Idealization of Motherhood and How It Has Undermined All Women* (New York: Free Press, 2004).

53. Marie Ashe, "The 'Bad' Mother in Law and Literature: A Problem of Representation," *Hastings Law Journal* 43 (1992): 1017–1037; Molly Ladd-Taylor and Lauri Umansky, eds., *Bad Mothers: The Politics of Blame in Twentieth-Century America* (New York: New York University Press, 1998).

54. Ellen Lewin, *Lesbian Mothers: Accounts of Gender in American Culture* (Ithaca, NY: Cornell University Press, 1993); Loretta J. Ross, "African-American Women and Abortion, 1800–1870," in *Theorizing Black Feminisms: The Visionary Pragmatism of Black Women*, edited by Stanlie M. James and Abena P. A. Busia (New York: Routledge, 1993), 141–159; Kath Weston, *Families We Choose: Lesbians, Gays, Kinship* (New York: Columbia University Press, 1991).

55. *Field Reporter* (1968), quoted in Ellen Baumler, "The Making of a Good Woman: Montana and the National Florence Crittenton Mission," *Montana: The Magazine of Western*

History 53, no. 4 (2003): 52. *Field Reporter* was the newsletter of the Florence Crittenton Association of America.

56. Women's Christian Association, Cleveland, *Annual Report, 1870*, quoted in Marian J. Morton, "Fallen Women, Federated Charities, and Maternity Homes, 1913–1973," *Social Service Review* 62, no. 1 (1988): 61.

57. Regina G. Kunzel, *Fallen Women, Problem Girls: Unmarried Mothers and the Professionalization of Social Work, 1890–1945* (New Haven, CT: Yale University Press, 1993); Ada Eliot Sheffield, *Case-Study Possibilities: A Forecast* (Boston: Research Bureau on Social Case Work, 1922).

58. Salvation Army Rescue Home, *Annual Report, 1893*, quoted in Morton, "Fallen Women," 63.

59. Baumler, "The Making of a Good Woman," 52.

60. Kunzel, *Fallen Women,* 10.

61. Henry D. Schumacher, "The Unmarried Mother: A Socio-Psychiatric Viewpoint," *Mental Hygiene* 4 (1927): 775–782.

62. *Florence Crittenton Bulletin* 4 (1929), 10, quoted in Regina G. Kunzel, "The Professionalization of Benevolence: Evangelicals and Social Workers in the Florence Crittenton Homes, 1915–1945," *Journal of Social History* 22, no. 1 (1988): 30.

63. Kunzel, "The Professionalization of Benevolence," 30–31.

64. Morton, "Fallen Women," 68.

65. Ibid., 69.

66. Ibid., 71.

67. Rickie Solinger, *Wake Up Little Susie: Single Pregnancy before Roe v. Wade* (New York: Routledge, 1992), 47.

68. George H. Finck, Beatrice Simcox Reiner, and Brady O. Smith, "Group Counseling with Unmarried Mothers," *Journal of Marriage and Family* 27, no. 2 (1965): 224–229.

69. Sarah Evan, "The Unwed Mother's Indecision about Her Baby as a Defense Mechanism," paper presented to the National Conference of Social Work, Philadelphia, Pennsylvania, May 23, 1957, in *Services to Unmarried Mothers* (New York: Child Welfare League of America, 1958), 20.

70. Ibid., 30.

71. Child Welfare League of America, *Standards for Services to Unmarried Mothers* (New York: Child Welfare League of America, 1960); National Council on Illegitimacy, *Unmarried Parenthood: Clues to Agency and Community Action* (New York: National Council on Illegitimacy, 1967); Salvation Army, *Services to Unmarried Parents and Their Children* (New York: Salvation Army National Headquarters, 1962); Helen E. Terkelson, *Counseling the Unwed Mother* (Englewood Cliffs, NJ: Prentice-Hall, 1964); Leontine Young, *Out of Wedlock: A Study of the Problems of the Unmarried Mother and Her Child* (New York: McGraw-Hill Book Company, 1954).

72. Solinger, *Wake Up Little Susie,* 94.

73. For example, Baumler notes that "by the late 1940s the National Florence Crittenton Mission discouraged young mothers from keeping their babies, and by 1957, 98 percent of Helena's Crittenton teens chose to put their babies up for adoption through one of the state's four licensed agencies: the Montana Children's Home, State Welfare, Lutheran Social Services, and Catholic Charities"; "The Making of a Good Woman," 61. See also *A Girl Like Her,* dir. Ann Fessler, DVD, Women Make Movies, 2011.

74. Daniel Patrick Moynihan, *The Negro Family: The Case for National Action* (Washington, DC: Government Printing Office, 1965); Oscar Lewis, "The Culture of Poverty," *Scientific American* 215, no. 4 (1966): 19–25.

75. Solinger discusses this at length in *Wake Up Little Susie*, 41–85.

76. Michelle Kahan, "Put Up on Platforms: A History of Twentieth-Century Adoption Policy in the United States," *Journal of Sociology and Social Welfare* 33, no. 3 (2006): 51–72.

77. Elizabeth Siegel Watkins, *On the Pill: A Social History of Oral Contraceptives, 1950–1970* (Baltimore, MD: John Hopkins University Press, 1998).

78. Laura Kaplan, *The Story of Jane: The Legendary Underground Abortion Service* (Chicago: University of Chicago Press, 1997); Leslie J. Reagan, *When Abortion Was a Crime: Women, Medicine, and the Law, 1867–1973* (Berkeley: University of California Press, 1998).

79. Ruth I. Pierce, *Single and Pregnant* (Boston: Beacon Press, 1970); Jean Renevoize, *Going Solo: Single Mothers by Choice* (London: Routledge and Kegan Paul, 1985).

80. Riane Tennenhaus Eisler, *Dissolution: No-Fault Divorce, Marriage, and the Future of Women* (New York: McGraw-Hill Book Company, 1977), 5.

81. William L. Anderson and Derek W. Little, "All's Fair: War and Other Causes of Divorce from a Beckerian Perspective," *American Journal of Economics and Sociology* 58, no. 4 (1999): 901–922.

82. Naomi Miller, *Single Parents by Choice: A Growing Trend in Family Life* (New York: Plenum Press, 1992), 103. For recent U.S. divorce data, see Casey E. Copen, Kimberly Daniels, Jonathan Vespa, and William D. Mosher, "First Marriages in the United States: Data from the 2006–2010 National Survey of Family Growth," accessed September 10, 2016. http://www.cdc.gov/nchs/data/nhsr/nhsr049.pdf.

83. California was the first state to legalize no-fault divorce; its legislature passed the California Family Law Act in 1970. Eisler, *Dissolution*; Lenore J. Weitzman, *The Divorce Revolution* (New York: The Free Press, 1985).

84. Susan Faludi, *Backlash: The Undeclared War against American Women* (New York: Crown Publishers, 1991).

85. Quoted in ibid., 232.

86. Toni L'Hommidieu, *The Divorce Experiences of Working and Middle Class Women* (Ann Arbor: UMI Research Press, 1984), 8–9.

87. Terry Arendell, *Mothers and Divorce: Legal, Economic, and Social Dilemmas* (Berkeley: University of California Press, 1986); Robert Weiss, *Going It Alone: The Family Life and Social Situation of the Single Parent* (New York: Basic Books, 1979).

88. Arendell, *Mothers and Divorce*, 128.

89. Moynihan, *The Negro Family*; Lewis, "The Culture of Poverty"; Charles Murray, *Losing Ground: American Social Policy, 1950–1980* (New York: Basic Books, 1984).

90. Rickie Solinger, "Dependency and Choice: The Two Faces of Eve," in *Whose Welfare?* ed. Gwendolyn Mink (Ithaca, NY: Cornell University Press, 1999), 7–35.

91. Gary L. Bauer, *The Family: Preserving America's Future* (Washington, DC: U.S. Department of Education, 1986). Associate professor Lawrence Mead, a political scientist at New York University, used the word "semisocialized" in his testimony at a congressional hearing; see *Workfare versus Welfare: Hearing before the Subcommittee on Trade, Productivity, and Economic Growth of the Joint Economic Committee, Ninety-Ninth Congress, Second Session, April 23, 1986* (Washington, DC: Government Printing Office, 1986), 99.

92. Murray Edelman, *Constructing the Political Spectacle* (Chicago: University of Chicago Press, 1988); William J. Clinton, "Statement on Signing the Personal Responsibility and Work Reconciliation Act of 1996," August 22, 1996, *The American Presidency Project*, accessed August 27, 2016, http://www.presidency.ucsb.edu/ws/?pid=53219; Ruth Sidel, "The Enemy Within: A Commentary on the Demonization of Difference," *American Journal of Orthopsychiatry* 66, no. 4 (1996): 490–496.

93. Bette J. Dickerson, *African-American Single Mothers: Understanding Their Lives and Families* (Thousand Oaks, CA: Sage Publications, 1995); Elaine Bell Kaplan, *Not Our Kind of Girl: Unraveling the Mythos of Black Teenage Motherhood* (Berkeley: University of California Press, 1997); Valerie Polakow, *Lives on the Edge: Single Mothers and Their Children in the Other America* (Chicago: University of Chicago Press, 1993).

94. Josh Levin, "The Welfare Queen," *Slate*, December 19, 2013, http://www.slate.com/articles/news_and_politics/history/2013/12/linda_taylor_welfare_queen_ronald_reagan_made_her_a_notorious_american_villain.html.

95. Lucy A. Williams, "Race, Rat Bites, and Unfit Mothers: How Media Discourse Informs Welfare Legislation Debate," *Fordham Urban Law Journal* 22, no. 4 (1994): 1159–1196; Franklin D. Gilliam Jr., "The 'Welfare Queen' Experiment: How Viewers React to Images of African-American Mothers on Welfare," *Nieman Reports* 53, no. 2 (1999), https://escholarship.org/uc/item/17m7r1rq#page-3. For more on the concept of the controlling image, see Collins, *Black Feminist Thought*, 68.

96. For more on the racism and New Right politics, see Martin Gilens, *Why Americans Hate Welfare: Race, Media, and the Politics of Antipoverty Policy* (Chicago: University of Chicago Press, 1999); and Kenneth J. Neubeck and Noel A. Cazenave, *Welfare Racism: Playing the Race Card against America's Poor* (New York: Routledge, 2001).

97. Quoted in Tobin Beck, "Quayle 10 Years After Murphy Brown," *Washington Times*, May 9, 2002.

98. Ibid.

99. Richard Lacayo and Jordan Bonfante, "This Land Is Your Land . . . This Land Is My Land," *Time*, May 18, 1992, 28; "Trapped in Eddies of Poverty," *Christian Science Monitor*, February 3, 1986, 21; David Holmstrom, "Gangs That 'Secede' from Society," *Christian Science Monitor*, January 18 1991, 10.

100. Carl S. Taylor, *Dangerous Society* (East Lansing: Michigan State University Press, 1990).

101. Christopher Farnell and Karen Pennar, "Commentary: Welfare Reform Won't Patch Up Poor Families," *Business Week*, January 23, 1995, 78.

102. "Excerpt from Vice President's Speech on Cities and Poverty," *New York Times*, February 12, 1990; Rev. John Carty, "As You Were Saying," *Boston Herald*, August 28, 1994; Steven V. Roberts, "America's New Crusade," *US News & World Report*, August 1, 1994.

103. Laurence Lynn, "Ending Welfare as We Know It," *The American Prospect*, Fall 1993, http://prospect.org/article/ending-welfare-reform-we-know-it.

104. Robin Toner, "Dukes Takes His Anger into 1992 Race," *New York Times*, December 5, 1991.

105. Kim Phillips, "Papa Don't Preach," *In These Times*, September 16, 1996.

106. Tom Coakley, "Scalded 5-Year-Old Is Disfigured for Life, Prosecutor Says," *Boston Globe*, March 24, 1994.

107. Ibid.

108. Robert Rector, "God and the Underclass," *National Review* 48, no. 10 (1996): 30.

109. Williams, "Race, Rat Bites, and Unfit Mothers," 1163.

110. Murray, *Losing Ground*, 9.

111. Robert J. Samuelson, "Can't Be Reformed," *Newsweek*, March 27, 1995, 47.

112. For example, Leon Dash wrote an eight-part, front-page story entitled, "Rosa Lee's Story," for the *Washington Post*. The first installment was published on September 18, 1994, and daily installments followed through September 25, 1994.

113. Steven Waldman, "Taking on the Welfare Dads," *Newsweek*, June 20, 1994, 34.

114. Christina Nitong, "Work, or Else: Welfare Moms Strive to Meet the Ultimatum," *Christian Science Monitor*, July 1, 1996, 10.

115. David Beasley, "Births out of Wedlock Will Get Sisters Locked Up," *Atlanta Constitution*, November 21, 1987.

116. David Holmstrom, "Census: Nuclear Family Fading," *Christian Science Monitor*, September 13, 1994.

117. Maureen Dowd, "Moynihan Opens Major Drive to Replace Welfare Program," *New York Times*, January 24, 1987.

118. Kay S. Hymnowitz, "Real Life on the Teen Mommy Track: The Middle-Class 'Script' Gets No Reading in the Inner City," *Washington Post*, November 13, 1994; Joe Frolik, "Brave New World: Single Motherhood Loses Stigma for Children of the Sexual Revolution," *Cleveland Plain Dealer*, November 30, 1993.

119. Farnell and Pennar, "Commentary," 78; Holmstrom, "Census: Nuclear Family Fading," 2.

120. George Gilder, "End Welfare Reform as We Know It," *American Spectator* 28, no. 6 (1995): 24–25.

121. Frolik, "Brave New World."

122. Gilder, "End Welfare Reform as We Know It," 25.

123. Bernard Weinraub, "Reagan Is Pushing the Welfare Issue," *New York Times*, February 16, 1986; Gilder, "End Welfare Reform as We Know It," 25.

124. William Tucker, "The Moral of the Story," *The American Spectator*, October 1996, 22.

125. Dorian Friedman, "The Flawed Premise of Welfare Reform," *U.S. News & World Report*, September 11, 1995, 32.

126. Marilyn Gardner, "When the Mothers Are Also Children," *Christian Science Monitor*, March 18 1991, 13.

127. Joanne Jacobs, "Who Needs Marriage? Children Do," *Atlanta Journal Constitution*, February 24, 1991.

128. Ibid.

129. Ibid.

130. Jane Gross, "Poor Seekers of Good Life Flock to California, as Middle Class Moves Away," *New York Times*, December 29, 1991; Dirk Johnson, "Rethinking Welfare: Interstate Migration," *New York Times*, May 8, 1989; "Welfare Reform-Bridging the Gap between the States," *Christian Science Monitor*, April 7, 1986.

131. Joseph Perkins, "Without Dads, Cycle of Dependency Continues," *Atlanta Constitution*, June 23, 1993.

132. Charles M. Sennott, "Welfare Program under Fire," *Boston Globe*, February 24, 1994; Mike Barnicle, "Ventura Fated to Be a Symbol," *Boston Globe*, October 6, 1994; Heather MacDonald, "Welfare's Next Vietnam," *City Journal* 5, no. 10 (1995), accessed August 26, 2016, http://www.city-journal.org/html/welfare%E2%80%99s-next-vietnam-12166.html.

133. See Abramovitz, *Regulating the Lives of Women*; Randy Albeda and Ann Withorn, eds., *Lost Ground: Welfare Reform, Poverty, and Beyond* (Boston: South End Press, 2002); Sharon Hays, *Flat Broke with Children: Women in the Age of Welfare Reform* (New York: Oxford University Press, 2003); Francis Fox Piven, ed., *Work, Welfare, and Politics: Confronting Poverty in the Wake of Welfare Reform* (Eugene: University of Oregon Press, 2002); Gwendolyn Mink, *Welfare's End* (Ithaca: Cornell University Press, 1998); Ruth Sidel, *Keeping Women and Children Last: America's War on the Poor* (New York: Penguin Books, 1996); and Valerie Polakow, Sandra S. Butler, Luisa Stormer Deprez, and Peggy Kahn, eds., *Shut Out: Low Income Mothers and Higher Education in Post-Welfare America* (Albany: State University of New York Press, 2004).

134. Nancy Naples, *Grassroots Warriors: Activist Mothering, Community Work, and the War on Poverty* (New York: Routledge, 1998); Ruth Sidel, *Unsung Heroines: Single Mothers and the American Dream* (Berkeley: University of California Press, 2006).

135. Vivian Adair and Sandra L. Dahlberg, *Reclaiming Class: Women, Poverty, and the Promise of Higher Education in America* (Philadelphia: Temple University Press, 2003); Lori Holyfield, *Moving Up and Out: Poverty, Education, and the Single Parent Family* (Philadelphia: Temple University Press, 2002).

136. Kathryn Edin and Maria Kafalas, *Promises I Can Keep: Why Poor Women Put Motherhood Before Marriage* (Berkeley: University of California Press, 2005); Margaret Nelson, *The Social Economy of Single Motherhood: Raising Children in Rural America* (New York: Routledge, 2005); Ellen Lewin, *Lesbian Mothers: Accounts of Gender in American Culture* (Ithaca, NY: Cornell University Press, 1993).

137. The Carnegie Tier One classification is assigned to postsecondary institutions with a significant focus on research.

138. Kristina Hunken, "Economic Decisions of Single Mothers Pursuing Postsecondary Education" (MA thesis, Texas Woman's University, 2007).

139. Such critiques were central to the volume *This Bridge Called My Back: Writings by Radical Women of Color*, edited by Cherríe Moraga and Gloria Anzaldúa (New York: Kitchen Table Press, 1980).

CHAPTER 2   TRYING TO MAKE ENDS MEET

1. Terri D. Heath and Dennis K. Orthner, "Stress Adaptation among Male and Female Student Parents," *Journal of Family Issues* 20, no. 4 (1999): 557–587.

2. Melody Ann Schobert, "Single Parents Who Are College Students: A Descriptive Study Incorporating Academic and General Self-Concept" (Ph.D. diss., University of Iowa, 2000).

3. Ibid.

4. Center for Women Policy Studies, *From Poverty to Self-Sufficiency: The Role of Postsecondary Education in Welfare Reform* (Washington, DC: Center for Women Policy Studies, 2002).

5. Vivyan C. Adair, "Poverty and the (Broken) Promise of Higher Education," *Harvard Educational Review* 71, no. 2 (2001): 217–239.

6. Min Zhan and Shanta Pandey, "Economic Well-Being of Single Mothers: Work First or Postsecondary Education?" *Journal of Sociology and Social Welfare* 31, no. 3 (2004): 87–113.

7. Peggy Kahn and Valerie Polakow, "Struggling to Live and to Learn: Single Mothers, Welfare Policy, and Post-Secondary Education in Michigan," in *Shut Out: Low Income Mothers and Higher Education in Post-Welfare America*, edited by Valeria Polakow, Sandra S. Butler, Luisa Stormer Duprez, and Peggy Kahn (Albany: State University of New York Press, 2004), 1–18.

8. For further discussion of this and related stereotypes that were central to welfare reform, see Kenneth J. Neubeck and Noel A. Cazenave, *Welfare Racism: Playing the Race Card against America's Poor* (New York: Routledge, 2001); Karen Seccombe, *"So You Think I Drive a Cadillac?" Welfare Recipients' Perspectives on the System and Its Reform* (Boston: Allyn and Bacon, 1999), 48–73; and Lucy A. Williams, "Race, Rat Bites, and Unfit Mothers: How Media Discourse Informs Welfare Legislation Debate," *Fordham Urban Law Journal* 22, no. 4 (1994): 1159–1196.

9. John Immerwahr and Tony Foleno, *Great Expectations: How the Public and Parents—White, African American, and Hispanic—View Higher Education* (San Jose, CA: National Center for Public Policy and Higher Education, 2000), http://www.highereducation.org/reports/expectations/expectations.shtml.

10. Catherine Pelissier Kingfisher uses the phrase "the American welfare trap" to describe the ways structural forces in American culture, specifically steady decreases in "economic opportunities and assistance," make it difficult for low-income women to escape poverty. Kingfisher, *Women in the American Welfare Trap* (Philadelphia: University of Pennsylvania Press, 1996), 1–15.

11. "Per-Semester Tuition and Fees for Fall 2004 and Spring 2005," *University of Iowa Office of the Registrar*, accessed August 27, 2004, http://www.registrar.uiowa.edu/tuition/2004-05FallSpring.pdf.

12. "Tuition," Kirkwood Community College Enrollment Services, accessed July 30, 2004, http://www.kirkwood.cc.ia.us/registration/tuition/html.

13. This was the maximum amount awarded in 2004, the time of my interviews with Joanna. For more information about Pell Grants and federal financial aid guidelines, see James B. Stedman, *Federal Pell Grant Program of the Higher Education Act* (Washington, DC: Congressional Research Service, 2004); and "Federal Pell Grant," *Federal Student Aid*, accessed March 15, 2012, http://studentaid.ed.gov/PORTALSWebApp/students/english/PellGrants.jsp.

14. Alan Finder, "Decline of the Tenure Track Raises Concerns," *New York Times*, November 20, 2007.

15. "Classification of Residents and Non-Residents for Admission and Tuition Purposes," *University of Iowa Office of the Registrar*, accessed November 21, 2004, http://www.registrar.uiowa.edu/residency/wresreg.aspx.

16. Interest rates for student loans depend on the type of loan and the date of loan disbursement. At present, interest rates range from 3.4 percent to 8.5 percent; "Here's Your Guide to Repaying Your Federal Student Loans," *Federal Student Aid*, accessed November 17, 2015, http://studentaid.ed.gov/PORTALSWebApp/students/english/repaying.jsp.

17. Ibid. Repayment can generally be deferred until a student leaves the university. In addition, there is a grace period for repayment of student loans, generally between six and nine months from the time the student leaves the institution because he or she has graduated or has withdrawn.

18. According to the USDA Center for Nutrition and Policy Promotion, the greatest expenditures on children from birth through age seventeen are expenses for housing, food, health care, and education; U.S. Department of Agriculture, Center for Nutrition and Policy Promotion, *Expenditures on Children by Families, 2012*, accessed March 13, 2014, http://www.cnpp.usda.gov/sites/default/files/expenditures_on_children_by_families/crc2012.pdf.

19. H. Russell Bernard, *Research Methods in Cultural Anthropology* (Newbury Park, CA: Sage Publications, Inc., 1988).

20. David Super, *Background on the Food Stamp Program* (Washington, DC: Center for Budget and Policy Priorities, 2001).

21. Randy Albelda and Ann Withorn, eds., *Lost Ground: Welfare Reform, Poverty, and Beyond* (Cambridge, MA: South End Press, 2002); Jane L. Collins and Victoria Mayer, *Both Hands Tied: Welfare Reform and the Race to the Bottom of the Low-Wage Labor Market* (Chicago: University of Chicago Press, 2010); Sharon Hays, *Flat Broke with Children: Women in the Age of Welfare Reform* (New York: Oxford University Press, 2003); Ruth Sidel, *Keeping Women and Children Last: America's War on the Poor* (New York: Penguin Books, 1998); Gwendolyn Mink, ed., *Whose Welfare?* (Ithaca, NY: Cornell University Press, 1999); Francis Fox Piven, ed., *Work, Welfare, and Politics: Confronting Poverty in the Wake of Welfare Reform* (Eugene: University of Oregon Press, 2002).

22. "Pay and Manage Your Loan," accessed 10 September 2016, https://www.salliemae.com/student-loans/managing-your-loans/pay-and-manage-your-loan/.

CHAPTER 3   CLOCKS AND CALENDARS

1. Stan Nussbaum, *American Cultural Baggage: How to Recognize and Deal with It* (Maryknoll, NY: Orbis Books, 2005), 20.

2. The only exception is when someone indicates a time *en punto*, or "exactly." If a business meeting was scheduled for 8 A.M. *en punto*, all participants would be expected to be present and ready promptly at 8 A.M.

3. This was the tuition rate Isabella recalled being charged in 2003.

4. The Texas Core Curriculum, sometimes referred to as the Texas General Education Core Curriculum, applies to all undergraduate degree programs and aims to provide a liberal arts foundation regardless of the specific degree a student may go on to complete. The core curriculum requires students to complete between forty-two and forty-eight credits, including courses in English rhetoric/composition, communications, mathematics, natural sciences, humanities, visual and performing arts, and the social sciences. Core curriculum courses transfer between institutions of higher education and it is common for many students to complete the Texas Core Curriculum requirements at a two-year or community college before transferring to a four-year institution. See "The Texas General Education Core Web Center," *Texas Higher Education Coordinating Board,* accessed February 23, 2015, http://statecore.its .txstate.edu/.

5. "Skills to Employment/IowaWorks: Creating Futures—Workforce Investment Act," *Kirkwood Community College,* accessed June 21, 2004, http://www.kirkwood.edu/creatingfutures.

6. As is typical of many college courses, Beth's classes met either on a Monday-Wednesday-Friday schedule or a Tuesday-Thursday schedule.

7. Sharon Hays, *The Cultural Contradictions of Motherhood* (New Haven, CT: Yale University Press, 1996).

8. Gwendolyn Mink, *Welfare's End* (Ithaca, NY: Cornell University Press, 1998), 103; Susan J. Douglas and Meredith W. Michaels, *The Mommy Myth: The Idealization of Motherhood and How It Has Undermined Women* (New York: The Free Press, 2004), 181.

9. James B. Maas with Megan L. Wherry, David J. Axelrod, Barbara R. Hogan, and Jennifer A. Blumin, *Power Sleep: The Revolutionary Program That Prepares your Mind for Peak Performance* (New York: Villard 1998); Michael H. Bonnet and Donna L. Arand, "How Much Sleep Do Adults Need?" *National Sleep Foundation,* 2012, http://www.sleepfoundation.org/article/white-papers/how-much-sleep-do-adults-need.

10. "Sleep Deprivation," *Postgraduate Medicine* 112, no. 4 (2002): 115–116.

11. L. Robert Kohls, *Values American Live By* (Washington, DC: Meridian House International, 1984), 2.

12. Monica Bauerlein and Clara Jeffrey, "All Work and No Pay: The Great Speedup," *Mother Jones,* July/August 2011, http://motherjones.com/politics/2011/06/speed-up-american-workers -long-hours.

13. Dave Gilson, "Overworked America: 12 Charts That Will Make Your Blood Boil," *Mother Jones*, July/August 2011, http://motherjones.com/politics/2011/06/speedup-americans -working-harder-charts.

14. Kathy Peel, *The Family Manager Takes Charge: Getting on the Fast Track to a Happy, Organized Home* (New York: Perigee Books, 2003), 3.

15. Janet Lehman, "9 Back to School Behavior Tips: How to Set up a Structure That Works," *Empowering Parents*, 2016, accessed September 16, 2016, http://www.empoweringparents .com/9-Back-to-School-Tips-for-Parents.php?&key=Routine-And-Structure; Rocks in My Dryer, "Managing the After-School Crunch," *Parenting*, 2008, accessed September 16, 2016, http://www.parenting.com/blogs/parenting-post/managing-after-school-crunch; "Time Management Tips for Thanksgiving: 6 Smart Shortcuts to Save Time during the Holiday Season," *Parenting*, accessed September 16, 2016, http://www.parenting.com/article/time -management-tips-for-thanksgiving; Katrina Brown Hunt, "The Best Time to Have #2 (or #3!)," *Parents*, accessed September 16, 2016, http://www.parents.com/pregnancy/considering -baby/another/best-time-to-have-2-or-3-babies/; Lewis Cohen, "Let Them Play," *Mothering*, December 25, 2010, accessed September 16, 2016, http://www.mothering.com/articles/let -them-play/; Valentina Sgro, *Organize your Family's Schedule in No Time* (Indianapolis: Que (Pearson) Publishing, 2004).

16. For example, Deutsch and colleagues demonstrated that increased paternal participation can have a positive impact on children's self-esteem. Similarly, Michael E. Lamb has argued that fathers play a crucial role in child development. In addition, Kyle Pruett and Marsha Kline Pruett indicate that although mothers and fathers typically have different approaches to parenting, there is much to be gained from the combination of these approaches. Francine M. Deutsch, Laura J. Servis, and Jessica D. Payne, "Paternal Participation in Child Care and Its Effects on Children's Self-Esteem and Attitudes toward Gender Roles," *Journal of Family Issues* 22, no. 8 (2001): 1000–1024; Michael E. Lamb, *The Role of the Father in Child Development*, 5th ed. (Hoboken, NJ: Wiley, 2010); Kyle Pruett and Marsha Kline Pruett, *Partnership Parenting: How Men and Women Parent Differently and How It Helps Your Kids and Can Strengthen Your Marriage* (New York: Da Capo Press, 2009).

17. Hochschild's landmark study is perhaps most often cited in regard to these issues. However, earlier work by both Szalai and by Baruch and Barnett provide important insight into the gendered division of labor in families, as does more recent work by Gornick and Meyers and by Treas and Drobnic. Arlie Russell Hochschild, *The Second Shift: Working Parents and the Revolution at Home* (New York: Viking, 1989); Alexander Szalai, ed., *The Use of Time: Daily Activities of Urban and Suburban Populations in Twelve Countries* (The Hague: Mouton, 1972); Grace K. Baruch and Rosalind Barnett, "Correlates of Fathers' Participation in Family Work: A Technical Report," Working Paper no. 106, Wellesley College Center for Research on Women, Wellesley, Massachusetts, 1983; Janet C. Gornick and Marcia K. Meyers, eds., *Gender Equality: Transforming Family Divisions of Labor* (Brooklyn, NY: Verso, 2009); Judith Treas and Sonja Drobnic, *Dividing the Domestic: Men, Women, and Household Work in Cross-National Perspective* (Stanford, CA: Stanford University Press, 2010).

18. Hochschild, *The Second Shift*, 3.

19. Jillian M. Duquaine-Watson, "All You Need Is Love: Representations of Maternal Emotion in *Working Mother* Magazine," in *Mother Matters: Motherhood as Discourse and Practice*, edited by Andrea O'Reilly (Toronto: Association for Research on Mothering, 2004), 125–138.

20. For an early discussion of the relationship between self-concept and academic performance, see William Watson Purkey, *Self-Concept and School Achievement* (Englewood Cliffs, NJ: Prentice Hall, 1970); and Ernest T. Pascarella, Elizabeth J. Whitt, Marcia I. Edison,

Amaury Nora, Linda Serra Hagedorn, Patricia Yeager, and Patrick T. Terenzini, "The 'Chilly Climate' for Women and Cognitive Outcomes during the First Year of College," paper presented at the annual meeting of the Association for the Study of Higher Education, Memphis, Tennessee, October 31–November 3, 1996, accessed August 10, 2016, http://files.eric.ed .gov/fulltext/ED402847.pdf. For the link between positive self-esteem and job performance and job satisfaction, see Timothy A. Judge and Joyce E. Bono, "Relationship of Core Self-Evaluation Traits—Self-Esteem, Generalized Self-Efficacy, Locus of Control, and Emotional Stability—with Job Satisfaction and Job Performance: A Meta-Analysis," *Journal of Applied Psychology* 86, no. 1 (2001): 80–92.

CHAPTER 4   NAVIGATING AMERICA'S CHILD CARE CRISIS

1. Mary Frances Berry, *The Politics of Parenthood: Child Care, Women's Rights, and the Myth of the Good Mother* (New York: Viking 1993); William T. Gormley Jr., *Everybody's Children: Child Care as a Public Problem* (Washington, DC: Brookings Institute, 1995); Angela Browne Miller, *The Day Care Dilemma: Critical Concerns for American Families* (New York: Plenum Press, 1990); Diane Lindsay Reeves, *Child Care Crisis* (Santa Barbara, CA: ABC-CLIO, Inc., 1992).

2. Hamilton Cravens, *Before Head Start: The Iowa Stations and America's Children* (Chapel Hill: University of North Carolina Press, 1993); Emilie Stoltzfus, *Citizen, Worker, Mother: Debating Public Responsibility for Child Care after the Second World War* (Chapel Hill: University of North Carolina Press, 2003).

3. Edward F. Zigler, Katherine Marsland, and Heather Lord, *The Tragedy of Child Care in America* (New Haven, CT: Yale University Press, 2009), 1–2.

4. George Thurman, *Day Care . . . An Emerging Crisis* (Springfield, IL: Charles C. Thomas Publishers, 1980), 120.

5. U.S. Department of Health and Human Services, "Child Care and Development Fund," March 2012, http://www.acf.hhs.gov/sites/default/files/occ/ccdf_factsheet.pdf.

6. Ibid.

7. "About Child Care," *Child Care Aware of America*, accessed June 17, 2015, http://usa .childcareaware.org/families-programs/about-child-care/.

8. Ibid.

9. "America After 3PM: Key Findings," *Afterschool Alliance*, accessed June 15, 2015, http:// www.afterschoolalliance.org/documents/AA3PM_Key_Findings_2009.pdf.

10. According to statistics from Realty Trac, foreclosure rates in 2009 "increased to a record 2.8 million, a 21% rise over 2008 and 120% over 2007." Daren Blomquist, "A Record 2.8 Million Properties Receive Foreclosure Notices in 2009," *RealtyTrac*, accessed September 16, 2016, http://www.realtytrac.com/landing/2009-year-end-foreclosure-report.html.

11. "Increase in Unemployment Rate, in January 2009," *U.S. Bureau of Labor Statistics*, February 10, 2009, http://www.bls.gov/opub/ted/2009/feb/wk2/art02.htm.

12. The U.S. Census Bureau reported that in 2009, "14.3 percent of the U.S. population had an income below their respective poverty thresholds. The number of people in poverty increased to 42.9 million." Alemayehu Bishaw and Suzanne McCartney, "Poverty: 2008 and 2009," *American Community Survey Briefs*, September 2010, http://www.census.gov/ prod/2010pubs/acsbr09-1.pdf.

13. A March 2009 survey by the *Wall Street Journal* and the National Conference of State Legislatures found that welfare rolls had increased in twenty-three of the thirty most populous

states in the United States and that nationally, the number of families receiving food stamps was 19 percent higher than the previous year; Sara Murray, "Numbers on Welfare See Sharp Increase," *Wall Street Journal*, June 22, 2009.

14. Child Care Aware of America, *Parents and the High Cost of Child Care: 2014 Report* (Arlington, VA: Child Care Aware of America, 2014).

15. Katherine Sell, Sarah Zlotnick, Kathleen Noonan, and David Rubin, *The Effect of Recession on Child Well-Being* (Philadelphia: Research Institute at Children's Hospital of Philadelphia, 2010), http://fcd-us.org/sites/default/files/Effect%20of%20Recession%20on%20Child%20Well-Being.pdf.

16. Valerie Polakow, *Who Cares for Our Children? The Child Care Crisis in the Other America* (New York: Teachers College Press, 2007), 22.

17. Child Care Aware of America, *Parents and the High Cost of Child Care*, 22.

18. Ibid.

19. Ibid.

20. Rachel A. Gordon and P. Lindsay Chase-Lansdale, "Availability of Child Care in the United States: A Description and Analysis of Data Resources," *Demography* 38, no. 2 (2001): 300.

21. Bruce Weber, "Rural Poverty in the United States," PowerPoint presentation at the Rural Communities Initiative Academy, Kansas City, MO, September 4, 2008, https://peerta.acf .hhs.gov/sites/default/files/public/uploaded_files/Rural%20HHS%20Academy%20Sept08 .pdf.

22. For example, Gordon and Chase-Lansdale found that families living in mixed-income urban areas had greater access to child care than families living in poor urban areas; Gordon and Chase-Lansdale, "Availability of Child Care in the United States."

23. "5 Steps to Choosing Care," *Child Care Aware of America*, accessed June 18, 2015, http:// childcareaware.org/parents-and-guardians/child-care-101/5-steps-to-choosing-care.

24. "Choosing a Child Care Center," *Healthy Children*, November 21, 2015, accessed June 17, 2015, http://www.healthychildren.org/english/family-life/work-play/Pages/Choosing-a-Childcare -Center.aspx; National Resource Center for Health and Safety in Child Care and Early Education, *A Parent's Guide to Choosing Safe and Healthy Child Care* (Aurora, CO: National Resource Center for Health and Safety in Child Care and Early Education, 2015), http://nrckids.org/ default/assets/file/parentsguide.pdf. See also Richard Fiene, "13 Indicators of Quality Child Care: Research Update," *U.S. Department of Health and Human Services, Office of the Assistant Secretary for Planning and Evaluation*, May 1, 2002, accessed May 25, 2015, http://aspe.hhs.gov/ hsp/ccquality-ind02/; and Deborah Lowe Vandell and Barbara Wolfe, *Child Care Quality: Does It Matter and Does It Need to Be Improved?* (Madison, WI: Institute for Research on Poverty, 2000).

Most states publish brochures or pamphlets or maintain websites that are intended to help parents choose high-quality child care for their children. For examples, see Connecticut Department of Public Health, "Parent Guidelines for Choosing a Child Day Care Program," accessed June 14, 2015, http://www.ct.gov/dph/lib/dph/daycare/pdf/CDC_brochure.pdf; New Mexico Children, Youth, and Families Department, "Parents' Guide to Selecting Quality Child Care," accessed May 25, 2015, https://cyfd.org/docs/parentsguide_childcare_0213lr.pdf.

25. Dylan Silver, "Kindertown Preschool Could Shut Down Friday," *Tahoe Daily Tribune*, June 22, 2011.

26. Lauren Rosenthal, "State Closes Three Child Care Facilities in Washington County," *Pittsburgh Post-Gazette*, July 1, 2011.

27. Laura Riparbelli, "Three Arrested for Death of Toddler in Overheated Day care Van," *ABC News*, June 21, 2011, http://abcnews.go.com/US/arrested-death-toddler-hot-daycare-van/story?id=13895335.

28. Elizabeth Mehren, "Study Finds Most Child Care Lacking," *Los Angeles Times*, April 8, 1994.

29. Robert D. McFadden, "Harsh Report on Day Care Death Finds Dangerous Flaws in System," *New York Times*, October 8, 2004.

30. National Institute of Child Health and Human Development, *The NICHD Study of Early Child Care and Youth Development: Findings for Children up to Age 4½ Years* (Washington, DC: U.S. National Institutes of Health, 2006), 9, https://www.nichd.nih.gov/publications/pubs/documents/seccyd_06.pdf.

31. For example, school officials in Adams County, Pennsylvania, faced the possibility of cutting middle school sports teams as a means of reducing costs; Scot Andrew Pitzer, "Superintendents Mulling Middle School League," *GettysburgTimes.com*, July 2, 2011. Similarly, the Keller Independent School District, just east of Dallas, was forced to cut numerous extracurricular programs in response to $16 million in budget cuts; Sandra Engelland, "Keller District to Cut Teachers, Programs after Tax Election Failed," *Star-Telegram*, June 20, 2011.

32. Lealan Jones, Lloyd Newman, and David Isay, *Our America: Life and Death on the South Side of Chicago* (New York: Washington Square Press, 1997).

33. For more information, see "4Cs: Community Coordinated Child Care," *Iowa4CS*, 2012, http://www.iowa4cs.com/.

34. According to federal student financial aid regulations, students must be enrolled at least half-time in order to qualify for any type of federal financial aid, including loans, grants, and work-study; U.S. Department of Education, "Basic Eligibility Criteria," 2012, accessed June 14, 2015, http://studentaid.ed.gov/eligibility/basic-criteria.

35. University of Iowa Office of the Provost, *Handbook for Teaching Assistants* (Iowa City: University of Iowa, 2004).

36. While government-sponsored programs such as Promise Jobs did provide child care assistance to parents seeking postsecondary education and training, program guidelines define individuals who have already completed a bachelor's degree as ineligible for child care grants. Iowa Department of Human Services, "Promise Jobs," accessed June 14, 2015, http://dhs.iowa.gov/reports/promise-jobs-reports.

37. Alison J. Pugh, "Windfall Child Rearing: Low-Income Care and Consumption," *Journal of Consumer Culture* 4, no. 2 (2004): 229–249.

38. Filling out an application at one of the Head Start centers in Johnson County automatically puts an applicant on a "master waiting list" for all Head Start sites in the county. They are contacted when they reach the top of the waiting list and an opening arises, regardless of whether or not the opening is at the specific site where they applied.

39. Rachel Schumacher and Kate Irish, "What's New in 2002? A Snapshot of Head Start Children, Families, Teachers, and Programs," Policy Brief No. 1, Center for Law and Social Policy, Washington, DC, 2003, https://archive.org/stream/ERIC_ED475970#page/no/mode/2up.

40. In 2003, the year Samantha applied to Head Start, the federal poverty guidelines were $8,860 annually for the first person and $3,080 for each additional person. Thus, for a family of two such as Samantha and Athena, the federal poverty threshold was $11,940. U.S. Department of Health and Human Services, "The 2003 HHS Poverty Guidelines," December 1, 2003, http://aspe.hhs.gov/poverty/03poverty.htm.

41. According to the U.S. Department of Health and Human Services, child needs include such factors as "mental retardation, health impairments, visual handicaps, hearing impairments, emotional disturbances, speech and language impairments, orthopedic handicaps and learning disabilities." Family needs could include such factors as refugee status, a parent with a disability, a parent who is being abused by their spouse or domestic partner, a parent who is incarcerated, or a parent who is abusing drugs or alcohol. U.S. Department of Health and Human Services, "Head Start: Selection Process," accessed June 3, 2015, https://eclkc.ohs.acf.hhs.gov/hslc/standards/hspps/1305/1305.6%20Selection%20process.htm.

42. Cravens, *Before Head Start*, 251.

43. Johnson County Council of Governments, *JCCOG Johnson County Services Directory* (Iowa City, IA: Johnson County Council of Governments, 2003).

44. For more information about United Action for Youth programs and resources, see the organization's website, http://www.unitedactionforyouth.org/content/.

45. Ibid.

46. WIC, or Women, Infants, and Children, is a supplemental nutrition program facilitated by the Food and Nutrition Service, an agency of the U.S. Department of Agriculture. For more information about the program, see "Women, Infants, and Children (WIC)," http://www.fns.usda.gov/wic/women-infants-and-children-wic.

47. Birthright of Iowa City offers a variety of services that include pregnancy testing, maternity and baby clothing, adoption and legal aid support, short-term housing, and pro-life speakers. For more information about the services provided by Birthright, see "Our Services," *Birthright International*, 2013, accessed August 11, 2016, http://www.birthright.org/htmpages/services.htm.

48. "What We Do," *The Nest of Johnson County: Healthy Babies, Healthy Beginnings*, accessed March 18, 2004, http://nestjc.blogspot.com/. Unfortunately, The Nest of Johnson County was forced to close in early 2011 due to inadequate funding. "Unfortunate News," January 31, 2011, http://nestjc.blogspot.com/.

49. The federal poverty guideline, which is used as the income-eligibility guideline for participation in Head Start, was $12,120 for a family of two in 2003. Amber says that working thirty-five hours a week at $7.00 per hour, she made "around $13,000 during 2003," approximately $800 above the eligibility guideline. U.S. Department of Health and Human Services, "The 2003 HHS Poverty Guidelines," December 1, 2003, https://aspe.hhs.gov/2003-hhs-poverty-guidelines.

50. Kirkwood Community College does not provide lactation rooms or breastfeeding lounges on the Cedar Rapids campus or the Iowa City campus.

51. As of June 2015, the UI Family Services office maintained thirty-three lactation rooms on the UI campus including locations in academic and administrative buildings, UIHC, and the Veterans Hospital. For more information and a list of these rooms, see the University of Iowa Family Services Office, "Lactation Room," accessed June 4, 2015, http://maps.uiowa.edu/amenity/lactation-room.

52. The CCAMPIS grant is available to institutions of higher education through the U.S. Department of Education and is intended to help support the child care needs of low-income students, particularly those who are eligible for Pell Grants; "Child Care Access Means Parents in School Program," *U.S. Department of Education*, accessed March 16, 2014, http://www2.ed.gov/programs/campisp/index.html.

53. "School Age Children's Enrichment Program," *Texas Woman's University*, June 2, 2016, http://www.twu.edu/housing/clubhouse.asp.

54. Kirkwood Kids, the only Kirkwood-affiliated child care, is located on the Kirkwood Cedar Rapids campus. For a current list of UI-affiliated child care centers, see "Child Care," *University of Iowa Human Resources*, accessed November 13, 2015, http://hr.uiowa.edu/family-services/child-care.

55. Phil Ciciora, "On-Campus Child Care Needed for Increasing Number of Student-Parents," *Illinois News Bureau*, February 22, 2010, http://news.illinois.edu/news/10/0222childcare.html.

56. Kevin Miller, Barbara Gault, and Abby Thorman, *Improving Child Care Access to Promote Postsecondary Success among Low-Income Students* (Washington, DC: Institute for Women's Policy Research, 2011).

CHAPTER 5   MOTHERING ALONE IN A CHILLY CLIMATE

1. Lawrence H. Summers, "Remarks at NBER Conference on Diversifying the Science and Engineering Workforce," Cambridge, MA, January 14, 2005, http://www.harvard.edu/president/speeches/summers_2005/nber.php.

2. John Hennessey, Susan Hockfield, and Shirley Tilghman, "Women and Science: The Real Issue," *Boston Globe*, February 12, 2005.

3. "ASA Statement on the Causes of Gender Differences in Science and Math Career Achievement," *Footnotes*, March 2005, accessed August 24, 2016, http://www.asanet.org/sites/default/files/savvy/footnotes/mar05/indexthree.html.

4. National Organization for Women, "NOW Calls for Resignation of Harvard University's President," January 20, 2015, accessed September 16, 2016, http://wiseli.engr.wisc.edu/archives/NOW.pdf.

5. Marcella Bombadieri, "Harvard Aims to Spur Advancement of Women," *Boston Globe*, February 4, 2005.

6. Institutional climate refers to the relative degree of inclusion and support that a particular institution provides to specific groups, such as women or other historically marginalized and underrepresented populations. Institutions that provide little support and/or where marginalization is prevalent are said to have a chilly climate.

7. Thomas J. Hibino to Dorothy K. Robinson, June 15, 2012, accessed September 15, 2015, http://www2.ed.gov/about/offices/list/ocr/docs/investigations/01112027-a.pdf.

8. Bernice R. Sandler and Roberta M. Hall, *The Classroom Climate: A Chilly One for Women?* (Washington, DC: Project on the Status of Women of the Association of American Colleges, 1982), 2, emphasis in the original.

9. Kathryn M. Moore, "Women's Access and Opportunities in Higher Education: Toward the Twenty-First Century," *Comparative Education* 23 no. 1 (1987): 30.

10. Ernest T. Pascarella, Elizabeth J. Whitt, Marcia I. Edison, Amaury Nora, and Linda Serra Hagedorn, "The 'Chilly Climate' for Women and Cognitive Outcomes during the First Year of College," paper presented at the annual meeting of the Association for the Study of Higher Education, Memphis, Tennessee, October 31–November 3, 1996, ERIC ED402847, accessed August 10, 2016, https://archive.org/stream/ERIC_ED402847#page/no/mode/2up; Bernice R. Sandler, *The Campus Climate Revisited: Chilly for Women Faculty, Administrators, and Graduate Students* (Washington, DC: Project on the Status of Women of the Association of American Colleges, 1986), 3; American Association of University Women, *Tenure Denied: Cases of Sex Discrimination in Academia* (Washington, DC: American Association of University Women, 2004).

11. Lois Banner, Eileen Boris, Mary Kelley, Annette Kolodny, Cecelia Tichi, and Lillian Schlissel, "Personal Lives and Professional Careers: The Uneasy Balance," report of the Women's Committee of the American Studies Association, Washington, DC, American Studies Association, 1988.

12. Constance Coiner and Diana Hume George, *The Family Track: Keeping Your Faculties While You Mentor, Nurture, Teach, and Serve* (Urbana: University of Illinois Press, 1998); Annette Kolodny, "Creating the Family-Friendly Campus," in *Failing the Future: A Dean Looks at Higher Education in the Twenty-First Century* (Durham, NC: Duke University Press, 1998), 131–158.

13. Anna Atkinson, "Under the Circumstances: Single Motherhood in an Academic Culture of Doubt," *Chronicle of Higher Education* 5, no. 2 (2003): 29–34; Joanne S. Frye, "Making a Living, Making a Life," *Journal of the Association for Research on Mothering* 5, no. 2 (2003): 21–28; Anne Trubek, "From Spousal Hire to Single Mom," *Chronicle of Higher Education* 50, no. 24 (2004): C1+. In recent years, the *Chronicle of Higher Education* has published a number of articles that explore how motherhood affects the personal and professional lives of married female academics. For example, see Catherine Evans, "So Why Are You Really Leaving?" *Chronicle of Higher Education* 49, no. 35 (2004): C4; Laura E. Skandera Trombley, "The Facts of Life for an Administrator and a Mother," *Chronicle of Higher Education* 50, no. 20 (2003): B12+; Robin Wilson, "How Babies Alter Careers for Academics," *Chronicle of Higher Education* 50, no. 15 (2003): 1+.

14. Sandler and Hall, *The Classroom Climate*, 10.

15. Joanne Detore-Nakamura, "Dissertation Distress: A Room of One's Own with a Crib and a Computer," *Journal of the Association for Research on Mothering* 5, no. 2 (2003): 57–61; Ann Steele, "When to Procreate," *Chronicle of Higher Education* 49, no. 44 (2003): C4.

16. Marriage promotion policies were intended to entice unmarried parents to wed, specifically poor couples who wished to receive a monthly cash grant through TANF. Such policies encouraged marriage by providing a financial incentive to couples who wed, typically through an increase in their monthly TANF grant. Aly Parker, "Can't Buy Me Love: Funding Marriage Promotion versus Listening to Real Needs in Breaking the Cycle of Poverty," *Review of Law and Social Justice* 18, no. 2 (2009): 493–536; Phoebe G. Silag, "To Have, To Hold, To Receive Public Assistance: TANF and Marriage-Promotion Policies," *Journal of Gender, Race, and Justice* 7 (2003): 413, 415.

17. Child exclusion policies, also known as "family cap" policies, were implemented in twenty-three states as part of their welfare reform legislation and were intended to control reproduction among those receiving public assistance. These policies denied benefits to children who were born to families already receiving assistance, to children for whom paternity had not been established, to children born to mothers under the age of eighteen, and to children born to single mothers who were not living with their parents. Such policies were criticized as inhumane and as posing potential harm to poor children. See Radha Jagannathan and Michael J. Camasso, "Family Caps and Nonmarital Fertility: The Racial Conditioning of Policy Effects," *Journal of Marriage and Family* 65, no. 1 (2003): 52–71; Shelley Shark and Jodie Levin-Epstein, *Excluded Children: Family Caps in a New Era* (Washington, DC: Center for Law and Social Policy, 1999); and M. J. Zaslow, K. A. Moore, J. L. Brooks, P.A. Morris, K. Tout, Z. A. Redd, and C. A. Emig, "Experimental Studies of Welfare Reform and Children," *The Future of Children* 21, no. 1 (2002): 78–95.

18. For additional discussion of the stereotypes of single mothers that were central to the American welfare reform debates, see Gwendolyn Mink, ed., *Whose Welfare?* (Ithaca, NY: Cornell University Press, 1999); Jill S. Quadagno, *The Color of Welfare: How Racism Undermined the War on Poverty* (New York: Oxford University Press, 1994); Ruth Sidel, *Keeping*

Women and Children Last: America's War on the Poor (New York: Penguin, 1996); Lucy A. Williams, "Race, Rat Bites, and Unfit Mothers: How Media Discourse Informs Welfare Legislation Debate," *Fordham Urban Law Journal* 22, no. 4 (1995): 1159–1196.

19. Erving J. Goffman, *Stigma: Notes on the Management of Spoiled Identity* (Englewood Cliffs, NJ: Prentice-Hall, 1963), 2–3.

20. Stephanie Coontz, *The Way We Never Were: American Families and the Nostalgia Trap* (New York: Basic Books, 1992); Robert Page, *Stigma* (New York: Routledge, 1984), 72–128. Page notes that unmarried mothers challenge Christian doctrine in two significant ways—by having sexual relationships outside marriage and by posing a threat to the institution of family based on heterosexual coupling.

21. Karen Seccombe, *"So You Think I Drive a Cadillac?" Welfare Recipients' Perspectives on the System and Its Reform* (Boston: Allyn and Bacon, 1999), 48–73.

22. Gerard Falk, *Stigma: How We Treat Outsiders* (Amherst, NY: Prometheus Books, 2001), 151–172; Sharon Hays, *Flat Broke with Children: Women in the Age of Welfare Reform* (New York: Oxford University Press, 2003); John Horton and Linda Shaw, "Opportunity and Control: Living Welfare Reform in Los Angeles County," in *Work, Welfare, and Politics: Confronting Poverty in the Wake of Welfare Reform*, ed. Frances Fox Piven (Eugene: University of Oregon Press, 2002): 197–212; Paul Spicker, *Stigma and Social Welfare* (London: St. Martin's Press, 1984); Gideon Yaniv, "Welfare Fraud and Welfare Stigma," *Journal of Economic Psychology* 18 (1997): 435–451.

23. In *Stigma*, Falk differentiates between "existential" and "achieved" stigma. He argues that the former describes a condition or identity the person did not cause or cannot control, such as mental illness, race, or homosexuality, and that the latter refers to persons who have "earned a stigma because of their conduct and/or because they contributed heavily to attaining that stigma," such as drug addicts, prostitutes, and criminals. Within this framework, single motherhood would be regarded as an achieved stigma.

24. Goffman, *Stigma*.

25. Page, "Stigma and the Unmarried Mother," 20.

26. Goffman, *Stigma*, 14; Melvin C. Ray, "Effects of Stigma on Intergroup Relations," *Journal of Social Psychology* 129, no. 6 (1989): 855–857; Edwin M. Schur, *Labeling Women Deviant: Gender, Stigma, and Social Control* (Philadelphia: Temple University Press, 1983).

27. Lee W. Larson, "The Great USA Flood of 1993," paper presented at the conference Destructive Water: Water-Caused Natural Disasters—Their Abatement and Control, Anaheim, California, June 24–28, 1996, accessed August 10, 2016, http://www.nwrfc.noaa.gov/floods/papers/oh_2/great.htm.

28. Ibid.

29. For example, on March 20, 2004, the University of Iowa Student Government, the University of Iowa Family Services Office, and the Student Family Community Group co-sponsored a "movie break" for student families, a free event that included a showing of *The Tigger Movie* and cookies. International Women's Club, "For UI Student Families: Movie Break—Free and Fun!" *International Women's Club Newsletter*, March 2004, 3.

30. James Baetke, "Hawkeye Residents Detail Substandard Living Conditions," *Daily Iowan*, May 7, 2003; Stacy Rossman, "UI Moves to Remedy Hawkeye Complaints," *Daily Iowan*, June 13, 2003.

31. University Apartments Residents Action Committee, "Support Needed for Hawkeye Court," *Daily Iowan*, April 15, 2003.

32. University of Iowa Resident Services Facilities and Operations, "Capital Projects," accessed June 19, 2015, http://housing.uiowa.edu/facilities/capitalprojects.htm.

33. Matthew Moss, "UI Tentatively Plans New Apts," *Daily Iowan*, October 29, 2003.

34. Thomas Kane, Jack Collins, and Jeff Janz, "Report of the External Review Team," accessed June 19, 2015, http://www.housing.uiowa.edu/pubs/UI-UH-external-review-report-fa09.pdf.

35. University of Iowa Office of Student Life, "Housing: Aspire at West Campus," *University of Iowa: Division of Student Life*, accessed June 20, 2015, http://housing.uiowa.edu/aspire-west -campus.

36. "Aspire at West Campus," accessed June 20, 2015, http://www.aspireatwestcampus.com/.

37. Vanessa Miller, "University of Iowa Representatives Voted for Graduate Housing Rent Increases," *The Gazette*, December 16, 2015.

38. The Johnson County Local Homeless Coordinating Board identified the lack of afford-able housing for low-income populations as a significant concern; see Ashley Hoffman, "Group Searches for Funds for Housing Aid," *Daily Iowan*, June 12, 2003. The limited availabil-ity of low-income housing in the Iowa City community received significant media attention when it was learned that thirty-four UI student athletes—who receive monthly housing and food allowances from the university—were living at Pheasant Ridge Apartments, a taxpayer-subsidized housing complex for needy families; see Lee Rood, "Students Take Housing from the Poor," *Daily Iowan*, June 20, 2004.

39. I borrow the term "learning community" from bell hooks, who describes it as a class-room that "creates a communal context for learning" and is fostered by the recognition of different voices and experiences and by a conscious effort to consistently incorporate those voices and experiences in the learning process. *Talking Back: Thinking Feminist, Thinking Black* (Boston: South End Press, 1994).

40. According to hooks, a key element of a learning community is the dismantling of tradi-tional classroom power dynamics and recognizing that all members of the community—both professor and students—can and do teach.

41. The UNT system has three campuses: the main campus in Denton, the UNT Health Sci-ence Center in Fort Worth, and UNT Dallas.

42. This information was provided to me by the family services coordinator at TWU. Kame-sha Ross, phone conversation with the author, August 17, 2011.

43. "School Age Children's Enrichment Program," *Texas Woman's University: Department of University Housing and Residence Life*, accessed June 15, 2011, http://www.twu.edu/housing/ clubhouse.asp.

44. Kathryn Edin and Laura Lein, *Making Ends Meet: How Single Mothers Survive Welfare and Low-Wage Work* (New York: Russell Sage Foundation, 1997); Hays, *Flat Broke with Children*; Piven, *Work, Welfare, and Politics*.

CONCLUSION

1. Dana Bash and Tom LoBianco, "Jeb Bush: Children of Single Parents Face 'Huge Chal-lenge,'" *CNN Politics*, June 11, 2015, http://www.cnn.com/2015/06/11/politics/bush-single -mothers-explanation/.

2. "We Fill Our Culture with Garbage, and We Reap the Result," *Bobby Jindal for President*, October 6, 2015, accessed November 17, 2015, https://www.bobbyjindal.com/jindal-we-fill -our-culture-with-garbage/.

3. Terry Shropshire, "Ben Carson Says Children of Single Parents Get on Welfare, Become Criminals," *Atlanta Daily World*, October 12, 2015, http://atlantadailyworld.com/2015/10/12/ ben-carson-says-children-of-single-parents-get-on-welfare-become-criminals/.

4. Sally C. Curtin, Stephanie J. Ventura, and Gladys M. Martinez, "Recent Declines in Non-Marital Childbearing in the United States," NCHS Data Brief no. 162, National Center for Health Statistics, Hyattsville, Maryland, 2014, http://www.cdc.gov/nchs/products/databriefs/db162.htm.

5. Ami R. Moore and Doug Henry, "Experiences of Older Informal Caregivers to People with HIV/AIDS in Lomé, Togo," *Aging International* 30, no. 2 (2005): 147–166.

6. Christina Wassom, "'It Was Like a Little Community': An Ethnographic Study of Online Learning and Its Implications for MOOCs," *EPIC: Ethnographic Praxis in Industry Conference Proceedings* 1 (September 2013): 186–199.

7. Susan Squires and Bryan Byrne, *Creating Breakthrough Ideas: The Collaboration of Anthropologists and Designers in the Product Development Industry* (Santa Barbara, CA: Praeger, 2002).

8. For the history of applied ethnography, see Pertti J. Pelto, *Applied Ethnography: Guide to Field Research* (Walnut Creek, CA: Left Coast Press, 2013).

9. Christa Craven and Dána-Ain Davis, eds., *Feminist Activist Ethnography: Counterpoints to Neoliberalism in North America* (Lanham, MD: Lexington Books, 2013).

10. Barbara Gault, Lindsey Reichlin, Elizabeth Reynolds, and Meghan Froehner, "4.8 Million College Students Are Raising Children," *Institute for Women's Policy Research Fact Sheet*, November 2014, http://www.luminafoundation.org/files/resources/college-students-raising-children.pdf.

11. Only California had a total postsecondary population that exceeded this number in 2008. U.S. Census Bureau, "Table 280: Degree-Granting Institutions, Number, and Enrollment by State, 2008," in *Statistical Abstract of the United States, 2012* (Washington, DC: U.S. Census Bureau, 2011), 180.

12. "Student-Athletes," *NCAA*, accessed October 12, 2015, http://www.ncaa.org/student-athletes.

13. Jonathan R. Alger, Jorge Chapa, Roxane Harvey Gudeman, Patricia Marin, Geoffrey Maruyama, Jeffrey F. Milem, José F. Moreno, and Deborah J. Wilds, *Does Diversity Make a Difference? Three Research Studies on Diversity in College Classrooms* (Washington, DC: American Association of University Professors, 2000), http://www.aaup.org/NR/rdonlyres/97003B7B-055F-4318-B14A-5336321FB742/0/DIVREP.PDF.

14. John P. Dugan, Michelle L. Kusel, and Dawn M. Simounet, "Transgender College Students: An Exploratory Assessment of Perceptions, Engagement, and Educational Outcomes," *Journal of College Student Development* 53, no. 5 (2012): 719–736; Zenen Jaimes Pérez and Hannah Hussey, "A Hidden Crisis: Including the LGBT Community When Addressing Sexual Violence on Campus," *Center for American Progress*, September 19, 2014, https://www.americanprogress.org/issues/lgbt/report/2014/09/19/97504/a-hidden-crisis/.

15. Nella Van Dyke and Holly J. McCammon, eds., *Strategic Alliances: Coalition Building and Social Movements* (Minneapolis: University of Minnesota Press, 2010).

16. Herbert Hoover used the phrase "rugged individualism" on October 28, 1928, during a speech made as part of his presidential campaign to express his belief that government support for the poor should be minimal and that the poor should seek the services of voluntary organizations and be taught self-reliance. See Herbert Hoover, "'Rugged Individualism' Campaign Speech," [1928], accessed August 11, 2016, *Digital History*, http://www.digitalhistory.uh.edu/disp_textbook.cfm?smtID=3&psid=1334.

17. Silvia Gilardi and Chiara Guglielmetti, "University Life of Non-Traditional Students: Engagement Styles and Impact on Attrition," *Journal of Higher Education* 82, no. 1 (2011): 33–34, http://www.researchgate.net/profile/Chiara_Guglielmetti/publication/233001913_University_Life_of_Non-Traditional_Students_Engagement_Styles_and_Impact_on_Attrition/links/0fcfd509b8bfd950f3000000.pdf.

18. Briana Boyington, "Prepare for College as a First Generation Student," *U.S. News & World Report,* April 20, 2015, http://www.usnews.com/education/best-colleges/articles/2015/04/20/prepare-for-college-as-a-first-generation-student.

19. Jeff Davis, *The First Generation Student Experience* (Sterling, VA: Stylus Publishing, 2010).

20. For example, many colleges have Living Learning Communities (LLCs) that help foster connections and a sense of community and promote academic engagement among students who have identified a specific academic major by housing them on the same floor or "wing" of a university residence hall, hosting social functions for such students, and setting up special sections of academic courses for LLC students.

APPENDIX

1. "Education Support Award Applications," *Patsy Takemoto Mink Foundation for Low Income Women and Children,* accessed November 7, 2015, http://www.patsyminkfoundation.org/edsupport.html.

2. "Rosenfeld Injury Lawyers' Annual Single Mother Scholarship," *Rosenfeld Injury Lawyers,* accessed October 28, 2015, http://www.rosenfeldinjurylawyers.com/news/single-mother-scholarship/.

3. "Scholarships," *Westminster College,* accessed November 25, 2015, https://www.westminstercollege.edu/financial_aid_undergraduate/?parent=4210&detail=4217.

4. "Kentucky Colonels Better Life Scholarship," *Jefferson Community and Technical College,* accessed November 21, 2015, https://jefferson.kctcs.edu/en/Costs_and_Financial_Aid/Scholarships/Offered/KY-Colonels.aspx.

5. Additional information about scholarships for single mothers attending the University of Wisconsin-Eau Claire can be found at "Foundation Scholarships," *My Bluegold: University of Wisconsin-Eau Claire,* accessed September 16, 2016, https://scholarships.apps.uwec.edu/scholarships?category=Nontraditional+Students.

6. "Hearst Foundation Gives Another $100,000 to TWU," *Dallas Business Journal,* April 22, 2002, accessed October 28, 2015, http://www.bizjournals.com/dallas/stories/2002/04/22/daily3.html.

7. Texas Woman's University, "William Randolph Hearst Application for Single Parents—Emergency Aid," accessed October 28, 2015, http://www.twu.edu/downloads/housing/Hearst_Application_Revised.pdf.

8. University Women's Association, "Helen's Special Fund—University Women's Association," *My Bluegold: University of Wisconsin-Eau Claire,* accessed November 15, 2015, https://scholarships.apps.uwec.edu/scholarships/1530.

9. "Child Care Subsidy Program for Student Families," *University of Iowa Family Services Office,* accessed October 14, 2015, http://hr.uiowa.edu/family-services/child-care-subsidy-student.

10. Ibid.

11. "Brown University Child Care Subsidy: Program Overview," accessed October 14, 2015, https://www.brown.edu/about/administration/human-resources/sites/human-resources/files/child-care-subsidy-overview-2016--10-20-15_0.pdf.

12. "Jim Sells Child Care Subsidy," *Portland State University,* accessed October 15, 2015, http://www.pdx.edu/students-with-children/jim-sells-childcare-subsidy.

13. "The Student Parent Child Care Subsidy Program," *Penn State Human Resources,* accessed October 17, 2015, http://ohr.psu.edu/child-care-subsidy/.

14. "Campus Children's Center," *Evergreen State College,* accessed November 13, 2015, http://www.evergreen.edu/childrenscenter/.

15. "Children's Center Rates," *Evergreen State College,* accessed November 13, 2015, http://www.evergreen.edu/childrenscenter/rates.htm.

16. "The Ohio State University Child Care Program," *Ohio State University Human Resources,* accessed November 10, 2015, https://hr.osu.edu/childcare/.

17. "University Community Childcare," *Iowa State University Human Resources,* accessed September 16, 2016, http://www.universitycommunitychildcare.org/index.html.

18. Jillian M. Duquaine-Watson, "Computing Technologies, the Digital Divide, and 'Universal' Instructional Methods," in *Pedagogy and Student Services for Institutional Transformation: Implementing Universal Design in Higher Education,* edited by Jeanne L. Higbee and Emily Goff (Minneapolis: University of Minnesota Press, 2008), 437–450.

19. "Single Parent Resources Information Networking Technology (SPRINT) Scholarship," *Texas Woman's University,* accessed November 11, 2015, http://www.twu.edu/housing/sprint -scholarship.asp. The SPRINT program was started in 2009 but was discontinued in 2012 when the three-year grant used to support the program expired.

20. College Board, *Trends in College Pricing 2004,* quoted in Robert Carbaugh and Koushik Ghosh, "Are College Textbooks Fairly Priced?" *Challenge* 48, no. 5 (2005): 95.

21. College Board, *Trends in College Pricing 2014,* accessed November 18, 2015, http://trends .collegeboard.org/sites/default/files/2014-trends-college-pricing-final-web.pdf.

22. Ben Popken, "College Textbook Prices Have Risen 1,041 Percent Since 1977," *NBC News,* August 6, 2015, accessed October 28, 2015, http://www.nbcnews.com/feature/freshman -year/college-textbook-prices-have-risen-812-percent-1978-n399926.

23. Mark J. Perry, "The New Era of the $400 Textbook, Which Is Part of the Unsustainable Higher Education Bubble," *AEI,* July 25, 2015, https://www.aei.org/publication/the -new-era-of-the-400-college-textbook-which-is-part-of-the-unsustainable-higher-education -bubble/.

24. Blake Paterson, "For Low-Income Students, the Cost of Books Can Be a Burden," *Harvard Crimson,* May 8, 2015; Carl Straumsheim, "Triaging Textbooks," *Inside Higher Education,* August 4, 2015.

25. Antioch University New England, "Antioch University New England (AUNE) Internal Sources for Scholarships and Grants," accessed October 28, 2015, http://www.antiochne.edu/ /financial/scholarships.

26. Paterson, "For Low-Income Students, the Cost of Books Can Be a Burden."

27. Laura M. Colorusso, "Programs Seek to Lower Cost of College Textbooks," *The Hechinger Report,* August 27, 2014, accessed October 28, 2015, http://hechingerreport.org/ programs-seek-lower-cost-college-textbooks/.

28. Mary Whitfill, "SGA Announces Online Textbook Exchange," *Huntington News,* October 30, 2014, accessed October 28, 2015, http://huntnewsnu.com/2014/10/sga-announces -online-textbook-exchange/.

29. Rachel Schumacher, *Prepping Colleges for Parents: Strategies for Supporting Student Parent Success in Postsecondary Education* (Washington, DC: Institute for Women's Policy Research, 2015), 8.

30. Mary Gatta, *Student Parents, Online Learning, and Community Colleges: Challenges and Promise* (Washington, DC: Institute for Women's Policy Research, forthcoming).

31. Kevin Miller, Frank Mayadas, Mary Gatta, and Alexandra Pickett, "Online Learning and Student Parents: Benefits, Challenges, and Future Directions," Webinar sponsored by the Institute for Women's Policy Research. February 27, 2012.

32. Andrea Solimeno, Minou Ella Mebane, Manuela Tomei, and Donata Francescato, "The Influence of Students and Teachers Characteristics on the Efficacy of Face-to-Face and Computer-Supported Collaborative Learning," *Computers & Education* 51 (2008): 109–128.

33. Duquaine-Watson, "Computing Technologies."

34. "Affordable and Accelerated," *University of Massachusetts Amherst University without Walls*, accessed October 20, 2015, https://www.umass.edu/uww/why-uww/affordable-and -accelerated.

35. Schumacher, *Prepping Colleges for Parents*, 8.

36. "Online & Regional Site Degrees, Certificate, and Certificate Preparation Programs," *Texas Tech University*, accessed October 28,2015, http://www.depts.ttu.edu/elearning/ programs/.

37. I. Elaine Allen and Jeff Seaman, *Learning on Demand: Online Education in the United States, 2009*, accessed October 28, 2015, http://files.eric.ed.gov/fulltext/ED529931.pdf.

38. Karen K. Inkelas, Zaneeta E. Daver, Kristen E. Vogt, and Jeannie Brown Leonard, "Living-Learning Programs and First-Generation College Students' Academic and Social Transition to College," *Research in Higher Education* 48, no. 4 (2007): 403–434; Ernest T. Pascarella, Christopher T. Pierson, Gregory C. Wolniak, and Patrick T. Terenzini, "First-Generation College Students: Additional Evidence on College Experiences and Outcomes," *Journal of Higher Education* 75, no. 3 (2004): 249–284; Louis M. Rocconi, "The Impact of Learning Communities on First Year Students' Growth and Development in College," *Research in Higher Education* 52 (2011): 178–193.

39. Gary R. Pike, "The Differential Effects of On- and Off-Campus Living Arrangements on Students' Openness to Diversity," *Journal of Student Affairs Research and Practice* 39, no. 4 (2002): 283–299.

40. Ray Gasser, "White Paper: Educational and Retention Benefits of Residence Hall Living," accessed October 29, 2015, http://www.webpages.uidaho.edu/eng207-td/Sources,%20Links/ Ed%20and%20Retention%20Gasser%20White%20Paper.htm; Megan Foley Nicpon, Laura Huser, Elva Hull Blanks, Sonja Sollenberger, Christie Befort, and Sharon E. Robinson Kurpius, "The Relationship of Loneliness and Social Support with College Freshmen's Academic Performance," *Journal of College Student Retention* 8, no. 3 (2006): 345–358.

41. Kevin Miller, Barbara Gault, and Abby Thorman, *Improving Child Care Access to Promote Postsecondary Success among Low-Income Parents* (Washington, DC: Institute for Women's Policy Research, 2011), 15, accessed November 03, 2015, http://www.iwpr.org/publications/pubs/ improving-child-care-access-to-promote-postsecondary-success-among-low-income-parents.

42. Ibid., 17; Scott Carlson, "Campus Child Care, a 'Critical Student Benefit,' Is Disappearing," *Chronicle of Higher Education*, May 18, 2015. The 2011 figure includes data for public, private nonprofit, and private for-profit institutions, including four-year programs, two-year programs, and programs less than two years in duration. See also Barbara Gault, Lindsey Reichlin, Elizabeth Reynolds, and Meghan Froehner, *Campus Child Care Declining Even as Growing Number of Parents Attend College* (Washington, DC: Institute for Women's Policy Research, 2014), accessed November 5, 2015, http://www.iwpr.org/ publications/pubs/campus-child-care-declining-even-as-growing-numbers-of-parents -attend-college.

43. Ibid.

44. Tracy Boswell, "Campus Child Care Centers,", accessed November 3, 2015, http://files.eric.ed.gov/fulltext/ED480466.pdf.

45. Augusta S. Kappner, *Across the Education Continuum: Child Care on the College Campus* (Cedar Falls, IA: National Coalition for Campus Children's Centers, 2002); UW Women's Studies Consortium Advisory Council, "Report on the Critical Importance of Childcare on All UW Campuses," September 23, 2010, accessed November 4, 2015, http://wsce-bulletin.blogspot.com/2012/12/report-on-critical-importance-of.html.

46. American Association of University Women, *Women in Community Colleges: Access to Success* (Washington, DC: American Association of University Women, 2013), 25.

47. "Children's Centers," *University of Michigan Human Resources*, accessed November 12, 2015, https://hr.umich.edu/benefits-wellness/family/childrens-centers; Wendy Frisch, "President's Child Care Initiative Meets Major Goals," *The University Record Online*, August 15, 2011, accessed November 12, 2015, http://ur.umich.edu/1011/Aug15_11/2530-presidents-child-care.

48. "MIT Dedicates New Koch Childcare Center," *MIT News*, October 4, 2013, accessed November 12, 2015, http://news.mit.edu/2013/mit-dedicates-new-koch-childcare-center-1004.

49. "Westwood Child Care Center," *Bright Horizons Early Education and Preschool*, accessed November 11, 2015, http://child-care-preschool.brighthorizons.com/CA/LosAngeles/uclawestwood.

50. Alison Hewitt, "Enrollment Is Ahead of Schedule at UCLA's Newest Child Care Center," *UCLA Today*, September 15, 2011, accessed November 11, 2015, http://newsroom.ucla.edu/stories/ucla-child-care-expansion-ahead-215111.

51. "Emory Child Care Network," *Emory Worklife Resource Center*, accessed November 12, 2015, http://www.worklife.emory.edu/quicklinks/childcarenetwork.html.

52. "Child Care Partners within 1.5 Miles of Campus: On and Near Campus," *University of Iowa University Human Resources*, accessed November 12, 2015, http://hr.uiowa.edu/family-services/child-care-near-campus.

53. "Caregivers Attending Montana Western," *Care.com University of Montana Western*, accessed November 4, 2015, https://www.care.com/edu/the-university-of-montana-western.

54. "About Us," *Northern Illinois University Campus Child Care*, accessed November 2, 2015, http://www.niu.edu/ccc/aboutus/index.shtml.

55. "Child Development Centers," *Tidewater Community College*, accessed September 16, 2016, http://www.tcc.edu/student-services/personal-support/child-care.

56. Ibid.

57. "School Age Children's Enrichment Program," *Texas Woman's University*, accessed November 4, 2015, http://www.twu.edu/housing/clubhouse.asp.

58. Miller, Gault, and Thorman, *Improving Child Care Access*, 13.

59. "Child Care at UT Dallas," UT Dallas, accessed November 5, 2015, http://www.utdallas.edu/childcare/; "About DIS," *Dallas International School*, accessed November 5, 2015, http://www.dallasinternationalschool.org/en/about_dis/.

60. "The Early Childhood Learning Center Programs, Inc.," *La Guardia Community College*, accessed November 7, 2015, http://ekfsf.laguardia.edu/Student-Services/Child-Care/.

61. "Well Back-Up Child Care and Mildly Ill Back-Up Child Care Offered by Helping Hands & More, Inc.," *University of Iowa University Human Resources*, accessed November 2, 2015, http://hr.uiowa.edu/family-services/caring-hands.

62. "Kids-Kare," *University of Wisconsin–Madison Office of Child Care and Family Resources*, accessed November 2, 2015, http://occfr.wisc.edu/kids-kare.htm.

63. "Back Up Child Care for UC Berkeley Student Parents," *University of California Berkeley*, accessed November 2, 2015, http://backupchildcare.berkeley.edu/.

64. "About the Service," *University of California Berkeley*, accessed November 3, 2015, http://backupchildcare.berkeley.edu/about-the-service/.

65. Amanda Haire and Christi McGeorge, "Negative Perceptions of Never-Married Custodial Single Mothers and Fathers: Applications of Gender Analysis for Family Therapists," *Journal of Feminist Family Therapy* 24, no. 1 (2012): 24–51; Joel F. Handler and Yeheskel Hasenfeld, *Blame Welfare, Ignore Poverty and Inequality* (New York: Cambridge University Press, 2007); Pew Research Center, *The Decline of Marriage and Rise of New Families* (Washington, DC: Pew Research Center, 2010), accessed November 27, 2015, http://www.pewsocialtrends.org/files/2010/11/pew-social-trends-2010-families.pdf.

66. Caryn McTighe Musil, Mildred Garcia, Cynthia A. Hudgins, Michael T. Nettles, William E. Sedlacek, and Daryl G. Smith, *To Form a More Perfect Union: Campus Diversity Initiatives* (Washington, DC: American Association of Colleges and Universities, 1999).

67. Kaustuv Basu, "Got Milk?" *Insider Higher Ed*, September 26, 2012, accessed November 28, 2015, https://www.insidehighered.com/news/2012/09/26/many-universities-still-have-ad-hoc-policies-about-lactation-resources.

68. Montez Pertonelli, "Breastfeeding on Campus," *The Student Parent Project, 2006*, reproduced in "UA Featured as a Best Practice Model for Student Parent Lactation Support," *University of Arizona Life & Work Connections*, accessed November 28, 2015, https://lifework.arizona.edu/cc/ua_featured_as_a_best_practice_model_for_student_parent_lactation_support. See also "Campus Lactation Spaces and Related Information," *University of Arizona Life & Work Connections*, accessed November 28, 2015, http://lifework.arizona.edu/cc/campus_lactation_list.

69. "Lactation Resources," *University of Michigan Human Resources*, accessed November 28, 2015, https://hr.umich.edu/benefits-wellness/family/work-life-resource-center/lactation-resources; "Lactation Room Setup Guide," *University of Michigan Human Resources*, accessed November 28, 2015, https://hr.umich.edu/benefits-wellness/family/work-life-resource-center/lactation-resources/lactation-room-setup-guide.

70. "Lactation Room Locations," *University of Iowa University Human Resources*, accessed November 28, 2015, http://hr.uiowa.edu/family-services/lactation-room-locations. For other models and strategies for making campuses more supportive for breastfeeding mothers, see Michele L. Vancour and Michel K. Griswold, *Breastfeeding Best Practices in Higher Education* (Plano, TX: Hale Publishing, 2014).

71. Jillian M. Duquaine-Watson, "'Pretty Darned Cold': Single Mother Students and the Community College Climate in Post-Welfare Reform America," *Equity & Excellence in Education* 40, no. 3 (2007): 229–240.

72. "Academic Rules," *Texas A&M University*, accessed December 2, 2015, http://student-rules.tamu.edu/academicrules.

73. "Attendance," *Texas A&M University*, accessed December 2, 2015, http://student-rules.tamu.edu/rule07.

74. "Make Up Work for Legitimate Absences: Twin Cities, Morris, Crookston, Rochester," *University of Minnesota*, accessed December 3, 2015, https://policy.umn.edu/education/makeupwork.

75. "Undergraduate Catalog 2016–2017: Syllabus, Attendance, Absences, and Assessment," *University of Maryland*, accessed August 11, 2016, http://www.umd.edu/catalog/index.cfm/show/content.section/c/27/ss/1584/s/1540.

76. Jillian M. Duquaine-Watson, "More Than Talk: Single Mothers Claiming Space and Subjectivity on the University Campus," in *Mothers Who Deliver: Feminist Interventions in Public and Interpersonal Discourse*, edited by Jocelyn Fenton Stitt and Pegeen Reichert Powell (Albany: State University of New York Press, 2010), 145–162.

77. "Women's Center," *Lakeland Community College*, accessed December 5, 2015, http://www.lakelandcc.edu/web/about/women-center-programs.

78. "Single Parents," *Utah Higher Education Assistance Authority*, accessed December 6, 2015, https://www.uheaa.org/singleparent/schools/UofU.html.

79. "Student Parents Also Raising Kids (SPARK)," *Texas Woman's University*, accessed December 6, 2015, http://www.twu.edu/commuter/spark.asp.

80. "Single Parent/Displaced Homemaker Services," *Western Nebraska Community College*, accessed December 6, 2015, https://www.wncc.edu/student-life/student-success/trio-programs/yessss/spin.

81. "Keys to Degrees: Educating Two Generations Together," *Endicott College*, brochure available at http://www.endicott.edu/Keys-Degrees-Prog.aspx, accessed August 11, 2016.

82. Richard Wylie, "Keys to Degrees: Educating Two Generations Together," document prepared for the Ascend Roundtable, The Aspen Institute, Washington, DC, March 29, 2011, accessed November 6, 2015, http://www.aspeninstitute.org/sites/default/files/content/docs/ascend/ascend-8-Wylie-Keys-Degrees-Educating-Two-Generations-Together.pdf.

83. David Vignernon, "Endicott College Keys to Degrees, Single Parent Program," PowerPoint presentation prepared for the 2nd annual symposium of CONNECT, Boston, Massachusetts, June 11, 2013, accessed November 7, 2015, http://www.connectnow.org/wp-content/uploads/2013/06/Keys-to-Degrees.pdf.

84. "Keys to Degrees: Educating Two Generations Together."

85. Vignernon, "Endicott College Keys to Degrees, Single Parent Program"; Pamela Young, "EMU 'Keys to Degrees' Program to Help Young Single Parents Earn Degree," *Eastern Michigan University*, accessed November 9, 2015, https://www.emich.edu/univcomm/releases/release.php?id=1294160558.

86. "Mothers Living & Learning," *College of Saint Mary*, accessed November 5, 2015, http://www.csm.edu/student-life/single-parent-success/mothers-living-learning; "Mothers Living & Learning Program Gains National Attention," *College of Saint Mary*, accessed November 5, 2015, http://www.csm.edu/alumnae-friends/ejourneys-mothers-living-learning-program-gains-national-attention.

87. "Madonna Hall: Home to College of Saint Mary's Mothers Living & Learning Program," *College of Saint Mary*, accessed November 18, 2015, http://www.csm.edu//student-life/campus-living/residence-halls/madonna-hall.

88. Kate Howard Perry, "Colleges' Devotion Benefits Moms," *Omaha World Herald*, May 27, 2014, accessed December 4, 2015, http://www.omaha.com/eedition/sunrise/articles/colleges-devotion-benefits-moms/article_96127e1e-6709-5421-b23e-ef86c9ce1953.html.

89. "Single Parent Success," *College of Saint Mary*, accessed December 15, 2015, http://www.csm.edu/student-life/single-mother-success-college.

90. "Spellman Child Development Center," *College of Saint Mary*, accessed December 8, 2015, http://www.csm.edu/student-life/single-parent-success/spellman-child-development-center.

91. "About the SPROUT Program," *SPROUT: Single Parents Reaching Out for Unlimited Tomorrows*, accessed August 26, 2016, https://bwsprout.wordpress.com/about/.

92. Ibid.

93. "BW Program Celebrates 20 Years of Sprouting Success," *Baldwin Wallace News & Events*, September 1, 2012, accessed December 2, 2015, https://www.bw.edu/news/2012/sprout-pogram-anniversary; Margaret Bernstein, "Plea for Single Moms Has a Lasting Impact at Baldwin-Wallace," *Cleveland.com*, February 8, 2012, http://www.cleveland.com/bernstein/index.ssf/2012/02/plea_to_help_single_moms_has_a.html.

94. "Bourger Women with Children Program," *Misericordia University*, accessed November 30, 2015, http://www.misericordia.edu/page.cfm?p=583.

95. "The Ruth Matthews Bourger Women with Children Program," *Misericordia University*, accessed November 30, 2015, http://www.misericordia.edu/uploaded/documents/futurestudents/wwc/wwc_misericordia_brochure.pdf.

96. "Single Parent Scholar Program," *Wilson College*, accessed December 2, 2015, http://www.wilson.edu/single-parent-scholar-program.

97. "Child Care Center," *Wilson College*, accessed December 5, 2015, http://www.wilson.edu/child-care-center-0.

98. "Single Parents Program: Overview," *Champlain College*, accessed December 5, 2015, http://www.champlain.edu/student-life/student-services/single-parents-program/single-parents-program-overview.

99. "What We Do," *Champlain College*, accessed December 12, 2015, http://www.champlain.edu/student-life/student-services/single-parents-program/what-we-do.

100. "The Single Parents Program Helps Families," *Champlain College*, accessed December 12, 2015, http://www.champlain.edu/student-life/student-services/single-parents-program/helping-families-single-parents-program.

BIBLIOGRAPHY

Abramovitz, Mimi. *Regulating the Lives of Women: Social Welfare Policy from Colonial Times to Present*. Cambridge, MA: South End Press, 1988.

Adair, Vivyan C. "Poverty and the (Broken) Promise of Higher Education." *Harvard Educational Review* 71, no. 2 (2001): 217–239.

Adair, Vivyan C., and Sandra L. Dahlberg, eds. *Reclaiming Class: Women, Poverty, and the Promise of Higher Education in America*. Philadelphia: Temple University Press, 2003.

Afterschool Alliance. "America after 3 P.M.: Key Findings." Accessed June 15, 2015. http://www.afterschoolalliance.org/documents/AA3PM_Key_Findings_2009.pdf.

Albeda, Randy, and Ann Withorn, eds. *Lost Ground: Welfare Reform, Poverty, and Beyond*. Boston: South End Press, 2002.

Alexakis, Georgia N. "Junior Will Face 2nd Custody Battle." *Harvard Crimson*, October 5, 1998. Accessed January 13, 2014. http://www.thecrimson.com/article/1998/10/5/junior-will-face-2nd-custody-battle/.

Alger, Jonathan R., Jorge Chapa, Roxane Harvey Gudeman, Patricia Marin, Geoffrey Maruyama, Jeffrey F. Milem, José F. Moreno, and Deborah J. Wilds. *Does Diversity Make a Difference? Three Research Studies on Diversity in College Classrooms*. Washington, DC: American Association of University Professors, 2000. Accessed December 13, 2015. http://www.aaup.org/NR/rdonlyres/97003B7B-055F-4318-B14A-5336321FB742/0/DIVREP.PDF.

Allen, I. Elaine, and Jeff Seaman. *Learning on Demand: Online Education in the United States, 2009*. Accessed October 28, 2015. http://files.eric.ed.gov/fulltext/ED529931.pdf.

American Association of University Women. *Tenure Denied: Cases of Sex Discrimination in Academia*. Washington, DC: American Association of University Women, 2004.

———. *Women in Community Colleges: Access to Success*. Washington, DC: American Association of University Women, 2013.

Anderson, William L., and Derek W. Little. "All's Fair: War and Other Causes of Divorce from a Beckerian Perspective." *American Journal of Economics and Sociology* 58, no. 4 (1999): 901–922.

Apple, Rima D. "Constructing Mothers: Scientific Motherhood in the Nineteenth and Twentieth Centuries." *Social History of Medicine* 8, no. 2 (1995): 161–178.

Arendell, Terry. *Mothers and Divorce: Legal, Economic, and Social Dilemmas*. Berkeley: University of California Press, 1986.

"ASA Statement on the Causes of Gender Differences in Science and Math Career Achievement." *Footnotes*, March 2005, accessed August 24, 2016, http://www.asanet.org/sites/default/files/savvy/footnotes/mar05/indexthree.html.

Ashe, Marie. "The 'Bad' Mother in Law and Literature: A Problem of Representation." *Hastings Law Journal* 43 (1992): 1017–1037.

Atkinson, Anna. "Under the Circumstances: Single Motherhood in an Academic Culture of Doubt." *Journal of the Motherhood Initiative for Research and Community Involvement* 5, no. 2 (2003): 29–34.

Banner, Lois, Eileen Boris, Mary Kelley, Annette Kolodny, Cecelia Tichi, and Lillian Schlissel. "Personal Lives and Professional Careers: The Uneasy Balance." Report of the Women's Committee of the American Studies Association. Washington, DC: American Studies Association, 1987.

Baruch, Grace K., and Rosalind Barnett. "Correlates of Fathers' Participation in Family Work: A Technical Report." Working Paper no. 106. Wellesley College Center for Research on Women, Wellesley, Massachusetts, 1983.

Bassin, Donna, Margaret Honey, and Meryle Mahrer Kaplan, eds. *Representations of Motherhood*. New Haven, CT: Yale University Press, 1994.

Bauer, Gary L. *The Family: Preserving America's Future*. Washington, DC: U.S. Department of Education, 1986.

Bauerlein, Monica, and Clara Jeffrey. "All Work and No Pay: The Great Speedup." *Mother Jones*. Accessed August 16, 2014. http://motherjones.com/politics/2011/06/speed-up-american-workers-long-hours.

Baumler, Ellen. "The Making of a Good Woman: Montana and the National Florence Crittenton Mission." *Montana: The Magazine of Western History* 53, no. 4 (2003): 50–63.

Bernard, H. Russell. *Research Methods in Cultural Anthropology*. Newbury Park, CA: Sage Publications, 1988.

Berry, Mary Frances. *The Politics of Parenthood: Child Care, Women's Rights, and the Myth of the Good Mother*. New York: Viking 1993.

Bishaw, Alemayehu, and Suzanne McCartney. "Poverty: 2008 and 2009." *American Community Survey Briefs*, September 2010. Accessed June 15, 2015. http://www.census.gov/prod/2010pubs/acsbr09-1.pdf.

Bonnet, Michael H., and Donna L. Arand. "How Much Sleep Do Adults Need?" National Sleep Foundation. Accessed August 28, 2013. http://www.sleepfoundation.org/article/white-papers/how-much-sleep-do-adults-need.

Boyington, Briana. "Prepare for College as a First Generation Student." *U.S. News & World Report*, April 20, 2015. Accessed December 14, 2015. http://www.usnews.com/education/best-colleges/articles/2015/04/20/prepare-for-college-as-a-first-generation-student.

Brachter, Timothy W. "Ireland V. Smith: Who Better Served a Child's Best Interests, Day Care Providers or Blood Relatives?" *University of Louisville Journal of Family Law* 34 (1995): 159–176.

Burchinal, Margaret R., Joanne E. Roberts, Rhodus Riggins Jr., Susan A. Zeisel, Eloise Neebe and Donna Bryant. "Relating Quality of Center-Based Child Care to Early Cognitive and Language Development Longitudinally." *Child Development* 71, no. 2 (2000): 339–357.

Carbaugh, Robert, and Koushik Ghosh, "Are College Textbooks Fairly Priced?" *Challenge* 48, no. 5 (2005): 95–112.

Carlson, Scott. "Campus Child Care, a 'Critical Student Benefit,' Is Disappearing." *Chronicle of Higher Education*, May 18, 2015.

Center for Women Policy Studies. *From Poverty to Self-Sufficiency: The Role of Postsecondary Education in Welfare Reform*. Washington, DC: Center for Women Policy Studies, 2002.

Child Care Aware of America. *Parents and the High Cost of Child Care: 2014 Report*. Arlington, VA: Child Care Aware of America, 2014.

Child Welfare League of America. *Standards for Services to Unmarried Mothers*. New York: Child Welfare League of America, 1960.

"Choosing a Child Care Center." *Healthy Children*. Accessed June 17, 2015. http://www.healthychildren.org/english/family-life/work-play/Pages/Choosing-a-Childcare-Center.aspx.

Clinton, William J. "Statement on Signing the Personal Responsibility and Work Reconciliation Act of 1996." August 22, 1996. *The American Presidency Project*, accessed August 27, 2016, http://www.presidency.ucsb.edu/ws/?pid=53219.

Coiner, Constance, and Diana Hume George. *The Family Track: Keeping Your Faculties While You Mentor, Nurture, Teach, and Serve*. Urbana: University of Illinois Press, 1998.

College Board. *Trends in College Pricing 2014*. Accessed November 18, 2015. http://trends.collegeboard.org/sites/default/files/2014-trends-college-pricing-final-web.pdf.

Collins, Jane L., and Victoria Mayer. *Both Hands Tied: Welfare Reform and the Race to the Bottom of the Low-Wage Labor Market*. Chicago: University of Chicago Press, 2010.

Collins, Patricia Hill. *Black Feminist Thought: Knowledge, Consciousness, and the Politics of Empowerment*. New York: HarperCollins, 1990.

Colorusso, Laura M. "Programs Seek to Lower Cost of College Textbooks." *Hechinger Report*, August 27, 2014. Accessed October 28, 2015. http://hechingerreport.org/programs-seek-lower-cost-college-textbooks/.

Coontz, Stephanie. *The Way We Never Were: American Families and the Nostalgia Trap*. New York: Basic Books, 1992.

Craven, Christa, and Dána-Ain Davis, eds. *Feminist Activist Ethnography: Counterpoints to Neoliberalism in North America*. Lanham, MD: Lexington Books, 2013.

Cravens, Hamilton. *Before Head Start: The Iowa Stations and America's Children*. Chapel Hill: University of North Carolina Press, 1993.

Crenshaw, Kimberlé. "Demarginalizing the Intersection of Race and Sex: A Black Feminist Critique of Antidiscrimination Doctrine, Feminist Theory, and Antiracist Politics." *University of Chicago Legal Forum* (1989): 139–167.

Curry, Lynne. "Modernizing the Rural Mother: Gender, Class, and Health Reform in Illinois, 1910–1930." In *Mothers and Motherhood: Readings in American History*, edited by Rima D. Apple and Janet Golden, 495–516. Columbus: Ohio State University Press, 1997.

Curtin, Sally C., Stephanie J. Ventura, and Gladys M. Martinez. "Recent Decreases in Non-Marital Childbearing in the United States." NCHS Data Brief no. 162, National Center for Health Statistics, Hyattsville, Maryland, 2014, http://www.cdc.gov/nchs/products/databriefs/db162.htm.

Davis, Jeff. *The First Generation Student Experience*. Sterling, VA: Stylus Publishing, 2010.

D'Emilio, John, and Estelle B. Freedman. *Intimate Matters: A History of Sexuality in America*. 2nd ed. Chicago: University of Chicago Press, 1998.

Detore-Nakamura, Joanne. "Dissertation Distress: A Room of One's Own with a Crib and Computer." *Journal of the Motherhood Initiative for Research and Community Involvement* 5, no. 2 (2003): 57–61.

Deutsch, Francine M., Laura J. Servis, and Jessica D. Payne. "Paternal Participation in Child Care and Its Effects on Children's Self-Esteem and Attitudes toward Gender Roles." *Journal of Family Issues* 22, no. 8 (2001): 1000–1024.

Dickerson, Bette J. *African-American Single Mothers: Understanding Their Lives and Families*. Thousand Oaks, CA: Sage Publications, 1995.

Douglas, Susan J., and Meredith W. Michaels. *The Mommy Myth: The Idealization of Motherhood and How It Has Undermined Women*. New York: The Free Press, 2004.

Dugan, John P., Michelle L. Kusel, and Dawn M. Simounet. "Transgender College Students: An Exploratory Assessment of Perceptions, Engagement, and Educational Outcomes." *Journal of College Student Development* 53, no. 5 (2012): 719–736.

Duquaine-Watson, Jillian M. "All You Need Is Love: Representations of Maternal Emotion in *Working Mother* Magazine." In *Mother Matters: Motherhood as Discourse and Practice*, edited by Andrea O'Reilly, 125–138. Toronto: Association for Research on Mothering, 2004.

———. "Computing Technologies, the Digital Divide, and 'Universal' Instructional Methods." In *Pedagogy and Student Services for Institutional Transformation: Implementing Universal Design in Higher Education*, edited by Jeanne L. Higbee and Emily Goff, 437–450. Minneapolis: University of Minnesota Press, 2008.

———. "More Than Talk: Single Mothers Claiming Space and Subjectivity on the University Campus." In *Mothers Who Deliver: Feminist Interventions in Public and Interpersonal Discourse*, edited by Jocelyn Fenton Stitt and Pegeen Reichert Powell, 145–162. Albany: State University of New York Press, 2010.

———. "'Pretty Darned Cold': Single Mother Students and the Community College Climate in Post-Welfare Reform America." *Equity & Excellence in Education* 40 (2007): 229–240.

Edelman, Murray. *Constructing the Political Spectacle*. Chicago: University of Chicago Press, 1988.

Edin, Kathryn, and Maria Kafalas. *Promises I Can Keep: Why Poor Women Put Motherhood Before Marriage*. Berkeley: University of California Press, 2005.

Edin, Kathryn, and Laura Lein. *Making Ends Meet: How Single Mothers Survive Welfare and Low-Wage Work*. New York: Russell Sage Foundation, 1997.

Eisenberg, Marlene, and Kirby Deater-Deckard. "Measurement of Quality in Child Care Centers." *Early Childhood Research Quarterly* 9, no. 2 (1994): 131–151.

Eisler, Riane Tennenhaus. *Dissolution: No-Fault Divorce, Marriage, and the Future of Women*. New York: McGraw-Hill Book Company, 1977.

Evan, Sarah. "The Unwed Mother's Indecision about Her Baby as a Defense Mechanism." Paper presented to the National Conference of Social Work, Philadelphia, PA, May 23, 1957. In *Services to Unmarried Mothers*. New York: Child Welfare League of America, 1958.

Evans, Catherine. "So Why Are You Really Leaving?" *Chronicle of Higher Education*, May 9, 2003.

Eyer, Diane. *Motherguilt: How Our Culture Blames Mothers for What's Wrong with Children*. New York: Random House, 1996.

Falk, Gerhard. *Stigma: How We Treat Outsiders*. Amherst, NY: Prometheus Books, 2001.

Faludi, Susan. *Backlash: The Undeclared War against American Women*. New York: Crown Publishers, Inc., 1991.

Farnell, Christopher, and Karen Pennar. "Commentary: Welfare Reform Won't Patch Up Poor Families." *Business Week*, January 23, 1995.

Fiene, Richard. "13 Indicators of Quality Child Care: Research Update." Accessed May 25, 2015, http://aspe.hhs.gov/hsp/ccquality-ind02/.

Finck, George H., Beatrice Simcox Reiner, and Brady O. Smith. "Group Counseling with Unmarried Mothers." *Journal of Marriage and Family* 27, no. 2 (1965): 224–229.

Fogg, Piper. "Family Time: Why Some Women Quit Their Coveted Tenure-Track Jobs." *Chronicle of Higher Education*, June 13, 2003.

———. "The Not-So-Lazy Days of Summer: While Some in Academe Enjoy the Good Life, Others Sweat It Out." *Chronicle of Higher Education*, July 26, 2002.

Friedman, Dorian. "The Flawed Premise of Welfare Reform." *U.S. News & World Report*, September 11, 1995.

Frye, Joanne S. "Making a Living, Making a Life." *Journal of the Motherhood Initiative for Research and Community Involvement* 5, no. 2 (2003): 21–28.

Gasser, Ray. "White Paper: Educational and Retention Benefits of Residence Hall Living." Accessed October 29, 2015. http://www.webpages.uidaho.edu/eng207-td/Sources, %20Links/Ed%20and%20Retention%20Gasser% 20White%20Paper.htm.

Gatta, Mary. *Student Parents, Online Learning, and Community Colleges: Challenges and Promise.* Washington, DC: Institute for Women's Policy Research (forthcoming).

Gault, Barbara, Lindsey Reichlin, Elizabeth Reynolds, and Meghan Froehner. *Campus Child Care Declining Even as Growing Number of Parents Attend College.* Washington, DC: Institute for Women's Policy Research, 2014. Accessed November 5, 2015. http://www.iwpr .org/publications/pubs/campus-child-care-declining-even-as-growing-numbers-of -parents-attend-college.

———. "4.8 Million College Students Are Raising Children." *Institute for Women's Policy Research Fact Sheet,* November 2014. Accessed December 14, 2015. http://www .luminafoundation.org/files/resources/college-students-raising-children.pdf.

Gilardi, Silvia, and Chiara Guglielmetti. "University Life of Non-Traditional Students: Engagement Styles and Impact on Attrition." *Journal of Higher Education* 82, no. 1 (2011): 33–34.

Gilder, George. "End Welfare Reform as We Know It." *American Spectator* 28, no. 6 (1995): 24–25.

Gilens, Martin. *Why Americans Hate Welfare: Race, Media, and the Politics of Antipoverty Policy.* Chicago: University of Chicago Press, 1999.

Gilliam, Franklin D., Jr. "The 'Welfare Queen' Experiment: How Viewers React to Images of African-American Mothers on Welfare." *Nieman Reports* 53, no. 2 (1999). Accessed August 29, 2014. https://escholarship.org/uc/item/17m7r1rq#page-3.

Gilson, Dave. "Overworked America: 12 Charts That Will Make Your Blood Boil." *Mother Jones.* Accessed August 16, 2014. http://motherjones.com/politics/2011/06/speedup -americans-working-harder-charts.

Goffman, Erving J. *Stigma: Notes on the Management of Spoiled Identity.* Englewood Cliffs, NJ: Prentice-Hall, 1963.

Gordon, Rachel A., and P. Lindsay Chase-Lansdale. "Availability of Child Care in the United States: A Description and Analysis of Data Resources." *Demography* 38, no. 2 (2001): 299–316.

Gormley, William T., Jr. *Everybody's Children: Child Care as a Public Problem.* Washington, DC: Brookings Institute, 1995.

Gornick, Janet C., and Marcia K. Meyers, eds. *Gender Equality: Transforming Family Divisions of Labor.* Brooklyn, NY: Verso, 2009.

Grant, Julia. *Raising Baby by the Book: The Education of American Mothers.* New Haven, CT: Yale University Press, 1998.

Haire, Amanda, and Christi McGeorge. "Negative Perceptions of Never-Married Custodial Single Mothers and Fathers: Applications of Gender Analysis for Family Therapists." *Journal of Feminist Family Therapy* 24, no. 1 (2012): 24–51.

Handler, Joel F., and Yeheskel Hasenfeld. *Blame Welfare, Ignore Poverty and Inequality.* New York: Cambridge University Press, 2007.

Hays, Sharon. *The Cultural Contradictions of Motherhood.* New Haven, CT: Yale University Press, 1998.

———. *Flat Broke with Children: Women in the Age of Welfare Reform.* New York: Oxford University Press, 2003.

Heath, Terri D., and Dennis K. Orthner. "Stress Adaptation among Male and Female Student Parents." *Journal of Family Issues* 20, no. 4 (1999): 557–587.

Heffner, Elaine. *Mothering: The Emotional Experience of Motherhood after Freud and Feminism.* New York: Doubleday, 1978.

Henderson, Heike. "Cancer, Children, and Career." *Chronicle of Higher Education,* November 16, 2004.

Hickman, Christine B. "The Devil and the One Drop Rule: Racial Categories, Africa Americans, and the U.S. Census." *Michigan Law Review* 95, no. 5 (1997): 1161–1265.

Hochschild, Arlie Russell. *The Second Shift: Working Parents and the Revolution at Home.* New York: Viking, 1989.

Holyfield, Lori. *Moving Up and Out: Poverty, Education, and the Single Parent Family.* Philadelphia: Temple University Press, 2002.

hooks, bell. *Talking Back: Thinking Feminist, Thinking Black.* Boston: South End Press, 1994.

Hoover, Herbert. "'Rugged Individualism' Campaign Speech." [1928.] *Digital History.* Accessed December 16, 2015. http://www.digitalhistory.uh.edu/disp_textbook.cfm?smtID=3&psid=1334.

Horton, John, and Linda Shaw. "Opportunity and Control: Living Welfare Reform in Los Angeles County." In *Work, Welfare, and Politics: Confronting Poverty in the Wake of Welfare Reform,* edited by Frances Fox Piven, 197–212. Eugene: University of Oregon Press, 2002.

Hunken, Kristina. "Economic Decisions of Single Mothers Pursuing Postsecondary Education." MA thesis, Texas Woman's University, 2007.

Immerwahr, John, and Tony Foleno. *Great Expectations: How the Public and Parents—White, African American, and Hispanic—View Higher Education.* San Jose, CA: National Center for Public Policy and Higher Education, 2000. Accessed November 18, 2015. http://www.highereducation.org/reports/expectations/expectations.shtml.

"Increase in Unemployment Rate, in January 2009." *U.S. Bureau of Labor Statistics,* February 10, 2009. http://www.bls.gov/opub/ted/2009/feb/wk2/art02.htm.

Inkelas, Karen K., Zaneeta E. Daver, Kristen E. Vogt, and Jeannie Brown Leonard. "Living-Learning Programs and First-Generation College Students' Academic and Social Transition to College." *Research in Higher Education* 48, no. 4 (2007): 403–434.

Jacobs, Susan Beth. "The Hidden Gender Bias behind 'The Best Interest of the Child' Standard in Custody Decisions." *Georgia State University Law Review* 13, no. 3 (1996): 845–901.

Jagannathan, Radha, and Michael J. Camasso. "Family Caps and Nonmarital Fertility: The Racial Conditioning of Policy Effects." *Journal of Marriage and Family* 65, no. 1 (2003): 52–71.

Jones, Lealan, Lloyd Newman, and David Isay. *Our America: Life and Death on the South Side of Chicago.* New York: Washington Square Press, 1997.

Judge, Timothy A., and Joyce E. Bono. "Relationship of Core Self-Evaluation Traits—Self-Esteem, Generalized Self-Efficacy, Locus of Control, and Emotional Stability—with Job Satisfaction and Job Performance: A Meta-Analysis." *Journal of Applied Psychology* 86, no. 1 (2001): 80–92.

Kahan, Michelle. "Put Up on Platforms: A History of Twentieth-Century Adoption Policy in the United States." *Journal of Sociology and Social Welfare,* 33, no. 3 (2006): 51–72.

Kahn, Peggy, and Valerie Polakow. "Struggling to Live and to Learn: Single Mothers, Welfare Policy, and Post-Secondary Education in Michigan." In *Shut Out: Low-Income Mothers and Higher Education in Post-Welfare America,* edited by Valeria Polakow, Sandra S. Butler, Luisa Stormer Duprez, and Peggy Kahn, 1–18. Albany: State University of New York Press, 2002.

Kaplan, Elaine Bell. *Not Our Kind of Girl: Unraveling the Mythos of Black Teenage Motherhood.* Berkeley: University of California Press, 1997.

Kaplan, Laura. *The Story of Jane: The Legendary Underground Abortion Service*. Chicago: University of Chicago Press, 1997.

Kappner, Augusta S. *Across the Education Continuum: Child Care on the College Campus*. Cedar Falls, IA: National Coalition for Campus Children's Centers, 2002.

Kerber, Linda K. "The Republican Mother: Women and the Enlightenment—An American Perspective." *American Quarterly*, 28, no. 2 (1976): 187–205.

Kingfisher, Catherine Pelissier. *Women in the American Welfare Trap*. Philadelphia: University of Pennsylvania Press, 1996.

Kohls, Robert L. *Values American Live By*. Washington, DC: Meridian House International, 1984.

Kolodny, Annette. *Failing the Future: A Dean Looks at Higher Education in the Twenty-First Century*. Durham, NC: Duke University Press, 1998.

Kunzel, Regina G. "The Professionalization of Benevolence: Evangelicals and Social Workers in the Florence Crittenton Homes, 1915–1945." *Journal of Social History* 22, no. 1 (1988): 21–43.

Ladd-Taylor, Molly. *Raising a Baby the Government Way: Mothers' Letters to the Children's Bureau, 1915–1932*. New Brunswick, NJ: Rutgers University Press, 1986.

Ladd-Taylor, Molly, and Lauri Umansky, eds. *Bad Mothers: The Politics of Blame in Twentieth-Century America*. New York: New York University Press, 1998.

Lamb, Michael E. *The Role of the Father in Child Development*. 5th ed. Hoboken, NJ: Wiley, 2010.

Leavitt, Judith Walzer. *Brought to Bed: Childbearing in America, 1750–1950*. New York: Oxford University Press, 1986.

Levin, Josh. "The Welfare Queen." *Slate*, December 19, 2013. Accessed March 18, 2014. http://www.slate.com/articles/news_and_politics/history/2013/12/linda_taylor_welfare_queen_ronald_reagan_made_her_a_notorious_american_villain.html.

Lewin, Ellen. *Lesbian Mothers: Accounts of Gender in American Culture*. Ithaca, NY: Cornell University Press, 1993.

Lewis, Oscar. "The Culture of Poverty." *Scientific American* 215, no. 4 (1966): 19–25.

L'Hommidieu, Toni. *The Divorce Experiences of Working and Middle Class Women*. Ann Arbor: UMI Research Press, 1984.

Litt, Jacquelyn S. *Medicalized Motherhood: Perspectives from the Lives of African-American and Jewish Women*. New Brunswick, NJ: Rutgers University Press, 2000.

Lynn, Laurence. "Ending Welfare as We Know It." *The American Prospect*. Fall 1993. Accessed August 28, 2014. http://prospect.org/article/ending-welfare-reform-we-know-it.

Maas, James B., with Megan L. Wherry, David J. Axelrod, Barbara R. Hogan, and Jennifer A. Blumin. *Power Sleep: The Revolutionary Program That Prepares Your Mind for Peak Performance*. New York: Villard 1998.

MacDonald, Heather. "Welfare's Next Vietnam." *City Journal* 5, no. 10 (1995). Accessed August 26, 2016. http://www.city-journal.org/html/welfare%E2%80%99s-next-vietnam-12166.html.

May, Elaine Tyler. *Barren in the Promised Land: Childless Americans and the Pursuit of Happiness*. New York: Basic Books, 1995.

Miller, Angela Browne. *The Day Care Dilemma: Critical Concerns for American Families*. New York: Plenum Press, 1990.

Miller, Kevin, Barbara Gault, and Abby Thorman. *Improving Child Care Access to Promote Postsecondary Success among Low-Income Students*. Washington, DC: Institute for Women's Policy Research, 2011.

Miller, Kevin, Frank Mayadas, Mary Gatta, and Alexandra Pickett. *Online Learning and Student Parents: Benefits, Challenges, and Future Directions.* Webinar sponsored by the Institute for Women's Policy Research. Monday, February 27, 2012.

Miller, Naomi. *Single Parents by Choice: A Growing Trend in Family Life.* New York: Plenum Press, 1992.

Mink, Gwendolyn. *Welfare's End.* Ithaca, NY: Cornell University Press, 1998.

——, ed. *Whose Welfare?* Ithaca, NY: Cornell University Press, 1999.

Moore, Ami R., and Doug Henry. "Experiences of Older Informal Caregivers to People with HIV/AIDS in Lomé, Togo." *Aging International* 30, no. 2 (2005): 147–166.

Moore, Kathryn M. "Women's Access and Opportunities in Higher Education: Toward the Twenty-First Century." *Comparative Education* 23, no. 1 (1987): 23–34.

Moraga, Cherríe, and Gloria Anzaldúa, eds. *This Bridge Called My Back: Writings by Radical Women of Color.* New York: Kitchen Table Press, 1980.

Morton, Marian J. "Fallen Women, Federated Charities, and Maternity Homes, 1913–1973." *Social Service Review* 62, no. 1 (1988): 61–82.

Moynihan, Daniel Patrick. *The Negro Family: The Case for National Action.* Washington, DC: Government Printing Office, 1965.

Murray, Charles. *Losing Ground: American Social Policy, 1950–1980.* New York: Basic Books, 1984.

Musil, Caryn McTighe, Mildred Garcia, Cynthia A. Hudgins, Michael T. Nettles, William E. Sedlacek, and Daryl G. Smith. *To Form a More Perfect Union: Campus Diversity Initiatives.* Washington, DC: American Association of Colleges and Universities, 1999.

Naples, Nancy. *Grassroots Warriors: Activist Mothering, Community Work, and the War on Poverty.* New York, Routledge, 1998.

National Council on Illegitimacy. *Unmarried Parenthood: Clues to Agency and Community Action.* New York: National Council on Illegitimacy, 1967.

National Institute of Child Health and Human Development. *The NICHD Study of Early Child Care and Youth Development: Findings for Children up to Age 4½ Years.* Washington, DC: U.S. National Institutes of Health, 2006.

National Resource Center for Health and Safety in Child Care and Early Education. *A Parent's Guide to Choosing Safe and Healthy Child Care.* Aurora, CO: National Resource Center for Health and Safety in Child Care and Early Education, 2015. Accessed June 28, 2015. https://www.nichd.nih.gov/publications/pubs/documents/seccyd_06.pdf.

Nelson, Margaret. *The Social Economy of Single Motherhood: Raising Children in Rural America.* New York: Routledge, 2005.

Neubeck, Kenneth J., and Noel A. Cazenave. *Welfare Racism: Playing the Race Card against America's Poor.* New York: Routledge, 2001.

Nicpon, Megan Foley, Laura Huser, Elva Hull Blanks, Sonja Sollenberger, Christie Befort, and Sharon E. Robinson Kurpius. "The Relationship of Loneliness and Social Support with College Freshmen's Academic Performance." *Journal of College Student Retention* 8, no. 3 (2006): 345–358.

Nussbaum, Stan. *American Cultural Baggage: How to Recognize and Deal with It.* Maryknoll, NY: Orbis Books, 2005.

Page, Robert. *Stigma.* New York: Routledge, 1984.

Parker, Aly. "Can't Buy Me Love: Funding Marriage Promotion versus Listening to Real Needs in Breaking the Cycle of Poverty." *Review of Law and Social Justice* 18, no. 2 (2009): 493–536.

Pascarella, Ernest T., Christopher T. Pierson, Gregory C. Wolniak, and Patrick T. Terenzini. "First-Generation College Students: Additional Evidence on College Experiences and Outcomes." *Journal of Higher Education* 75, no. 3 (2004): 249–284.

Pascarella, Ernest T., Elizabeth J. Whitt, Marcia I. Edison, Amaury Nora, Linda Serra Hagedorn, Patricia Yeager, and Patrick T. Terenzini. "The 'Chilly Climate' for Women and Cognitive Outcomes during the First Year of College." Paper presented at the annual meeting of the Association for the Study of Higher Education, Memphis, Tennessee, October 31–November 3, 1996. Accessed August 10, 2016. http://files.eric.ed.gov/fulltext/ED402847.pdf.

Peel, Kathy. *The Family Manager Takes Charge: Getting on the Fast Track to a Happy, Organized Home.* New York: Perigee Books, 2003.

Pelto, Pertti J. *Applied Ethnography: Guide to Field Research.* Walnut Creek, CA: Left Coast Press, 2013.

Pérez Zenen, Jaimes, and Hannah Hussey. "A Hidden Crisis: Including the LGBT Community When Addressing Sexual Violence on Campus." *Center for American Progress,* September 19, 2014. Accessed December 13, 2015. https://www.americanprogress.org/issues/lgbt/report/2014/09/19/97504/a-hidden-crisis/.

Perry, Mark J. "The New Era of the $400 Textbook, Which Is Part of the Unsustainable Higher Education Bubble." *AEI.* July 25, 2015. https://www.aei.org/publication/the-new-era-of-the-400-college-textbook-which-is-part-of-the-unsustainable-higher-education-bubble/.

Pew Research Center. *The Decline of Marriage and Rise of New Families.* Accessed November 27, 2015. http://www.pewsocialtrends.org/files/2010/11/pew-social-trends-2010-families.pdf.

Pierce, Ruth I. *Single and Pregnant.* Boston: Beacon Press, 1970.

Pike, Gary R. "The Differential Effects of On- and Off-Campus Living Arrangements on Students' Openness to Diversity." *Journal of Student Affairs Research and Practice* 39, no. 4 (2002): 283–299.

———. "The Effects of Residential Learning Communities and Traditional Residential Living Arrangements on Educational Gains during the First Year of College." *Journal of College Student Development* 40, no. 3 (1999): 269–284.

Pilgrim, David. "Jezebel Stereotype." Accessed February 17, 2014. http://fir.ferris.edu:8080/xmlui/bitstream/handle/2323/4778/Jezebel%20Stereotype.pdf?sequence=1.

Piven, Francis Fox, ed. *Work, Welfare, and Politics: Confronting Poverty in the Wake of Welfare Reform.* Eugene: University of Oregon Press, 2002.

Polakow, Valerie. *Lives on the Edge: Single Mothers and Their Children in the Other America.* Chicago: University of Chicago Press, 1993.

———. *Who Cares for Our Children? The Child Care Crisis in the Other America.* New York: Teachers College Press, 2007.

Polakow, Valerie, Sandra S. Butler, Luisa Stormer Deprez, and Peggy Kahn, eds. *Shut Out: Low Income Mothers and Higher Education in Post-Welfare America.* Albany: State University of New York Press, 2004.

Pruett, Kyle, and Marsha Kline Pruett. *Partnership Parenting: How Men and Women Parent Differently and How It Helps Your Kids and Can Strengthen Your Marriage.* New York: Da Capo Press, 2009.

Pugh, Alison J. "Windfall Child Rearing: Low-Income Care and Consumption." *Journal of Consumer Culture,* 4, no. 2 (2004): 229–249.

Purkey, William Watson. *Self-Concept and School Achievement.* Englewood Cliffs, NJ: Prentice Hall, 1970.

Quadagno, Jill S. *The Color of Welfare: How Racism Undermined the War on Poverty*. New York: Oxford University Press, 1994.

Ray, Melvin C. "Effects of Stigma on Intergroup Relations." *Journal of Social Psychology* 129, no. 6 (1989): 855–857.

Reagan, Leslie J. *When Abortion Was a Crime: Women, Medicine, and the Law, 1867–1973*. Berkeley: University of California Press, 1998.

Rector, Robert. "God and the Underclass." *National Review* 48, no. 10 (1996): 30–33.

Reef, Catherine. *Poverty in America*. New York: Infobase Publishing, 2007.

Reeves, Diane Lindsay. *Child Care Crisis*. Santa Barbara, CA: ABC-CLIO, 1992.

Renevoize, Jean. *Going Solo: Single Mothers by Choice*. London: Routledge and Kegan Paul, 1985.

Rich, Adrienne. *Of Woman Born: Motherhood as Experience and Institution*. New York: Bantam, 1976.

Roberts, Steven V. "America's New Crusade." *US News & World Report*, August 1, 1994.

Rocconi, Louis M. "The Impact of Learning Communities on First Year Students' Growth and Development in College." *Research in Higher Education* 52 (2011): 178–193.

Ross, Loretta J. "African-American Women and Abortion, 1800–1870." In *Theorizing Black Feminisms: The Visionary Pragmatism of Black Women*, edited by Stanlie M. James and Abena P. A. Busia, 141–159. New York: Routledge, 1993.

Ryan, Bernard, Jr. "Baby Maranda Case: 1994." *law.jrank.org*. Accessed January 11, 2014. http://law.jrank.org/pages/3612/Baby-Maranda-Case-1994.html.

Salvation Army. *Services to Unmarried Parents and Their Children*. New York: Salvation Army National Headquarters, 1962.

Samuelson, Robert J. "Can't Be Reformed." *Newsweek*, March 27, 1995.

Sandler, Bernice R. *The Campus Climate Revisited: Chilly for Women Faculty, Administrators, and Graduate Students*. Washington, DC: Project on the Status of Women of the Association of American Colleges, 1986.

Sandler, Bernice R., and Roberta M. Hall. *The Classroom Climate: A Chilly One for Women?* Washington, DC: Project on the Status of Women of the Association of American Colleges, 1982.

Schobert, Melody Ann. "Single Parents Who Are College Students: A Descriptive Study Incorporating Academic and General Self-Concept." PhD diss., University of Iowa, 2000.

Schumacher, Henry D. "The Unmarried Mother: A Socio-Psychiatric Viewpoint." *Mental Hygiene* 4 (1927): 775–782.

Schumacher, Rachel. *Prepping Colleges for Parents: Strategies for Supporting Student Parent Success in Postsecondary Education*. Washington, DC: Institute for Women's Policy Research, 2015.

Schumacher, Rachel, and Kate Irish. "What's New in 2002? A Snapshot of Head Start Children, Families, Teachers, and Programs." Policy Brief No. 1, Center for Law and Social Policy, Washington, DC, 2003. https://archive.org/stream/ERIC_ED475970#page/no/mode/2up.

Schur, Edwin M. *Labeling Women Deviant: Gender, Stigma, and Social Control*. Philadelphia: Temple University Press, 1983.

Seccombe, Karen. *"So You Think I Drive a Cadillac?" Welfare Recipients' Perspectives on the System and Its Reform*. Boston: Allyn and Bacon, 1999.

Sell, Katherine, Sarah Zlotnick, Kathleen Noonan, and David Rubin. *The Effect of Recession on Child Well-Being*. Philadelphia: Research Institute at Children's Hospital of Philadelphia, 2010.

Sgro, Valentina. *Organize Your Family's Schedule in No Time.* Indianapolis: Que, 2004.

Shark, Shelley, and Jodie Levin-Epstein. *Excluded Children: Family Caps in a New Era.* Washington, DC: Center for Law and Social Policy, 1999.

Sheffield, Ada Eliot. *Case-Study Possibilities: A Forecast.* Boston: Research Bureau on Social Case Work, 1922.

Sidel, Ruth. "The Enemy Within: A Commentary on the Demonization of Difference." *American Journal of Orthopsychiatry* 66, no. 4 (1996): 490–496.

———. *Keeping Women and Children Last: America's War on the Poor.* New York: Penguin Books, 1996.

———. *Unsung Heroines: Single Mothers and the American Dream.* Berkeley: University of California Press, 2006.

Silag, Phoebe G. "To Have, To Hold, To Receive Public Assistance: TANF and Marriage-Promotion Policies." *Journal of Gender, Race, and Justice* 7 (2003): 413–438.

"Sleep Deprivation." *Postgraduate Medicine* 112, no. 4 (2002): 115–116.

Smith, Dorothy E. "The Standard North American Family: SNAF as an Ideological Code." *Journal of Family Issues* 14, no. 1 (1993): 50–65.

Solimeno, Andrea, Minou Ella Mebane, Manuela Tomei, and Donata Francescato. "The Influence of Students and Teachers Characteristics on the Efficacy of Face-to-Face and Computer-Supported Collaborative Learning." *Computers & Education* 51 (2008): 109–128.

Solinger, Rickie. "Dependency and Choice: The Two Faces of Eve." In *Whose Welfare?* edited by Gwendolyn Mink, 7–35. Ithaca, NY: Cornell University Press, 1999.

———. *Wake Up Little Susie: Single Pregnancy before Roe v. Wade.* New York: Routledge, 1992.

Spain, Daphne, and Suzanne M. Bianchi. *Balancing Act: Motherhood, Marriage, and Employment among American Women.* New York: Russell Sage Foundation, 1996.

Spicker, Paul. *Stigma and Social Welfare.* London: St. Martin's Press, 1984.

Squires, Susan, and Bryan Byrne. *Creating Breakthrough Ideas: The Collaboration of Anthropologists and Designers in the Product Development Industry.* Santa Barbara, CA: Praeger, 2002.

Stedman, James B. *Federal Pell Grant Program of the Higher Education Act.* Washington, DC: Congressional Research Service, 2004.

Steele, Ann. "When to Procreate." *Chronicle of Higher Education,* July 11, 2003.

Stoltzfus, Emilie. *Citizen, Worker, Mother: Debating Public Responsibility for Child Care after the Second World War.* Chapel Hill: University of North Carolina Press, 2003.

Straumsheim, Carl. "Triaging Textbooks." *Inside Higher Education,* August 4, 2015.

Summers, Lawrence H. "Remarks at NBER Conference on Diversifying the Science and Engineering Workforce." Cambridge, MA, January 14, 2005. http://www.harvard.edu/president/speeches/summers_2005/nber.php.

Super, David. *Background on the Food Stamp Program.* Washington, DC: Center for Budget and Policy Priorities, 2001.

Swigart, Jane. *The Myth of the Bad Mother: The Emotional Realities of Mothering.* New York: Bantam, 1991.

Szalai, Alexander, ed. *The Use of Time: Daily Activities of Urban and Suburban Populations in Twelve Countries.* The Hague: Mouton, 1972.

Taylor, Carl S. *Dangerous Society.* East Lansing: Michigan State University Press, 1990.

Terkelson, Helen E. *Counseling the Unwed Mother.* Englewood Cliffs, NJ: Prentice-Hall, 1964.

Thornton, Saranna. "Where—Not When—Should You Have a Baby?" *Chronicle of Higher Education,* October 8, 2004.

Thurman, George. *Day Care . . . An Emerging Crisis.* Springfield, IL: Charles C. Thomas Publishers, 1980.

Trattner, William. *From Poor Law to Welfare State: A History of Social Welfare in America*. New York: Free Press, 1998.

Treas, Judith, and Sonja Drobnic. *Dividing the Domestic: Men, Women, and Household Work in Cross-National Perspective*. Stanford, CA: Stanford University Press, 2010.

Trombley, Laura E. Skandera. "The Facts of Life for an Administrator and a Mother." *Chronicle of Higher Education*, September 5, 2003.

Trubek, Anne. "When a Spousal Hire Becomes a Single Mom." *Chronicle of Higher Education*, February 20, 2004.

U.S. Census Bureau. "Table 280: Degree-Granting Institutions, Number, and Enrollment by State, 2008." In *Statistical Abstract of the United States, 2012*. Washington, DC: U.S. Census Bureau, 2011.

U.S. Department of Agriculture, Center for Nutrition and Policy Promotion. *Expenditures on Children by Families, 2012*. Accessed March 13, 2014. http://www.cnpp.usda.gov/sites/default/files/expenditures_on_children_by_families/crc2012.pdf.

Ulrich, Laurel Thatcher. *A Midwife's Tale: The Life of Martha Ballard, Based on Her Diary, 1785–1812*. New York: Vintage Books, 1990.

Vancour, Michele L., and Michel K. Griswold. *Breastfeeding Best Practices in Higher Education*. Plano, TX: Hale Publishing, 2014.

Van Dyke, Nella, and Holly J. McCammon, eds. *Strategic Alliances: Coalition Building and Social Movements*. Minneapolis: University of Minnesota Press, 2010.

Vandell, Deborah Lowe, and Barbara Wolfe. *Child Care Quality: Does It Matter and Does It Need to Be Improved?* Madison, WI: Institute for Research on Poverty, 2000.

Wasson, Christina. "'It Was Like a Little Community': An Ethnographic Study of Online Learning and Its Implications for MOOCs." *EPIC: Ethnographic Praxis in Industry Conference Proceedings* 1 (September 2013): 186–199.

Watkins, Elizabeth Siegel. *On the Pill: A Social History of Oral Contraceptives, 1950–1970*. Baltimore: John Hopkins University Press, 1998.

Weiner, Lynne Y. "Reconstructing Motherhood: The La Leche League in Postwar America." *Journal of American History* 80, no. 4 (1994): 1357–1381.

Weiss, Robert. *Going It Alone: The Family Life and Social Situation of the Single Parent*. New York: Basic Books, 1979.

Weitzman, Lenore J. *The Divorce Revolution*. New York: The Free Press, 1985.

Weston, Kath. *Families We Choose: Lesbians, Gays, Kinship*. New York: Columbia University Press, 1991.

White, Dorothy Gray. *Ar'n't I a Woman? Female Slaves in the Plantation South*. 2nd ed. New York: W. W. Norton, 1999.

Williams, Joan. "The Subtle Side of Discrimination." *Chronicle of Higher Education*, April 14, 2003.

Williams, Lucy A. "Race, Rat Bites, and Unfit Mothers: How Media Discourse Informs Welfare Legislation Debate." *Fordham Urban Law Journal* 22, no. 4 (1994): 1159–1196.

Wilson, Robin. "Are Faculty Members Overworked?" *Chronicle of Higher Education*, November 5, 2004.

———. "How Babies Alter Careers for Academics." *Chronicle of Higher Education*, December 5, 2003.

———. "Papers and Pampers: The Challenges of Attending a Scholarly Meeting, Children in Tow." *Chronicle of Higher Education*, December 13, 2002.

———. "Timing Is Everything: Academe's Annual Baby Boom." *Chronicle of Higher Education*, June 25, 1999.

Wong, Venessa. "Foreclosures: An Increase of 21% in 2009 and Climbing." *Bloomberg Business Week*, January 14, 2010. Accessed June 15, 2015. http://www.businessweek.com/lifestyle/content/jan2010/bw20100113_985068.htm.

Workfare versus Welfare: Hearing before the Subcommittee on Trade, Productivity, and Economic Growth of the Joint Economic Committee, Ninety-Ninth Congress, Second Session, April 23, 1986. Washington, DC: Government Printing Office, 1986.

Wylie, Richard. "Keys to Degrees: Educating Two Generations Together." Document prepared for the Ascend Roundtable: The Aspen Institute, Washington, DC: March 29, 2011. Accessed November 6, 2015. http://www.aspeninstitute.org/sites/default/files/content/docs/ascend/ascend-8-Wylie-Keys-Degrees-Educating-Two-Generations-Together.pdf.

Yaniv, Gideon. "Welfare Fraud and Welfare Stigma." *Journal of Economic Psychology* 18 (1997): 435–451.

Young, Leontine. *Out of Wedlock: A Study of the Problems of the Unmarried Mother and Her Child.* New York: McGraw-Hill, 1954.

Zaslow, Martha J., K. A. Moore, J. L. Brooks, P. A. Morris, K. Tout, Z. A. Redd, and C. A. Emig. "Experimental Studies of Welfare Reform and Children." *The Future of Children: Special Issue on Children and Welfare Reform* 21, no. 1 (2002): 78–95.

Zhan, Min, and Shanta Pandey. "Economic Well-Being of Single Mothers: Work First or Postsecondary Education?" *Journal of Sociology and Social Welfare* 31, no. 3 (2004): 87–113.

Zigler, Edward F., Katherine Marsland, and Heather Lord. *The Tragedy of Child Care in America.* New Haven, CT: Yale University Press, 2009.

INDEX

AA. *See* Alcoholics Anonymous

abortion, 16, 28–29, 99, 124, 146, 148

absentee fathers, 31, 46–47, 53, 62–63, 69, 86, 94, 98, 119, 125, 146–147, 182–183

academic "bridge" programs, 190

academic probation, 57

adoption, 16, 27–28

after-school programs. *See* before- and after-school programs

Aid to Families with Dependent Children (AFDC), 70, 144

Alcoholics Anonymous (AA), 48

alcoholism. *See* drug abuse

alternative high school, 8, 86–87, 103

American Academy of Pediatrics, 114, 115

American Bar Association, 94

American dream, as cultural narrative, 45, 189

American Public Health Association, 115

American Revolution, 20

American welfare trap, 45

Back-Up Child Care (University of California–Berkeley), 207

"bad mothers," 24, 30

bastard, 3–5, 22

bastardy laws, 22

before- and after-school programs, 112–113, 119, 121, 137, 153, 181

Bigelow Cooperative Day Care, 15

birth control: failure of, 28–29, 73, 146, 152; lack of use among interviewees, 8, 47, 53, 93

Birthright of Iowa City, 130

Blackboard. *See* online education

bootstraps ideology, 79, 189

Bourger Women with Children Program (Misericordia University), 211

Brazelton, T. Berry, 23

Bush, Jeb, 182–183

Calvinism, 21

Campus Child Care (Northern Illinois University), 205

Campus Children's Center (Evergreen State College), 199

Cap and Gown Scholarship (Antioch University New England), 200

CAPRA: Computer Access Promoting Retention and Achievement, 200

Cardinal Mooney High School, 16

Caregivers Network (University of Montana), 205

Carson, Ben, 183

Cashen, Raymond R., 17

CCAMPIS: Child Care Access Means Parents in School, 135

Chemelski, John, 15

childbearing, as a civic duty, 20

child care: availability, 50–51, 113–114, 119, 133, 171–173, 203; benefits of on-campus, 203–204; commonly cited problems in the U.S., 111–115; cost of, 50–51, 67, 102, 113, 120–122; as detrimental to child well-being, 15, 17; as educational expense, 138–139; quality of, 51, 113, 114; sliding fee scales, 199–200; subsidies, 61, 112, 121, 135, 172, 199–200; university-affiliated, 15, 117, 137, 139–140, 172–173; in U.S. compared to other countries, 112; waiting lists, 117–118, 119, 127–128, 134–135, 137–138. *See also individual program names*

Child Care and Development Fund (CCDF) Block Grant, 112

Child Care Aware of America, 113

Child Care Partners Program (UI), 204

Child Care Program (Ohio State University), 199

Child Care Subsidy Program (Brown University), 199

Child Care Subsidy Program for Student Families (UI), 199

Child Care Tuition Assistance Program (University of Wisconsin), 206–207
child custody: amici curiae, 17–18; and best interests of the child, 15, 17–18; father's rights, 19; legal battles related to, 14–15, 17–18, 62; move-away case, 15; shared custody, 18; visitation rights, 16
child exclusion policies, 36, 144
chilly climate of higher education, 142–144
choice, rhetoric of in American politics, 28–31
City Colleges of Chicago, 115
Civil Rights Act of 1964, 185
class schedules, flexible scheduling options, 72, 201–202
Collin College, 91
Community Coordinated Child Care (4Cs), 117
computer labs, on campus, 77, 96–97
Concern for Women, 130
coverture, 20
credit card debt, among interviewees, 62–63

Dahl, Roald, 45
Daily Iowan (campus newspaper, UI), 60
David H. Koch Childcare Center (MIT), 204
deadlines, in postsecondary institutions, 82–83
Designing Women (television sitcom), 35–36
division of labor. See gendered division of labor
divorce: among interviewees, 7, 39, 45, 71, 74, 90, 98, 101, 110, 119, 125, 152, 159, 170; and downward economic mobility afterward, 45, 98; no-fault divorce laws, 29–30; rates in the U.S., 29–30
domestic violence, 7, 16, 46, 73–74
drug abuse, 46–48, 73–74
Duke, David, 32

Early Childhood Learning Center Programs, Inc. (La Guardia Community College), 206
eLearning. See online education
emergency funds for single parents, 68, 198–199
Emory Childcare Network (Emory University), 204

employment, of interviewees while pursuing postsecondary education, 7, 50, 60, 71–73, 89, 92, 103, 104–106, 118, 131–132
English Poor Law of 1601, 22
Enlightenment, 20
ethnography, 11–12, 37, 40, 184
Evening Child Care Program (University of Texas at Dallas), 206
excused absences, within postsecondary institutions, 135–136, 154–156, 168, 182, 208
extracurricular activities, of interviewees' children, 7–8, 110–111, 115

Families and Work Institute, 114
family: decline of, 11; ideals in colonial America, 19. See also family values
family values, 12, 17, 144
Federal Emergency Management Agency (FEMA), 66
Federal Student Aid (FSA), 9
Federal Student Aid Report (SAR), 68
Federal Supplemental Educational Opportunity Grant (FSEOG), 132
FEMA. See Federal Emergency Management Agency
feminism, 34–35
filius nullius, 22
first-generation college students, 7, 190–191. See also academic "bridge" programs
food stamps, 9, 70, 74, 78, 116
foster care, 16
Free Application for Federal Student Aid (FAFSA), 132, 191
Friends (television sitcom), 31

GED. See General Educational Development degree
gendered division of labor, 100, 107–108. See also gender roles
gender roles: in colonial America, 19–20; in late twentieth-century America, 33–36; in post-Revolution U.S., 20–21. See also gendered division of labor
General Educational Development (GED) degree, 49, 86, 133
"good mothering": American ideals of, 12, 23–24, 108; as financially expensive, 12; and influence of "scientific motherhood," 23; as "intensive mothering," 23, 97; as

labor intensive, 12; as racialized, 27–28; in twentieth-century America, 23
grade point average (GPA), of interviewees: higher than 3.0, 6, 74, 89, 92, 129, 137; lower than 3.0, 9, 57, 166
Graduate Record Examination (GRE), 52
Great Awakening, 20
Great Depression, 26

Hall, Roberta, 143
Harvard University, 13–15, 142
Hawkeye Community College, 94
Head Start programs, 126–128, 132, 138, 181
Health Systems Children's Center (UM), 204
Helen's Special Fund (University of Wisconsin–Eau Claire), 198
Heritage Foundation, 30
heteronormativity, 145
higher education. *See* chilly climate of higher education
homelessness, among interviewees, 65–66, 68
housing: affordability of, off-campus, 14, 162; affordability of, on-campus, 162–163, 165; family housing, on-campus, 17, 87, 162–165, 171, 202–203; lack of availability, on-campus, 14; poor condition of, on-campus, 162–165. *See also* Section 8 Housing Assistance
Hurricane Katrina, 63–66

Illinois Department of Public Health, 116
illness: of interviewees, 120, 124–125, 156; of interviewees' children or family members, 69–70, 98–100, 116–118, 135–136
income sources, of interviewees: alimony, 45, 110; child support, 45, 71, 110, 120, 153; community programs, 59, 61, 66, 75, 130–131, 174; general list of, 43–44; government programs, 44, 70, 74–75, 94; illegal activities, 77–78; sale of personal possessions, 59; student loans, 45–46, 50–51, 59, 67, 120, 153. *See also* employment, of interviewees; Pell Grant; scholarships; teaching assistantship; work-study
Infant Care (booklet), 23
intersectionality, 19, 24, 190
Iowa Department of Human Services, 9, 60–61, 70, 74, 94, 121

Iowa Department of Public Health, 117
Iowa Right to Life Committee, 130
Iowa State University child care centers, 199–200
Iowa Western Community College, 125
Iowa Workforce Development Program, 103–104
Ireland, Jennifer, 16–19
Ireland Smith, Maranda Kate, 16–18

James E. "Pete" Peterson Memorial Scholarship (Westminster College), 198
Jezebel stereotype, 21
Jim Sells Childcare Subsidy (Portland State University), 199
Jindal, Bobby, 183
Job Training Partnership Act of 1980, 94
John Birch Society, 30

Kentucky Colonels Better Life Scholarship (Kentucky Community and Technical College System), 198
Keys to Degrees: Educating Two Generations Together (Endicott College), 209–210
Kids-Kare (University of Wisconsin), 206
Kirkwood Community College, 38
Kirkwood Kids (Kirkwood Community College), 117–118, 134
Kohls, L. Robert, 106

lactation rooms, at postsecondary institutions, 135, 149–150, 207–208
Leach, Penelope, 23
Limited Benefit Plan, 75
Long Beach City College, 13

Macomb Community College, 17
Maggiore, Bailey Marie Theresa, 14–15
Maggiore, Theresa (Bailey's grandmother), 15
Maggiore, Tommaso, 13–15
marriage: as financial strategy, 73; promotion policies, 144, 169–170; social acceptance of, 20
Marshalltown Community College, 72–73
"master status," as an element of stigma, 157, 168–169
matrix of domination, 19, 214n25

McKinley, William, 25
media coverage of single mothers, 31–36
Medicaid, 9, 62, 70, 116
Melton, Maxine, 32
Michigan Court of Appeals, 18
Mildly Ill Back-Up Child Care Program (UI), 206
mother-blaming, 11, 48
motherhood: American cultural ideals of, 19; in colonial America, 19–22; as experience and institution, 19; and identity, 19–22; in post-Revolution U.S., 20–22; in the twentieth-century, 23–36
Mothers Living & Learning Program (College of Saint Mary), 210
Murphy Brown (television sitcom), 31, 35–36

Nagin, Ray, 64
National Association of Child Care Resource and Referral Agencies, 114
National Center for Health Statistics (NCHS), 183
National Florence Crittenton Mission, 25
National Institute of Child Health and Human Development, 114–115
The Nest, 130
New Deal social policies, 26
New Right, 30
nonmarital childbearing, rates of, 183
non-traditional college students, 7, 11, 190
North Campus Children's Center (UM), 204
North Central Texas College, 7

Ocon, Gina, 13–15
online education, 38, 92–93, 180, 201–202

passing, as a technique of stigma management, 155–157
"pathology" of the Black family, 27
Patsy Takemoto Mink Education Support Award, 197–198
Pell Grant, 9, 50, 67, 91, 104, 132, 153
Personal Responsibility and Work Opportunities Reconciliation Act of 1996, 36, 37, 69, 74, 80, 144
Pincus, Gregory, 28
postsecondary education: as avenue out of poverty, 12, 43–44, 57, 66, 72, 91, 179; as economic investment, 43–45, 76, 86–87,

108, 179; as strategy for career advancement, 179; as type of "good mothering," 12, 37, 45, 79, 91, 159, 179; as type of mothering work, 12, 37, 54–55, 159, 179
poverty: culture of, 27, 30; threshold, 46, 127
privilege, 19–20, 111, 180–181
probation. *See* academic probation
Promise Jobs (PJ), 9–10
psychoanalytic theory, 23, 27

Quayle, Dan, 31

rape, of slave women, 21
Reagan, Ronald, 31, 44
reproductive labor, during slavery in the U.S., 21
reproductive technologies, 34
republican mother, 20
residency regulations, as related to tuition, 59–60
residential maternity homes, 25–28
residential programs, for single mothers attending postsecondary institutions, 209–212
responsibility, as theme narratives of interviewees, 6, 48, 95–96, 109
Revolutionary War. *See* American Revolution
RioLearn (Rio Salado College), 202
Roe v. Wade, 28
Rosenfeld Injury Lawyers' Annual Single Mother Scholarship, 198
rugged individualism, 189
Ruth Matthews Bourger Women with Children Program. *See* Bourger Women with Children Program

Salvation Army, 61, 66
Sandler, Bernice, 143
schedules. *See* class schedules, flexible scheduling options
scholarships, 6, 13, 16, 52–53, 57, 74, 91, 106, 146, 197–198
second shift, 108
Section 8 Housing Assistance, 70, 75, 116
Section 418 of the Social Security Act, 112
sexism, in higher education, 141–144, 149–150
Shalala, Donna, 32
single adults in colonial America, 19–20

single mothers: and agency, 85, 155–158, 165, 167–170, 182, 186–187; as "bad mothers," 24–28, 30–33, 182–183; bashing of, 19; blaming of, 31–36, 182–183, 189–191; and concerns about relationships with children, among interviewees, 8, 97, 100, 106, 108–109, 181; as consequence of poverty, 25; dual identities as single mothers and college students, 6, 43, 88–89, 95; educational concerns of, 43; as "heroines," 187–188; as "irresponsible," 33–34; media coverage of, 31–36; as political spectacle, 31, 182–183; and relationships with family, 7, 9, 27–28, 46–48, 52–53, 86–87, 123–126, 128–133, 147; self-concept of, 109, 146, 152; social isolation of, among interviewees, 10, 51–52, 93, 108, 158, 170–176; stereotypes of, 11, 27–28, 30–37, 44, 80, 146, 168–170, 182; stigmatization of, 3, 5, 30–31, 34, 70, 144–146, 148–149, 155–158, 160, 165, 167–170, 176, 177–178, 182; as threat to American values, 30–36; as "uppity," 34–36

Single Mothers Achieving Real Triumph (SMART) (Lakeland Community College), 208–209

Single Parent Scholar Program (Wilson College), 211

Single Parents Program (Champlain College), 211–212

sleep deprivation, 105

Smith, Steven, 16–18

social work profession, focus on single mothers, 25–26

speedup, in the workplace, 107

SPiN: Single Parents Network (Western Nebraska Community College), 209

Spock, Benjamin, 23

SPRINT: Single Parent Resource Information Networking Technology (Texas Woman's University), 200

SPROUT: Single Parents Reaching Out for Unlimited Tomorrows (Baldwin Wallace University), 210–211

Standard North American Family (SNAF), 19

stereotypes: of African American women, 21, 27–28, 31–34; of college students, 6,

95–96; of single mothers, 11, 27–28, 30–37, 44, 80, 146, 168–170, 182

storytelling, 1, 10, 11

student loans: as debt, 46, 104; emergency loans, 68, 198–199; "maxing out" of, 56, 60, 75, 154; repayment of, 46, 56, 63, 75–76, 80–81; as strategy for reducing credit card debt, 62–63

Student Parent Child Care Subsidy Program (Pennsylvania State University), 199

student parents, as part of postsecondary student population, 139

Summers, Lawrence H., 141–142

support for single mothers, from family and friends: child care, 16, 64, 69, 94, 104–105, 108, 112, 121, 125–126, 127, 128–133, 156, 166, 181; educational expenses, 125–126; housing and living expenses, 49–51, 69, 104–105, 125–126, 154; withdrawal or lack of support, 9, 59, 68, 94, 126, 147, 166

TCC Child Development Center (Tidewater Community College), 205

teaching assistantship, 53, 55–56, 98–99, 120–121, 147–148

Temporary Aid to Needy Families (TANF), 56, 75, 116, 144

Texas Department of Family and Protective Services, 172

Texas Woman's University (TWU), 38; The Clubhouse, 172–173, 205; Lowry Woods Community, 171; Office of Commuter and Non-Traditional Student Services, 174; Single Parents Student Organization (SPSO), 174–176; SPRINT: Single Parent Resource Information Networking Technology, 200; Student Parents Also Raising Kids (SPARK), 175–176, 209; William Randolph Hearst Endowment for Students/Parents, 198

textbooks, cost of, 69, 77, 200–201

third shift, 103–106, 166

time management: American attitudes toward, 83–85, 106–108; Costa Rican attitudes toward, 83–84; lack of leisure time among interviewees, 7–8, 10, 89, 93, 99, 102, 108; strategies for, among interviewees, 87–90, 92, 95–97, 101–102, 104–106

Title IX of the Education Amendments of
1972, 142, 185
Towsley Children's House (UM), 204
traditional college students, definition of, 190
tuition: as key factor in choice of college,
49–50, 67, 72; and residency regulations,
59–60; rising rates of, 60

UE-COGS (UI graduate student union), 55, 148
UI. *See* University of Iowa
UM. *See* University of Michigan
Umpqua Community College, 183
United Action for Youth, 130
United Way, 130
University of Iowa (UI), 38; Child Care
Partners Program, 204; Child Care Subsidy
Program for Student Families, 199; Family
Services Office, 61, 121–122, 126, 135, 162,
199, 204; Mildly Ill Back-Up Child Care
Program, 206; Student Counseling Services,
78, 177; Well Back-Up Child Care, 206
University of Michigan (UM), 16–18; Health
Systems Children's Center, 204; North
Campus Children's Center, 204; Towsley
Children's House, 204
University of North Texas, 171
University of Utah Women's Center, 209
University of Wisconsin–Eau Claire, 198
University without Walls (Amherst Univer-
sity), 202
unmarried women, as a burden in colonial
America, 19–20
U.S. Department of Education, 63, 190
U.S. Department of Education Office for
Civil Rights, 142

U.S. Department of Health and Human
Services, 114
U.S. Information Agency and the Meridian
International Center, 106
U.S. News & World Report rankings, best col-
leges and hospitals, 152

Ventura, Clarabel, 32

welfare: fraud, 78; magnet states, 36; reform,
36, 37, 69, 74, 80, 144; and stereotypes of
single mothers, 33–36
"welfare queen," 31, 35, 44
Well Back-Up Child Care (UI), 206
Westwood Child Care Center (UCLA), 204
WIC. *See* Women, Infants, and Children
nutritional program
William Randolph Hearst Endowment for
Students/Parents (Texas Woman's University), 198
windfall child rearing, 122
Winthrop, John, 22
withdrawal from college or university, 18, 57,
151, 152, 166
Women, Infants, and Children (WIC) nutritional program, 61, 62, 130
women's movement in the U.S., 29–30
Workforce Investment Act (WIA) of 1998, 94
Workforce Solutions Office of the Texas
Workforce Commission, 172
work-study, 160, 173
Worldwide eLearning (Texas Tech University), 202

Yale University, 142

ABOUT THE AUTHOR

JILLIAN M. DUQUAINE-WATSON is Senior Lecturer II and head of the master's program in interdisciplinary studies at the University of Texas at Dallas. She is an award-winning educator whose research and teaching interests include poverty, international development, social change and social movements, American culture, educational practices and policies, motherhood, and reproductive technologies.